# Studies in Latin American Ethnohistory & Archaeology

## Joyce Marcus, General Editor

Volume I  *A Fuego y Sangre: Early Zapotec Imperialism in the Cuicatlán Cañada, Oaxaca,* by Elsa M. Redmond. Memoirs of the Museum of Anthropology, University of Michigan, No. 16 (1983). $15.

Volume II  *Irrigation & the Cuicatec Ecosystem: A Study of Agriculture & Civilization in North Central Oaxaca,* by Joseph W. Hopkins III. Memoirs of the Museum of Anthropology, University of Michigan, No. 17 (1984). $15.

Volume III  *Aztec City States,* by Mary G. Hodge. Memoirs of the Museum of Anthropology, University of Michigan, No. 18 (1984). $15.

Volume IV  *Conflicts over Coca Fields in XVIth-Century Perú,* by María Rostworowski de Diez Canseco. Memoirs of the Museum of Anthropology, University of Michigan, No. 21 (1988). $19.50

Volume V  *Tribal and Chiefly Warfare in South America,* by Elsa M. Redmond. Memoirs of the Museum of Anthropology, University of Michigan, No. 28 (1994).

MEMOIRS OF THE MUSEUM OF ANTHROPOLOGY
UNIVERSITY OF MICHIGAN
NUMBER 28

Studies in Latin American
Ethnohistory & Archaeology

Joyce Marcus, General Editor

Volume V

# Tribal and Chiefly Warfare in South America

by

Elsa M. Redmond

ANN ARBOR
1994

*Cover illustration. Sixteenth-century woodcut illustration of a Tupinaquin attack against the Tamoio settlement of Ubatuba, on the coast of Brazil, that was witnessed by Hans Staden during his captivity there in 1555. Staden recounted how twenty-five canoes of warriors attacked Ubatuba with bows and arrows to the sound of horns. The male defenders took up armed positions behind the settlement's palisade while the women and children remained helplessly in the center, unable to flee. Human head trophies can be seen atop tall posts at one end of the village's palisade. Redrawn from Staden 1944:64.*

This series is partially supported by a grant-in-aid No. 4453 from the Wenner-Gren Foundation for Anthropological Research, whose Director of Research, Lita Osmundsen, offered both encouragement and help during the preparation of the grant proposal.

© 1994 by the Regents of the University of Michigan
The Museum of Anthropology
All rights reserved

Printed in the United States of America
ISBN 0-915703-35-1

The University of Michigan Museum of Anthropology currently publishes three monograph series: Anthropological Papers, Memoirs, and Technical Reports. We have over seventy titles in print. For a complete catalog, write to Museum of Anthropology Publications, 4009 Museums Bldg., Ann Arbor, MI 48109-1079, or call (313) 764-0485.

Library of Congress Cataloging-in-Publication Data

Redmond, Elsa M.
　　Tribal and chiefly warfare in South America / by Elsa M. Redmond.
　　　p. cm. — (Memoirs of the Museum of Anthropology, University
of Michigan ; no. 28) (Studies in Latin American ethnohistory &
archaeology ; v. 5)
　　Includes bibliographical references.
　　ISBN 0-915703-35-1 (alk. paper)
　　1. Indians of South America—Warfare. 2. Chiefdoms—South
America. 3. South America—Antiquities. 4. Shuar Indians—Warfare.
Yanomamo Indians—Warfare. I. Title. II. Series. III. Series:
Studies in Latin American ethnohistory & archaeology ; v. 5.
GN2.M52 no. 28
[F2230.1.W37]
306 s—dc20
[303.6′6′08998]　　　　　　　　94-18061

The paper used in this publication meets the requirements of the ANSI Standard Z39.48-1984 (Permanence of Paper)

# Introduction to Volume V

*by Joyce Marcus*

This volume, the fifth in our series entitled Studies in Latin American Ethnohistory & Archaeology, is the product of more than a decade of research by Elsa Redmond. Redmond has been amassing ethnohistoric, ethnographic, and archaeological data on warfare in Latin America, particularly northern South America. Taken together, those data have increasingly convinced her that warfare played a major role in the cultures of many tribes and chiefdoms throughout the region. When Redmond compared and evaluated those data, she began to see important differences between tribal and chiefly warfare, as well as striking similarities shared by groups at the same sociopolitical level. Specifying these differences and similarities is one of Redmond's most valuable contributions (see Chapter 4).

In this volume we learn of tribal warfare among the Jívaro and Yanomamö, chiefly warfare among groups in Colombia and Panama, and the archaeological evidence for similar warfare patterns from a wide range of sites in the New World. We also see Redmond tackle the role of warfare in the evolution of chiefdoms. She suggests that warfare spurred the development of chiefdoms by turning some renowned warriors into powerful chiefs (see Chapter 7).

To maximize the data of northern South America and lower Central America, Redmond had to wear three different hats—that of ethnologist, ethnohistorian, and archaeologist. Wearing her ethnologist's hat, she surveyed the extensive ethnographic literature for northern South America, focusing on several themes: the motivations for warfare; the preparations for battle; the weapons used; the timing and seasonality of battles; the location of battles; the range of associated rites (such as headshrinking, ritual bathing, making of poison to tip arrows, cannibalism); the injuries and losses in human life on both sides; and the gains (booty, captives, land, wives).

Wearing the hat of an ethnohistorian, Redmond searched sixteenth- and seventeenth-century documents with the idea of collecting detailed, eyewitness reports of groups who had only recently come into contact with the Spaniards. Those ethnohistoric data are extremely important, since a few scholars (e.g., Ferguson 1990, 1992) have attributed the region's endemic warfare to contact with Europeans. Redmond's data and those of others (Carneiro 1981, 1991; Spencer 1991) strongly suggest such conflict is prehispanic.

Redmond's ethnographic and ethnohistoric studies reveal dimensions of warfare that the archaeological record does not preserve—the range of motives, the size of the military forces, the number of losses, the location of various pre-battle and post-battle rites, the number of women taken, the seasonality of warfare, and so forth. Redmond shows that South American tribesmen plan their raids for the dry season, since intervillage travel is more difficult during the rainy season. They even go so far as to conduct raids on enemy villages at the end of the dry season in order to postpone the enemy's counterraid until the following dry season. Although archaeologists often find it difficult to document the seasonality of warfare, a preference for dry season warfare can also be shown for the ancient Maya, because sufficient hieroglyphic texts exist for certain centuries (Marcus 1992:430–433). Without such texts, the task is much tougher.

Finally, wearing the hat of an archaeologist, Redmond began to consider how archaeologists could improve their research designs to increase the likelihood of recovering more information about warfare. She proposes a comprehensive research design that focuses on increasingly larger units of study—from the feature to the household, to the community, to the region, and to the interregional level. The current strategy of excavating mounds or making test pits only in the very center of a site would rarely reveal the kinds of evidence she has documented with ethnohistoric and ethnographic data. Archaeologists often fail to look for features on the periphery of sites, such as palisades of wooden logs, cane, vines, and lianas which form a ring circumscribing the settlement. Furthermore, archaeologists have virtually no methods for documenting battles that took place in between settlements. Sadly, survey is unlikely to recover such data.

Ethnologists and ethnohistorians have much to learn from this book because of its strong comparative approach and its integration of different lines of evidence. For their part, archaeologists will profit from the following kinds of evidence that Redmond presents:

(1) *Boundary markers, buffer zones, or no-man's-lands.* When extensive regions have been surveyed and mapped, it has sometimes been possible to locate boundaries between social and political units (e.g., DeBoer 1981; Redmond 1983). Such boundaries may be completely human-made, or they may be minimal modifications of the natural landscape.

(2) *Fortifications.* These include moats, deep hidden trenches filled with sharpened stakes set in their floors, timber palisades lashed together by vines, or earthen walls (Spencer and Redmond 1992; Spencer 1991). There may be inner and outer palisades, or concentric rings of defensive features, increasing the chances of recovering such constructions.

(3) *Burial and skeletal data.* Having a large skeletal population for study is an advantage. Evidence of pre-mortem and postmortem trauma are both important. Healed wounds and fractures might indicate participation in battles. Unhealed fractures such as parry fractures and skull fractures might indicate death was caused in battle. Postmortem treatment, such as cut marks on the cervical vertebrae, might indicate decapitation. Keeping skulls and mandibles as trophies is also known. If many victims of war were carried off by the enemy, left on the battlefield, or buried outside the site being excavated, victims of warfare may be underestimated.

(4) *Weapons.* Chipped-stone projectiles used as arrow, spear, or dart points, stone axes, and broadswords studded with obsidian blades are potentially recoverable. If made of wood, cane, or vegetal fiber, weapons such as lances, spears, arrows with feathers, clubs, and slings would be difficult to recover.

(5) *Settlement pattern changes.* Abrupt changes in the location of sites, such as a shift of all sites from the valley floor to defensible hilltop locations, may suggest concern for defense and the threat of warfare. The abrupt abandonment of many houses in a village with no evidence of reoccupation is another example (e.g., Redmond 1983).

(6) *Burned buildings or sites.* Widespread burning of several scattered and noncontiguous buildings; evidence of whole artifacts, whole vessels, and food discarded and abandoned on the floors of burned houses might be recoverable. Unburied skeletons, lying abandoned on house floors, could be further evidence.

(7) *Abrupt or drastic changes in the cultural sequence.* The complete interruption of local ceramic or architectural styles, especially if they are replaced by those of another polity, has been used to infer warfare in various parts of the world (e.g., Spencer 1982; Redmond 1983; Webster 1993).

(8) *Iconography.* Artistic scenes that show weapons, warriors fighting, men with warpaint, nude or bound prisoners, and so on, have been used as evidence of warfare. At the chiefly level, we might expect more of these depictions because of the endemic rivalry and competition between chiefs. Stone monument galleries displaying hundreds of nude and mutilated prisoners, such as those constructed at Cerro Sechín in Peru and Monte Albán in Mexico, come to mind.

This volume should serve as a catalyst for scholars interested in the diversity of prestate warfare patterns, and as a challenge to archaeologists concerned with the role of warfare in the evolution of complex societies.

# Bibliography

Carneiro, Robert L.
- 1981 The chiefdom: precursor of the state. In: The Transition to Statehood in the New World, edited by Grant D. Jones and Robert R. Kautz, pp. 37–79. Cambridge: Cambridge University Press.
- 1991 The nature of the chiefdom as revealed by evidence from the Cauca Valley of Colombia. In: Profiles in Cultural Evolution: Papers from a Conference in Honor of Elman R. Service, edited by A. Terry Rambo and Kathleen Gillogly, pp. 167–190. Anthropological Papers of the Museum of Anthropology, University of Michigan, No. 85. Ann Arbor.

DeBoer, Warren R.
- 1981 Buffer zones in the cultural ecology of aboriginal Amazonia: an ethnohistorical approach. American Antiquity 46:364–377.

Ferguson, R. Brian
- 1990 Blood of the Leviathan: western contact and warfare in Amazonia. American Ethnologist 17(2):237–257.
- 1992 A savage encounter: western contact and the Yanomami war complex. In: War in the Tribal Zone, edited by R. Brian Ferguson and Neil L. Whitehead, pp. 199–227. Santa Fe, N.M.: School of American Research.

Marcus, Joyce
- 1992 Mesoamerican Writing Systems: Propaganda, Myth, and History in Four Ancient Civilizations. Princeton: Princeton University Press.

Redmond, Elsa M.
- 1983 A Fuego y Sangre: Early Zapotec Imperialism in the Cuicatlán Cañada, Oaxaca. Studies in Latin American Ethnohistory & Archaeology, Volume I. Memoirs of the Museum of Anthropology, University of Michigan, No. 16. Ann Arbor.

Spencer, Charles S.
- 1982 The Cuicatlán Cañada and Monte Albán: A Study of Primary State Formation. New York: Academic Press.
- 1991 Coevolution and the development of Venezuelan chiefdoms. In: Profiles in Cultural Evolution: Papers from a Conference in Honor of Elman R. Service, edited by A. Terry Rambo and Kathleen Gillogly, pp. 137–165. Anthropological Papers of the Museum of Anthropology, University of Michigan, No. 85. Ann Arbor.

Spencer, Charles S. and Elsa M. Redmond
- 1992 Prehispanic chiefdoms of the western Venezuelan llanos. World Archaeology 24(1):134–157.

Webster, David
- 1993 The study of Maya warfare: what it tells us about the Maya and what it tells us about Maya Archaeology. In: Lowland Maya Civilization in the Eighth Century A.D., edited by Jeremy A. Sabloff and John S. Henderson, pp. 415–444. Washington, D.C.: Dumbarton Oaks Research Library and Collection.

# Contents

**Introduction to Volume V** ............................................................... v
**Figures** ................................................................................... x
**Tables** .................................................................................... xi
**Acknowledgments** ......................................................................... xii

**Chapter 1   Introduction** ................................................................ 1
    Uncentralized tribes and centralized chiefdoms ......................................... 1

**Chapter 2   Tribal Warfare Patterns** ..................................................... 3
    Jívaro Warfare ........................................................................ 3
        The nature and objectives of warfare ............................................. 3
        Preparations for war ............................................................. 3
        Organization of war parties ...................................................... 5
        Warfare strategies, weapons, and tactics ......................................... 5
        Defensive strategies ............................................................. 8
        Post-war rituals and practices .................................................. 10
        Mortuary treatment .............................................................. 12
    Yanomamö Warfare ..................................................................... 15
        The nature and objectives of warfare ............................................ 15
        Preparations for war ............................................................ 15
        Organization of war parties ..................................................... 16
        Warfare strategies, weapons, and tactics ........................................ 17
        Defensive strategies ............................................................ 19
        Post-war rituals and practices .................................................. 21
        Mortuary treatment .............................................................. 22

**Chapter 3   Chiefly Warfare Patterns** ................................................... 25
    Warfare in the Cauca Valley .......................................................... 25
        The nature and objectives of warfare ............................................ 25
        Preparations for war ............................................................ 27
        Organization of war parties ..................................................... 27
        Warfare strategies, weapons, and tactics ........................................ 28
        Defensive strategies ............................................................ 29
        Post-war rituals and practices .................................................. 30
        Mortuary treatment .............................................................. 31
    Tairona Warfare ...................................................................... 32
        The nature and objectives of warfare ............................................ 32
        Preparations for war ............................................................ 32
        Organization of war parties ..................................................... 34
        Warfare strategies, weapons, and tactics ........................................ 34
        Defensive strategies ............................................................ 36
        Post-war rituals and practices .................................................. 37
        Mortuary treatment .............................................................. 37

    Warfare among the Panamanian Chiefdoms ................................................. 37
        The nature and objectives of warfare ................................................. 39
        Preparations for war ................................................. 40
        Organization of war parties ................................................. 41
        Warfare strategies, weapons, and tactics ................................................. 42
        Defensive strategies ................................................. 45
        Post-war rituals and practices ................................................. 46
        Mortuary treatment ................................................. 48

**Chapter 4 Tribal Versus Chiefly Warfare** ................................................. 51
    Objectives ................................................. 51
    Organization ................................................. 51
    Pre-War Rituals ................................................. 52
    Offensive Tactics ................................................. 53
    Defensive Tactics ................................................. 54
    Post-War Rituals ................................................. 55
    Funerary Treatment of Warriors ................................................. 56

**Chapter 5 The Archaeology of Tribal Warfare** ................................................. 57
    Investigating Warfare Archaeologically ................................................. 57
    Archaeology of Tribal Warfare ................................................. 59
        Preparations for war ................................................. 59
        Pre-war rituals ................................................. 62
        Warfare tactics ................................................. 62
        Defensive tactics ................................................. 69
        Post-war rituals ................................................. 74
        Mortuary treatment ................................................. 79

**Chapter 6 The Archaeology of Chiefly Warfare** ................................................. 83
    Preparations for War ................................................. 83
    Arrow Poisons ................................................. 84
    Pre-War Rituals ................................................. 87
    Organization of War Parties ................................................. 89
    Warfare Tactics ................................................. 93
    Defensive Tactics ................................................. 96
    Post-war Rituals ................................................. 102
    Ritual Cannibalism ................................................. 103
    Display of Human War Trophies ................................................. 108
    Mortuary Treatment ................................................. 109

**Chapter 7 Conclusion** ................................................. 117
    The Authority of Tribal War Leaders and Warring Chiefs ................................................. 117
    The Ideological Motives of Warfare ................................................. 118
    The Alternating Roles of Warfare and Exchange ................................................. 120
    Warfare and the Development of Centralized Societies ................................................. 123
        Sources of power ................................................. 124
        Legitimation of power ................................................. 127
        Favorable conditions ................................................. 128
        Conclusion ................................................. 130

**Bibliography** ................................................. 133
**Notes** ................................................. 143
**Appendix: Author's Translations of Spanish Text** ................................................. 145

# Figures

1. Locations of tribes and chiefdoms ................................................................. 4
2. Jívaro warrior wearing ear tubes and carrying lance ................................... 6
3. Jívaro warrior wearing ear tubes and carrying lance ................................... 7
4. Jívaro warriors wearing feather ornaments .................................................. 7
5. Jívaro warrior in war dress with lance and shield ........................................ 8
6. Armed Jívaro warriors on a raid ................................................................... 9
7. Jívaro household .......................................................................................... 10
8. Jívaro man preparing spikes of a dead-fall trap ......................................... 11
9. Conical head-cooking jars ........................................................................... 12
10. Jívaro human-head trophies ...................................................................... 13
11. Jívaro warrior at victory feast ................................................................... 14
12. Jívaro burial inside house .......................................................................... 16
13. Yanomamö face-painting styles ................................................................. 18
14. Yanomamö *teri* with defensive palisade .................................................. 21
15. Map of Colombia showing major river valleys ......................................... 26
16. Cauca Valley chiefdoms ............................................................................. 27
17. Tairona chiefdoms and their neighbors in the Sierra Nevada de Santa Marta ............. 33
18. Isthmus of Panama and its sixteenth-century chiefdoms ........................ 38
19. Spearthrower illustrated by Oviedo y Valdés ........................................... 45
20. Archaeological framework for investigating warfare .............................. 58
21. Ostra site ..................................................................................................... 60
22. Activity areas in Tsamirku's house ............................................................ 61
23. Jívaro poison pot ........................................................................................ 62
24. Jívaro cylinder seals ................................................................................... 63
25. Jívaro manioc-beer jar ............................................................................... 63
26. Jívaro drinking bowl .................................................................................. 63
27. Baniva overnight camp .............................................................................. 64
28. Gallina Anasazi mortality profile .............................................................. 67
29. Cabezas Largas ossuary .............................................................................. 68
30. Sample III sites in Long House Valley, A.D. 1250-1300 ......................... 70
31. Jívaro settlement pattern ........................................................................... 72
32. The Mascarenas site ................................................................................... 73
33. Sandoval village .......................................................................................... 75
34. Bg 88 tower site with subterranean tunnels and tower ........................... 76
35. Grave 23, Asia ............................................................................................. 77
36. Grave 42, Asia ............................................................................................. 77
37. Grave 48, Asia ............................................................................................. 77
38. Grave 10, Asia ............................................................................................. 77
39. Hafted stone ax ........................................................................................... 78

40. Pit 16, Asia ... 81
41. House C1 at Paloma ... 80
42. Basalt-column precinct, El Caño ... 88
43. Conch-shell trumpets from Cerro Brujo ... 90
44. Late Polychrome jars with human effigy covers from Grave 24, Sitio Conte ... 91
45. Late Polychrome human effigy jar covers from Graves 5 and 24, Sitio Conte ... 92
46. Late Polychrome effigy jar covers from Grave 26 and Trench I, Sitio Conte ... 93
47. A Tairona gold pendant of a male figure wearing headdress, helmet, nose plug, carrying double-spiraled baton ... 93
48. A Tairona gold pendant of a male figure from San Pedro de la Sierra, Ciénaga ... 94
49. A Tairona gold pendant of a male figure wearing helmet, nose plug, carrying double-spiraled baton ... 95
50. Muisca *tumbaga tunjo* figure of a warrior ... 95
51. Muisca gold pendant of a male figure ... 96
52. *Tumbaga* pendant from Grave 5, Sitio Conte of double-warrior figures ... 97
53. Cast-gold pendant from Chiriquí province of double-warrior figures with bat attributes ... 97
54. Scene from a Moche vessel from Trujillo, Moche Valley ... 98
55. Scene from a Moche vessel from Chimbote, Santa Valley ... 98
56. Stone-slab staircase at Pueblo Bernardo ... 100
57. Regional center of Gaván, encircled by oval earthwork topped by palisade ... 101
58. Human maxilla from Cottonwood Creek, Utah with "blown-out" front teeth ... 103
59. Carved stone column of male captive, El Caño ... 104
60. Splintered long-bone shafts from Burnt Mesa, New Mexico ... 108
61. Incised human astralagus from Nahuange ... 110
62. Plan of Grave 13, Sitio Conte ... 111
63. Plan of Grave 19, Sitio Conte ... 112
64. Bundle of stingray spines, bone awls, chipped-stone blade, gold chisels, and ear rods in Grave 19, Sitio Conte ... 113
65. Carved bone staff head from Gairaca, Colombia ... 114
66. Plan of the skeletons in Grave 26, Sitio Conte ... 115

# Tables

1. Inventories of perishable weapons encountered in looted tombs in Hoya del Quindío, Colombia ... 84
2. Tally of trophy heads and wives acquired by Jívaro warriors and war leaders ... 126

# Acknowledgments

This study of South American warfare began in 1984, in concert with an archaeological field project that Charles Spencer and I were carrying out in Barinas, Venezuela, where likely archaeological manifestations of chiefly warfare were turning up. With the advice and encouragement of Joyce Marcus in 1987, the investigation was broadened to include Panamanian warfare. Along the way, Elizabeth Brumfiel, Richard Cooke, and Robert Carneiro provided me with opportunities to express my arguments in shorter form and to receive some welcome feedback from colleagues.

The research upon which the study is based would not have been possible without the help of Bob Vrecenak and Lynn Sweet of the Interlibrary Loan Department of the Homer Babbidge Library at the University of Connecticut. I also wish to thank Sarah Granato of the American Museum of Natural History Library for her patience in introducing me to that library and its many resources. James Chase, Bruce Bradley, John Topic, and Richard Cooke were generous in sending me unpublished manuscripts, which were extremely useful for writing the chapters on the archaeology of tribal and chiefly warfare. Charles Meyers spurred my investigation of arrow poisons by sending me a number of articles on the subject. Robert D. Drennan, Carlos Fitzgerald, and Michael Brown helped me track down some information about arrow poisons and body paint.

David Kiphuth and Diana Salles drafted many of the figures presented here. For their help in securing and reproducing figures from published sources, I wish to thank the American Philosophical Society, Jaymie Brauer, Carmen Collazo of the Photographic Collection at the American Museum of Natural History Library, Donna Dickerson and Kaye Wild of the Peabody Museum of Archaeology and Ethnology at Harvard University, Frédéric Engel, Paul Goldstein, Martha Hill of the Peabody Museum of Natural History at Yale University, Diana Lubick of the Museum of Northern Arizona, Betty Meggers, Anna Roosevelt, Christy Turner II, Laila Williamson, and David Wilson.

As this project nears its completion I wish to thank Charles Spencer, Robert Carneiro, and Joyce Marcus for their useful criticisms and unending support of this endeavor. I can also reflect upon the possibility that the inspiration for this study may have originated long ago, when I ventured into the Amazonas Territory of Venezuela in the company of William Parker Redmond (1918–1992) and Marcel Griot C. (1924–1991). With them I was fortunate enough to encounter many village headmen, including a Yanomamö war leader at Ocamo in 1979, so it is fitting that I dedicate this volume to their memory.

# Chapter 1

# Introduction

When Kalervo Oberg (1955) established his sequence of lowland South American societies, he concentrated on the social and political organization of tribes and chiefdoms, and he noted that the tribe-to-chiefdom transition in lowland South America was associated with pronounced differences in the nature of warfare and intertribal relationships (Oberg 1955:192). Certainly no other single research topic has spurred as many ethnologists to conduct field studies among the militant Amerindian groups that remain in the upper Orinoco and Amazon river basins (Chagnon 1968a, 1983; Lizot 1977; Shapiro 1972; Harner 1972; Ross 1980, 1984; Siverts 1975; Murphy 1960; Siskind 1973; Gross 1979). Moreover, Stirling's remark about Jívaro warfare could well apply to all of these warring groups: "they have merely retained a custom and a war pattern that was widespread in northwestern South America at the time of the conquest" (Stirling 1938:41).

Interest in traditional South American warfare patterns has been heightened recently by some ethnologists who have raised the possibility that aboriginal warfare was dramatically transformed in the face of European contact in the late fifteenth and sixteenth centuries (Ferguson 1990b, 1992a, 1992b; Whitehead 1990, 1992). Ferguson goes so far as to contest the militant nature of many aboriginal Amerindian groups, including the Jívaro and the Yanomamö, claiming that their internecine warfare is a result of their interaction with European nations. Significantly, however, he does allow that "it is an indisputable fact that warfare existed in Amazonia before the arrival of Europeans" (Ferguson 1990b:238) and that "archaeology provides unmistakable evidence of war among sedentary village peoples, sometimes going back thousands of years" (Ferguson 1992a:113). It seems that our full understanding of aboriginal South American warfare—and of the degree to which it was transformed in post-Contact times—will have to await the collection of information about warfare as it was practiced by Amerindian groups in pre-Columbian times. Such information will have to be garnered for the most part by archaeologists.

With a few and notable exceptions (Lathrap 1970; Morey and Marwitt 1975; De Boer 1981), however, archaeologists have seemingly neglected warfare in their discussions of the integration and dynamics of prehistoric lowland South American societies. One reason for this may be the considerable problem of archaeological preservation in the humid tropical forests and savanna grasslands of Amazonia. As one leading proponent of warfare as a major factor in the development of chiefdoms in the Circum-Caribbean area has asked: "What evidence would an archaeologist digging in Yanomamö territory five hundred years from now find of the acute and recurring warfare among them today?" (Carneiro 1981:75).

In this volume I will address this question. I will begin by examining the patterns of warfare conducted by the Yanomamö and several other tribal and chiefly societies in northern South America. I will outline the continuities and differences between the warfare strategies of uncentralized tribes and centralized chiefdoms, and will propose some archaeological manifestations of each. In the concluding chapter I will show how the distinctive characteristics of chiefly warfare relate to the development of centralized decision making. Although archaeologists are beginning to recognize the role that intersocietal relationships such as warfare and exchange can play in the internal dynamics of these societies, they have concerned themselves principally with the latter (Wright 1977; Braun 1986; Lathrap 1973; Helms 1979; Shennan 1982; Spencer 1982). Consequently, this study of tribal and chiefly warfare strategies should help to redress the current imbalance in the treatment of "trading and raiding" relationships among these prestate societies.

### *Uncentralized Tribes and Centralized Chiefdoms*

In his cross-cultural study of political centralization and warfare, Otterbein distinguished between the centralized political systems of chiefdoms and the uncentralized political systems of tribes (Otterbein 1970:4, 18). I wish to elaborate upon that dichotomy further by contrasting the nature of decision making in tribes and chiefdoms. Tribes, like chiefdoms, are made up of villages and households. Although the member communities of a tribe recognize their common descent, language, and other tribal customs, they remain politically autonomous. Decisions are made by consensus, in a lengthy, circuitous process that Johnson has named "sequential decision making" (Johnson

1982:403). For example, among the Yanomamö of the Parima highlands, all adult males are involved in deciding when and where to gather wild foods; whether to build a new village *shabono;* or how to conduct the marriage of a kinswoman. The opinions of male and female elders are highly respected, and mature wives and sisters express their views on most matters as well. But once a decision has been reached, each man is still free to do what he pleases (Smole 1976:70).

This is not to say that tribes lack leaders. There is a limitless supply of potential leaders who can emerge by virtue of their prowess, cunning, eloquence, hunting skills, curing powers, diplomacy, and even their luck at being in the right place at the right time (Sahlins 1968:22; Fried 1967:33–34; Werner 1980:105–111, 121–158). But the decision-making authority of these leaders is episodic and specific in nature. Even village headmen or recognized "big men" cannot overstep the arduous process of sequential decision making and exert decision-making authority apart from their fellow kinsmen, cronies, and allies. As we shall see, they recruit and lead war parties not by force but by example, and their plans can be readily challenged by participating warriors. In the absence of any kind of centralized decision making, "it seems remarkable that a tribe remains a tribe" (Service 1962:104).

Chiefdoms, by contrast, are autonomous political units comprising a number of villages or communities under the permanent control of a paramount chief (Carneiro 1981:45). They overcome the limitations of sequential decision making and are marked by what Peebles and Kus call "a higher-level ritually sanctioned homeostat—the chief" (Peebles and Kus 1977:430). The chief fills a formal, hereditary office at the apex of a regional administrative hierarchy of local chiefs whence he exerts decision-making authority for the chiefdom as a whole. The nature of decision making in chiefdoms is thus centralized and hierarchical in what Johnson refers to as a "simultaneous hierarchy" (Johnson 1982:409). The chief simultaneously coordinates the production, distribution, and exchange of material goods and services for the entire cultural system, with the help of a ritual calendar of feasts over which he presides (Earle 1978:188–189; Peebles and Kus 1977:425–427). He also participates in interregional alliances with neighboring chiefs for the purposes of exchange and warfare (Flannery 1968; Friedman and Rowlands 1978; Helms 1979; Spencer 1982:42–58; Wright 1977:382–383). In distinguishing between the organizational capacities of tribal big-men and chiefs, Sahlins notes: "A chief is a true authority: his is the power of the group rather than the person, given by the structural obligations of others to honor and obey him" (Sahlins 1968:26–27).

A corollary of the chiefdom's centralized decision-making hierarchy, however, is the absence of internal administrative specialization, which sets the chiefdom apart from societies of greater complexity. According to Wright (1977:381), the decision-making process of a chiefdom is externally differentiated into decision making on the local and central (or regional) levels, but is not internally specialized. Unlike the decision-making bodies of states, which are centralized, hierarchical, and internally differentiated into specialized bureaucratic components, the one-man show associated with chiefdoms precludes an internally specialized administrative organization. The chief, for example, has the authority to recruit warriors and stockpile supplies for warfare, but there are no standing armies or military depots at his disposal, in contrast to the specialized military forces and facilities that can be mobilized momentarily by the rulers of states.

Faced with the daunting task of centralized decision making, the chief's strategy is to walk the fine line between encouraging local chiefs to handle their own community affairs and risking political insurrection on the local level. How does the chief overcome this "central regulatory dilemma" (Spencer 1987:376) and maintain regional political allegiance?

The chief relies upon the sanctification of his authority; by virtue of his divine descent, he maintains privileged access to the supernatural world, whence his demands ultimately emanate. The chief's exalted position of leadership is legitimized by his identification with divine forces and is reflected in his dominant role in ritual activities.

He also consolidates his authority by building close alliances with village chiefs, sometimes by means of actual kinship ties with these cadet members of the chiefly lineage. Or he may actively pursue marriage alliances to broaden his network of ties with local chiefs.

Very often, these alliances are reaffirmed by the reciprocal flow of material goods between the paramount chief and individual village chiefs. In return for surplus mobilized on the local level and sent periodically to the regional paramount center, the paramount chief rewards the local chiefs with exotic prestige items, which he obtains through prestige-good exchange with the paramount chiefs of neighboring and distant polities (Spencer 1982:44–51; Helms 1979:31–32, 75; Earle 1978:181–182).

Finally, as we shall see, warfare serves the chief in this regard. For example, Helms has suggested that sixteenth-century Panamanian chiefs pursued warfare with neighboring groups "as a political occasion or activity in its own right that served to highlight the contenders as men of prestige and of 'power,' quite apart from booty or loot gained" (Helms 1979:32). Of course, the division of the spoils of war, including captives, can also augment the chief's political position at home (Gibson 1974:132–133; Carneiro 1981:61, 65) in the same way that the bestowal of prestige goods enhances the loyalty of his supporters and cements his alliances with lesser chiefs. Not surprisingly, in their survey of the functions of leaders in prestate New World societies, Feinman and Neitzel (1984:49–56) discovered that two-thirds of Central and South American leaders conduct war-related activities.

# Chapter 2

# Tribal Warfare Patterns

Long-distance raiding (Métraux 1949:384; Harner 1972:182; Chagnon 1983:170) is the type of primitive warfare I will be examining here. Other forms of hostility fall into the category of individual feuds or personal vendettas, which can exist between members of the same community or between separate communities within the same tribe (Divale 1973). Feuds erupt in the form of individual contests that range from bewitching tactics to chest-pounding or side-slapping duels and club fights, which usually stop short of drawing blood. They are designed to avenge personal offenses, such as wife stealing or food theft, and in the case of the Yanomamö, are not intended to kill the opponent (Chagnon 1983:170–174). Even the Jívaro, whose feuding includes the assassination of individuals, distinguish between these local hostilities and true warfare (Harner 1972:116, 180–183).

The following review of Jívaro and Yanomamö warfare strategies will address a series of variables relating to the organization, leadership, and implementation of secret raids among autonomous tribal villages. In addition to these organizational attributes, I will examine the technological aspects of tribal warfare, in terms of the weapons and facilities used. Beginning with the objectives of raiding, I will consider the preparations for war, the recruitment and organization of war parties, the raiding tactics and weapons themselves, and the frequency and seasonality of warfare. I will also discuss the defensive measures undertaken by the attacking village and target village alike, as well as the responses by the latter to the actual raid and the resulting mortality figures. Finally, I will describe the post-raid rituals, including the mortuary treatment of warriors and other victims of warfare. Such a complete treatment of the organizational, tactical, and ritual aspects of tribal warfare, followed by a similarly complete examination of chiefly warfare, should enable us to evaluate the role warfare plays in the internal sociopolitical dynamics of tribes and chiefdoms.

## *Jívaro Warfare*

### The nature and objectives of warfare

Warfare among the Jívaro in the upper Amazon basin of southeastern Ecuador and northern Peru (Figure 1) consists largely of headhunting raids that are spurred by aggrieved individuals' desire for blood revenge. Headhunting raids are conducted beyond the tribe's boundaries, against groups "that speak differently" (Harner 1972:183), who are located up to six days' travel away (or thirty days' canoeing, by one account in Up de Graff 1923:223). The principal objective is to kill as many members of the enemy settlement as possible and seize their heads as trophies (*tsantsa*). After completing that objective, the raiders often ransack the houses, removing their valuables; the loot includes blowguns, quivers, dart poison, machetes, steel axes, ammunition, bead necklaces, featherwork, and dogs (Harner 1972:187; Drown and Drown 1961:98). Although women and children might be taken captive following a raid, more often than not they wind up as shrunken heads at some point along the journey homeward (Harner 1972:186; Drown and Drown 1961:98; Cotlow 1953:119, 243). Seizing territory is not an objective of Jívaro warfare (Harner 1972:182). As we shall see, Jívaro warfare tactics involve spending as little time as possible in the hated land of their enemies, "filled as it is with evil spirits" (Cotlow 1953:144).

### *Preparations for war*

With the aim of avenging the death of a kinsman who was killed in warfare or whose death is attributed to the bewitching tactics of the enemy (Stirling 1938:75; Harner 1972:143–144, 157; Karsten 1935:406–407; Cotlow 1953:47, 130, 151), an aggrieved household begins drumming up interest among tribesmen to participate in a retaliatory raid. The preparations for war begin when a renowned warrior (*kakáram*) agrees to lead a raiding party. By virtue of having killed several times, a *kakáram* is recognized as the leader of the expedition into enemy territory, although no special title is conveyed upon him. The members of the war party generally obey his orders, but only for the duration of the raid. Sometimes there will be more than one war leader, depending upon the composition of the raiding party (Harner 1972:183–185).

Some months before the planned raid, the *kakáram* lines up a respected male elder to host the first victory celebration upon the

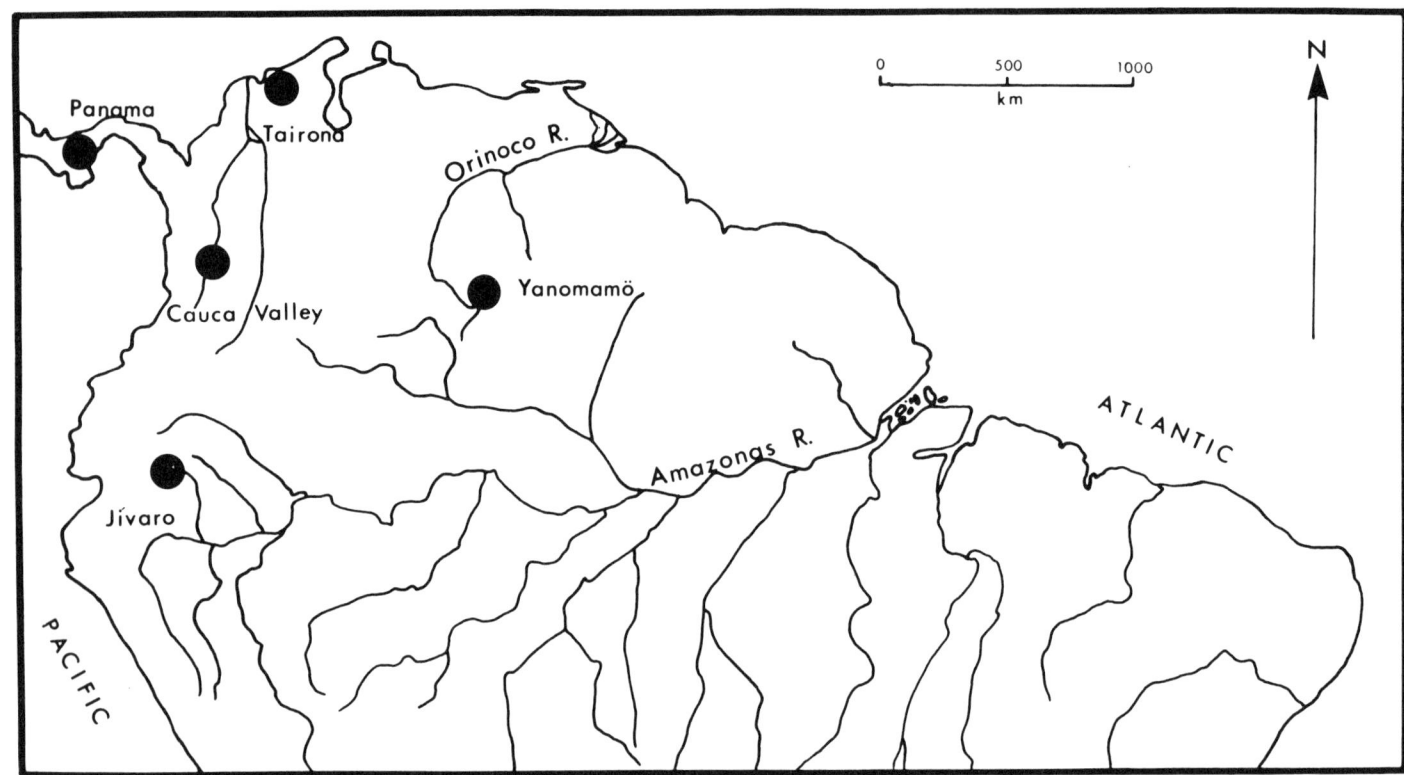

*Figure 1.* Map of northern South America and lower Central America with the locations of the tribes and chiefdoms that are the subjects of this study.

return of the headhunting party. Members of the raiding party will build the host a large house for the victory feast over the succeeding months. Two weeks or so before the raid, the war leader dispatches scouts into enemy territory to reconnoiter the target settlement. He also sends younger kinsmen to neighboring villages to recruit warriors for the war party. The recruitment process includes door-to-door canvassing, soliciting support to defeat a common enemy, even presenting a formal war challenge. The war leader relies upon his renown and resorts to his skills in the art of oratory and persuasion as he goes about recruiting tribesmen for the raid (Harner 1972:184; Up de Graff 1923:252–253; Drown and Drown 1961:77–78; Hendricks 1988:223).

The resulting war party usually consists of thirty to fifty men; earlier size estimates of Jívaro raiding parties tend to be larger than later ones. Kelekna described Achuara Jívaro raiding parties in the late 1970s as consisting of as few as two or three men or as many as several canoe-loads of warriors (Kelekna 1981:94). Harner, who last visited the Untsuri Shuara Jívaro in 1969, states that a war party rarely exceeded forty men (Harner 1972:184, 204). Missionary Frank Drown, who has lived among the Shuara Jívaro since 1946, accompanied a raiding party launched against the Achuara Jívaro and described the recruitment of "nearly a hundred men" for the raiding party, which dwindled to fifty men by the time they reached the enemy settlement, due to the departure of those members of the party who had suffered dreams of defeat and death (Drown and Drown 1961:78). In 1945 filmmaker Lewis Cotlow encountered a raiding party of twenty-five warriors drawn by the signal drum from settlements four to five miles away on the eve of their departure, and later reported twenty warriors at the actual scene of the raid (Cotlow 1953:38, 143, 146). Turn-of-the-century adventurer F.W. Up de Graff encountered a joint Aguaruna and Antipas Jívaro war party composed of fifty-five canoes and some two hundred men in October of 1899. It was a military alliance formed to raid the Huambisa Jívaro and led by an Aguaruna and Antipas war leader respectively (Up de Graff 1923:250–253). According to Harner (1972:204), Shuara Jívaro raiding parties could number up to 400 or 500 warriors at this time. The largest recorded alliance of Jívaro war parties produced the great uprising of 1599, when 20,000 Jívaro, led by the famed war leader Quirruba and two deputy war captains, attacked Sevilla del Oro and other Spanish settlements in Jívaro territory, and succeeded in terminating Spanish rule there (Stirling 1938:16–18).

Along with the decreasing size of raiding parties over time is a decline in the frequency of Jívaro warfare. Whereas headhunting raids occurred on almost a monthly basis at the turn of the century, today the Shuara Jívaro rarely conduct more than one raid every year (Harner 1972:204). I recovered little direct information on the seasonality of Jívaro warfare, perhaps because there is no distinct dry season in the humid forested foothills of

Jívaro territory (Harner 1972:47–48). It has been suggested that in the past the Jívaro were encroached upon by floodplain populations who moved inland during the rainy season (Ross 1980:41), a development that certainly would have intensified intertribal warfare at this time of year.

On the eve of the raid, the warriors are summoned by the signal for war on the log drum to the newly constructed celebration house (Figure 2). They drink manioc beer and the hallucinogenic *natéma*. They stand in rows to exchange formal war chants with the host or war leader, complete with bloodcurdling cries, foot-stomping and weapon-thrusting movements (Harner 1972:184; Karsten 1935:283–286; Cotlow 1953:143–144). According to Cotlow (1953:143, 242), the war leader always takes the hallucinogenic *natéma* or *maikua* drink before a raid in order to learn from the "old ones," or mythical ancestors (Karsten 1935:447–448), whom he encounters in his dreams, whether the planned raid will succeed. The importance of seeking visionary knowledge, which the Jívaro express as "seeing," by taking *natéma* or *maikua* before going to war is underscored by the Shuara warrior Tukup', who claimed that a warrior who goes to war without seeing and knowing who his enemy is, is likely to be killed (Hendricks 1993:164–165, 290). If the outcome appears favorable, the members of the raiding party reassemble at dawn in a formal lineup of warriors and perform a final round of war cries. Jars of manioc beer are placed before them for breakfast, whereupon they file out silently to war.

*Organization of war parties*

Overnight camps are pitched along the trail to the target village. Generally they consist of simple lean-tos and hearths, which are constructed in less than an hour at nightfall. A group of scouts remains ahead in their own overnight outpost; their job is to locate the enemy village, and if possible, to count the resident warriors (Up de Graff 1923:265–266). In the joint Aguaruna-Antipas raiding party that Up de Graff accompanied, he noted: "By day they mingled so that there was no distinguishing the two parties, but by night they camped apart, suspicious, probably, of each other for they are natural enemies" (Up de Graff 1923:253). Their overnight camps consist of separate groups of shelters, each with a hearth, surrounded by a cleared strip, and spaced some thirty yards (27.42 m) apart (Up de Graff 1923:263–264). Incidentally, this was precisely the strategy adopted by the representatives of four Jívaro groups who assembled at the Sepa River and camped there overnight for the purposes of filming a victory feast dance; after the dancing each group left the clearing and went off in a different direction to its own shelter in the forest (Cotlow 1953:225–233). During allied war parties, pairs of close relatives are responsible for protecting one another from attack by other members of the expedition (Harner 1972:185). Any women along on the war expedition remain at one of these camps (Cotlow 1953:147).

At the last overnight camp before reaching the enemy settlement, the warriors dress for war. They apply black paint from the *sua* fruit (*Genipa americana*) to their faces and bodies for camouflage, for recognition by other members of the attacking party, and for courage (Drown and Drown 1961:78–79; Up de Graff 1923:264; Karsten 1935:288–289). According to Karsten (1935:288–289; cf. Harner 1972:2–4), their war dress included feather head ornaments and hair knots, ear tubes, jaguar-teeth necklaces, and belts of human hair or snake skin (Figure 3). Cotlow, who was impressed by their war dress, said "it was an unbelievable sight, for the men were painted with much black *sua* and had their hair dressed with their finest feathers. If their heads were to be taken, they would at least look their best!" (Cotlow 1953:144) (Figure 4). For armor they carried a round shield of *ceiba* wood (*Ceiba bombax*) and formerly of tapir or manatee skin, which today they reserve for ceremonial occasions (Figure 5) (Stirling 1938:79, 86–87; Harner 1972:205).

*Warfare strategies, weapons, and tactics*

The key to the success of the nocturnal or matutinal raid is the element of surprise. The raiding party approaches to within earshot of the target village—to within ten yards (9.14 m), by one account (Up de Graff 1923:270)—and waits for the inhabitants to emerge from their houses (Figure 6). Large allied raiding parties will break up into member groups for the ambush. At just the right moment, they storm the village, attacking the inhabitants with their lances, bayonet-style, or opening fire with their shotguns. Kelekna points out that the most experienced warrior takes aim first, followed immediately by the other warriors (Kelekna 1981:95).

Prior to the introduction of the shotgun in the 1850s, the Jívaro used wooden lances six to eight feet (1.83 to 2.44 m) long for warfare. They were made from the hard black wood of the *chonta* palm (*Bactris, Iriartea, Giulielma*), and tipped with *chonta* wood, bone, and more recently, with iron points (Stirling 1938:79, 85–87; Cotlow 1953:34). Even in this century, the lance persists alongside the shotgun, perhaps because it is believed to possess certain magical powers (Drown and Drown 1961:83; Harner 1972:186; Stirling 1938:86–87). Indeed, Cotlow described a raid that occurred in 1945 in which the raiders and defenders threw aside their firearms and fought hand-to-hand with lances (Cotlow 1953:146). The legacy of the lance in Jívaro warfare is implicit in the phrase "carrying the lance," which continues to be the way they express "going to war" in the age of firearms (Hendricks 1993:150–151).

Other weapons attributed to the Jívaro include spears and spear-throwers, bows and arrows, double-pointed palm throwing-sticks, copper axes, and blowguns and poisoned darts. Stirling claimed that the blowgun darts tipped with a variety of plant poisons (*curare*) were used only for hunting game and never for warfare—a taboo adhered to by the Jívaro in the seventeenth century according to Jesuit priest Francisco Figueroa. Karsten observed the same custom of not using the blowgun and poisoned darts in war, although he was told that in former times the Jívaro used them in war, and Harner mentions that they were formerly

*Figure 2.* Jívaro warrior wearing ear tubes and carrying a lance. [By G. K. Cherrie (1920), Neg. #212864. Courtesy of the American Museum of Natural History.]

used in the defense of a household during an attack (Stirling 1938:78–79, 84–85; Zikmund and Hanzelka 1963:260; Karsten 1935:155, 159; Harner 1972:57, 205).

If the village has a defensive palisade, or if the inhabitants have anticipated the presence of the raiding party and remain boarded-up in their houses, it is difficult to carry out a surprise attack. Other tactics will be resorted to under these circumstances. The raiding party may have to lay in wait and hold the boarded-up inhabitants under siege until the occupants are forced by hunger to emerge for provisions; as many as sixty or seventy persons were held under siege during a prolonged war among the Achuara Jívaro in the late 1970s (Kelekna 1981:95–96, 225). The war leader has to weigh the factor of waiting for the right time to attack against the anxiety of his warriors, who might abandon the endeavor altogether. As Cotlow learned, "it is not easy to storm a *jivaría*. Asapi [the war leader] could besiege the house, keeping his enemies inside until they ran out of food and opened the door. But he had no patience for a long siege and feared that some of his men had even less and would leave after a short while. He had to strike while they were angry and hot-tempered, brave and lusting after blood and *tsantsa*" (Cotlow 1953:145). In this case when barking dogs had alerted the inhabitants that an enemy raiding party had approached, the raiders retreated noisily, only to turn back silently through the forest to the target village and wait to attack the unsuspecting inhabitants as they emerged from their houses (Cotlow 1953:145–146). Alternatively, the raiders might set fire to the thatched roofs with firebrands. As the inhabitants try to escape, they are killed and beheaded, man, woman, and child alike (Karsten 1935:289–291; Up de Graff 1923:270–274; Drown and Drown 1961:79–97; Harner 1972:186; Kelekna 1981:95–96).

The Jívaro also resort to treachery in their quest for revenge. In the guise of visiting, trading, and feasting with their targeted victim, the plotters will choose the right moment to catch the victim off guard and kill him. Kelekna reported the following example of treachery in the assassination of a great Achuara Jívaro warrior, Pinchu:

After many years of warring, an enemy group approached him seemingly in an attempt to end hostilities. Pinchu was formally invited to establish a trading relationship. He accepted and visited the house of his former foe. After a day or two of negotiations, a feast was given to celebrate the occasion. That night, Pinchu and his party pleasantly drunk with nijiamanch were surrounded and gunned down in their sleep. [Kelekna 1981:97]

The kill-all strategy practiced by Jívaro raiding parties is reflected in the available mortality figures. A recent mortality sample of over 250 Achuara Jívaro in the upper Morona River revealed that 59% of the adult males, 27% of the adult females, and 12% of children's deaths were homicides (Ross 1980:46;

*Figure 3.* Jívaro warrior with lance in Zamora, Ecuador. [By G.K. Cherrie (1920), Neg. #212859. Courtesy of the American Museum of Natural History.]

*Figure 4.* Jívaro warriors wearing face paint and feather ornaments, in Ecuador. [By William Bell Taylor (1907–1909), Neg. #125199. Courtesy of the American Museum of Natural History.]

1984:96). Achuara warfare in 1959–1960 alone accounted for some eighty deaths (Ross 1980:46). Cotlow's account of a single raid against a village on a tributary of the Morona River suggests that no fewer than eighteen men, women, and children were killed by a party of twenty raiders in a period of fifteen minutes. Since some of the victims were relatives of the raiders, their heads could not be taken, and since "no Jívaro is interested in a child's head or a woman's" (Cotlow 1953:146), only nine heads were severed. Finally, in the single aforementioned Aguaruna-Antipas raid in 1899, eleven Huambisa heads (both male and female) were secured (Up de Graff 1923:274–275). If the previous example is any indication of the actual number of victims relative to the number of heads taken, then it is likely that there were more than eleven victims of this allied raid.

The sought-after heads are severed, sometimes while the victims are still alive, with a tool kit that includes lance points, stone axes, split bamboo knives, sharpened clam shells and *chonta*-wood or steel machetes. An incision is made on the victim's chest and the skin is rolled back. The muscles are cut through, and then the lance or knife is thrust between two vertebrae low on the neck "as close to the trunk as possible" (Karsten 1935:294; Stirling 1938:50, 55; Cotlow 1953:146–147, 127; Zikmund and Hanzelka 1963:269). Then the trophy-takers sling the heads by their long hair over their shoulders or string them by passing lengths of stripped bark or palm fronds through their mouths and out at the neck for the trip home (Up de Graff 1923:274–275; Cotlow 1953:147; Drown and Drown 1961:97).

If circumstances permit, the raiders loot the enemy settlement. The booty includes utilitarian and exotic trade items. In the aftermath of one raid witnessed by Up de Graff: "Nothing was too small to escape the Aguarunas' attention. They cleaned out the house from end to end, every man keeping for himself all he could lay hands on" (Up de Graff 1923:274–275). Sometimes they will set fire to the looted houses before retreating "swiftly and silently" (Cotlow 1953:234).

The taking of war captives is not a general practice among the

*Figure 5.* Jívaro warrior wearing feather headdress, ear tubes, and jaguar-teeth necklace, and carrying lance and wooden shield. [Drawn from Karsten 1935: Plate XXVI:1.]

Jívaro. There are instances of women and children being abducted, and cases of men seeking additional, younger wives by abducting them from enemy settlements after a raid (Cotlow 1953:119, 144, 243). But war captives are not considered great prizes. For one thing, they do not submit readily to their captors, and often escape. Also, the Jívaro prefer to seize women from within the tribe, since they look upon the members of foreign tribes with dislike and distrust. Finally, a warrior who wishes to take a woman or young girl home as an extra wife must contend with the likelihood that she might be killed and beheaded by other members of the raiding party or by fellow tribesmen at home (Harner 1972:186–187; Drown and Drown 1961:98–102; Karsten 1935:291; Up de Graff 1923:276, 282).

*Defensive strategies*

Ross (1980:47) attributes the "pulsating nature of Achuara settlement" to the effects of warfare. Jívaro settlement patterns have traditionally consisted of neighborhoods made up of small, dispersed households that are located no closer than a half-hour's walk through the forest from each other, and that tend to be spaced between one hour to one day's walk or canoe trip apart (Figure 7). They are usually located in defensible positions overlooking the headwaters of tributary streams (Ross 1980:49; Descola 1981:626; Zeidler 1983:160; Cotlow 1953:8, 114; Meggers 1971:62).

According to Ross (1980:54), warfare sets a lower limit on the sizes of these isolated communities, below which they become vulnerable to attack. The average Jívaro household contains nine persons, but it can range up to 30 or more occupants (Harner 1972:77–79; Ross 1980:49; Descola 1981:626; Zeidler 1983:164).

As warfare intensifies, the settlement pattern experiences the following developments. One response to an actual attack or to an expected attack involves fortifying a settlement by erecting a palisade of thick *chonta* trunks, approximately 2.5–3 m tall, around it (Karsten 1935: Plate X(3–4), 81, 261; Stirling 1938:59; Ross 1984:103; Drown and Drown 1961:158; Cotlow 1953:145; Kelekna 1981:46). The actual construction of Jívaro houses is defensive in design, for the walls are built of palmwood staves, with intervening cracks that allow the inhabitants to peer out and fire at any attackers. In time of war interior partitions of *chonta* poles and slats might be added within the houses themselves (Karsten 1935:261; Stirling 1938:59–60; Ross 1984:103; Harner 1972:43–44, 206; Kelekna 1981:46; Zikmund and Hanzelka 1963:152–153, 260). This may be the type of defensive measure taken by an Achuara group in anticipation of a Shuara raid when they built a large house "with double walls" (Hendricks 1993:57). From inside their boarded-up houses, the defenders await the raiders and when barking dogs announce their arrival the defenders are prepared, hurling insults and firing shotguns at the enemy. If the raiders proceed with their attack and storm the settlement, the defenders confront the raiders with their lances in defensive face-to-face combat. Alternatively, however, the

*Figure 6.* Jívaro warriors on a raid. [By Lewis Cotlow (1945). Courtesy of the Yale Peabody Museum of Natural History.]

defenders might escape from their houses during the attack and flee into the forest (Cotlow 1953:145–147).

Before shotguns became generally available in the early part of this century, the Jívaro constructed war towers at one end of their houses. Karsten (1923:4, 1935:262) described them as towers made of *chonta* trunks, some twenty to thirty meters tall, which supported a small room, about four meters square in area, which could be reached by climbing a notched log. Stirling described another such tower associated with a fortified settlement:

> Just off the end of the building which was evidently considered least vulnerable there was a small room barely 15 feet [1.39 m] square which was protected on all sides in the same manner, but was raised about 20 feet [6.10 m] from the ground, supported by four stout posts and placed conveniently near the little door of the main building so that one could at once step on a notched tree trunk and climb to safety throwing the ladder away. These places are used for the safety of women and children in times of raiding and as a final refuge. Should the enemy try to climb to the hut, a shower of rocks is dropped down upon them, a supply being kept ready for that purpose.... However, the purpose of the structure is primarily as a protection for the women while the male occupants of the jívaria fight the enemy with their lances and shields. [Stirling 1938:60]

According to Harner (1972:205), poisoned blowgun darts and double-pointed throwing sticks were also fired at the enemy from these house towers. With the introduction of shotguns, however, these towers no longer served as a means of defense from armed attackers, who could make ready targets of their occupants, and they have disappeared entirely.

Another traditional defensive tactic involved the sounding of a log drum, which alerted nearby households of an attack, and summoned a defensive fighting force. The sounding of these signal drums represented the power of a giant anaconda spirit, who was called forth to help in the defense and subsequent retaliatory attack. Today, the discharge of a firearm serves the same purpose (Karsten 1935:110–112, 264; Cotlow 1953:143; Whitten 1976:219, 1978:852; Harner 1972:206; Kelekna 1981:95). In this way, one household that expected an enemy raid in 1945 had assembled a defensive fighting force of 18 warriors from neighboring communities (Cotlow 1953:146).

The Jívaro continue to erect a variety of traps and deadfalls with hidden poison-tipped lances and sharpened *chonta* sticks at strategic points around their settlements and along major trails leading to their households (Figure 8). Tunnels and foxholes are also dug inside the houses for protection and escape (Stirling 1938:59; Karsten 1935:262–263; Cotlow 1953:5–6; Harner 1972:206).

Sometimes, however, warfare intensifies to the point where

*Figure 7.* Unusual bird's-eye view of a Jívaro household on the the upper Santiago River, Ecuador. This is the house of the war leader (*curaca*) Peruche (see Table 2; Cotlow 1953:114). [By Lewis Cotlow (1945). Courtesy of the Yale Peabody Museum of Natural History.]

the inhabitants of a household find it necessary to abandon their settlement and seek refuge elsewhere. A number of neighboring Achuara households will unite and construct a large, fortified settlement under the influence of a great man, who is recognized as a great warrior and as a leader in times of war. These nucleated settlements can consist of a single fortified structure that is large enough to house up to 60 people, or a group of separate houses encircled by a palisade. Such defensive nucleation occurred along the Río Corrientes in 1977, when two fortified settlements were established under the influence of two allied war leaders; one of them housed 46 refugees and the other protected a small group of temporary houses that sheltered 72 people (Descola 1981:638). In the late 1970s, when Kelekna arrived in the Achuara Jívaro settlement of Yapitentsa, east of the Makuma River, she reported that its large population of 78 people consisted of wartime refugees from the north who had joined together for the purposes of defense (Kelekna 1981:25). The Shuara warrior Tukup' described this long-term Achuara practice in his narrative (1982):

> Long ago the Achuar
> never lived alone.

> Many Achuar lived together in one house,
> and indeed, these enemies lived together there.
> They still live together this way. [Hendricks 1993:54]

Wartime settlement nucleation is generally short-lived, however, never lasting for more than three or four years, after which the large fortified settlements are abandoned. New neighborhoods are formed as wartime refugees resettle in new communities (Descola 1981:638; Ross 1980:47, 49, 53).

Another consequence of escalating hostilities is the creation of unoccupied buffer zones, more than one day's travel and often some three days' travel in breadth, between enemies. These no-man's-lands are rich in game and in other wild resources because their exploitation is considered risky and undesirable. Natural barriers such as mountain ranges and vast swamp forests (*aguajals*) also help to separate hostile groups and to reduce conflict (Ross 1980:47–48, 53; Descola 1981:627–628; Cotlow 1953:145).

*Post-war rituals and practices*

For the raiders, the post-raid rituals begin along the trail home from war, at the first of a series of camps where the headtakers

*Figure 8*. Jívaro man attaching the palm-wood spikes of a comblike *tambunchi* trap on a trail in order to thwart raiders. [By Lewis Cotlow (1945). Courtesy of the Yale Peabody Museum of Natural History.]

stop to prepare the heads as trophies (*tsantsa*). These trophy-processing camps are usually situated along water courses, outside enemy territory, where the raiders are in relative safety from any pursuing enemies, and where they occasionally have cached ceramic jars for that purpose. Here the raiders will reunite with any women who have accompanied them on the war expedition. Those warriors who have killed gather around the heads that have been placed on a shield or on a large leaf and receive a blast of tobacco juice in their nostrils from the oldest warrior(s). Henceforth, these headtakers must practice certain purification observances, which include abstinence from certain foods, sex, weapons, and personal adornment (Drown and Drown 1961:98–101; Karsten 1935:294, 299–309; Up de Graff 1923:276–277; Cotlow 1953:124).

Several large fires are lighted at the trophy-processing camp, and while any women present prepare food, the headtakers begin processing their head trophies. With a sharp bamboo knife they cut neatly through the scalp from the base of the neck to the crown and skin the heads, using the knife to free the flesh from the skull when necessary. After this procedure, which takes fifteen minutes, the skulls are discarded; they are either cast away in the river or left behind at the trophy-processing camp. The eyelids of the skins are sewn shut, and *chonta* pins are used to seal the lips shut. The headskins are lowered by the hair into conical ceramic jars of water, one for each head. These cooking jars measure some 18 inches (46 cm) in diameter and 18 inches (46 cm) tall (Figure 9) (see Karsten 1935: Plates XXXI-XXXII) and the conical base is supported by stones. When the water reaches the boiling point, the shrunken heads are removed from the jars, which are discarded. The heads are filled with heated pebbles and sand collected nearby in order to sear the interior and to shrink the head further. Additional preparation of the trophy heads involves shrinking them further, to about the size of a large orange, by filling them with hot sand and pebbles and rubbing their exteriors with heated flat stones and charcoal to seal, to shape, and to decorate them. The shrunken heads are then hung by a lance over the fire to harden and blacken. These trophy-processing activities are either completed at a single camp over a period of a day or two, or they are carried out intermittently along the way home (Harner 1972:187–189; Drown and Drown 1961:98; Up de Graff 1923:277–280; Karsten 1936:294–296; Cotlow 1953:147–149).

A series of *tsantsa* feasts crown a successful raid. So important are these victory feasts to the Jívaro that when it is not

*Figure 9.* Ceramic cooking jars used to prepare trophy heads. These wide-mouthed, conical black vessels measure 18 inches (46 cm) in diameter and are approximately 18 inches (46 cm) tall. [Drawn from Karsten 1935: Plates XXXI, XXXII.]

possible to retrieve the enemy's head at the scene of the raid, either because the victim is a relative of one of the raiders or because a defensive counterattack prevented the killer from taking his victim's head, the killer uses a sloth's head as a substitute (Karsten 1935:298; Cotlow 1953:141–142; Harner 1972:148–149). The first of these feasts is held at the newly constructed house of the elder who agreed beforehand to act as host. The second *tsantsa* feast is celebrated a year later at one of the killers' houses, and the third and final feast, also hosted by a headtaker, is the most sumptuous of all. Up to 150 people from the local neighborhoods are summoned by the host's signal drum to attend the victory feasts. The guests paint their faces and arms red (with ground *Bixa orellana* seeds) and wear feather and monkey-fur headdresses, ear sticks, lip plugs, and necklaces of shells, bird bone, and jaguar teeth. After being formally greeted, they consume enormous quantities of manioc beer, boiled manioc, plantains, meat, and fish (Harner 1972:190–192; Karsten 1935:334–338; Cotlow 1953:124–125).

The killers continue their purification observances, which entail receiving tobacco juice in their nostrils and completing the trophy heads. On these occasions their bodies are decorated with black *Genipa* paint that is rolled on with a wooden cylindrical instrument (*payánga*), which used to be made out of clay, into which circular motifs are incised that produce rolled-out designs (Figure 23). Their black body paint signals their status as killers and provides them with a certain measure of protection against disease and witchcraft (Karsten 1935:306, 310–311, 429). All night chanting, dancing, lance thrusting, *natéma* drinking, and sexual revelry mark what "tend to be viewed by the Jívaro as the pinnacles of their social lives" (Harner 1972:193).

On the final day of feasting, the *tsantsa* (or *tsantsas*) undergo their final preparation; the lips are tied with long cotton strings, and the ears are sometimes decorated with small toucan feathers (Figure 10). Occasionally, some of their hair is removed to make additional trophies, such as gourd *tsantsas* or belts. After the victory feasts, however, the *tsantsas* lose much of their value and wind up as mere keepsakes. If not lost they are hung from the house beams, worn on social occasions, exchanged, even laid to rest with the headtaker upon his death (Stirling 1938:78; Harner 1972:147, 191; Drown and Drown 1961:101; Karsten 1935:361; Up de Graff 1923:282–283; Cotlow 1953:40).

Enormous prestige and supernatural power accrue to the headtakers upon the conclusion of the *tsantsa* feasts. By virtue of hosting the feasts, they augment their reputation and largesse, in spite of the fact that their family's resources will be depleted as a consequence of their generosity as hosts. Harner notes that the primary purpose of the *tsantsa* feast "is to acquire prestige, friendship, and obligations through being recognized as an accomplished warrior and, through the feasting, by being a generous host to as many neighbors as possible" (Harner 1972:191–192). Their trophy heads indicate that they are killers or "powerful ones" (*kakáram*) who possess much *arutam* power, and who are respected by friend and foe alike (Figure 11). The term *arutam* refers to the "old ones," to the first ancestors of the Jívaro who were great warriors (Karsten 1935:448), and therefore whose enormous power is sought by their living descendants. This *arutam* power is considered to increase the headtaker's physical and mental strength as well as his resistance to disease and death (Harner 1972:139, 91). By means of further killing and headtaking a *kakáram* will accumulate further *arutam* power and will become "very powerful" (*ti kakáram*) and a leader of war parties. By the time a distinguished warrior reaches this point in his career of seeking *arutam* power, he may already be elderly. Most Jívaro leaders, who are referred to as "old" men or "big" men (*untä*), have achieved this position in recognition of their career as killers and hosts (Harner 1972:110–115, 191; Siverts 1975:665; Stirling 1938:75; Up de Graff 1923:282).

*Mortuary treatment*

The Jívaro bury their dead in their houses, either in graves 2.5–3 feet (.76–.91 m) under the house floor or in hollow log coffins on low scaffolds above the floor or suspended from the roof. Burial treatment varies according to the individual's sex and age. When the male head of household dies, he is buried between the house's two central roof supports in the male *tankamash* end of the house. He will be buried either under the floor or above it in a large hollowed-out balsa log tied closed with bark strips or vines and aligned east-west, with his head to the east (Figure 12). His body is adorned with black body paint and glass-bead necklaces and wrapped in cloth, and his funerary accompaniments include his *chonta* lance, his blowgun, his round stool, and any *tsantsa* still in his possession. Other personal effects, including his quiver of darts and his gourds of cotton and poison, are

*Figure 10.* Jívaro human-head trophies (*tsantsas*), Ecuador. [By Kay C. Lenskjold (March, 1921), Neg. #38750. Courtesy of the American Museum of Natural History.]

*Figure 11*. Jívaro warrior at a victory feast, wearing the shrunken head of the enemy he has killed. [Drawn from Karsten 1935: Plate XXVIII.]

suspended overhead in his monkey skin bag. A large basket of cooked manioc and meat is also hung above the head of the deceased; a jar of manioc beer is placed on the floor. Otherwise, the house is stripped, swept clean, and then abandoned. Subsequent family burials might be included in the family mausoleum, which will be tended by their descendants (Karsten 1935:458–459, Fig.11; Harner 1972:166–167; Descola 1981:620; Cotlow 1953:8–10; Kelekna 1981:63).

There is some diversity of opinion as to the mortuary treatment of warriors killed during a raid. Karsten (1935:292, 460) describes the rapid burial of victims near the scene of their death, and especially those victims who have been killed with the lance and beheaded. Frank Drown described the hasty burial of a member of a Shuara Jívaro raiding party along the trail while retreating from enemy territory (Drown and Drown 1961:98). According to Harner (1972:168), the victims of a headhunting raid are granted the usual burial of someone their sex and age.

Occasionally, a great warrior (a *kakáram*, or an *untä*), who is believed to possess much *arutam* power (Harner 1972:112), receives special funerary treatment. According to Karsten (1935:458), his body is seated on a stool in a subterranean pit alongside a central roof support of his house, together with his lance, food, and manioc beer. Harner (1972:168–169) describes the temporary burial above ground of the body seated on his stool, propped up against a central roof support and surrounded by a palm stave enclosure. The stool is a clear expression of his power; only heads of households and headmen have the right to sit on such stools, a right that in Jívaro myths is associated with a position of power and authority (Hendricks 1988:230). After a designated period of ritual visits by sons who seek the deceased's *arutam* power, the body is buried in the usual way. Filmmaker Lewis Cotlow recorded a similar funerary treatment among the Huambisa of the Santiago River in 1940. He entered the abandoned house where a deceased leader lay in a hollowed-log coffin that was suspended on end from the roof; unlike ordinary men who were laid to rest in a horizontal position, this leader was accorded an upright position, "like a good *curaka*" (Cotlow 1953:9). Cotlow was told that the deceased's descendants would visit his grave every month and bring food and manioc beer for two years. By that time, the deceased, who in life had been a brave warrior and a taker of many heads, and who therefore was entitled to become a jaguar, could take care of himself (Cotlow 1953:10–11).

## Yanomamö Warfare

### The nature and objectives of warfare

To the Yanomamö of the upper Orinoco basin on the border of Venezuela and Brazil (Figure 1), "warfare proper is the raid" (Chagnon 1983:170). The sequence of chest-pounding or side-slapping duels, club fights and spear fights that precede it are but formal, sometimes prearranged, alternatives to warfare. And unlike intravillage conflicts between competing or growingly hostile factions, which can be resolved ultimately by the fissioning of a community into separate villages (Lizot 1988:558–559), outright warfare takes place *between* villages. Intervillage raids can occur between unrelated and related communities, which tend to be spaced at least two or three days' walk apart (Chagnon 1968a:117, 135). The minimum distance between neighboring Yanomamö villages is a few hours' to a day's walk, but some warring villages can be located as much as ten days' travel away (Chagnon 1968a:117, 1983:43; Lizot 1988:522, 524). Valero recorded travel of several days, to six, nine, and eleven days for the sequence of Yanomamö raiding parties that abducted her at various points during her life in captivity among a half-dozen Yanomamö groups (Valero 1984:33, 74–76, 79, 486–487).

Revenge killing is the primary incentive for conducting a raid on another village. Ideally, the raiding party will kill one or more male inhabitants of the enemy village—the headman and other recognized warriors are considered the most desirable targets—in order to avenge the death by sorcery or outright murder of a kinsmen at their hands. Adultery and wife stealing can precipitate intervillage warfare, as can food theft, but only after a long round of fights, with fists, then with clubs, has failed to resolve these transgressions. Sometimes these club fights escalate to fights with fine wooden broadswords, spears, and increasingly today, with axes and machetes, which can provoke further hostilities (Chagnon 1983:7, 170–174, 176; Chagnon and Bugos 1979:216; Cocco 1972:356–362, 366–370; Valero 1984:201–204, 323–325, 345, 465–466).

Abducting young women from an enemy village is considered by the members of the raiding party to be a supplementary benefit or bonus of a successful raid, and very occasionally, a raid is launched for that purpose alone. Nevertheless, the abduction of women is practiced only when the circumstances of the raiders' retreat allow the dragging and guarding of reluctant female captives, who slow them down, and some of whom are apt to escape. Looting the enemy village is another outcome of a successful raid (Chagnon 1983:175–176, 180, 1988, 1990:51; Valero 1984:27, 45–49, 142; Lizot 1988:540–541, 559). Acquiring land resources is neither an objective nor a consequence of Yanomamö warfare (Chagnon 1968a:110–113; Smole 1976:79; Lizot 1977:515).

### Preparations for war

The preparations for war begin when a renowned warrior, sometimes the village headman, decides to raid another village. Chagnon alludes to the intensity of raiding among the Yanomamö, "who live in a chronic state of warfare" (Chagnon 1983:7): one village in Chagnon's study area was raided some twenty-five times in fifteen months (Chagnon 1968a:141, 1983:180). On a regional scale, however, the frequency of raiding varies; villages along the tribe's periphery may enjoy many years without raids, but closer to the tribal heartland it is rare for several years to pass without intervillage warfare. Here raids tend to take place weeks or even months apart, although the Yano-

Figure 12. Jívaro subfloor burial inside a house at Andoas at the junction of the Bobonaza and Pastaza Rivers, Ecuador. [Neg. #128027. Courtesy of the American Museum of Natural History.]

mamö have been known to launch a counterraid the day after an attack upon their village (Chagnon 1983:71; Smole 1976:49; Valero 1984:342, 419–420).

Most raids occur during the dry season, when intervillage travel is relatively easy. When the leader of a successful Shamatari raid against the Shekerei-teri encountered some Karawë-tari allies who happened to be visiting the village he scolded them for being there: "Ustedes sabían que este es el tiempo bueno para ir a hacer la guerra" (Valero 1984:70). Conversely, when some Pishaasi-teri came to invite a renowned Puunapiwei-teri war leader to join their raiding party against the Shama-tari, he declined to go because it was the rainy season (Valero 1984:434). Chagnon did record two raids during the rainy season: one raid was scheduled for the early rainy season in order to allow time for war preparations, but also to reduce the possibility of a counterraid until the succeeding dry season, hence as a defensive tactic; another raid occurred near the end of the rainy season (Chagnon 1983:5, 77, 179, 186).

One of the first preparations for war involves clearing new gardens away from the village in anticipation of the counterraids that the planned raid will foment. Indeed, the deteriorating relations between two neighboring villages in 1988 were such that one of the groups was beginning to clear additional gardens at a distant site and was planning to move there soon (Chagnon 1990:97). Alternatively, the villagers make arrangements to move near the established gardens of a relative. Sometimes a new communal structure (*shabono*) is constructed and fortified with wooden slats at the base of the roof and encircled by a tall palisade of tree trunks tied together with lianas (Chagnon 1983:178–180; Biocca 1970:276; Valero 1984:44, 153, 422–423).

In the event of an ad hoc raid, when there is not enough time for these preparations, the women are sent out to garden and to collect firewood in anticipation of the counterraid, which will prevent anyone from leaving the village (Valero 1984:328, 342, 370). A palisade of pashuba (*Iriartea exorrhiza*) trunks might be erected hastily about four yards (3.66 m) from the *shabono* and surrounded by a 100-yard (91.41 m)-wide cleared, burned strip (Biocca 1970:203–204; Valero 1984:169, 339).

*Organization of war parties*

Although there are no formal war leaders in Yanomamö society, "it is the wisest and boldest whose opinion prevails" (Lizot 1985:183). The village headman or another distinguished warrior commonly possesses the necessary qualities to organize and lead a war party; they are recognized as being *waiteri,* or fierce, by virtue of having killed one who has killed, and more (Chagnon 1983:6, 122–124; Biocca 1970:66; Cocco 1972:393). Valero relates the invitation made to her *waiteri* husband by another group to lead their raiding party: "You are *waiteri,* you are famous everywhere; you have killed Waika, you have fought against Shiriana; now you must go there. We will show you the way to the Shamatari and you must avenge our dead. If you kill a Shamatari, we will give you one of our women" (Biocca 1970:316; see also Valero 1984:462, 485).

The raiding party convenes for a feast, especially when it involves members of allied villages (Chagnon 1968a:136). Due mainly to travel considerations, these feasts—like the ensuing raids—are held principally during the dry season. By joining in a feast, which sometimes includes the ritual consumption of the individual's ashes whose death they wish to avenge, the host village and its guests pledge their alliance in war (Lizot 1985:178–179, 1988:525, 559–561; Valero 1984:359–361, 370; Smole 1976:26). A mock attack is staged with a grass or log dummy set up in the village clearing, while the raiders encircle the village stealthily. At the signal of the war-party leader, the raiders shoot at the target and simulate their subsequent retreat (Chagnon 1968a:136, 1983:181; Valero 1984:147, 370).

On the evening before the raiding party departs a formal warrior lineup is held in the village clearing. The maximum number of participating raiders recorded is fifty men (Chagnon 1983:182;

Valero 1984:148) and "nearly 40 men" (Lizot 1985:182) all of which represent allied war parties. Although Chagnon (1983:187) cites ten men as the smallest size for a raiding party to be effective, other sources describe village war parties of ten, six, and five men (Biocca 1970:43; Cocco 1972:400; Valero 1984:340, 419). One renowned Puunapiwei-teri warrior is said to have carried out a hit-and-run counterraid on his own against an enemy village (Valero 1984:420).

One by one the participating warriors line up, their faces and bodies painted black with wet or masticated charcoal, soot, and occasionally a prepared plant dye (Figure 13) (Cocco 1972:125, 385; Lizot 1988:514–516; Valero 1984:231, 275, 462). They knock their bows and arrows and utter wild animal calls. The village headman stands by acting as a drillmaster, making sure that the warriors are in a straight line facing in the direction of the enemy. A series of war cries are shouted into the night and repeated before the line breaks up for the night.

At dawn the raiders blacken their bodies again and check their arrowpoints and bowstrings while the women of the village prepare the roasted plantains, manioc cakes, and tobacco that the members of raiding party will carry in their vine hammocks. When the headman signals for the final lineup to begin, the respective war parties from each village align themselves for the allied war party. After a final war cry, the raiders march out of the village in single file. According to Cocco (1972:385–386), at the head of the line are young *waiteri* warriors of short stature, followed by the other raiders, including the leader of the war party. In the rear are the novices, who are participating in their first raid (cf. Chagnon 1968a:138, 1983:184). The warriors range from approximately fifteen to forty years in age. As the members of an allied war party file out of the village they are intentionally intermingled to form the single departing line. They stop only to pick up the bundles of provisions, which the women have left for them along the trail leading away from the village (Chagnon 1983:181–182; Valero 1984:148–149, 370; Cocco 1972:384–386; Lizot 1985:180).

As a rule some men must remain in the village to protect the women while the raiding party is away. During allied war parties this male home guard might include men from allied villages (Valero 1984:33–34, 371; Chagnon 1968a:138).

*Warfare strategies, weapons, and tactics*

The raiding party proceeds at a relaxed pace since the goal of the first day is to reach within an hour's walk of the target village. By dusk the raiders stop and establish an overnight camp along the trail. The nature of these overnight camps depends upon their distance from the enemy village. At a certain radius away they pitch simple lean-tos (*tapirís*) and hang their vine or bark-strip hammocks near hearths. The activities at these overnight camps include hunting, collecting, firing arrows at grass or log dummies, and body painting (Cocco 1972:226, 387; Lizot 1985:182, 1988:525, 559; Valero 1984:32, 51, 241, 342). But if the overnight camp is within easy striking distance of the target village, the raiders take the precaution of sleeping on the ground without lighting fires (Chagnon 1983:184; Smole 1976:86; Valero 1984:340–341, 433).

By this point in the expedition some of the members of the raiding party will have abandoned the effort, citing ominous animal calls, dreams, and other inauspicious signs, as well as illnesses and sore feet, as reasons for dropping out. Sometimes the leader of the raiding party will decide to turn back, and so too will the entire party. In view of these developments, it is not surprising to learn that raiding parties often fail before reaching enemy territory (Chagnon 1983:183–186, 1988:987; Lizot 1988:559; Valero 1984:242, 419–420).

At dawn the raiding party breaks up into groups of four to six men who approach their attacking positions near the entrances, trails, water sources, gardens, and hunting grounds of the enemy village (Chagnon 1983:184; Valero 1984:149). The raiders lie in wait, sometimes for a day or two, in a squatting position behind a tree with an arrow poised in their bows for the attack (Biocca 1970:56; Valero 1984:341). Indeed, it is evident from Valero's repeated use of the term "*flechar*" that to the Yanomamö making war or raiding means killing with arrows (Valero 1984:123, 319, 328, 365, 506). Their bowstaves are five to six feet (1.52–1.83 m) long and made of hard palm wood (*Bactris gasipaes, Jessenia bataua, Geonoma* sp.) and the arrow shafts, six to eight feet (1.83–2.44 m) long, of cultivated cane (*Gynerium sagittatum*). The six or seven arrows that warriors carry to war have different arrowpoints; bamboo and palm-wood points predominate, but bone points are also used. Most of the arrowpoints, including the extra points that they carry in their bamboo quivers, are tipped with *curare* poison (*Strychnos guianensis*), which is used especially for warfare (Lizot 1988:516–517; Cocco 1972:317; Chagnon 1983:46–48; Smole 1976:30, 178; Valero 1984:70, 260, 307, 353).

The Yanomamö also inflict harm on the enemy in other ways. By sprinkling the noxious powder (*aroari, waka moshi*) of a cultivated tuber (*Cyperus corymbosus*)—sometimes mixed with processed armadillo parts—on the arrows' feathers or by blowing it through tubes the raiders allegedly increase their chances of killing the unsuspecting enemy (Cocco 1972:185, 370, 386–387, 408–409; Lizot 1988:572; Chagnon 1983:67; Valero 1984:137, 224, 397, 512). Valero observed several other bewitching tactics used by the Shama-tari against their enemies. A small bundle containing dirt taken from outside an enemy village is passed from man to man and repeatedly pounded at an afternoon narcotic-taking (*yopo*) session; the dirt might also be sprinkled on a sherd and heated or moistened. Sometimes the fangs of the poisonous fer-de-lance are used at these sessions, thrust into the bundle of dirt and flung in the direction of the enemy (Valero 1984:82–83). Today the Yanomamö also threaten to burn red fabric and break glass near their enemies' *shabono* in order to inflict a deadly epidemic upon them (Valero 1984:470, 506).

The principal raiding tactic is to ambush one or more key male inhabitants as they emerge from the village to relieve themselves, bathe, collect water, garden, gather or hunt. To kill the headman

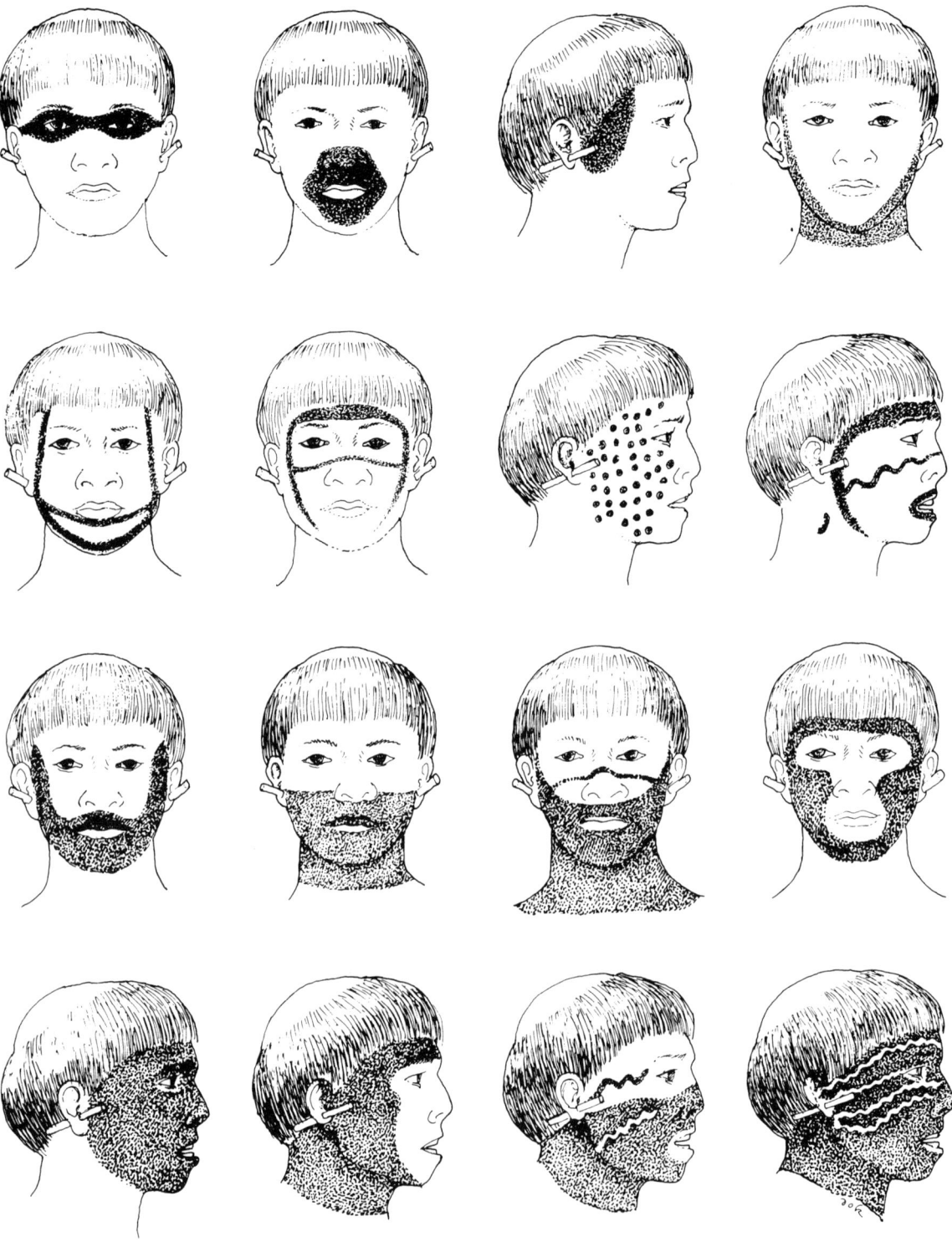

*Figure 13.* Face-painting styles worn by Yanomamö warriors. [Redrawn from Cocco 1972:128.]

or another *waiteri* warrior is a great deed. The killing of women, children, and old men, however, is looked down upon by the Yanomamö, although it happens occasionally. After one such raid by the Shama-tari against the Shekerei-teri that resulted in a devastating number of casualties, including women and children, the leader of the raiding party scolded his bloodthirsty warriors for having killed too many: "No estoy contento . . . No me explico cómo mataron a toda esa gente. Qué de muertos en aquel shapono! Flecharon hombres, mujeres, niños . . . Ustedes no debían matar como mataron" (Valero 1984:77, 48–50, 69–70, 329, 344, 353; Chagnon 1983:23, 180, 184–185, 189; Cocco 1972:388, 396). As soon as the volley of arrows has been fired, the raiders retreat quickly, sometimes abducting women and children of the victims (Lizot 1988:559–561; Chagnon 1968a:138, 1983:175–176; Cocco 1972:388; Valero 1984:69–72, 123, 341, 487).

The Yanomamö conduct nocturnal attacks occasionally using different tactics and weapons. One strategy involves shooting arrows into the *shabono* indiscriminately in the hope of striking an inhabitant. The arrowpoints used in these nocturnal attacks are not tipped with *curare,* because in the night it is difficult to hit and because the night dew waters down the poison (Valero 1984:347–348). Fire-tipped arrows are sometimes employed to set fire to the village and rout the inhabitants, whereupon they can be spotted easily and attacked (Cocco 1972:388; Valero 1984:332). To this end, the village of Tayari-teri was set ablaze by a Pishaasi-teri raiding party in 1980, forcing the inhabitants to flee and run for cover (Chagnon 1990:100; Lizot 1989:28–29).

The effectiveness of these matutinal and nocturnal attacks is surpassed by the sporadically-hosted treacherous feast. A treacherous feast is planned by two or three allied villages, one of which hosts a feast for the invited guests from another village. For example, Valero overheard the plans of a war alliance among the Namowei-teri, the Irota-teri, and the Shama-tari against the Pishaasi-teri in order to seek revenge for the Pishaasi-teri's killing of the Namowei-teri headman. The allied plan called for the Pishaasi-teri being invited to three feasts by the Shama-tari. At the third feast, the unsuspecting Pishaasi-teri guests, especially their headman and most *waiteri* men, would be killed by their hosts, which is precisely what ensued (Valero 1984:369, 386, 432). At some point during a treacherous feast, the hosts and their allies assail the hapless male guests with axes, clubs, machetes, bowstaves, and arrows. Those who try to flee are met with a volley of arrows from archers positioned outside the *shabono.* Although the wives and children of the victims are usually spared from death, some of them might be taken captive and distributed among the victors. The impact of a treacherous feast is great; in one such feast recorded by missionary James Barker in 1951, fifteen adult males from a single village were massacred (Chagnon 1968a:141, 138–139, 1983:3, 175; Valero 1984:234–235).

According to Chagnon, the secret raids and treacherous feasts conducted by the Yanomamö are "a phenomenon that affects all aspects of their social organization, settlement pattern, and daily routines. It is not simply 'ritualistic' war: at least one-fourth of all adult males die violently" (Chagnon 1983:5). In a mortality sample of 240 adult Yanomamö in Chagnon's study area, warfare accounted for 22.5% of all male deaths and 5.9% of all female deaths (Chagnon 1968a:140). But within the Yanomamö area the number of violent deaths varies, which reflects the aforementioned variation in the frequency of raiding between villages in the heartland and those along the tribe's periphery. For the Namowei-teri Yanomamö at the juncture of the Mavaca, Ocamo and Orinoco rivers, warfare and mortal duels account for 27% of all adult male deaths and 8% of all adult female deaths. Warfare among the Shama-tari Yanomamö who inhabit the uppermost reaches of the Mavaca River is more intense; 41% of all adult males and 5% of all females die in raids and duels (Chagnon 1974:160; Ross 1980:46; cf. Chagnon 1983:79). Other available mortality figures reflect lower intensities of warfare. During his fifteen years among the Namowei-teri Yanomamö, missionary Luis Cocco recorded the violent death of 25 men out of a sample of 2,000 Yanomamö (Cocco 1972:393). Among Yanomamö villages north of the Orinoco River, warfare accounts for 10–24% of male deaths (Lizot's figures cited in Albert 1989:637). For a single highland Yanomamö village of 210 inhabitants in the Parima massif, Smole recorded seven deaths during a two-year period; of the three adult males who died during this period, only one individual was killed during a raid (Smole 1976:49, 74).

The most immediate response by the inhabitants of a village under attack is to flee into the surrounding forest (Valero 1984: 46, 70, 354, 432). Following a successful attack, the raiders may proceed to loot the deserted *shabono* of its hammocks, baskets, ceramic and gourd containers, adornments, cotton, hallucinogens, and plantains, among other desirables. Steel machetes and axes have become highly prized booty. Any female prisoners are assembled and guarded at this time. Before retreating, the raiders might smash some ceramic jars and set fire to the village (Valero 1984:29, 70–72; Cocco 1972:388, 390).

*Defensive strategies*

Warfare is a major factor in the settlement mobility of the Yanomamö (Chagnon 1968a:118; Lizot 1977:505; Hames 1983:396–397, Table 13.2). In a society that lives under the constant threat of warfare, mobility is a defensive strategy to escape from enemy attacks (Lizot 1988:552). Lizot might well have had the village of Daiyari-teri in mind when he wrote this because that is precisely the strategy that this village adopted after a successful ambush during their war in 1980 with the Bisaasi-teri (Chagnon 1990:100). Indeed, picking up and moving is such a predictable outcome of warfare that it is used by respected male villagers to discourage their peers from precipitating a new round of warfare: "Por estar matando gente, fíjense cómo nosotros hemos tenido que venirnos de Kōnata, de Warëta, de Namowei, de Hahoyaope, para ahora vivir lejos de los demás Yanomami, pasando tanto trabajo. Ahora que estamos de paz, no debemos buscar más pleitos. Si volvemos a guerrear, tendremos que abandonar estos conucos, irnos para otros lugares y comenzar de nuevo" (Valero 1984:227). Just the anticipation of an enemy raid can prompt a village to move and establish a new *shabono,* and repeated raids upon a village will almost certainly lead to that settlement's relocation. The members of the village might seek temporary refuge at or near an allied village while they conduct their mourning ceremonies for the dead, clear new gardens, and establish a new *shabono* (Chagnon 1983:75; Valero 1984:207–208, 434). As described by Valero, such an arrangement might include the erection of a strong palisade by the hosts to protect the refugees (Valero 1984:339, 348–349, 362). North of the Orinoco River, allied villages will coordinate their movements as a defensive measure (Lizot 1988:524).

Valero documented several instances when the fear of an enemy raid encouraged a village headman to invite allies to a feast. It is a defensive strategy, a way of seeking safety by means of the temporary gathering of allies. Also, the presence of relatives of the enemy among the invited guests can serve to deter the anticipated raid by the enemy. Very often, in fact, the invited guests can be persuaded to take up longer residence at the host's village after the feast has concluded (Valero 1984:404, 413, 434–435).

The anticipation of enemy raids can prompt several allied villages to fuse and erect a single fortified *shabono,* since there is a minimal settlement size of approximately 45 people below which a village becomes vulnerable to attack (Chagnon 1968a:138; 1983:74, 180). In Valero's words, "tan poquitos, era peligroso quedarse allí" (Valero 1984:387). Fear of enemy raids in early 1966 prompted two highland Yanomamö villages (*teri*), for example, to move to a single *shabono* in a poorly-drained location along the edge of the Niyayoba savanna. Two other villages joined them there by the end of that year and erected another *shabono* alongside the former, with a single palisade that enclosed both structures in the form of a figure eight. In 1968 the four *teri* raised a single large *shabono* a few hundred yards south out on the Niyayoba savanna (Figure 14) (Smole 1976:93). Indeed, the intensity of warfare is partially reflected in the degree of population nucleation reached by intervillage fusion; some Shama-tari Yanomamö villages with their aforementioned higher rates of violent death have up to 400 inhabitants, whereas Namowei-teri Yanomamö villages remain below 200 people and average between 80–90 inhabitants (Chagnon 1983:79). Even the 35 villages in Lizot's central Yanomami study region that average 63 inhabitants today apparently derived from two larger, original communities, whose population at the turn of the century are estimated to have been 150 and 250 inhabitants, and thus approximated the sizes of the aforementioned Yanomamö villages to the south. The more nucleated central Yanomamö communities in the past were probably a consequence of village fusion spurred by more intense intervillage warfare then (Lizot 1977:501–502, 1988:521–524, 559).

When the Yanomamö select a new location for a village, their primary consideration is its security (Chagnon 1983:52; Smole 1976:58; Valero 1984:491, 507). Indeed, the Witokaya-theri's move away from their productive, maize-bearing gardens prompted Valero to remark: "no sé por qué los Witokaya-theri después abandonaron ese lugar; tal vez por miedo a los Hii-theri" (Valero 1984:442). The Kōhōrōshi-tari moved and established a new *shabono* seventeen days from their former village—far enough, they thought, to avoid a raid by their enemies, the Karawë-tari (Valero 1984:44). The Shama-tari Yanomamö, who are considered to be more militant, space their villages farther apart than the Namowei-teri Yanomamö, in keeping with their tendency to live in large, nucleated settlements. They may be located a three or four days' walk away from their closest neighbors (Chagnon 1979:93, 1983:43, 79). A different settlement pattern exists north of the Orinoco River, where Yanomamö communities range from 20 to 150 inhabitants today, and are thus smaller than those to the south. Yet they are spaced less than a day's walk apart, which makes their alliances, joint movements, and intervillage fusion easier to achieve (Lizot 1988:521–524, 559). As a matter of fact, when a Namowei-teri village fissioned in 1973–1974, the daughter village was erected just yards away from the original village in anticipation of raids from common enemies (Chagnon 1979:121).

In addition to maintaining a certain distance from neighboring villages and especially from enemy villages, uninhabited buffer zones and topographic barriers such as rugged hills and rivers also serve to separate them from neighbors and enemies. Yanomamö villages in the Parima mountains might seem to be closely spaced in terms of linear distance, but intervillage travel considerations here are tempered by the rugged terrain that must be negotiated (Smole 1976:47, 78; Chagnon 1983:179, 1979:93–94).

Yanomamö villages take other defensive measures, principally, constructing palisades 8 to 10 ft (2.44–3.05 m) tall of trunks lashed tightly with lianas a few feet outside the base of the *shabono's* sloping roof. Occasionally, they erect double palisades (Chagnon 1983:56; Smole 1976:67; Biocca 1970:203–204; Valero 1984:339, 415, 420; Cocco 1972:388). One village encircled by rock outcrops used them as a natural palisade, fortifying the intervening spaces with a wooden palisade (Valero 1984:348–349). Palm fronds are used to seal the gaps between the trunks of the palisade and to fortify campsites. Stacks of firewood or wooden slats protect the base of the roof—especially in the absence of a palisade—and are sometimes used as interior barricades, along with stacks of plantains or large baskets. The village entrances are covered by extending the palisade, or with dry brush and palm fronds (Chagnon 1983:10, 56; Valero 1984:329, 332, 339, 518). The importance of the palisade for defense is illustrated by Valero's comments in the aftermath of two raids, that had it not been for the village palisade, many more inhabitants would have been wounded and killed (Valero 1984:418, 476).

Beyond the palisade they clear from 16.5 to 100 yards (15.24–91.41m) of the surrounding forest that will soon sprout a thick undergrowth "which the enemy cannot penetrate.... Among the trees which they had cut down the enemy would make a noise,

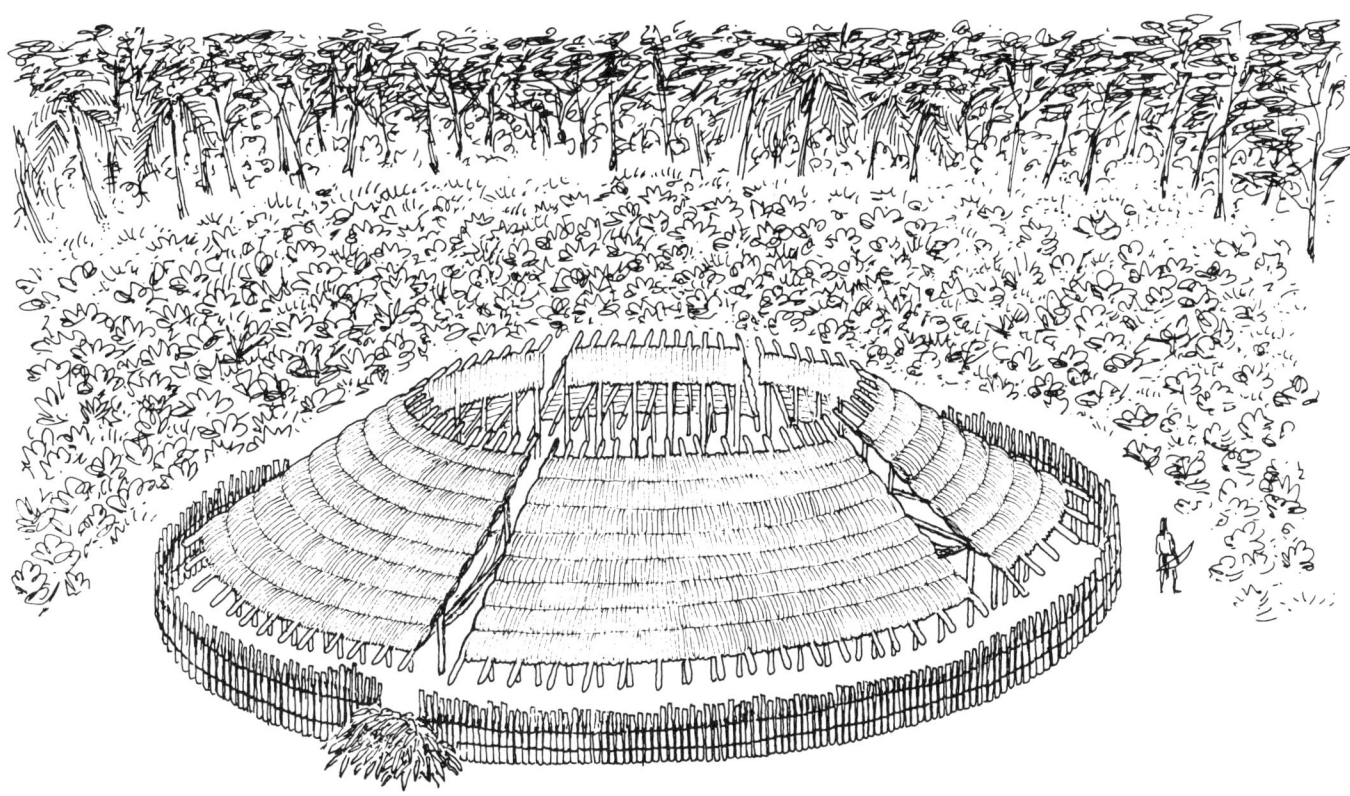

*Figure 14.* Artist's reconstruction of a Yanomamö *shabono* ringed by a defensive palisade and a cleared strip. [After Chagnon 1968: Fig.2-4 and Smole 1976:59–63.]

by stepping on the dry burnt branches and the men would hear and so shoot them" (Biocca 1970:204; see also Valero 1984:169; Smole 1976:68). Trails leading to the village are guarded and thorny branches are scattered across them at dark to deter a nocturnal raid (Valero 1984:153, 342, 518). In a final defensive tactic, women place a curse on the attackers by blowing the magical powder *aroari* in their direction, which has allegedly fatal properties. This may cause the attackers to take flight (Cocco 1972:386; Valero 1984:397).

*Post-war rituals and practices*

Purification rituals for the victorious raiders begin on the way home from war. They stop to bathe and adorn themselves with red body paint and feather ornaments. Those warriors who have killed, however, must bathe downstream and their bodies are scrubbed with fern leaves. They fasten little sticks in their ear lobes, and at their wrists and calves, which they use to scratch their bodies and to eat with. Their two-week to month-long purification observances (*unokaimou*) include ritual bathing, leaf scrubbings, and fasting, eating only roasted plantains and some honey. They sleep in isolated vine hammocks, and abstain from body painting, hallucinogens, and sex. By means of these purification rituals the killers cleanse themselves and seek protection from the revengeful spirits of their victims during the period of time before the latter are cremated. They must counteract the effects of supernaturally incorporating their victims' flesh and blood into their bodies during this uneasy *unokaimou* period. They should not participate in warfare, for the Yanomamö believe that those who have killed are easier targets at this time. The end of the killers' confinement is marked by a bath, a tonsure, fresh body painting, new feather adornments, animal-skin armbands and headbands. Finally, the killers remove their vine hammocks, scratching sticks and other items used during their purification rituals and take them out to tie up as bundles high up in a tree in the forest (Valero 1984:52, 74–75, 77–79, 82–83, 342–343, 376; Cocco 1972:390–393; Chagnon 1983:186, 1988:987; Albert 1989:638).

Having performed the *unokaimou* observances, these distinguished warriors are referred to henceforth as *unokai* and held in great esteem. By participating in future raids and carrying out more killings, their renown will increase to the point where they gain the reputation of being *waiteri* (fierce): "A good warrior—a *waiteri* man—enjoys a superior status; people respect him, fear him; he is influential in the political affairs of his community and his opinion is taken into consideration" (Lizot 1985:183). Chagnon has demonstrated that distinguished warriors also have more wives, either by abducting them from raided villages or by the customary marriage alliances between allies in which they are sought out as mates. Indeed, *waiteri* men are so attractive and so bold that they can openly seduce other men's wives, even to the point of breaking incest taboos. By the same token they can suppress any attempts by other men to seduce their wives. Due to their greater marital success, moreover, these distinguished warriors have more offspring (Chagnon 1979:101, 105, 1988:989–990, 1990:53; Valero 1984:79).

All Yanomamö headmen are *unokai* and most are *waiteri*, almost by necessity; "they are simultaneously peacemakers and valiant warriors. Peacemaking often requires the threat or actual use of force and most headmen have an acquired reputation for being *waiteri*" (Chagnon 1983:6; Chagnon 1988:988). Lizot uses "brave," "tough," "intrepid," "bold," and "stoic" to define the qualities of a *waiteri* man, and he emphasizes the person's ability to weigh matters rather than to erupt in anger, to have the courage to confront others, and to endure physical and psychic suffering (Lizot 1989:32–33). Chagnon has pointed out that these men's *waiteri* qualities include their ferocity, coerciveness, vindictiveness, and aggressiveness, as well as their willingness to use force to advance their own cause or those of close kinsmen. Accordingly, these men have more wives, children, and therefore, more kinsmen than do other adult males in their villages (Chagnon, Flinn, and Melancon 1979:317–319; Chagnon 1988:988, 1990:53).

All Yanomamö men seek to become distinguished warriors and to be considered *waiteri*. Many *waiteri* men boast of their prowess and of the superior status they have earned in war, as the following quotations illustrate:

> Soy hombre valiente. A mí me da fuerza el Espíritu báquiro. Yo no tengo compasión de nadie. Hasta a mi hijo lo puedo matar. Matar gente es un placer para mí. [Valero 1984:225]

> Yo soy valiente, el más valiente de los Puunapiwei-theri. Donde yo voy, derramo sangre de hombre. Por eso los Mahekotho-theri siempre me invitan a ir a pelear con ellos. [Valero 1984:462]

The superior status and positions of leadership achieved by distinguished warriors are constantly challenged by younger, *waiteri*-seeking men. It is only by carrying out additional and sometimes daring exploits that they can preserve their reputation. Sometimes the very fear of failing to appear *waiteri* will incite them to participate in revenge raids, even when they least want to (Chagnon 1983:188; Valero 1984:336, 410, 517; Cocco 1972:400; Lizot 1985:183). As Lizot points out,

> la lógica implacable del sistema exige que el status adquirido y la bravura sean permanentemente cuestionados, de tal manera que ellos no logran mantenerse sino a base de hazañas cada vez más arriesgadas. En el horizonte se perfila la sombra de la muerte, sistema terriblemente eficaz ya que impide el establecimiento de cualquier poder real. [Lizot 1988:556]

*Mortuary treatment*

The Yanomamö show concern for returning the victims of raids home. Wounded raiders are carried in bark strips or hammocks slung from poles in the middle of the retreating file of warriors, who take turns bearing them home. If it is possible, the retreating warriors stop to extract the wounded's arrowpoints with quartz flakes and peccary teeth, and to treat their wounds. The retreating warriors might launch counterattacks against any enemy pursuers in order to give time for the wounded to be carried away (Valero 1984:37, 51–52, 150). Dead raiders or the victims of an ambush are carried back to the village in bark slings or in hammocks hung from poles, whereupon their remains are cremated. Although circumstances do not always permit it, the Yanomamö prefer cremating the dead on a funeral pyre of split logs in the village clearing (Valero 1984:355, 366; Cocco 1972:389). This is especially the case upon the death of headmen, as the following quotations by their immediate relatives make clear:

> Yo no voy a quemar a mi papá lejos del shapono. . . . No es un muerto cualquiera. Por más lejos que estemos, hay que cargarlo para quemarlo en el shapono. [Valero 1984:261]

> No voy a pilar los huesos aquí en el monte. Quiero pilarlos en mi shapono. . . . El fue hombre grande. Sus huesos no se pueden pilar aquí. [Valero 1984:358]

All Yanomamö are accorded the same funerary ritual. The body is adorned with body paint and feathers, and a fresh wad of tobacco is inserted into the deceased's mouth. As the relatives assemble in the village clearing the belongings of the dead are publicly displayed and the rectangular funeral pyre is lighted. Still in its hammock, the body is placed on the pyre and covered by a layer of logs. Some of the deceased's belongings will be thrown into the fire as well, adding to the intended obliteration of the deceased (Valero 1984:262–263; Lizot 1988:572). When the body is completely incinerated and the pyre has cooled, the relatives collect the charred bone fragments, which are then ritually pulverized until the powdered bone passes through a sieve and is poured into small gourds (*cuias*), which are sealed with beeswax or with the white down of the sparrowhawk or some other bird of prey and distributed among the closest kinsmen. Upon receiving the cremated remains of the deceased war victim, they swear that they will avenge his death. At a later date, the deceased's remains will be consumed in a specially prepared plantain soup as part of a formal mourning ceremony (*reaho*). The ashes and charcoal from the funeral pyre are collected and buried away from the village along a stream. The area where the funeral pyre was erected is swept—indeed scraped—clean and fresh dirt is brought to resurface the area, which is then covered with leaves (Chagnon 1983:106; Valero 1984:263–265, 358–360, 369; Cocco 1972:444–454; Lizot 1985:23–30, 1988:546).

Distinguished warriors and headmen are accorded elaborate and repeated *reahos*; kinsmen and allies gather periodically from afar to partake in their ritual consumption, for many years after their death. Most significantly perhaps, these mourning ceremonies are often held on the eve of a revenge raid—"to make the raiders *hushuwo* ("feel anger verging on violence") and fill them with resolve" (Chagon 1988:986). They thereby serve to perpetuate warfare (Valero 1984:226, 358–360, 369; Chagnon 1983:106, 186–187; Smole 1976:26; Lizot 1988:559).

# Chapter 3

# Chiefly Warfare Patterns

Although chiefdoms were widespread in the Intermediate Area at the time of the Spanish Conquest in the sixteenth century, making it a prime area for the investigation of aboriginal chiefdoms (Earle 1987), they were virtually exterminated in the Colonial period. We are fortunate to have some accounts written by the earliest explorers and missionaries who penetrated the area, whose direct observations of the societies they were subduing include lengthy descriptions of chiefly warfare. Although much of the warfare described in these sixteenth-century ethnohistoric accounts was directed against the Spanish forces, the accounts nevertheless give some picture of the warfare strategies developed by these centralized societies in prehispanic times. To those critics who might reject, because of their inherent Colonial-period biases, the use of these ethnohistoric accounts to glean valuable information about aboriginal warfare patterns, I cite the words of a fellow ethnohistorian of northern South American Amerindians who has responded to similar criticisms of the historical sources by pointing out that if we reject these accounts, "then there seems little alternative to a wholesale rejection of all the historical evidence presented . . . , to say nothing of the attempt to write history at all" (Whitehead 1988:180). Consequently, I hope to show how useful a careful reading of these sources can be for the comparative study of warfare among the tribes and chiefdoms of northern South America and lower Central America (Service 1968:166; Steward and Faron 1959:174–177; Steward 1948: xv; Carneiro 1981:38–41).

I will be reviewing the warfare conducted by the chiefdoms of the Cauca Valley and the Sierra Nevada de Santa Marta in northern Colombia, and those of eastern and central Panama, all designated "militaristic chiefdoms" by Steward and Faron because "although the component villages of these chiefdoms were more or less self-sufficient . . . , they united under a supreme chief to conquer lands, exact tribute from people, and take captives. . . . Warfare was crucial to religion in supplying human victims for blood sacrifice in temple rites, and for cannibalism. It was also an essential factor in achieving social status" (Steward and Faron 1959:177). These militaristic chiefdoms conducted surprise raids against their enemies, which as we shall see, ranged from small-scale ambushes to attacks waged by fighting forces of over 10,000 warriors. As in the previous discussion of tribal warfare patterns, I will examine the objectives of their warfare, their preparations for war, and the size and organization of their war parties. I will also review their warfare strategies and tactics, their means of defense, and the consequences of warfare, including the post-raid rituals and mortuary treatment of warriors and captives.

*Warfare in the Cauca Valley*

At the time of the Spanish Conquest, a number of independent chiefdoms flourished the length of the Cauca River valley from Popayán to Cácares (Figure 15). It is clear from Trimborn's ethnohistoric study (1949:244–251, 256–257) that most of the Cauca Valley chiefdoms exhibited centralized decision-making authority on the local and regional (tribal) levels (Figure 16). Sometime prior to the Conquest, however, two supraregional chiefdoms (Taylor 1975:78; Spencer 1982:10–11) emerged at the northern and southern ends of the river valley, with their paramount centers at Guaca and Popayán. Interpolity relationships were shaped by marriage alliances, exchange and warfare (Trimborn 1949:257–258, 275–277).

*The nature and objectives of warfare*

A state of chronic warfare existed among the Cauca Valley chiefdoms. Entire polities fought against one another, by means of every available military and extramilitary tactic in what amounted to all-out warfare. Although revenge motives certainly spurred their counterattacks, the principal objectives of their warfare were acquisitive in nature. They enlarged their territories by seizing conquered land. They were also interested in controlling certain natural resources and trade routes. The major booty they sought was war captives, who served as slaves, as exchange items, and as sacrificial victims. A final objective was to keep expanding polities in the region at bay in the apparent belief that the best defense was a strong offense (Trimborn 1949:280–284, 288, 368–369).

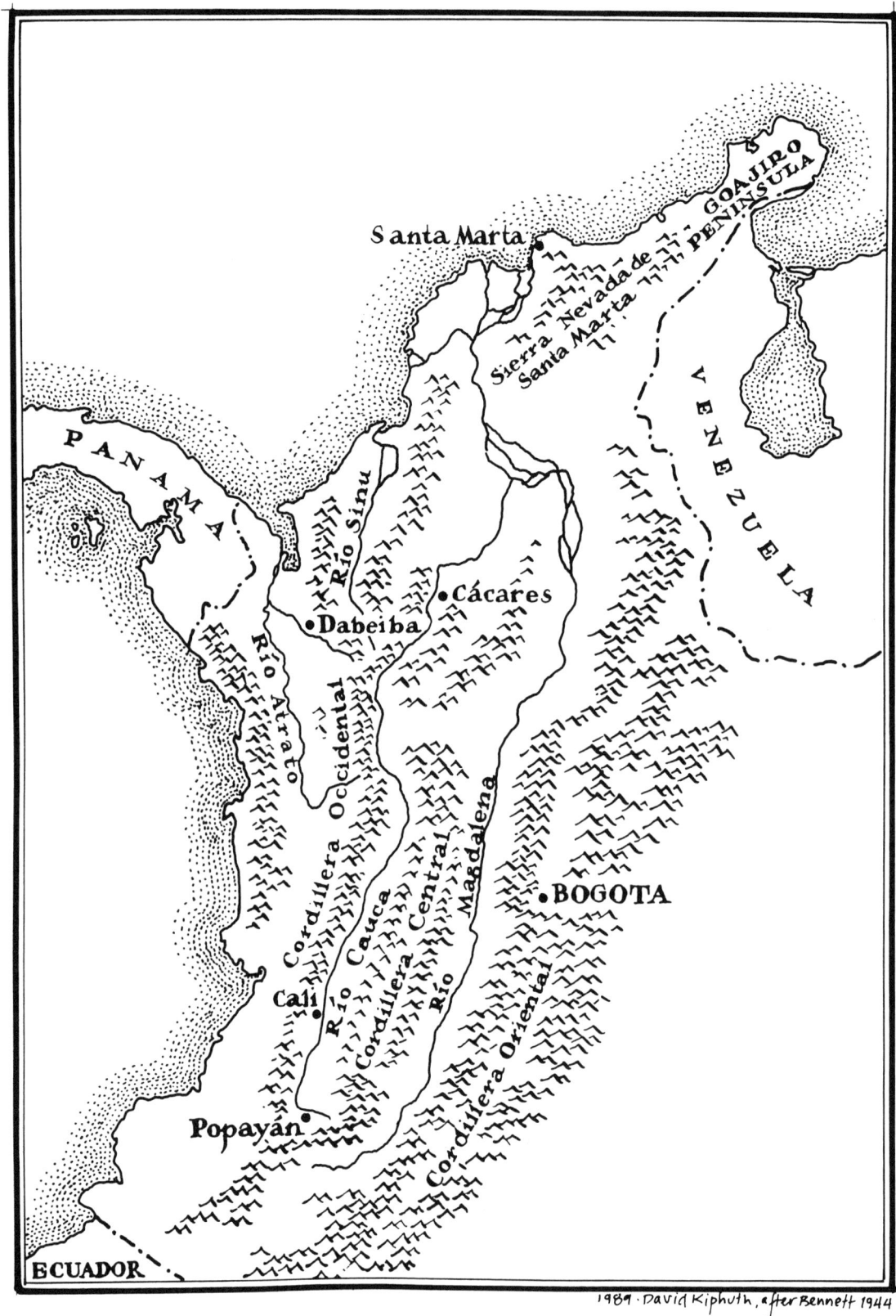

*Figure 15.* Map of Colombia showing the major mountain ranges and river valleys. [Redrawn from Bennett 1944:18.]

ors among neighboring allies. Sometimes mercenaries were recruited to fight in return for a share of the spoils. For example, the mountain Pijao, who were known for their warlike tendencies, fought as mercenaries for a number of other polities (Andagoya 1945:439; Trimborn 1949:282, 332).

The sources refer occasionally to war councils attended by regional chiefs, such as the one held at the paramount center of Guaca prior to a Spanish incursion. The gathered chiefs sought the counsel of supernatural forces by means of rituals and sacrificial bloodletting; a fierce feline figure appeared before them and called them to arms (Cieza de León 1853:364; Simón 1892b:88, 177; Trimborn 1949:296–297). Amid rituals and feasts, military alliances were established between neighboring chiefs and war stratagems were decided upon to defeat a common enemy. The plans were then proclaimed in the form of songs (*areytos*), which were performed with dancing and drinking. At the end of such inebriated feasts between allies, the chiefs and their men competed in mock attacks and jousted with shields and spears. The participants formed teams of thirty or more men, who in turn rushed forward, crying "batatabati, batatabati," which means "come on, let's play!" and jousting with spears until many were wounded and some were dead (Andagoya 1865:75, 1945:436; Cieza de León 1853:375; Simón 1892b:331; Trimborn 1949:242–243, 332–334).

The preparations for war included stockpiling armaments and provisions. The members of a military alliance, for example, cultivated certain fields collectively to this end. The Spaniards described settlements in the Cauca Valley that had storehouses of weapons and provisions, including water stored in canoes, troughs, and vessels (Castellanos 1850:528, 555–559; Trimborn 1949:294, 327–330, 345). In preparation for war, the Catío chief's fortified center was ready with abundant lances, darts, arrows, stones, javelins, and storehouses of food, jars full of fermented beverages, and canoes full of rainwater (Simón 1892b:271). Fighting forces were mobilized, whose numbers roughly reflected the size of the independent chiefly polities in the region, the extent of their military alliances, and the particular military maneuver they anticipated. The available size estimates of their war parties range from minimums of 100 to 500 warriors to maximums of 1,000–10,000 men. And the fighting force raised by the paramount chief at Guaca against the Spaniards was variously estimated to have ranged from as few as 10,000 to as many as 30,000 men (Trimborn 1949:141–142, 335–337; Cieza de León 1853:364, 374, 384; Andagoya 1865:78).

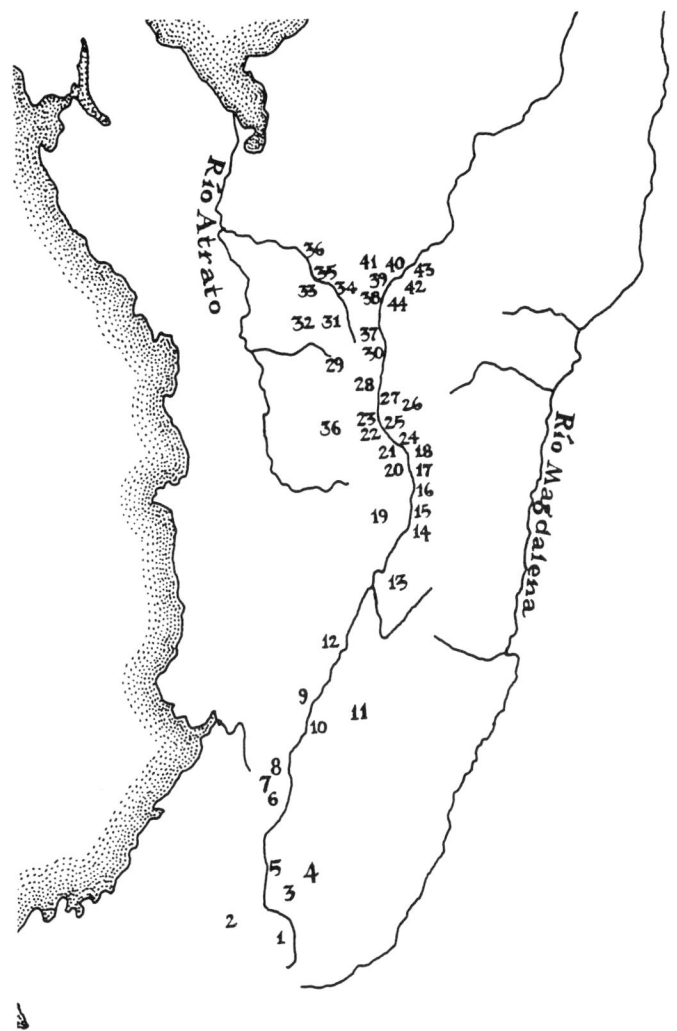

1. Coconuco
2. Timbío
3. Guambia
4. Paez
5. Aguales
6. Jamundí
7. Timba
8. Lile
9. Gorrones
10. Buga
11. Pijao
12. Chanco
13. Quimbaya
14. Carrapa
15. Picara
16. Pozo
17. Paucura
18. Arma
19. Anserma
20. Caramanta
21. Cartama
22. Corí
23. Iraca
24. Cenufana
25. Pueblo-Llano
26. Aburrá
27. Torvura
28. Curume
29. Penco
30. Hevéjico
31. Nore
32. Tatabe
33. Dabeiba
34. Guaca
35. Sierra de Abibe
36. Catío
37. Buriticá
38. Pequí
39. Norisco
40. Ituango
41. Guacuceco
42. Guarcama
43. Nutave
44. Tahamí

*Figure 16.* The Cauca River Valley, Colombia, with the chiefdoms that inhabited it in the sixteenth century. [Redrawn from Trimborn 1949:65.]

## Preparations for war

The chiefs were the supreme military commanders who made all the decisions concerning warfare. They dispatched scouts to monitor the enemy settlements and positions and to recruit warri-

## Organization of war parties

War parties were organized into units led by military captains (*cabras*). They obeyed the local or regional chief (*saco*), who was the supreme military commander. In a society that was differentiated into chiefly elite, commoners, and slaves, the *cabras* enjoyed many sumptuary privileges associated with the chiefly elite, despite the fact that they were not always drawn from that sector of society (Trimborn 1949:196–198, 337). In the case of the paramount chiefdoms centered at Guaca and Popayán the sources mention special war leaders who commanded the allied troops led by local and regional captains; in both instances, these war leaders were younger brothers of the paramount chief. Other war leaders were nephews and sons-in-law of the paramount chief (Cieza de León 1853:364; Castellanos 1850:394–395; Simón 1892b:84–85, 331; Trimborn 1949:256–257, 337–339).

The ranking of warriors was denoted by the gold and feather insignia, the hair styles and the red (*Bixa orellana*) and black (charcoal, pitch) body-painting they wore to war. Mixed with turpentine, their war paint could be detected by its smell. Moreover, each chiefdom was distinguished by different body-painting styles and accoutrements. We are told that in times of war, Catío warriors cut their hair (Castellanos 1850:506; Trimborn 1949:323; Simón 1892b:171, 326, 379, 1892c:19). Apparently, in some parts of the Cauca Valley they used human hair to fashion big round shields, described as being well made and painted, that they jousted with and carried to war (Cieza de León 1853:375; Trimborn 1949:323; Castellanos 1850:458). Depending on a warrior's rank, his war dress might have included plumed headbands, helmets, breastplates, armbands, necklaces, ear plugs, nose plugs, and other gold and feather ornaments (Cieza de León 1853:371, 375; Castellanos 1850:395, 458; Trimborn 1949:317–327). Indeed, when the Spaniards first encountered the warriors of Arma, they saw warriors armed with gold from head to foot (Cieza de León 1853:371). Finally, chiefs like paramount Utibará of Guaca were further distinguished by the fact that they were carried to war in gold-inlaid litters (Castellanos 1850:395; Cieza de León 1853:364; Simón 1892b:84–85; Trimborn 1949:217–218). The significance of their military accoutrements is illustrated in Oviedo's account of Martín de Murga's treacherous death during a feast at a chiefly center south of the Gulf of Urabá hosted by Chief Bea, who first donned his gold diadem, necklace, and gold-embellished club (*macana*) before mobilizing his warriors and dragging Murga's body out of the settlement (Oviedo y Valdés 1853:74).

*Warfare strategies, weapons, and tactics*

Led by their chiefs and captains, the troops of warriors proceeded with determination to war. When Andagoya's detachment approached Apirama's troops for an open attack some five leagues from Popayán, he was impressed by their order and precision; "they awaited their approach on a plain, formed in close column, with as much precision as could have been seen in Italy, to the number of twelve thousand" (Andagoya 1865:78). They favored nocturnal or matutinal attacks on enemy settlements. At the signal, the warriors rushed forward "con singular orden, en escuadrones compuestos, compases de piés y a nueve por hilera, con sus sobresalientes, todos ferocísimos, aljabas llenas de flechas venenosas, picas de tostadas puntas, macanas durísimas de palma" (Simón 1892c:69). As they surrounded the target settlement, their intimidation tactics included setting it on fire with torches, sounding their drums, blowing their conch-shell trumpets or instruments made out of human long bones, and emitting war cries ("Hu, hu, hu"). To the din produced by these noisemakers, the attackers added insults and invectives; these included calling the enemy *umes* ("women") and other more insulting expressions. They were also known to poison the enemy's water springs and ravage their cultivated fields (Cieza de León 1853:371–374, 455; Cieza de León 1881:26; Simón 1892b:333, 1892c:14, 70; Trimborn 1949:288–292, 351–354, 358–363).

Another common warfare strategy was the ambush. As enemy forces traversed narrow passes or river fords a hidden war party overwhelmed them with similar attacking tactics. Spanish detachments serving as rearguard were often ambushed and routed (Trimborn 1949:356–358; Andagoya 1865:79; Simón 1892c:73). Cieza de León also witnessed the ambushing of an Indian in a maize field by four others, who attacked him with clubs (Cieza de León 1853:365–366; cf. Trimborn 1949:401).

The open battles and ambushes they waged could last several hours or more. Moreover, repeated raids constituted an offensive strategy. Nightly or daily attacks—nightly and daily attacks in one instance—were a way to wear down the enemy. Benalcázar's troops withstood up to five attacks in one day from the same opposing forces during their passage through the eastern Cauca Valley from the south (Trimborn 1949:363; Simón 1892b:123, 342, 1892c:70).

Warriors in the Cauca Valley fought with a variety of long-range weapons. Palm-wood darts were hurled as were spears with spear-throwers and arrows with bows. Their spear-throwers enabled them to fling spears rodeo-style at the enemy, and were consequently feared and deemed a *mala arma* by the Spaniards (Cieza de León 1853:375). Some groups in the northern Cauca Valley and in adjacent regions to the north and west coated the tips of their darts and arrows with poison. This *mala yerba,* as the chroniclers referred to it, was actually a poison brew that was concocted out of a variety of ingredients, the recipe for which Cieza de León learned about from a Chief Macuriz in the coastal settlement of Bahaire in the province of Cartagena (see Chapter 6). They took the roots of the manchineel tree (*Hippomane mancinella*) and cooked them in ceramic containers to produce a paste, to which they might add ants, spiders, caterpillars, bat wings, the head and tail of the small saltwater *tamborino* fish, toads, snakes, manchineel apples, and other plants and roots. The concoction proved so noxious that it was prepared over fires at a safe distance from their settlements by female slaves or by other women held in low regard (Cieza de León 1853:361–362). During his subsequent journey in 1537 inland from the coastal settlement of San Sebastián de Buenavista on the Gulf of Urabá over the Serranía de Abibe and southward to Antioquía across some 53 leagues Cieza de León noted that the inland groups in the Cauca Valley, when they did fight with bows and arrows, didn't use this *mala yerba,* so as not to contaminate the victims' flesh (Cieza de León 1853:363, 374; Simón 1892b:177, 180, 1892c:22). Other sources indicated that the Guazuceco, Ituango, Nutave, Norisco, Pequí, Tahamí, Buriticá, Ibijico, Corí, and Catío who inhabited the lower Cauca Valley and surrounding regions (see Figure 16) fought with darts and arrows tipped with plant and animal poisons (Castellanos 1850:506, 520, 524, 526; Simón 1892b:380, 1892c:13, 19, 71; Trimborn 1949:303, 310). Other references to the Catío, however, noted that they didn't use poison (Castellanos 1850:556; Simón 1892b:273, 326).

In face-to-face combat they wielded palm-wood clubs, which are described by an anonymous chronicler as "unos palos de palma negra, muy duro, largos de braza y media, que llaman macanas, ancho de cuatro dedos, con dos filos a un cabo y a otro" (Trimborn 1949:297–298). These *macanas* were also made from another native hardwood that is described only as a "palo blanco, recio" (Cieza de León 1853:369). They struck blows with these clubs by holding them with both hands, much like broadswords (Cieza de León 1853:364). Another weapon was the palm-wood lance, some 30 spans long, whose sharp, fire-hardened point was suitable for stabbing (Cieza de León 1853:384; Trimborn 1949:297–312). Andagoya's account of his encounter with Apirama's warriors reveals some of their combat tactics with these weapons:

> 12,000 hombres con picas de mas de 40 palmos arriba, y debajo de las picas que tenian caladas, entre dos picas había uno de un montante que allá se dice macana, los cuales salian de entre el escuadron de las picas a pelear, se tornaban a retraer debajo de las picas, y los de caballos jamas pudieron romper por ninguna parte ni dar lanzada. [Andagoya 1945:439]

Between every two warriors armed with lances were warriors with clubs, who stepped forward to fight and then retreated behind the line of fixed lances. Similarly, Utibará's 20,000 warriors confronted Francisco de César's men in the province of Guaca in an impenetrable column of lance-thrusting warriors (Castellanos 1850:395; Simón 1892b:86).

Females participated in these raids, carrying standards, drums, weapons, and other provisions. Their standards consisted of long, narrow sheets of cloth that were studded with many small, round, and star-shaped gold ornaments and tied to lances (Cieza de León 1853:375, 371; Simón 1892b:179). The accompanying women incited the warriors with their war cries and drum beats and hurled insults at the opposing forces. They also supplied the strong rope to tie the captives, and the sharpened flint or cane knives, axes, and other implements to decapitate and dismember the victims of the raid (Castellanos 1850:458; Cieza de León 1853:367, 373; Simón 1892b:85; Trimborn 1949:120–121, 286–288).

The Cauca Valley chiefdoms were also capable of establishing false truces and betraying their allies (Cieza de León 1853:371). Many times their peace treaties proved to be a delaying tactic, which gave them time to plan new attacks. Treacherous tactics were used to lure the enemy into a trap or ambush. An allied attack by the Nutaves and Tahamís against Valdivia's fortified settlement began with a few Indians entering the settlement with their usual tribute, only to open the doors for the remaining force of 500 warriors, concealed outside, to launch their attack (Simón 1892c:19, 68–69). On at least two occasions the attackers hid clubs and knives in their seemingly unarmed bundles of tribute and offerings; at the appropriate moment they withdrew their weapons and whipped the helpless enemy (Castellanos 1850:540, 542; Simón 1892b:374–376, 1892c:18; Trimborn 1949:366–368). Similarly, during a feast held for Martín de Murga and his men south of the Gulf of Urabá they were assailed by their hosts, who dealt them blows on the back of the head and killed them with the very axes that the Spaniards had bestowed upon them earlier. Their Indian bearers were seized and branded as slaves (Oviedo y Valdés 1853:74).

*Defensive strategies*

Warfare was so chronic in the Cauca Valley that laborers in the province of Pozo, when cultivating their fields, held a club to clear the fallow in one hand, and a lance to fight in the other (Cieza de León 1853:373). In anticipation of war, the Cauca Valley chiefdoms practiced a variety of defensive measures. Scouts monitored enemy movements and warned of any advance. Obstacles were laid along the trail that the enemy was expected to traverse, such as pitfalls studded with sharp palm-wood stakes. Special figures fashioned from roots were also placed on the trail in order to bewitch the enemy or deter them (Trimborn 1949:340–342, 354–355; Cieza de León 1853:374; Castellanos 1850:458, 555; Simón 1892b:271).

The settlements themselves were fortified in various ways. It is not clear from the ethnohistoric accounts whether all the smallest villages dispersed within a regional chiefdom's territory erected defensive palisades. Cieza de León described the Arma's settlement pattern as consisting of many big round houses scattered across the valley floor and then plazas located on low ridges or piedmont spurs. The latter were no doubt their chiefly centers, for Cieza de León goes on to describe how these defensible hilltop plazas were further fortified by palisades of thick trunks, which they erected in rows "de veinte en veinte por su órden y compás, como calles" (Cieza de León 1853:371, see also 372–373). Some of these ridgetop centers are referred to as mountain fortresses where the inhabitants of the valley floor sought refuge in times of war. Here the chiefs and their retinue resided alongside a central plaza that was enclosed by a thick, impregnable cane palisade. Within the fortified plaza stood tall wooden platforms, sometimes roofed over with matting, which served as watchtowers as well as sacrificial altars (Cieza de León 1853:368–369, 372–374; Castellanos 1850:458, 555; Simón 1892b:101; Trimborn 1949:129, 344–351).

In the mountains west of the Cauca Valley the Spaniards described fortified tree houses (*barbacoas*) that were built in trees or atop wooden scaffolds consisting of more than 200 thick posts over 7 m tall and featuring elaborate ramparts and loopholes and palm-thatched roofs and that housed many people (Cieza de León 1853:365, 378; Oviedo y Valdés 1852:455; Andagoya 1865:76; Castellanos 1850:555; Simón 1892b:105, 271; Trimborn 1949:344–345). Oviedo y Valdés (1853:50, 131) reported similarly fortified settlements along the Atrato River that consisted of *barbacoas* erected atop strong posts of black palm wood. To reach their raised houses, the nimble inhabitants of these tree houses used ladders fashioned out of clinging tree vines. When the Spaniards asked them why they erected their settlements this way they responded that these *barbacoas* offered a means of defense against the fire and fury of their enemies (Oviedo y Valdés 1852:455, 1853:131). So impregnable were they that after two days of fighting with artillery, more than 200 Spanish soldiers under Johan de Tavira's command were still unable to overwhelm the defenders of one such settlement. Only after the inhabitants escaped one night did the Spaniards climb and enter the spacious fortress, which easily accommodated them.

In response to an imminent or an actual attack, the inhabitants frequently evacuated the settlement and fled to safe, defensible locations. In times of war the inhabitants of Anserma, for example, sought refuge atop a steep cliff (Cieza de León 1853:369). Women, children, and the elderly were evacuated beforehand if there was enough time. They hid valuables, if they could, by removing them from the village or by burying them. In some instances they set fire to their houses before taking flight (Cieza de León 1853:366; Simón 1892b:109, 112, 179). Sometimes they would even destroy their fields to make it difficult for the enemy forces to provision themselves (Cieza de León 1853:382–383). This policy of retreating rather than defending their settlements is reflected in the numerous abandoned or destroyed villages that the Spanish expeditions encountered throughout the Cauca Valley (Cieza de León 1853:375; Trimborn 1949:285, 290–295). The subsequent defense of a settlement included taking up strategic positions at narrow passes and river fords to impede the enemy's advance. From these defensible positions or from their hilltop fortresses, the defenders hurled spears, darts, arrows, stones and rocks, sometimes with the help of slings, at the enemy. They launched boulders, timbers, and thick, pointed jabs downslope toward the attackers (Cieza de León 1853:374, 384, 455; Castellanos 1850:401, 405, 555, 557; Simón 1892b:198, 271–273; Trimborn 1949:313–315, 354–355). Boiling water and hot coals were also used as short-range projectiles against the attackers (Oviedo y Valdés 1852:455; Castellanos 1850:405; Simón 1892b:105). By means of these defensive tactics, the warriors defending Nobobarco's fortress successfully outlasted and repelled the enemy for some 39 days (Simón 1892b:276–278). Retreating to higher, rough ground was the last resort in an attack (Andagoya 1865:78).

A related defensive strategy involved circumventing the advancing forces and effectively cutting off the enemy's retreat, thereby ambushing them in gorges or other strategic locations. In several instances the defenders waited for the enemy to cross a bridge and then promptly felled it with stone axes. Likewise, they surrounded and ambushed the enemy's rearguard (Trimborn 1949:355–358; Andagoya 1865:78–79).

*Post-war rituals and practices*

For the raiders, the post-war rituals began at the scene of combat or immediately thereafter with the execution and dismemberment of victims and war captives. To begin with, their battlefields were strewn with the bodies of those killed in combat; during one attack alone, a fighting force of more than 700 warriors lost up to 300 men (Simón 1892c:69–71). But live victims were bound with rope and clubbed to death in a kneeling, face-down position; they succumbed to their fate unflinchingly. Children were held by their feet and their heads were bashed against a rock face. The victors' quest for sacrificial victims was so great that in the aftermath of an attack the victors would pass over the battleground, searching for victims "like rabbits" amid the vegetation and outcrops (Cieza de León 1853:373). The victims were then decapitated and dismembered with flint or cane knives. According to Simón, "les cortaban las cabezas y dividían en cuartos sus cuerpos, y aun en menores piezas, porque participasen más del despojo de la victoria" (Simón 1892b:202). The victorious warriors drank the victims' blood and consumed their hearts and entrails on the spot. The victims' heads and quarters were sent back to their villages to be cooked by boiling or roasting, although their female companions sometimes brought the containers and utensils along to the battleground for this purpose. Great victory feasts were celebrated upon the war party's return from war, at which they cooked and consumed their victims' flesh, drank chicha, and danced (Andagoya 1945:433–434, 436; Cieza de León 1853:366, 372–373; Simón 1892b:85, 1892c:21–22; Trimborn 1949:388–397).

Those war captives spared from their death and dismemberment on the battlefield were bound and taken home, for use as slaves, for exchange, and for sacrifice. Many war captives were bound and kept in reed cages within the chief's precinct where they were fattened up for use in later sacrifices. Cieza de León informs us, for example, that at the door of the paramount chief of Paucura's residence stood a life-size wooden male figure with arms outstretched towards the east, for whom two victims were sacrificed every week. From the tall ritual platforms that dominated the chief's enclosure they tied their prisoners of war and left some of them hanging, while they ripped open the chests of others with flint knives in order to offer their hearts to the great wooden cult figure (Cieza de León 1853:371–372, 380; Simón 1892b:177, 327). Male, female, and child captives were thus sacrificed. Cieza also described the piece-by-piece sacrifice over a period of days of Pedro de Añasco, who was taken captive by an allied force of Yalcones and Páez Indians, in what must have been considered explicit torture: "un día le cortaban un brazo y otro le sacaban un ojo, y en otro le cortaban los lábios, y así se fue consumiendo el ser que tenía de hombre, hasta que se le acabó la vida y fue sepultado en los vientres de los que le mataron" (Cieza de León 1881:43). The victims' body fat was used as fuel for lamps, and the remaining body parts were consumed (Simón 1892c:173; Trimborn 1949:389–390, 417–418).

The available mortality figures reflect the extent of these post-war rituals. After their allied victory over the Pozo, the warriors of Carrapa and Picara sacrificed more than 300 captives and sent more than 200 loads of human flesh to their settlements. A subsequent raid by the Paucura against the Pozo ended with the sacrifice of 200 Pozo victims. And after a successful counterattack by the Pozo against their enemies, Chief Perequita and his retinue alone sacrificed 100 victims in one day (Cieza de León 1881:30–31, 33; Cieza de León 1853:372–374; Simón 1892b:178; Trimborn 1949:388).

The heads, limbs, hands, and feet of their enemies became war trophies, which the victors displayed in public. Even their flayed skins and innards were stuffed with flesh or ashes like sausages and exhibited. These war trophies were hung from the doors of the chief's residence as well as from those of other members of the chiefly elite, including military captains. They were also attached to stakes on the sacrificial platform, atop the thick posts of the chiefly enclosure, and on top of the settlement's defensive palisade (Andagoya 1945:434; Cieza de León 1853:364, 368, 378; Simón 1892b:116, 121; Trimborn 1949:369–372, 375). At the paramount center of Caramanta the cane posts supporting the trophy heads stood alongside carved wooden slabs that depicted fierce human and feline figures (Cieza de León 1853:367). In the process of describing Picara's chiefly enclosure Cieza de León commented on the terrifying effect of such displays:

> A las puertas de las casas de los caciques hay plazas pequeñas, todas cercadas de las cañas gordas, en lo alto de las cuales tienen colgadas las cabezas de los enemigos, que es cosa temerosa de verlas, segun están muchas, y fieras con sus cabellos largos, y las caras pintadas de tal manera, que parescen rostros de demonios. Por lo bajo de las cañas hacen unos agujeros por donde el aire puede respirar cuando algun viento se levanta; hacen gran sonido, paresce música de diablos. [Cieza de León 1853:374]

The awesome effect produced by this display of their enemies' heads, still wearing the face paint for war sometimes, was heightened by the noisemakers pierced along the base of the surrounding palisade (Simón 1892b:121, 171).

Paramount chiefs stored their human trophies in special public buildings or charnels, where the skeletal parts and sometimes the flayed skins of their enemies were neatly displayed. According to Andagoya,

> Halláronse en las casas principales del señor de esta provincia de Lili, en alto tanto como tres o cuatro estados dentro de la casa al redonda de la principal sala, puestos en cantidad de 400 hombres o los que cabían en aquella sala, desollados y llenos de ceniza, y sin que les faltase figura ninguna y sentados en una silla juntos unos con otros con las armas que les prendían puestas en las manos, como si estuviesen vivos. [Andagoya 1945:436]

Writing about the same large, round, thatched charnel with a single entrance and four skylights that dominated the great paramount chief Petecuy's center in the valley of Lile, Cieza de León added that the faces of the stuffed figures were fashioned out of wax, a practice that he also observed in the province of Pozo, where inside their houses the chiefly elite displayed rows of life-size wooden figures that were topped with skulls fleshed out with wax. Adjacent to Petecuy's principal charnel, where a great number of hands and feet were also hung, Petecuy had another storehouse full of cadavers, skulls, and other skeletal remains (Cieza de León 1853:373, 380, 1881:27). Other charnels contained kettledrums made from the flayed skins of war captives; there were as many as 680 such drums in the charnels at one paramount center (Oviedo y Valdés 1851:217–218).

These post-war rituals and the public display of war trophies practiced by the Cauca Valley chiefdoms reinforced the social and military ranking of warriors. Warriors who had killed were distinguished by a hair cut, by one account (Trimborn 1949:323). Wounded warriors who distinguished themselves in war wore their wounds proudly. They were deemed noble and enjoyed certain privileges. They took home a share of the bodies of those they had killed in war (Simón 1892b:202, 1892c:21). The display of human trophies outside their residences also attested to their war deeds (Trimborn 1949:198, 372). The ritual sacrifice and consumption of enemy warriors killed during or after an attack was another unmistakable token of victory (Andagoya 1865:75; Cieza de León 1853:364; Simón 1892b:84). The warriors who partook were imbued with the dead warriors' innate power, which further augmented their standing. Their valor, which was lauded by the Spaniards, is epitomized by the case of an illustrious Pijao warrior, who consented to his ritual sacrifice and cannibalism by his fellow warriors, so that they might acquire his power:

> en señalándose uno con valentía en la guerra ó en otra ocasion, le mataban con grande gusto del valiente y lo hacian pedazos y daban uno á comer á cada uno de los demás indios, con que decian se hacian valientes como aquél lo era. [Simón 1882:7]

The notion of acquiring the deceased's innate power through the consumption of his flesh was so ingrained that a warrior who lacked initiative or courage was chided by being told that his flesh would never be worthy of ritual consumption (Simón 1882:7; Trimborn 1949:378–381, 413–414).

As the supreme military commander, we have seen how the chief presided over large-scale ritual sacrifices in his chiefly precinct. Indeed, Tateepe, the chief of Buriticá, was said to eat only human flesh (Trimborn 1949:401). A chief's greatness was also measured by the number of human trophies and kettledrums he possessed; in addition to adorning his residence and enclosure with these symbols of victory, he erected special structures to display them. When the Spaniards inquired about the chiefly practice of displaying such a multitude of human trophies, they were told that these trophies were symbols of a chief's military victories, and therefore, constituted his greatness (Cieza de León 1853:380).

*Mortuary treatment*

Upon their death, war leaders and military captains were accorded special burial in tombs with offerings (Trimborn 1949:198, 228, 368). When paramount chief Utibará's war leader, Quinunchú, was killed during a battle against Francisco

César's expedition, his fellow warriors sounded their retreat and carried his body home in Utibará's litter; the bodies of other fallen chiefs or military leaders were also claimed and returned home (Simón 1892b:86–87, 1892c:74). The right to have their bodies returned home for burial was an elite privilege not accorded to common warriors, whose bodies were left strewn on the battlefield. Chiefs received lengthy mourning ceremonies, followed by an elaborate burial in tombs that were often located under the floors of their residences or in the adjacent plaza. Sometimes a chief's body was placed in a hammock, desiccated over a fire, wrapped in mantles, and thus preserved above ground for several years before being buried. Their rich funerary accompaniments included their gold and feather adornments, weapons, and jars of food and fermented drink, as well as wives and war captives, who were sacrificed to serve as chiefly burial retainers (Trimborn 1949:203, 226–232; Cieza de León 1853:362, 365, 368, 369; Simón 1892c:173).

## Tairona Warfare

Similar warfare patterns existed among the mosaic of chiefdoms designated the Tairona and their neighbors who inhabited the coastal plains and the narrow river valleys of the Sierra Nevada de Santa Marta at the time of the Spanish Conquest (Figure 17). Each densely populated valley was ruled by a paramount chief (*naoma*), who had the authority to declare war, to mobilize war parties, to summon manpower for public building projects, and to exact tribute. Subject village chiefs (*mohánes*) and lineage heads carried out the paramount chief's wishes on the local level, for which they were rewarded. Relationships between the Tairona chiefdoms and their neighbors were regulated by exchange and warfare. The paramount chiefs of Bonda and Posigueica were especially powerful in the sixteenth century, and apparently exhibited greater centralized authority on the regional and interregional levels (Reichel-Dolmatoff 1977:93–94). According to Piedrahita, the Tairona were by far the most complex and powerful polity in the Sierra Nevada de Santa Marta area, "sin que se hallase nación alguna dentro de este término y del que corre desde las cumbres más altas hasta las riberas del mar, que no estuviese a la protección o dominio de dichos tairones, con más o menos sujeción a sus armas" (Piedrahita 1942:125, 155, 185; Castellanos 1850:258, 270, 322, 293; Reichel-Dolmatoff 1951:72–75, 88–90; Reichel-Dolmatoff 1953:18–22; Nicholas 1901:614; Simón 1892b:365–366, 1892c:192, 217; Oyuela 1987:213; Castaño 1987:235).

### The nature and objectives of warfare

The Tairona conducted revenge raids to avenge the deaths of relatives and ancestors. Paramount chiefs waged wars in order to seek revenge, to gain control over natural resources, such as fishing rights, and to maintain and expand their territories (Castellanos 1850:350, 341; Simón 1892c:42, 181; Reichel-Dolmatoff 1951:91). In a discussion with his war leader over an impending attack, the paramount chief of Bonda mentioned his desire to maintain the honor and greatness of his polity by seeking victory in war (Castellanos 1850:334). Looting was a favorable outcome of a successful raid; the booty included gold, precious stones and weapons. In at least two cases, Tairona war parties sought women as captives, as concubines (Castellanos 1850:333, 335–336). Enemy skulls and other human trophies were also sought in war (Oviedo y Valdés 1852:355; Castellanos 1850:293).

### Preparations for war

Paramount chiefs announced an impending attack and summoned fighting forces by blowing conch-shell trumpets and sounding drums. The sound of the drum could be heard over great distances. It sounded one signal to be on the alert and another for an actual attack. This system of communication enabled chiefs to mobilize the valley's inhabitants at a moment's notice (Piedrahita 1942:132; Castellanos 1850:273, 295–296; Simón 1891:47; Aguado 1916:148). Scouts and spies gathered information regarding the size and location of the enemy's force. In one instance, a spy recorded the size of the enemy's evident fighting force with maize kernels and literally handed this information to the chief (Castellanos 1850:343; Simón 1892c:35, 208). Upon declaring war, the chief sent messengers to allied villages with arrows that signaled his intentions (Simón 1892c:181, 186).

Paramount chiefs also convened war councils with their allies for the purpose of calling them to arms and planning their allied military stratagems. Sometimes they had to convince their allies of their common purpose in war, "por grado ó por fuerza" (Simón 1892c:29, 47, 189, 1892b:366–367; Castellanos 1850:279, 328, 353). And in one instance, the war council broke up in a disagreement between the participating chiefs over the war party's leadership (Simón 1892c:208). The participating chiefs awaited the augury delivered by the supernatural to their diviners. Chiefly war councils usually ended with victory celebrations at which the gathered chiefs celebrated their expected allied victory in war with dancing and drinking (Simón 1892c:205–206).

At the conclusion of their war councils, they began their preparations for war in earnest. Many fields of maize were planted in order to have abundant food supplies to last the war's duration. The roads and trails leading to their settlements were guarded or obstructed in order to impede the enemy's expected retaliatory attacks. Bows and arrows were manufactured, along with strong arrow poisons (Simón 1892c:205–206). The stockpiling of armament and provisions for war was evident at a paramount center, where Oviedo (1852:354) described a chief's arsenal that contained many bows and countless bundles of arrows, and many balls or nuts of pitch-black arrow poison, feather headdresses, and drums. At another paramount center up the Don Diego River valley in the Tairona heartland, the Spaniards discovered abundant supplies of shelled maize and other provisions, "por ser el más abundante y rico de toda aquella tierra, de quien

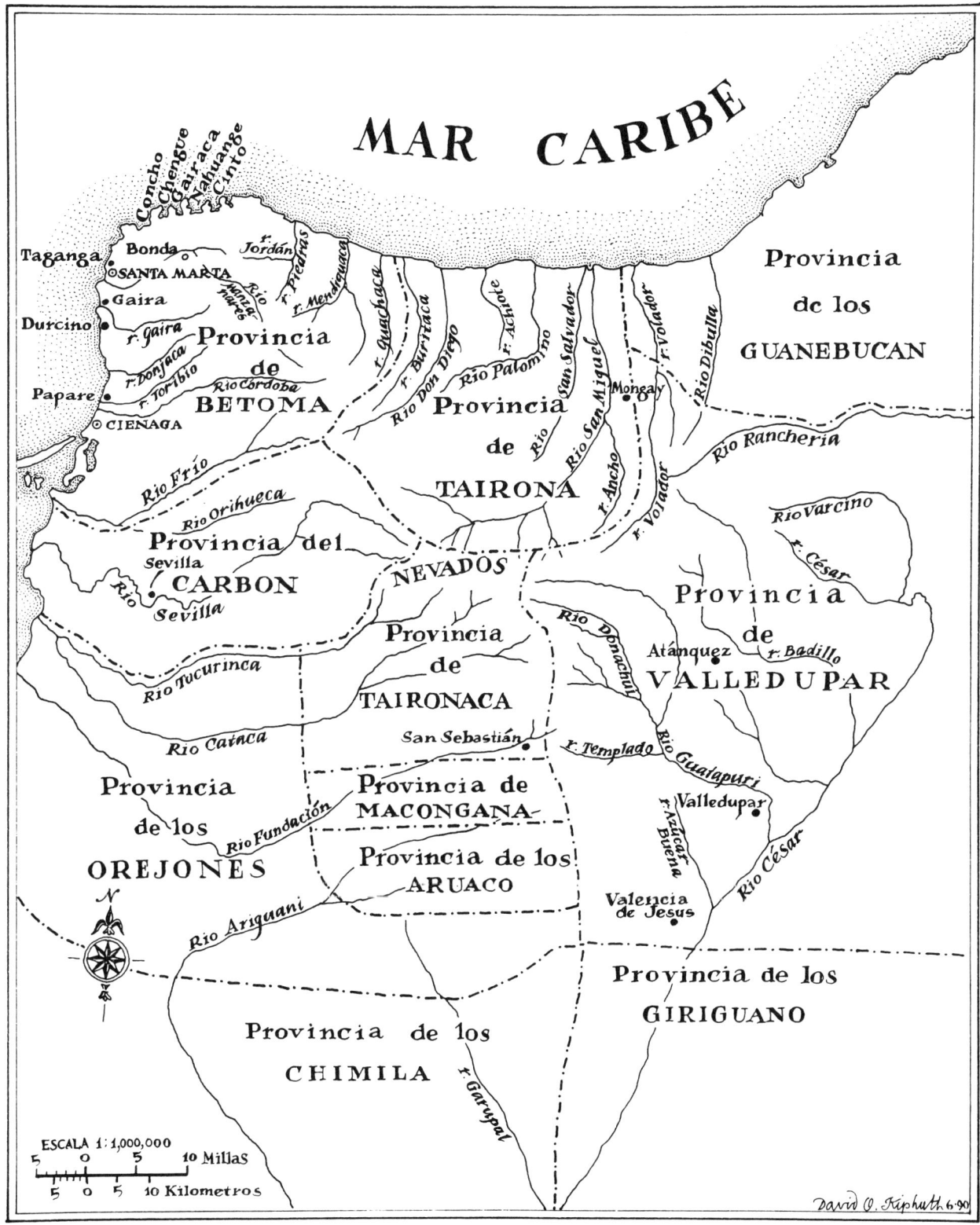

*Figure 17.* The Sierra Nevada de Santa Marta, Colombia, with the Tairona chiefdoms and their neighbors in the sixteenth century. [Redrawn from Reichel-Dolmatoff 1953.]

era la corte y cabecera" (Simón 1892b:355). On the local level, bows and arrows were evidently stockpiled in the chief's sanctuary, as Fray Tomás de Morales observed in a house of worship at Mahancique, near Bonda, on the eve of an allied attack in 1599 (Simón 1892c:206). Elsewhere Simón alluded to the practice of preparing piles of stones, for use as missiles, at their hilltop positions (Simón 1891:39, 43).

*Organization of war parties*

Tairona chiefs led war parties and fought in the vanguard. As Simón (1892c:189) put it, the chief was the nerve center and the root of all war. Their war parties consisted of troops of warriors under the command of military captains. War parties ranged in size from small guerrilla units of eight to ten warriors, as Reichel-Dolmatoff (1951:91) characterized them, to estimated fighting forces from 500 to more than 3,000 men. For one attack against the Spaniards, the paramount chief of Pocigueica drew an allied fighting force of more than 20,000 warriors (Castellanos 1850:270, 343, 357; Cieza de León 1853:364; Simón 1892c:35, 51, 207; Aguado 1916:104; Reichel-Dolmatoff 1951:77, 91).

In the case of large-scale allied attacks, chiefs jointly commanded a wing of the allied forces. This organization was evident in an attack led by paramount chief Marocando with 15 allied chiefs against García de Lerma's force. Similarly, Tupe chief Coro Ponaimo's allied attack in the Valle de Upar was made up of four separate fighting units, commanded by Coro Ponaimo and three war leaders designated by him. At least one of the war leaders in these allied attacks is referred to as the paramount chief's brother while the others were allied chiefs and military captains (Castellanos 1850:270, 297, 353; Simón 1892c:46–47; Reichel-Dolmatoff 1951:91). For one large-scale allied attack, Jeriboca's chief, Cotocique, designated his son, Dioena, and possibly another son or close ally, Macheoena, as his war leaders, to the dismay of the other participating chiefs (Simón 1892c:208). When the paramount chief of Bonda led a large-scale attack against Spanish settlements in the province of Santa Marta, his war leader commanded the vanguard, he led the rearguard, and another war leader or military captain of his followed with an additional force (Simón 1892c:27–28). Finally, their military order became evident in the aftermath of a raid on the paramount center of Bonda; the paramount chief was killed, and his war leader, subject chiefs (*mohánes*), and military captains directed the defense and rout of the enemy (Castellanos 1850:340–342; Simón 1892c:32).

The members of a war party anointed their naked bodies with red paint, made by grinding *bija* (*Bixa orellana*) seeds and tree resins. This red war paint was also referred to by the Spanish chroniclers as a *betún colorado* ("red polish"). According to Castellanos, the preparation of this war paint produced a strong odor that could be detected from afar, which alerted neighboring groups of an impending attack (Castellanos 1850:273–274, 320, 337; Simón 1892b:353, 1892c:206; Aguado 1916:132, 142).

Tairona warriors also donned feather headdresses and feather ornaments that radiated from their gold caps or helmets, such that collectively they resembled a dense reedbed when it sports its plume-tipped stalks (Castellanos 1850:343). They were resplendent in the gold headbands, ear and nose ornaments, necklaces, breastplates, armbands, and other gold ornaments. Military captains and chiefs displayed the feather and gold insignia of their rank (Aguado 1916:132; Castellanos 1850:270–271, 322–323, 343; Simón 1892b:355, 361, 1892c:35). They advanced to war and met the enemy in full attire:

> De largas plumas las cabezas llenas,
> Diademas de oro por las frentes,
> En los pechos chaguales ó patenas
> Que los rayos del sol hacen patentes,
> Con otras joyas de doradas venas
> De las orejas y nariz pendientes,
> Embijados, compuestos y lozanos
> Y con arcos y flechas en las manos. [Castellanos 1850:325]

Finally, when Macarona, the great paramount chief of Bonda, was trapped in his burning residence during an attack and consumed by fire, his body could be identified with certainty by his chiefly insignia (Castellanos 1850:340).

*Warfare strategies, weapons, and tactics*

Widely known as a warlike people, the Tairona exercised a variety of military tactics to achieve their objectives (Castellanos 1850:258; Simón 1891:39, 1892c:36; Reichel-Dolmatoff 1951:91). The ambush was the hallmark of their warfare strategies. Scouts monitored their territories and from hilltop lookout points they spied on enemy settlements and enemy movements. Troops guarded strategic routes, river fords, and trails through their rugged terrain. As enemy forces traversed such narrow corridors they suddenly met with a volley of poisoned arrows, darts, and stones from a large, hidden war party upslope. The ambush was principally a form of long-distance combat, directed at enemy forces out on foray as well as at enemy settlements. Although dawn or pre-dawn ambushes were frequent, Tairona war parties initiated attacks throughout the day or night in response to the enemy's whereabouts (Castellanos 1850:331, 321, 323, 294–295, 328–331; Simón 1891:41, 46–47, 1892b:354, 361, 1892c:36, 39–40, 186, 189–190; Aguado 1916:130, 141, 153, 155).

Another ambush tactic involved setting a trap for the enemy, in the form of a small number of warriors out in the open, awaiting the enemy's approach. Only when the enemy's force arrived, thinking that they could quickly dispatch the vastly outnumbered opposition, did the remaining members of a large fighting force—a thousand feather headdresses in one case—emerge and encircle the enemy (Castellanos 1850:329, 330–331; Simón 1891:7, 1892b:367–369).

All Tairona warriors were accomplished bowmen; in Castellanos' words, "arma comun de todos es la flecha" (Castellanos 1850:258). Their skill at shooting with the bow and arrow greatly impressed the Spaniards; evidently they honed their archery skills at grounds like the one that Simón described on a hilltop near the paramount center of Betoma, where they conducted mock attacks (Castellanos 1850:295, 349–350; Simón 1891:45, 1892c:42, 191–192). In the province of Santa Marta they made their arrow-points out of wood or stingray spines and anointed them with a deadly poison brewed from the manchineel (*Hippomane mancinella*) tree. Cieza de León's description of this poisonous concoction, which included plant and animal ingredients, applies to the Tairona of Santa Marta as well as to groups to the west in the province of Cartagena. In his account of García de Lerma and Pedro de Lerma's expeditions through Tairona territory around 1530, Aguado (1916:102) stated that all the native inhabitants of Santa Marta and of the adjacent mountains and provinces applied a deadly *hierba ponzoñosa* to their arrows, which I will describe in more detail in Chapter 6. The final product was a pitch-black paste or wax in the form of balls or nuts that ended up in the chief's storehouse. The use of poisoned arrows was widespread in the Tairona area, as it was among neighboring groups (Aguado 1916:98, 102, 128; Oviedo y Valdés 1852:353–354; Cieza de León 1853:361–362; Espinosa 1955:58; Castellanos 1850:258, 261, 270–271; Simón 1891:7, 19, 40, 1892b:284, 363, 367, 1892c:38). Of a battle waged at the paramount center of Cincorona in the mountainous Tairona heartland, however, Castellanos mentioned that:

Porque los moradores deste seno
No todas veces tienen a las manos
La yerba ni mortífero veneno
Usado de los indios comarcanos:
Dicen también que no prevalecía
Por ya participar de tierra fría. [Castellanos 1850:322]

It is possible that several kinds of arrow poison were used in warfare by the Tairona. Simón noted, as Castellanos alluded to above in verse, that the poison used by the Tairona of the interior sierra was apparently not as toxic as that used by coastal groups "por tocar en tierra fría" (Simón 1892b:357). This information also led Reichel-Dolmatoff to distinguish between the Tairona's use of two kinds of poison, a plant poison and an animal (cadaverine) poison (Reichel-Dolmatoff 1951:88). I will return to discuss the various arrow poisons used by the Tairona and other sixteenth-century groups in a later chapter.

When the Tairona launched open attacks upon enemy forces and settlements their warriors advanced in orderly formations led by captains, carrying bows, quivers of arrows, darts, and clubs. Castellanos described a Taironaca warrior's intrepid approach to combat in the following verses:

Cuando vieron bajar por un recuesto
Gandul empenachado bien dispuesto.

En todos sus meneos y semblante
Representaba singular soltura:
Tenía proporciones de gigante,
Y no menos feroz en la postura,

Con un carcax de flechas abundante,
Cubierta solamente la cintura,
Arco que de los hombros va pendiente,
Y en las manos macana prepotente.

Cada cual español está confuso
Viéndolo descender con tanta gana,
Con armas y pertrechos de su uso,
Que son el arco, flechas y macana. [Castellanos 1850:323]

The fighting force that Alonso de Lugo's men confronted in Bonda advanced in tight fighting units or squadrons, with their bows poised in their right hands, ready to shower the opposing force with arrows (Aguado 1916:148). The arrows they flung could penetrate any defensive armor and the large, heavy clubs that they wielded with both hands could smash shields. In view of both the piercing poisoned arrows directed at them from afar and the club blows (*macanazos*) that they endured in face-to-face combat, the Spaniards tried to protect themselves with stuffed cotton armor that reached down to their calves and helmets of stuffed cotton, leather, or best of all, steel (Castellanos 1850:257–258, 270–271, 322; Simón 1891:44, 1892b:356, 358–359, 1892c:187; Aguado 1916:139–140).

The war party's troops often converged upon the target settlement or force from different directions, all at once, or at staggered moments, according to the war leader's plan of attack. The separate troops waited for the sound of the war leader's trumpet before joining the attack. For example, paramount chief Marocando's allied forces advanced in two long wings in order to outflank García de Lerma's troops, while Marocando led the front line. Similarly, Tupe chief Coro Ponaimo commanded an allied fighting force against a settlement on the Guataporí River that consisted of four separate attacking units led by himself, his brother, and two allied chiefs or war leaders. When Tairona war parties ambushed the enemy in narrow passes, they deployed fighting units at strategic points to cut off the enemy's retreat. As they launched their attack they hollered deafening war cries and invectives, and sounded a variety of noisemakers, such as conch-shell trumpets, flutes fashioned from human long bones, and drums (Castellanos 1850:270–271, 280, 343, 355–356; Simón 1891:15, 20, 43, 1892b:355, 363, 1892c:27–28, 53; Aguado 1916:104, 142, 144). Whistling arrows were also hurled to confound the enemy (Castellanos 1850:258).

A common offensive tactic involved setting the enemy settlement afire with fire-tipped arrows. Although paramount centers were the principal target, other villages and hamlets in enemy territory were destroyed by fire as a way to reduce the enemy's source of provisions. The Spaniards soon adopted this tactic themselves in their campaigns against the Tairona (Castellanos 1850:337–339, 348, 350, 353–356; Simón 1891:20, 1892c:43, 46, 47–48, 207; Reichel-Dolmatoff 1951:87). The Tairona also laid waste to the enemy's fields to the same end (Simón 1892c:196; Castellanos 1850:355).

Tairona war parties were capable of regrouping and launching repeated attacks, irrespective of their losses. Even in the face of defeat, the members of the fighting force fought determinedly in a tight column; those warriors who had spent their arrows parried with their bows or came to blows with their clubs (Castellanos 1850:344; Simón 1891:40, 44, 1892c:36, 187, 214; Aguado 1916:143). Simón further described how in the heat of combat the warriors in the front line were animated by the sound of shell trumpets (Simón 1891:44).

Not only could they carry out retaliatory attacks within a matter of days, but they were also known to pursue daily attacks without interruption and sometimes more than that. In the territory of Carbon, for example, the warriors of Chief Zazagueica waged attacks over three successive days; after the first day's attack, which lasted more than two hours, the members of the war party retreated to fortified positions on nearby hilltops for the night, where their women and boys brought them food and drink (Simón 1892c:186–187). Another Tairona attack against a fortified center apparently lasted for two nights and two days. Alonso de Lugo's men endured repeated attacks at a narrow pass in the province of Bondigua over four days before giving up and retreating. Finally, Diego de Orozco's troops were forced to retreat after enduring three attacks in one day (Aguado 1916:155; Castellanos 1850:257–258, 343, 348; Simón 1892c:40, 26, 55).

The Tairona resorted to treachery in warfare, a tactic they used in a raid against a fortified Spanish settlement in the region of Bonda in 1575. The paramount chief, Macarona, sent a supply of timber to the settlement with his war leader, Coendo, whose contingent of twenty men carried axes rather than bows and arrows so as not to arouse the Spaniards' suspicion. When the Spanish lieutenant emerged to receive the tribute he was felled by Coendo's axe blow, whereupon the war party stormed the settlement. At that moment Macarona and 200 more warriors joined in the attack. A third unit of 300 warriors led by Jebo, another war leader or military captain of Macarona, followed and took up defensible positions on hilltops in order to launch a successive attack (Castellanos 1850:333–335; Simón 1892c:27–28). Other treacherous tactics included meeting the enemy peacefully and bestowing gifts upon them, or leading them to their settlement only later to catch the unsuspecting force off guard, ambushing them, killing them, and reclaiming their belongings (Castellanos 1850:279; Simón 1892c:54–56, 179).

*Defensive strategies*

The principal defensive measure practiced by the Tairona was their strategy of settlement location. Ridgetops were favorite places for their settlements, especially for their chiefly centers. The paramount center of Bonda, for example, was practically inaccessible; it could only be reached by ascending stone-slab stairways, so steep that horses could not climb them (Castellanos 1850:261, 255, 269, 295; Simón 1891:39, 1892c:201, 210; Oviedo y Valdés 1852:353; Aguado 1916:105). Moreover, we know that in 1599 the chiefly centers of Jeriboca, Macinga, and Macinguilla were further fortified with palisades of thick timbers (Simón 1892c:211–212). The inhabitants of subject villages sought refuge at these ridgetop centers in anticipation of an attack, as they did at the paramount center of Posigueica, which was considered to have been the largest fortified center in the Sierra Nevada de Santa Marta (Castellanos 1850:329, 357; Simón 1892b:367, 1892c:51).

To reach some of these mountaintop centers, mighty watercourses first needed to be traversed by suspension bridges or otherwise forded. The Tairona placed other obstacles to hinder the enemy's movements, such as intercepting, even demolishing, trails, and felling bridges. Thus, when Francisco González de Castro returned to cross the Don Diego River, the hanging bridge had been chopped down and his men were forced to swim across. They also studded the enemy's route with poison-tipped stakes. Finally, a noise-making obstacle was laid across Alonso de Lugo's route of retreat from Bondigua; it consisted of hollow gourds and bones hanging from strings stretching across the trail that Lugo's vanguard ran into in their nighttime retreat, thereby alerting the enemy (Castellanos 1850:321, 328; Simón 1892b:354, 1892c:205–206, 188; Aguado 1916:156).

In response to an attack the Tairona often evacuated their settlements, sometimes taking their provisions and setting their houses on fire before fleeing. This defensive strategy accounts for the number of abandoned, empty, and burned-down settlements encountered by the Spaniards throughout the Tairona area (Castellanos 1850:294, 321–323; Espinosa 1955:58; Simón 1891:16, 40, 43, 1892b:354–355, 360, 367, 1892c:179, 189, 211–213; Aguado 1916:104–105). The possibility that they buried their valuables before taking flight is raised by Alonso de Lugo's discovery of buried caches of gold inside houses at an abandoned settlement en route to La Ramada (Castellanos 1850:298). The practice of hiding their valuables before an impending attack is also noted by Aguado (1916:149) in his account of Alonso de Lugo's successful attack against the settlements of chiefs Arogare and Maruare (Biriburare) beyond Bonda and his seizure of more than 800 pounds of gold that the unsuspecting chiefs had not yet removed for safekeeping.

If they chose to defend their settlements, they sounded their conch-shell trumpets and drums and quickly armed and mobilized themselves. Amid great clamor they took up defensible positions, from which they hurled at the enemy boulders, poisoned arrows and, with the help of slings, fist-sized stones and larger rocks. They favored these long-distance forms of defensive warfare. In Castellanos's words,

> Porque viendo venir gentes armadas,
> El Arobaro luego tocó cuerno,
> A cuyo ronco son sobresaltadas
> Acuden las que son de su gobierno,
> Con tantos dardos, flechas y pedradas,
> Como gotas espesas en invierno,
> De tal manera, que quien vencer piensa
> Tiene por gran victoria su defensa. [Castellanos 1850:296]

Forced to retreat, the attackers were often pursued by the defenders, who fearlessly sought immediate revenge. Sometimes they intercepted the retreating force in narrow corridors and blocked their escape route. Only when they were vastly outnumbered or when their war leader was killed would the defenders cease their resistance and take flight (Castellanos 1850:261, 269, 273, 292–295; Simón 1891:40–42, 45, 48–49, 1892b:360, 369, 1892c:32–33, 210–212; Aguado 1916:104–106, 144).

*Post-war rituals and practices*

Following a successful raid the war party clubbed and dismembered the settlement's inhabitants—men, women, and children. Indeed, one chief of Bonda was said to have personally killed more than sixty individuals in war (Castellanos 1850:349; Simón 1892c:42). Simón (1892b:361) described a battlefield littered with dead bodies, weapons, and war spoils. The victors combed the scene of battle, searching for victims, going so far as to set fire to the underlying vegetation to uncover the bodies of their dead enemies. An open allied attack against an enemy force resulted in over ninety victims, and an allied attack against an enemy settlement resulted in more than fifty victims (Castellanos 1850:342, 355; Simón 1892c:34, 48). The victims' heads and limbs were part of the war spoils, as were their flayed skins, which they would stuff with straw. They also seized gold, precious ornaments, weapons, women, and provisions. If they had not already done so, the attackers set fire to the settlement before departing, in one case at the sound of a trumpet (Castellanos 1850:273, 277–278, 332–335, 354–356, 1892b:371, 1892c:46, 47–48, 56).

Back home, their post-war rituals and practices included the public and personal display of human trophies. They stored their war trophies in special structures or sanctuaries. They also displayed the skulls of their enemies on stakes that they erected in front of their residences and hung other human trophies inside their residences along with other war spoils as tokens of their bravery and victory in warfare. They bedecked themselves with necklaces of human teeth. As with other war spoils, the chief bestowed human trophies according to an individual's status or office, and sent them as gifts to neighbors and allies (Simón 1891:37, 1892b:366, 371, 1892c:42; Oviedo y Valdés 1852:355; Castellanos 1850:328, 332, 334).

The sixteenth-century sources differ concerning the possibility that the Indians of the province of Santa Marta consumed human flesh. Oviedo considered the inhabitants of the coast at the time of Pedrarias Dávila's arrival in 1514 to be anthropophagous "porque en algunas casas se hallaron aquel día tasajos é miembros de hombres ó de mugeres, assi como braços y piernas y una mano puesta y salada y enjairada" (Oviedo y Valdés 1852:355). But in writing about the Tairona of 1570, Simón maintained that they did not consume human flesh (Simón 1892b:356). As we shall see, however, their funerary customs did include acts of ritual endocannibalism.

Tairona warriors were rewarded for their war exploits in several ways. They received a share of the booty gained in war. Distinguished warriors became *manicatos,* and had the right to hang a long ponytail of human hair from their waists as a sign of their valor. They also donned elaborate feather ornaments for war and for other occasions (Simón 1892c:198; Reichel-Dolmatoff 1951:91; Castellanos 1850:322, 334–335). Finally, they took part in the special funerary rites for those killed in war, and upon their death, they were accorded similarly elaborate funerary rites.

*Mortuary treatment*

To die in war was the greatest glory. Although battlefields were strewn with the bodies of dead warriors (Simón 1892b:361), it seems that the bodies of some warriors killed in war were carried back home by their fellow warriors or were recovered later by their relatives (Castellanos 1850:342, 346; Simón 1892b:368). Mourning ceremonies were held over several days during which the deceased's bravery and achievements were extolled with lamentations and superlatives. We know that in Bonda a dead warrior's body was placed on a pyre and the drippings were collected in containers and drunk by his most outstanding fellow warriors. His ashes were deposited in a ceramic urn that was either stored in a special sanctuary of his family's residence or buried (Simón 1892c:34; Castellanos 1850:342). One reading of a passage by Simón describing Gonzalo Suárez's encounter with a war party in Charaima raises the possibility that some of the musical instruments that the Tairona sounded in warfare were made from the long bones of warriors killed in war (Simón 1891:43).

Members of the chiefly elite were honored with elaborate mourning ceremonies and were buried in stone-lined shaft tombs in a flexed or seated position with their gold ornaments, weapons, vessels of food and drink, women, and slaves (Castellanos 1850:258, 276, 356; Simón 1892c:218; Espinosa 1955:59; Reichel-Dolmatoff 1951:92). The mourning ceremonies accorded the dead could easily precipitate a new round of warfare, because very often when they recalled their relatives' deaths in war during their drinking bouts, they became incensed and determined to seek revenge (Simón 1892c:181).

### Warfare Among the Panamanian Chiefdoms

In the sixteenth century the militaristic chiefdoms of the Panamanian isthmus were within striking distance of their neighbors in northern South America. The Atrato River and its tributaries served as a major travel route across the isthmus to the northern Colombian Andes (Figure 18). Not surprisingly, therefore, close cultural ties existed between the Panamanian chiefdoms and those of northwestern Colombia—so close, in fact, that some scholars have posited their participation in a broad interregional network of exchange, marriage alliances, and warfare (Helms 1976:150–154; Lange and Stone 1984:5; Bray 1984:305–309). Helms has documented the nature of long-distance exchange between the chiefly elites of Panama and northern Colombia in the sixteenth century and earlier. From her study of the pertinent ethnohistoric, archaeological and ethnographic data, she con-

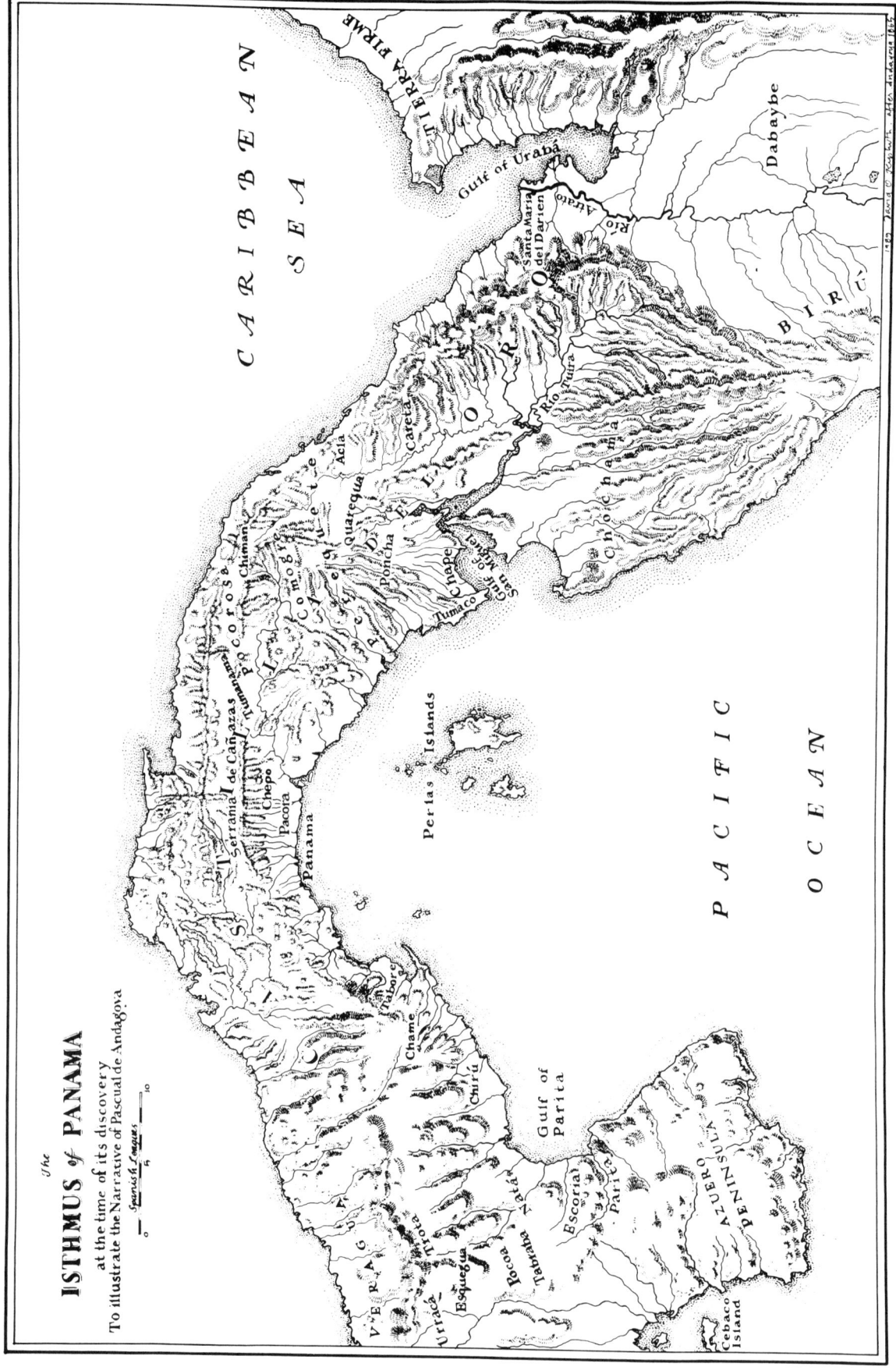

*Figure 18.* Map of the Isthmus of Panama, with the chiefdoms that inhabited it in the sixteenth century. [Redrawn from Andagoya 1865.]

cludes that the elites in pre-Columbian Panama and the northern Colombian Andes shared a common political ideology (Helms 1976:145–146, 153–160, 167–171).

The Cueva-speaking Indians are another case in point for they extended from eastern Panama to the Gulf of Urabá and the Western Cordillera of the Colombian Andes in the sixteenth century (Oviedo y Valdés 1855:117; Lothrop 1937:12; Cooke and Ranere 1992:294). For this reason, Oviedo y Valdés's informative account of the Cueva Indians in the twenty-ninth book of his *Historia General* (Oviedo y Valdés 1853:125–144) is used by scholars of both northern South American and lower Central American societies. Moreover, Oviedo y Valdés (1853:43, 1855:118) himself remarked on the rapid depopulation of the Indians who inhabited the Panamanian isthmus in the decade following Pedrarias Dávila's arrival and installation as governor of Castilla del Oro in 1514, a fact that renders his and his contemporaries' accounts all the more valuable.

My principal rationale for considering the Panamanian chiefdoms, however, is the exceptional ethnohistoric and archaeological data that exist about ancient Panamanian warfare. The sixteenth-century accounts of the Spanish expeditions and conquests in Panama by Oviedo y Valdés (1853, 1855), Las Casas (1951), Andagoya (1865), Espinosa (1864, 1873), and others offer eyewitness accounts of the large-scale attacks and ambushes (*guacábaras*) directed against them by the mighty paramount chiefs who ruled the provinces of Panama. These ethnohistoric sources provide an unusually complete picture of the warfare waged by the Panamanian chiefdoms at the time of the Spanish Conquest. Equally remarkable is the existing archaeological evidence relating to pre-Columbian chiefly warfare in Panama, which I will examine in a later chapter.

The sixteenth-century Spanish provinces of Castilla del Oro overlay a diversity of independent chiefdoms, whose territories varied in size according to the military might of their paramount chiefs. Perhaps the best known are the chiefdoms around Parita Bay in central Panama: Natá centered in the Chico-Grande-Coclé River drainage; Escoria on the Santa María River; Parita of the Parita-La Villa River drainages; Esquegua in the upper Gatú River; and Urracá in the upper Santa María highlands (Cooke and Ranere 1992:294).

In her authoritative ethnohistoric study of these Panamanian chiefdoms, Helms (1976:40–65) determined the supraregional territories ruled by the paramount chiefs (*quevís*) of Comogre, Chape, Escoria, Parita, and Veragua. From their chiefly centers (*bohíos*) these high chiefs presided over their subjects, who lived for the most part in small, dispersed settlements near their fields, under the control of local chiefs (*sacos*). The ties between the regional-level *quevís* (or *tibas*) and the lesser chiefs were governed by affinal ties, marriage alliances, exchange, and warfare. Outside their domains, the paramount chiefs of Panama participated in elite marriage alliances and prestige-good exchange networks with each other as well as with the chiefly elites of polities beyond the isthmus (Helms 1976:8–15, 40–66; Lothrop 1937:10–12, 14, 22; Oviedo y Valdés 1853:129).

*The nature and objectives of warfare*

The Panamanian chiefdoms also waged war against one another, due principally to the paramount chiefs' expansionist desires for land and power. Few were the instances when chiefs within a paramount chief's domain took up their arms to settle their differences, for the paramount chief had the authority to squelch any feuds that erupted within his territory. The high chief's ability to settle disputes was highlighted by his personal execution of any member of the elite who was convicted of some wrongdoing (Oviedo y Valdés 1853:129–130, 142; Andagoya 1865:13).

Warfare was directed against neighboring chiefdoms with an intensity that impressed their European adversaries. It was spurred in part by their deep-rooted hatred for one another, an enmity so great that it apparently superseded their feelings towards the Spanish *conquistadores* (Espinosa 1864:497). Their warfare was often ideologically motivated as well; as we shall see, they sought the counsel of supernatural forces before launching their military campaigns and believed that their warfare was divinely sanctioned (Oviedo y Valdés 1853:129).

According to Pietro Anghera (Anghera 1912:292), however, these interpolity enmities went hand in hand with their chiefs' ambitions. Powerful *quevís* waged expansionist conquest warfare against neighboring groups in order to enlarge their territories and bring more villages under their control. Chief Comogre's son is reported to have told the Spaniards that "we are ambitious, and we fight one against the other for power, each seeking to conquer his neighbour. This, therefore, is the source of frequent wars" (Anghera 1912:222). Oviedo y Valdés's observation that warfare was conducted to see which chief "terná mas tierra é señorio" (Oviedo y Valdés 1853:129) is illustrated by different accounts of their expansionist warfare. The great chief Parita, who controlled much of the eastern shores of the Azuero Peninsula ringing the Gulf of Parita, embarked upon a military campaign southward that succeeded in conquering the other chiefdoms on the Azuero Peninsula and incorporating them into his domain. In this way, Parita gained more land and more subjects, including warriors, which provided him with a decided advantage in his future wars (Helms 1976:59–60). The chiefs of the neighboring provinces of Careta and Acla on the Caribbean coast, who were brothers, were also at war with one another because one wished "to possess all" (Andagoya 1865:9). According to Andagoya (1945:396), the warlike Cueva chiefs fought repeatedly over the boundaries of their territories.

Through warfare the Panamanian chiefs sought to obtain access to fishing and hunting grounds and major trade routes. Not surprisingly, therefore, when Helms plotted the geographic locations of the Panamanian chiefdoms, she noted that "the domains of chiefs considered most powerful or prestigious were found to be located adjacent to major transportation arteries, either rivers or land trails" (Helms 1976:39, see also 33–34).

Rich were the spoils gained from war too, which included fine gold pieces and war captives, who became slaves. The paramount chief of the Perlas Islands would attack the mainland chiefdoms of Tumaco and Chape periodically with a great fleet of war canoes and carry off everything he found (Helms 1976:49). Prior to the arrival of the Spaniards, the chief of Parita had faced the threat of an army of foreigners from the north, but they had fallen ill and retired to a campsite. At dawn one morning Parita's troops descended upon their encampment, defeated them, killed them all, and took the spoil, which included much gold (Andagoya 1945:411). Later when the same chief of Parita ambushed Badajoz's camp, his warriors carried off much of the gold amassed by the Spaniards (Andagoya 1945:401). Both these military campaigns of Parita's illustrate a final objective of the warfare conducted by the Panamanian chiefdoms: defensive warfare that was intended to repel invaders.

*Preparations for war*

The Panamanian chiefs personally organized and directed their military campaigns. The importance of war as a chiefly activity is revealed by Oviedo y Valdés's remark that the chief occasionally took pleasure in cultivating corn and manioc, hunting, and fishing when he was not at war (Oviedo y Valdés 1853:133). Preparations for war began with the reports by scouts and spies regarding the location and strength of enemy forces. The chiefs dispatched messengers posthaste to warn their allies and convene war councils. These chiefly emissaries must have been carefully groomed for their role as spies and messengers, for were they to fall into the hands of their enemies, they never divulged any damaging information, even under torture (Espinosa 1864:496, 498; Las Casas 1951:393; Lothrop 1937:9; Oviedo y Valdés 1853:130).

The chiefs of a military alliance attended war councils in order to decide upon their joint war ventures. The sizes of these military alliances reflected the power of the paramount chief leading the venture as well as the nature of the enemy threat. Aside from the lure of defeating a common enemy, the paramount chief encouraged other chiefs to join in a military alliance with promises of a daughter in marriage or a share in the spoils (Helms 1976:43; Espinosa 1864:496). The Spanish sources principally mention the large-scale military alliances that were established by the paramount chiefs of Comogre, Escoria, Parita, and Urracá in order to resist them. The neighboring chiefs of Comogre and Pocorosa allied themselves for the purposes of attacking the Spanish port of Santa Cruz on the Caribbean Sea (Oviedo y Valdés 1853:46). When Gonzalo de Badajoz penetrated the province of Escoria during his expedition westward along the Pacific coast in 1515, the chief of Escoria warned his neighbor and brother-in-law, the great chief Parita. Together they mounted an allied military force that succeeded in attacking and looting Badajoz's camp and driving the surviving members of his expedition away (Oviedo y Valdés 1853:47–49). When Gaspar de Espinosa returned the following year to pursue the Spanish conquest of western Panama with greater force, Parita convened a war council in order to decide upon a strategy against Espinosa's troops. At this council meeting, a brother of Parita urged him not to yield to Espinosa by returning the gold seized from Badajoz's camp, but instead, to distribute Badajoz's gold to the chiefs who would join in a military alliance against the Spaniards. Most of the chiefdoms of Azuero Peninsula united under Parita's leadership to resist the Spanish forces (Espinosa 1864:495–496). And later in the 1520s during Pedrarias's campaign to subdue Urracá, whose territory extended across the mountains north of the Azuero Peninsula, this chief mounted a military alliance with his neighbor, Esquegua, that in time mobilized warriors from chiefdoms across both the Atlantic and Pacific watersheds—including the chiefdoms of Chiriquí, Vareclas and Burica—as well as the provinces surrounding the Spanish settlement at Natá (Las Casas 1951:395, 398; Lothrop 1937:8–9).

At these war councils the participating chiefs decided and agreed upon their allied military campaigns in the course of rituals and feasts. Their diviners (*tequinas*) were called upon to communicate with the supernatural being (*tuyra*) by means of rituals and sacrifices and counsel them as to the favorable moment to launch their attack. In Darien, their invocations to the supernatural included emitting animal calls and sounding a variety of noisemakers and instruments: "with their own noise, they joined that of several stones struck together, and of conch-shells, and of a sorry sort of drums made of hollow bambooes, which they beat upon; making a jarring noise also with strings fastened to the larger bones of beasts: and every now and then they would make a dreadful exclamation, and clattering all of a sudden, would as suddenly make a pause and a profound silence" (Wafer 1903:61). Upon receiving the *tequina's* augury, the gathered chiefs and other members of the chiefly elite attended a feast complete with drinking, dancing, and singing (Oviedo y Valdés 1853:127, 130). Espinosa (1873:41) described one such feast at the chiefly center of Natá that was attended by 1,500 or more people. It is likely that games were part of these chiefly gatherings, for Oviedo y Valdés (1853:159) and Espinosa (1864:510) reported that a ball game similar to the native *batey* game played in Hispaniola was played by Panamanian chiefdoms, and a game of *cañas* was played at a feast celebrated by Espinosa and the chief of Comagre (Espinosa 1864:470). On ritual occasions like these they sounded wooden drums, some of which were small enough for a man to carry but others required five or six men to carry them from the chief's house where they were stored. The objectives of their military alliance were established in song and performed to the accompaniment of drums; in this way their war stratagems were formally decreed—lest any carouser forget what was agreed to the next morning (Oviedo y Valdés 1853:130, 137, 142).

Having declared war, a chief's subsequent preparations for war included stockpiling armament and provisions, and mobilizing the desired fighting force. The storehouses within a chief's residence (*bohío*) were stocked with provisions, such as at the chiefly center of Comogre, which Anghera (1912:219) described as a timber and stone wall compound measuring some 450 feet (137 m) long by 240 (73 m) feet wide and containing various apartments and storerooms. Here the chief's provisions consisted of maize, roots, chile peppers, fruits, smoked deer and pork, dried fish, baskets of corn meal, herbs, and fermented drinks (*chichas*) made from maize, roots, and a variety of fruits (Helms 1976:11). When Espinosa attacked the chiefly center of Natá he seized a four months' supply of provisions, which included maize, dried fish, three hundred smoked deer, geese, and turkeys (Espinosa 1864:488; Lothrop 1937:6). A warring chief's armament was also readied; Espinosa remarked upon the fine armorers of the chief of Escoria, and for that matter, the weapons made by all the Panamanian chiefdoms, which I will describe later (Espinosa 1864:508). Chiefs in coastal or island locations also had canoes at their disposal, including some that could transport 60 or more men (Oviedo y Valdés 1853:159).

To summon his subjects the chief ordered his large drum beaten (Oviedo y Valdés 1853:142). And through his network of alliances with neighboring chiefs, a paramount chief like Parita could mobilize an allied fighting force in a day or two at the most (Espinosa 1873:25). The size estimates of the resulting war parties range from 200 to 4,000 warriors (Espinosa 1873:19–20; Oviedo y Valdés 1853:9, 117; Lothrop 1937:6; Helms 1976:43, 45). The war parties mobilized by island chiefs were assessed by the Spaniards on three occasions in terms of the number of war canoes, which if they could carry 60 men, convert to maximum fighting force estimates of 480, 540, and 1,080 warriors (Espinosa 1864:514–516; Oviedo y Valdés 1853:159). Finally, in his first encounter with Parita's forces, Espinosa's vanguard was encircled by what he later described as an "infinite" number of warriors (Espinosa 1864:496). A warring chief apparently had special barracks to lodge the warriors that he recruited from allied villages; Tumanama's center included two long houses, measuring 220 by 50 paces, that were used to shelter warriors when he made war (Anghera 1912:309). The legacy of these structures may be reflected in the war houses that the British traveler Lionel Wafer visited later in 1681 during his stay in Darien. Serving neighboring communities these war houses measured approximately 130 by 25 feet (39.6 by 7.6 m) with 10 foot-tall walls and thick wooden doors at each end. Their lack of interior partitions also made them different from ordinary residences (Wafer 1903:145–147).

*Organization of war parties*

The Panamanian chiefs organized and led their war parties. Andagoya (1945:403), for example, characterized the chief of Parita as a brave man who conquered neighboring provinces. During an open attack against Espinosa's troops this paramount chief came forward to fight, to throw lances, to incite his warriors, and to punish any men who retreated by beating them with a club (Espinosa 1864:497–498). Paramount chiefs commanded a two-tiered military hierarchy, composed of lesser chiefs (*sacos*) and military captains (*cabras*). In the case of several large-scale, allied military campaigns against Badajoz and Espinosa's forces special war leaders are mentioned, but in all these possible instances of a third tier of command the war leaders were brothers or a brother-in-law of the paramount chief (Espinosa 1864:494, 496, 508).

The command structure of their war parties is evident in Oviedo y Valdés's remark that "Quando van á la guerra, llevan sus caudillos ó capitanes: estos son sacos é cabras, é son ya hombres de expiriençia en las cosas de las armas quellos usan" (Oviedo y Valdés 1853:130). According to Lothrop (1937:22), the chiefs (*sacos*) appointed captains (*cabras*) who assembled, organized, and led troops of warriors. These military captains were warriors who in spite of their commoner status achieved the noble title of *cabra* by distinguishing themselves in warfare. In addition to being granted a military title and entry into the elite sector of society, *cabras* were rewarded with gifts of a territory to administer, women, and slaves. Their wives became *espaves*, a term used to distinguish the wives of paramount chiefs, lesser chiefs and other female members of the chiefly elite. Moreover, the title won by these outstanding warriors could be inherited by their sons on the condition that they, too, devoted themselves to warfare (Oviedo y Valdés 1853:129–130, 126; Espinosa 1864:479, 495; Lothrop 1937:22; Helms 1976:13).

The social and military ranking of their war parties was displayed on the battlefield by the headdresses, armor, gold insignia, and face and body paint that the chiefs, military captains, and warriors donned for war. In the first place, we are told that chiefs and their participating wives were carried to war in litters consisting of a hammock strung on a pole by a team of slave-bearers (Oviedo y Valdés 1853:126). When Chief Pocoa led a dawn ambush on Alonso de Vargas's campsite he was easily distinguished—aside from his position at the forefront of his 500 or more attacking warriors—by his great gold breastplate, which enabled him to be recognized by his warriors, his allies, and even by his enemies: "porque es costumbre en aquellas partes que los caçiques é hombres prinçipales traygan en la batalla alguna joya de oro en los pechos ó en la cabeça ó en los braços, para ser señalados é conosçidos entre los suyos é aun entre sus enemigos" (Oviedo y Valdés 1853:118). When Espinosa's men were attacked by Parita's warriors the Spaniards spotted and recognized Chief Parita as the leader of the advancing war party because he was bedecked with many gold disks, plates, and bracelets over his cotton tunic (Espinosa 1864:497). This distinction between the chiefly leaders of war parties and their men is also emphasized in Anghera's description of the confrontation between Vasco Nuñez de Balboa's and Chief Quarequa's armies. Quarequa "stepped out in front of his men, dressed, as were all his chiefs, while the rest of his people were naked" (Anghera 1912:284).

Their personal adornment included feather-crested headgear, gold breastplates, headbands, and armbands, shell and gold-bead necklaces, bracelets, anklets, and knee bands, gold earrings, gold nose-plugs, and nose plaques (Oviedo y Valdés 1853:138). In the succeeding century Wafer observed the chiefly elite in Darien wearing gold diadems, nose plaques, and multiple necklaces of teeth, shells, and beads on public occasions (Wafer 1903:140–

144). The practice of wearing these multiple necklaces was not restricted to the chiefly elite, only the "chains" of jagged animal teeth, which covered their chests. Although Wafer noted that these necklaces were not worn to war by warriors, in all likelihood these are precisely the insignia that Andagoya observed the brave warriors of Escoria wearing on the battlefield in 1516 (Andagoya 1945:404). According to Oviedo y Valdés, they prided themselves on their war dress: "en las cosas de la guerra he visto desta gente que se presçian mucho; ... é de ninguna manera tanto como en la guerra se presçian de paresçer gentiles hombres é yr lo mas bien aderesçados quellos pueden" (Oviedo y Valdés 1853:138). When high-ranking women (*espaves*) accompanied their husbands to battle, or in some cases were in positions of leadership and commanded war parties, they were similarly bedecked with splendid feather headgear, gold headbands, eagle ornaments, and heavy gold bars that served as pectorals to support their breasts, many of which were decorated in fine relief with bird motifs and other figures (Oviedo y Valdés 1853:126).

Their war dress was not complete without painting their faces and bodies with red *bixa* (*Bixa orellana*) and black *xagua* (*Genipa*) colors. Although this form of personal adornment was practiced by men and women both in times of war and peace, it was most frequently worn by warriors (Oviedo y Valdés 1853:138). Wafer described in some detail the art of face and body painting among the Indians of Darien. Women were the artists, who painted "birds, beasts, men, trees, or the like, up and down in every part of the body, more especially the face" (Wafer 1903:136) in vivid red, yellow, and blue colors. Before going to war, however, warriors had their faces painted red and the rest of their bodies painted in large spots of yellow and black—the colors of death and victory (Wafer 1903:137, 133; Helms 1976:95). Not only did this war paint signal their status as warriors but they also considered it a preventive measure for the upcoming venture that contributed to their well-being (Oviedo y Valdés 1853:138).

The related practice of tattooing their faces, chests and arms created an indelible badge of one's social rank. There was a difference between the tattoos worn by chiefs and other freemen and those branded on the faces of captives or slaves. Chiefs and other freemen wore tattoos on their lower faces (from the mouth and ears down), their arms, and their chests. This was a privilege that according to Wafer was limited to "scarce one in forty of them" (Wafer 1903:137). Captives or slaves were branded on their faces (from the mouth up) with the brand of their new overlord. The forcible tattooing of war captives (*pacos*) with the mark of their new overlord represented the stigma of their enslavement (Oviedo y Valdés 1853:138–139; Espinosa 1864:470; Lothrop 1937:13–14, 22–23).

*Warfare strategies, weapons, and tactics*

Chiefs and military captains led their troops to war in an orderly manner (Espinosa 1864:516–517). The only possible reference to the seasonality of warfare among the Panamanian chiefdoms is Anghera's remark that Chief Careca undertook a military campaign against his neighbor, Poncha, immediately after the sowing season, which would probably have corresponded to the late dry season or early rainy season (Anghera 1912:218). Moreover, Chief Chiorisos's emissaries appealed to Vasco Nuñez de Balboa for help in their defensive warfare against the powerful and expansionist Chief Tumanama, who attacked them yearly (Anghera 1912:307). Yet, the Cueva-speaking inhabitants east of the Gulf of San Miguel in the province of Chochama endured attacks "at every full moon" by warriors from Birú, a fact that underscores the chronic nature of warfare in the Isthmus in the early sixteenth century (Andagoya 1865:40).

The element of surprise was a tactic in two of their warfare strategies, which I shall distinguish as nocturnal raids and ambushes. The nocturnal attack most frequently related in the ethnohistoric literature is the one that Chief Parita masterminded against Badajoz's encampment in 1516. With the help of spies, Parita intentionally misinformed the Spaniards about his whereabouts and his storehouse of gold, and monitored the enemy's subsequent movements, waiting for the right moment to attack. Allied with his brother-in-law, the chief of Escoria, and other neighboring chiefs, Parita's forces raided Badajoz's camp at night, overwhelming its defenders, setting fire to the houses, and looting the hoard of gold that had been collected by Badajoz's expedition (Andagoya 1865:26, 1945:401; Oviedo y Valdés 1853:48; Lothrop 1937:6). Chief Parita had used this same tactic two years earlier, when he carried out a matutinal raid on the seaside camp of a large foreign army (Andagoya 1945:411).

Two other examples of nocturnal raids extend the chiefly practice of this war stratagem well into the period of Spanish settlement in the region. In 1527, Chief Trota and his ally, Pocoa, sent scouts to spy on Alonso de Vargas's expedition inland from Natá; they also sent emissaries to befriend and deceive the Spaniards further. A day or two later, these chiefs led a pre-dawn force of 500 or more warriors against Vargas's camp; with resounding war cries and a "rain" of spears they succeeded in killing the Spanish captain and half of his men, and driving the survivors back to Natá (Oviedo y Valdés 1853:117–118). During Governor Pedrarias's nine-year-long campaign against Chief Urracá the Spanish settlement at Natá endured several large-scale nocturnal attacks, including one in which Urracá's forces set fire to Natá (Las Casas 1951:395; Lothrop 1937:8–9). With their spearthrowers the night raiders flung spears and darts made of palm wood or cane, which were sometimes tipped with points that had hollow balls on their extremities and that whistled as they sailed toward their target, to spite the enemy (Oviedo y Valdés 1853:127; Lothrop 1937:20–21; Las Casas 1953:393).

The nocturnal raid was such an effective warfare strategy that the Spaniards soon adopted it themselves. During one of Vasco Nuñez de Balboa's forays inland from the Spanish settlement at Darien sometime after 1511 he befriended Chief Pochorroso and together their allied forces attacked Tumanama's chiefly center at night, "taking him completely by surprise, for he expected nothing" (Anghera 1912:308–309). In the course of Espinosa's first expedition across the Isthmus and toward the Azuero Peninsula in 1516 he began storming the chiefly centers at night, including Natá, where he subsequently established an outpost in the region (Espinosa 1864:478, 481, 484, 488). According to Wafer (1903:146), the Spaniards and their allies would set fire to the thatched roofs of fortified enemy settlements by flinging firebrands with bows in order to drive the inhabitants out of their fortifications.

Ambushes involved encircling or cornering the enemy in a restricted location such as a gorge or on a river bank and surprising the unsuspecting group with a mightier fighting force. Espinosa's first confrontation with Parita's forces occurred in the aftermath of such an ambush. Unknowingly guided by spies of Parita, Espinosa's vanguard resumed their march across Parita's territory one dawn. Upon fording a stream and emerging from its gallery forest the 80 Spaniards led by Captain Diego Albítez saw some warriors lying down on the open savanna ahead, and thinking that this was their only opposition they rushed forward to the attack. At that moment an "infinite" number of warriors sprang from forests on both sides of the savanna to encircle the Spaniards with a hailstorm of spears (Espinosa 1864:496–497).

Later during the Spaniards' campaign to subdue Chief Urracá, Espinosa's, Pizarro's, and Pedrarias's forces suffered many ambushes in the narrow passes of Urracá's mountainous territory (Lothrop 1937:8). When Espinosa decided to retreat from one arduous battle, he was pursued by some of Urracá's warriors and intercepted by others who awaited his retreat in a dangerous pass where they descended upon Espinosa and his men like "fierce lions" (Las Casas 1951:393–394). Under orders by Pedrarias to pursue Urracá, Captain Albítez fell into many such traps laid by Urracá along the route through the mountains, making it evident that repeated ambushes were another characteristic of Panamanian chiefly warfare. On their return from one fruitless search for Urracá in the sierra, Albítez's men were intercepted in a narrow river gorge by Urracá's warriors, who awaited the Spaniards on the river bank and cut off their escape route as they rushed to attack them with great war cries (Las Casas 1951:396).

In addition to nocturnal raids and ambushes, the Panamanian chiefdoms waged open advances and attacks in broad daylight. For example, the above-mentioned Urracá confronted Pedrarias and Pizarro's forces at the entrance to his ally Esquegua's fortified settlement for a day-long battle. Undaunted by Pedrarias's artillery, Urracá's allied forces came out to attack the Spaniards on four successive days with the same fury that they had displayed in their first encounter with Espinosa's men (Las Casas 1951:393, 395–396).

Pascual de Andagoya's account of the battles between the neighboring chiefs of Parita and Escoria is particularly informative in this regard because it describes chiefly warfare that was waged in prehispanic times. According to Andagoya, these neighboring chiefs, who later became allies to repel their common Spanish enemy, had long been at war with one another. The great chief of Parita wished to incorporate the territory of Escoria into his realm, but the brave warriors of Escoria succeeded in repelling his forces. Andagoya relates how Escoria's men entered Parita's territory to wage war, which lasted for eight days, and on each day a battle was fought. Although Parita's men held an advantage in being able to retire from the battlefield each day and send in fresh troops on successive days, Escoria's warriors were renowned for their armament, their strength, and their valor (Espinosa 1864:508).

In 1516 a series of such open attacks followed Parita and Escoria's joint nocturnal raid upon Badajoz's encampment. The next morning Badajoz encountered an arm of Parita's allied force proceeding "in war-like array" to the place where the survivors of the raid had fled. Badajoz defeated them, and expecting a return attack the following day by fresh troops summoned by Parita, he withdrew to Natá, home of his two guides on this fateful expedition into Parita's territory, only to be met with an encounter by Natá's warriors, who "came out to fight them with great fury" in a day-long battle (Andagoya 1865:26–27, Oviedo y Valdés 1853:48–49; Lothrop 1937:6).

After Badajoz's retreat it was Espinosa who succeeded in establishing an outpost at the chiefly center of Natá and who upon entering the province of Parita withstood multiple attacks by Parita's allied forces. Andagoya described their approach to a village where they expected to find the chief of Parita, "who came out to us to give us battle on a plain, and this battle was fought with great ferocity, and lasted from nine in the morning until an hour before sunset" (Andagoya 1865:29). In all likelihood Andagoya was referring to the six-hour-long battle that followed Parita's ambush of Espinosa's vanguard on the open savanna, during which Espinosa's men and their Indian allies defeated and pursued Parita's retreating warriors. Chief Parita himself led a return attack with additional forces; incited by his presence, his warriors threw themselves valiantly into combat with Espinosa's men, including his crossbowmen, "los cuales asaetaban é mataban mucho de los indios bravos, aunque los dichos indios tenian tanto esfuerzo, que no mataban uno, cuando ponian diez delante" (Espinosa 1864:497). In a later expedition headed by one of Espinosa's captains, Bartolomé Hurtado, to the island of Cabo (Coiba), the chief, upon hearing about the Spaniards' landing, arrived with eight canoes of armed warriors. They disembarked and approached Hurtado's men "en su ordenanza de la manera de alemanes" (Espinosa 1864:516) for the ensuing battle, which Espinosa characterized as "una bien rezia guacabara, ó batalla, los unos con los otros, la cual fue bien reñida" (Espinosa 1864:517).

Because battles like these took place in broad daylight, the Spanish accounts of them contain nuggets of information about the organization and nature of combat, including the use of weapons and armament, and the accompanying musical instruments and war cries. War parties proceeded to war and met the enemy forces in a highly organized, determined manner. In at least two encounters, Espinosa noted how the chiefly war parties were organized into fighting units or troops that assembled to fight in a large army or battalion. They proved to be very effective fighting units, for if the troops at the front suffered casualties, they were reinforced immediately by troops of warriors who were sent forward to take over, thereby forming and reforming a solid, fighting front (Espinosa 1864:488, 497).

According to Oviedo y Valdés (1853:127) and Andagoya (1945:395–396), the Cueva Indians fought with clubs (*macanas*), lances, and spears that they flung with spearthrowers. Their *macanas* were long, double-edged wooden broadswords, some that were wielded with one hand, and others so heavy that they required both hands to swing and thrust them in face-to-face combat (Oviedo y Valdés 1853:129; Andagoya 1945:396; Anghera 1912:217–218, 284, 301). Their lances were made of palm wood or *xagua* or other hardwood, with fire-hardened points. Some of the western Panamanian chiefdoms had particularly long lances made of hard, jet-black palm wood that Espinosa described as "fechas á la manera de picas, tan luengas é tan gruesas, como las que usan los alemanes, sembradas, obra de una vara de medir [or .836 m], hácia la punta, de dientes de tiburones é otros pescados" (Espinosa 1864:516). So tall were these lances that Oviedo y Valdés used their height as a standard for estimating the height of certain columnar cacti (Oviedo y Valdés 1853:143). Although we lack precise descriptions of how these lances were used in combat there are several references to hurling these weapons at the enemy (Espinosa 1864:515, 1873:38). Similarly, Anghera reported that in addition to using *macanas* in hand-to-hand combat "they likewise use pointed sticks hardened in the fire, bone-tipped javelins, and other projectiles" (Anghera 1912:218, see also 284, 301). And it is likely that they thrust their lances like pikes in the manner described by Andagoya for the Colombian chiefdoms (see above).

Panamanian warriors also fought with spears and darts flung with spearthrowers. As described and illustrated by Oviedo y Valdés (1853:127, 129, Lámina I) and shown in Figure 19, these well-made spearthrowers enabled them to hurl spears over great or short distances with great accuracy and force. The spears (*varas*) were made of black palm wood or of other hardwoods with fire-hardened sharp points that were capable of penetrating a victim's body all the way through (Oviedo y Valdés 1853:129; Anghera 1912:218, 284). Some spears were made of strong, smooth cane the thickness of the little finger or less with mounted barbed points of black palm wood; other spearpoints were made from animal bone and fish bone, including sawfish spikes and stingray spines, which inflicted festering wounds in their victims (Oviedo y Valdés 1853:129; Lothrop 1937:20). We have seen how some spearpoints had attached whistles that were occasionally used in long-distance or nocturnal attacks. During Espinosa's march into Esquegua's territory from the Gulf of Parita in 1519 he had two of his spies disguise themselves as Indians by removing their clothes and donning the spearthrowers and spears of the Indians (Espinosa 1873:36).

Panamanian warriors were not bowmen, according to Oviedo y Valdés (1853:127). The only references to the use of bows and arrows in warfare pertain to the chiefdoms of eastern Panama along the Caribbean coast and in the Gulf of Urabá. In describing the weapons used by the warriors of Careca (Quarequa), Anghera stated that they used bows and poisoned arrows, as was the case among the Indians to the east beyond the gulf (Anghera 1912:217–218, see also 284, 301). The poison was made from the fruit of a particular *mançanillo* tree (*Hippomane mancinella*) "con que se haçe la hierva de los caribes flecheros, assi en el golpho de Urabá como en la costa del Darien é de Acla" (Oviedo y Valdés 1853:143). The bow and arrow headed Wafer's list of the weapons used by the Indians of Darien in the seventeenth century, which was made up of "their bow and arrow, lance, hatchet, or macheat or long-knife" (Wafer 1903:160). They fashioned their arrowpoints out of black palmwood (Wafer 1903:97, 158). By this time, their lances, which Wafer characterized as "half pikes," were used principally on public occasions (Wafer 1903:60, 158)

The armament of Panamanian warriors included their armor and their shields. Warriors wore thick, padded cotton corsets that hung from their shoulders with elbow-length sleeves and reached down to their knees or lower; as thick as a mattress, this cotton armor was probably stiffened with brine (Espinosa 1864:516; Lothrop 1937:22). Hurtado encountered an entire war party armed with this cotton armor on the island of Cabo (Coiba). So thick and strong was their armor that crossbows could not pierce it; the Spaniards' artillery shots finally succeeded in ripping their protective armor apart (Espinosa 1864:516–517; cf. Lothrop 1937:22). The same war party featured warriors bearing lances studded with shark teeth and other warriors carrying round shields made of interwoven roots or strips of cane, "raizes de las de caña encabalgadas unas sobre otras é redondas" (Espinosa 1864:516). This description of armor-clad warriors fighting with lances alongside fellow warriors with shields evokes the group warfare tactic performed by Apirama's forces against Andagoya's expedition in the Cauca Valley.

Armed and orderly, the members of a war party carried musical instruments to battle, such as large conch-shell trumpets that sounded loudly, and drums (Oviedo y Valdés 1853:138). The war party described above that advanced determinedly towards Hurtado's force on the island of Cabo (Coiba) also toted fifes and drums (Espinosa 1864:516). Menacing calls and war cries were directed at the enemy force in the moment before the attack, best described by Anghera in his account of Gaspar de Morales's landing on one of the Perlas Islands. "The proud and formidable king of the island . . . advanced to meet them, escorted by a large number of warriors, and proffering menaces. Guazzaciara is their war-cry; when they utter this cry, they let fly their javelins. . . . Guazzaciara means a battle" (Anghera 1912:394). We have seen how Urracá's troops emitted such war cries when they ambushed Albítez's detachment in a narrow river pass. For this reason, the Spanish chroniclers adopted the term *guaçábara* to refer to the ambushes and battles that their expeditions encountered in Castilla del Oro (e.g., Oviedo y Valdés 1853:118, 129; Espinosa 1864:517).

Incited by their hatred of the enemy, the Panamanian warriors threw themselves en masse into combat and fought with an ardor

*Figure 19.* Spearthrower illustrated by Oviedo y Valdés (1853: Lámina I). [Reprinted by permission, from *Coclé: An Archaeological Study of Central Panama* (Lothrop 1937: Fig. 10b). Peabody Museum.]

that impressed the Spaniards (Espinosa 1864:497). When Urracá's warriors confronted Espinosa's force, "sáleles al encuentro con tanto esfuerzo y braveza como si fueran tigres o leones contra gatos que los rasguñaran" (Las Casas 1951:393). Furthermore, a guiding principle of their combat was "á los que pueden matar matan" (Oviedo y Valdés 1853:129). We have seen how under the leadership of their zealous chiefs and military captains they maintained a front line of fierce warriors irrespective of any losses they incurred. Andagoya provides a graphic portrayal of their face-to-face combat in his account of the outcome of the war between Escoria and Parita's forces, in which "finally, they threw away their arms, and closed in an embrace, biting each other. As those of Escoria were bigger and stronger than those of Paris, they worsted them" (Andagoya 1865:30).

Warring chiefs were capable of performing acts of deception and treachery in order to achieve their goals. A common strategy was to have spies intentionally captured by the enemy; this way they gained more information about the nature of the enemy force and they could befriend and deceive their captors with false information. Parita raided Badajoz's camp after having one of his spies captured by the Spaniards, who misinformed Badajoz and lured him away to a bigger pot of gold three or four leagues away (Andagoya 1865:26; Lothrop 1937:6). We have seen how Chief Pocoa, who became a trusted ally and peace negotiator for the Spaniards in their attempt to subdue Chief Trota, shortly thereafter led a pre-dawn raid together with Trota and 500 or more warriors against Alonso de Vargas's camp, knowing that Vargas was ill and that there were but 40 Spaniards therein (Oviedo y Valdés 1853:117–118; Lothrop 1937:9). After Espinosa's captain, Pablo Mexía, ransacked Chamna's village and took his wives and gold, Chamna agreed to meet Mexía and asked that a hammock-litter be sent for him. When he came a few days later, however, it was to lead an attack upon the Spaniards (Espinosa 1864:520).

*Defensive strategies*

In response to the state of chronic warfare between the Panamanian chiefdoms they fortified their settlements in various ways. We know little about the defensive measures practiced by the inhabitants of the many households, hamlets and small villages distributed across a chief's territory because the Spaniards principally visited and described the chiefly centers (*bohíos*) (Helms 1976:9). At the first sign of trouble, the inhabitants of settlements lacking fortifications probably fled and sought refuge at the nearest fortified settlement. The settlement pattern observed later by Wafer in Darien was made up of such scattered households and hamlets, always located on hilltops, that constituted a village or neighborhood. Aside from their elevated location, another precaution taken by the inhabitants of these wattle-and-daub households involved clearing the forest for "a bow's-shoot" (Wafer 1903:146) around them. In anticipation of warfare, however, the inhabitants of these isolated settlements sought safety elsewhere; sometimes they even moved their settlements (Wafer 1903:145). Only in the case of the fortified tree houses, or *barbacoas,* reported for the Atrato River drainage in the sixteenth-century provinces of Abraime, Teruy (Tuira?), and Tatuma in present-day Colombia do the inhabitants of these raised households appear to have remained to withstand enemy attacks.

The dispersed households of a village in seventeenth-century Darien shared a common war house or fort that they erected in a clearing on high ground. The dimensions of these rectangular wattle-and-daub war houses were five times the size of ordinary houses and they lacked interior partitions. Their walls were dotted with fist-sized holes through which they could shoot arrows at the approaching enemy and their entrances at each end were barricaded with foot-thick doors and interior buttresses (Wafer 1903:146–147).

The sixteenth-century chiefly centers manifested a variety of defensive measures. They too were often located on high ground or in other positions that could not be stormed easily, such as at the junction of rivers (Andagoya 1865:41, 44–45). And they were commonly defended by palisades of thick trunks, sometimes by two or even three such imposing palisades, that, according to Espinosa (1864:515), were difficult to scale and penetrate. The *bohío* of Comogre constructed "of beams cut from the trees, and securely fastened together. It was further strengthened by stone walls" (Anghera 1912:219). Helms (1976:9) also makes reference to defensive enclosures of columnar cactus in western Panama. Francisco Compañon, who was left to administer the Spanish settlement at Natá in 1520, made many attempts to subdue the great chief Urracá and his allies, who resided in impregnable palisaded centers in the mountains north of Natá (Las Casas 1951:394–398; Lothrop 1937:9).

Moreover, the fortifications of some chiefly centers included yet another line of defense in the form of an outer moat or ditch (*cava*). Espinosa described several of these fortified centers, including Chief Tabraba's, whose fortifications consisted of two palisades of thick, sprouting tree trunks—or "living barriers" as Lothrop (1937:14) referred to them—and a big moat (Espinosa 1864:510).

The two fundamental responses by a settlement's inhabitants to an anticipated or actual attack were to fight or to flee. When fleeing, settlements were abandoned, sometimes even chiefly centers such as Parita and Natá, whose chiefs were the first to escape (Espinosa 1864:474, 488, 515). If there was sufficient time, the fleeing inhabitants harvested their crops and either took these provisions along or hid them in underground caches (Espinosa 1864:478, 480, 495, 1873:17). Sometimes the inhabitants intentionally destroyed their chiefly centers by setting them on fire (Espinosa 1864:471). The morning after their hard-won victory over Parita in 1516, for example, Espinosa's expedition came upon his abandoned, burned-down paramount center where they found nothing to eat (Espinosa 1864:499; Andagoya 1865:29). And the story was much the same elsewhere, making for an effective defensive strategy that undercut Espinosa's conquest of western Panama: "thus the Spaniards found themselves masters of the field, but the Indians had managed to burn the neighboring towns and to destroy the provisions they contained" (Lothrop 1937:6). When they returned to Natá, they found that the chief of Natá had risen in revolt, setting fire to the center's palisade and harvesting the fields of ripe and unripe maize before taking flight with his followers. The chief of Natá had also sent emissaries to neighboring chiefs, asking them to revolt against the Spaniards and to hide all their food "porque no teniendo que comer, nos moririamos todos de hambre" (Espinosa 1864:511).

If the inhabitants of a target settlement decided to confront the attacking force, they usually placed their women, children, and the elderly in safety and stashed their goods. Urracá, for example, took this precaution before confronting Espinosa's forces in 1520 (Las Casas 1951:393; Lothrop 1937:8; see also Andagoya 1865:41). We have seen the sizes of the war parties that Urracá and other chiefs could mobilize on short notice, in reponse to an attack. No sooner had Bartolomé Hurtado and his detachment leapt ashore at dawn on the island of Caubaco (Cebaco) than the inhabitants called out and quickly mobilized a defensive force, in spite of the fact that their chief was away on a military campaign against some chiefs on the mainland (Espinosa 1864:513–514). And the communications between neighboring chiefs were so speedy that they could muster a large fighting force in a day or two (Espinosa 1873:25), or alternatively, opt to hide their provisions and take to the hills (Espinosa 1873:17, 1864:511, 519).

In the defensive warfare that followed an attack upon a fortified settlement, the defenders flung missiles at the attackers from within the fortifications, as did the defenders of Isla de Varones, who used stones, lances, and pikes against Hurtado's allied force (Espinosa 1864:515). The seventeenth-century inhabitants of Darien similarly barricaded themselves in their war houses during a raid and shot arrows at the attackers through the peepholes (Wafer 1903:146). These defensive tactics were also used by the Panamanian chiefs outside their fortified settlements to defend their territories; Esquegua's force repelled Pedro de Gómez and Espinosa's expeditions from his mountainous territory with stones, spears flung by spearthrowers, and lances (Espinosa 1873:34, 38).

If necessary, the defenders retreated to higher ground in the aftermath of an attack. Following the day-long battle between Espinosa and Parita's forces, Parita withdrew to a refuge on a steep, defensible hilltop, where his mounted Spanish pursuers could not reach him (Espinosa 1864:498–499). After battles on five successive days with Pedrarias's troops, Urracá retreated to a mountaintop stronghold above the Atra River, from where he mobilized more forces in order to ambush and rout the enemy (Las Casas 1951:396).

*Post-war rituals and practices*

Lothrop's characterization of Espinosa's men being "on the point of being cut to pieces" during their retreat from Urracá's territory is more than just a figure of speech (Lothrop 1937:8). Guided by their "a los que pueden matar matan" strategy, the post-war rituals practiced by Panamanian war parties began right on the battlefield, with the slaughter of the enemy. So many warriors were killed in the war between Escoria and Parita that when the Spaniards visited the battlefield "we found a great street entirely paved with the heads of the dead, and at the end of it a tower of heads which was such that a man on horseback could not see over it" (Andagoya 1865:31). Similarly, Acla, meaning "the bones of men," was the name given to the site of a battle between the chief of Careta and his brother over territorial gain;

"y por ser tanta la cantidad de los huesos que allí quedaron quedó el nombre a la provincia de los huesos" (Andagoya 1945:390, 1865:9).

The practice of dismembering the victims of war is corroborated by several independent references to the sacrificial practices of the Panamanian chiefdoms. The two sick Spanish men left behind by Espinosa in the province of Chinía (Chiman?) in the Serranía de Cañazas were ritually sacrificed "tajada á tajada" by the chiefs who had promised to care for them; to the accompaniment of singing and dancing, their hands and arms were cut off, little by little, until they were killed (Espinosa 1864:474). When spies were captured and pressed for information, they were accorded similar forms of torture (Oviedo y Valdés 1853:130). By the same token, thieves were punished by having their hands cut off and hung by a rope around their neck (Oviedo y Valdés 1853:129). Mutinous members of the elite were indicted and executed in public rituals that were presided over by the chief; first the chief delivered one or two blows to the victim's head with a *macana* or rammed his body with a lance or spear several times, before turning him over to be finished off by an executioner and discarded in the field (Oviedo y Valdés 1853:130, 142).

Victorious warriors stopped short of consuming the victims' body parts, and, in fact, abstained from eating meat of any kind. The ethnohistoric accounts of the Panamanian chiefdoms pointed out their dread of the neighboring Caribs, who were said to eat human flesh (Anghera 1912:221, 315; Andagoya 1865:44). And when an army of human flesh eaters approached the Azuero Peninsula from the north "this filled the people of all the districts through which they passed with fear. In one province, bordering on Paris, called Tauraba, they encamped on a plain, to which they took the boys of the neighbouring villages, that they might eat them" (Andagoya 1865:40). But we have seen how the chief of Parita caught them off their guard one morning at their seaside camp, "defeated them, and killed every one, so that none were saved" (Andagoya 1865:40).

The available mortality figures further support this picture of slaughter on the battlefield. The war casualties had been so great on the battlefield of Acla that when the Spaniards landed in that province, they met with no resistance (Andagoya 1945:390–391). In the battle that followed Parita's allied attack against Espinosa's expedition, during which Parita's warriors reportedly threw themselves tenfold into combat, Parita's allied forces incurred major losses, including the loss of twenty chiefs (Espinosa 1864:497–499).

Those victims not killed on the battlefield were captured and bound in their new status as prisoners of war. They were destined to become slaves (*pacos*) and to serve their new overlord as bearers, laborers, domestic servants, concubines, and sacrificial victims (Anghera 1912:298, 309; Oviedo y Valdés 1853:126, 134, 140; Espinosa 1873:27; Lothrop 1937:22–23; Helms 1976:14). War captives were desirable booty and were treated like a valuable commodity, much like gold. According to Helms (1976:66), war captives and gold were among the items exchanged between a paramount chief and his local chiefs. Victorious chiefs also distributed the gold and war captives as gifts to their allied chiefs, in order to maintain and build their interregional military alliances. Parita's brother recommended distributing the gold seized from Badajoz to the other members of Parita's military alliance; it would help them to mobilize a large enough military force with which to defeat the Spaniards (Espinosa 1864:496). Similarly, the son of Chief Comogre presented Vasco Nuñez de Balboa with gold and 70 captives when he asked the Spaniards' help to defeat the powerful chiefs who bordered his territory (Anghera 1912:220–223). And in 1519, Chief Queco of Parita sent Espinosa gold and four female slaves in order to reaffirm his recently established alliance with the Spaniards, whose help he requested to squelch a revolt by one of his chiefs, Quema (Espinosa 1873:60–69). This episode further illustrates the use of gold and slaves as ransom to retrieve chiefs and their wives captured in war (Espinosa 1873:27–28, 56, 61; Helms 1976:84).

The four slaves presented to Espinosa wore tattoos on their faces, a practice that the Spaniards consistently characterized as "branding." Upon their capture, prisoners of war were branded on their faces with the indelible mark of their new chiefly overlord and of their new status as slaves. Sometimes one of their incisors was extracted as another sign of their enslavement (Oviedo y Valdés 1853:74, 129, 138–139).

The fate of war captives was varied and uncertain, for they were subject both to exchange and further capture in the trading and raiding relationships of their overlords (Anghera 1912:222). The night that Vasco Nuñez de Balboa and Pochorroso's warriors raided Tumanama's center they came upon this chief in the company of "two men, his favourites, and eighty women, who had been carried off from different caciques by violence and outrage" (Anghera 1912:309). And when Espinosa finally came face-to-face with the great chief of Parita, laid out for burial in his *bohío*, he found some twenty war captives from Escoria and Chirú there too, bound with ropes around their necks, about to be sacrificed as burial retainers the following night (Espinosa 1873:27).

Other post-war rituals included the establishment of marriage alliances and peace treaties between the chiefly principals. Parita's sister became one of Escoria's wives after Escoria's victory over Parita; this marriage alliance marked the end of their war and proved to be a major mechanism in the formation of their subsequent military alliance against the Spaniards (Oviedo y Valdés 1853:47–48; Lothrop 1937:11; Helms 1976:58). Peace treaties were marked by great feasts complete with drinking, dining, and military jousting (Espinosa 1873:41; 1864:470).

Warriors practiced certain post-war observances. In Darien, warriors who had killed an enemy "cut off the hair even of their heads, it being a custom they have to do so by way of triumph, and as a distinguishing mark of honour to him who has killed a Spaniard, or other enemy. He also then paints himself black (which is not usual upon any other occasion) continuing painted of this colour till the first new-moon . . . after the fact is done" (Wafer 1903:132–133). Warriors were also distinguished from other members of society by their practice of not eating the meat of deer and tapir, only fish and iguanas (Andagoya 1945:404). Helms's review of the crested iguana in Cuna myths and its portrayal on ancient Panamanian goldwork and polychrome ceramics sheds light on warriors' consumption of iguanas. Helms concluded that the crested iguana represented a celestial culture hero who symbolized the competitive activities of chiefs, on and off the battlefield, and that in this way the iguana was part of the sacred traditions of the chiefly elite in pre-Columbian Panama (Helms 1976:97–108).

The battlefield was an important arena for social advancement in ancient Panamanian society. To begin with, military prowess and bravery were qualities that were highly esteemed. The warriors of Escoria were particularly respected and feared by their neighbors for their stature and their military prowess (Andagoya 1865:30). Cueva women sought out brave men, in part because they were aware of the advantages that accrued to them (Oviedo y Valdés 1853:133). Warriors who committed brave deeds in battle while wounded and in the presence of the chief were awarded a military title (*cabra*) by the chief. Andagoya reported that this title was bestowed upon "brave men renowned in war, who had killed an adversary, or had come wounded from the battle" (Andagoya 1865:12). Their prowess on the battlefield and the blood they shed there were thus the sources of their social advancement into the elite sector of society. As *cabras*, and their wives as *espaves*, they were entitled to privileges restricted to the chiefly elite (Oviedo y Valdés 1853:130). The sons of these distinguished warriors inherited the title and position of *cabra* on the condition that they pursue the art of war. This route to social advancement helps to explain the aforementioned ferocity with which a chief's warriors fought—especially in his presence (Espinosa 1864:497). It is not surprising to learn that from a very early age, boys honed their military skills by mastering the art of spear throwing and shooting with the bow and arrow (Wafer 1903:151; Lothrop 1937:27). By means of this system of promotion, suggested Lothrop, the chief kept himself surrounded by an energetic class of distinguished warriors or military captains: "although their ranks often must have been depleted in war, they were filled again by selection of the most fit" (Lothrop 1937:22).

*Mortuary treatment*

The mortuary treatment of warriors depended upon their social status in life and the circumstances of their death. Commoners and those prisoners of wars not destined to serve as burial retainers for their new overlords were deposited in a field or forest upon their death and left to the elements without burial (Oviedo y Valdés 1853:142). We have seen how the battlefield of Acla and the one that figured in the war between the chiefs of Escoria and Parita were littered with the bones of war victims and we have to conclude that most warriors killed in battle were left on the battlefield. Yet we also know that the number of warriors who died on the way home from the latter battlefield was so great that "por el camino hicieron silos donde echaban los muertos" (Andagoya 1945:404), a fact that points to the practice of hastily burying these warriors in underground pits along the route home, perhaps in mass graves.

Chiefs and other members of the chiefly elite, including *cabras*, were accorded various kinds of funerary treatment, which are described in detail by Lothrop (1937:43–48). One practice involved slowly roasting the body to the point of desiccation, adorning it with gold ornaments and armor, wrapping it in cotton mantles, and then placing it in a hammock strung in the chiefly *bohío*, sometimes in the very room where the individual slept, and other times in a special funerary chamber. This was the burial treatment accorded the great chief Parita, whose final resting place was visited by Espinosa in 1519, and hence recorded in detail (Espinosa 1873:23–25). His dried body was completely bedecked in gold armor and ornaments, from the gold helmet on his head to the greaves covering his legs, and wrapped in cotton mantles, the innermost one of which was tied with cords of human hair. At his head lay the body of a woman and another lay at his feet, both of whom wore many gold pieces; these women were probably wives of Parita who had taken their lives voluntarily by taking poison in order to accompany Parita in death, a sacrificial practice that could take the lives of up to forty or fifty of the chief's retainers (Oviedo y Valdés 1853:154–156; Andagoya 1945:394). Oviedo y Valdés himself oversaw the opening of two sepulchers inside the *bohío* of the chief of Guaturo that contained the bodies of two agricultural laborers who had taken their lives upon the death of the former chief, in order to serve him in the afterlife along with the maize and *macanas* that were found therein (Oviedo y Valdés 1853:154). In the case of Parita, his death was to be marked by human sacrifice on a large scale, for we have seen how inside the *bohío* were some twenty bound war captives who were to be sacrificed the following night, including a son of the chief of Pacara (Espinosa 1873:27).

The bodies of two of Parita's successors lay in hammocks alongside Parita, similarly adorned with gold armor and ornaments and wrapped in mantles. The placement of their bodies in Parita's *bohío*, called the Asiento Viejo by Espinosa (1873:20), exemplifies the practice of storing the desiccated bodies of chiefs in a special chiefly funerary chamber of the chief's *bohío* that was intended to display the bodies of the chief and his ancestors in the order of their succession (Oviedo y Valdés 1853:155). Vasco Nuñez de Balboa described one such chiefly charnel in the innermost sanctum of Chief Comogre's multi-roomed residence; the room was filled with the bodies of the ancestors of Comogre, who were preserved with great care, decorated with gold masks, and suspended with cotton ropes, according to the rank they had occupied in life (Anghera 1912:219). In those instances when a chief perished in a battle at sea or whose body for some reason couldn't be brought back to his territory, the space that he was to have occupied in the chiefly funerary chamber was left empty in memory of him (Oviedo y Valdés 1853:155).

The funerary treatment of Chief Pocorosa, observed first-hand by Andagoya, illustrates another kind of chiefly mortuary ritual, one that took place on the first anniversary of his death. A feast was celebrated in the chamber where the wrapped bundle containing Pocorosa's desiccated body had been suspended, and where the chief's weapons, miniature wooden models of his canoes, and his favorite foods were presented. They then took Pocorosa's remains and his possessions out to a plaza where his body and his belongings were burned and reduced to ashes (Andagoya 1945:395).

Finally, Oviedo y Valdés described the burial of chiefs in rectangular tombs a meter or more underground in which the body, adorned with its gold finery, was seated on a stone bench that lined the tomb. Gourd containers with water, maize, fruits, and flowers were placed in the tomb. The women chosen to accompany the deceased arrived and seated themselves on the bench beside him, bedecked with gold ornaments. After a day or two of mourning ceremonies during which the chief's virtues and lifetime achievements were recounted in song, with dancing, and drinking by all, the tomb was sealed with timbers and filled in with dirt, and the intoxicated female retainers were buried alive therein (Oviedo y Valdés 1853:156).

Helms has used certain Cuna concepts of chiefly leadership and power to interpret the differential treatment of the dead in the Panamanian chiefdoms. One of these is the Cuna concept of *niga*, a power that all are born with and that grows during an individual's lifetime, manifesting itself in acts of bravery, for example. Another is a power called *kurgin* that is responsible for the different skills possessed by individuals. The chiefly elite, with their greater inherent capacity for *niga* and *kurgin,* and therefore, greater sacred value or worth, deserved having their bodies preserved after death and receiving elaborate funerary rites, in contrast to commoners, who because of their lesser inherent capacities, were accorded mortuary treatment little different from that of the birds and beasts of the forest (Helms 1976:73–75).

The death of chiefs also prompted elaborate and sometimes prolonged mourning ceremonies, as in the case of Pocorosa's last rites. His son, the new chief, his relatives and other members of his retinue gathered to suspend the corpse over the fire to be roasted. Ten men remained there to oversee the roasting and drying of the body, concealed in long black mantles. From time to time during their vigil they sounded a kettledrum, and hollered, as they recounted the deceased's history. We have seen how on the anniversary of his death, another mourning ceremony was held with feasting and drinking, and in subsequent years as well, depending upon the individual's status (Andagoya 1945:395). Similar rites were intended to be celebrated for Chief Parita, attended by the new chief and other members of the elite. The mourning feast was to include the consumption of iguanas and fish, in keeping with the association of these foods with warriors, and in honor of Parita, the greatest war chief of all (Espinosa 1873:27).

Attendant upon the dead chief's funeral was the induction of the new chief, who was led by the elders to the room he was to occupy and placed in a hammock. There he presided over ceremonies lasting three or more days, during which he received his vassals, laden with gifts of food, and was instructed in his lineage's genealogy and past history by means of epic songs. The deeds of former chiefs were thus related, including the alliances and enemies of his father, the dead chief, thereby updating the oral history and setting the future course of relationships with neighboring chiefs. The new chief dispatched emissaries to friends and foes alike to announce his succession; although reconciliations with former enemies were sometimes achieved, more often than not his emissaries were seized and killed, thereby perpetuating the state of war (Oviedo y Valdés 1853:155–156).

# Chapter 4

# Tribal Versus Chiefly Warfare

Having examined the warfare patterns of certain South American tribes and chiefdoms in some detail, I wish to point out their distinctive features. To be sure, many of the offensive and defensive strategies associated with tribal warfare also figure in chiefly warfare: the ambush, the use of treachery, fire, and poison-tipped weapons, looting, trophy-taking, nucleated settlements, and defensive palisades are among them. Nevertheless, a systematic comparison of their warfare patterns turns up some notable differences in their objectives, their organization for war and their war parties, their offensive and defensive tactics, and their post-war practices and rituals. In the concluding chapter I will consider how their differing warfare strategies relate to the development of centralized authority in chiefdoms.

## *Objectives*

In the tribes reviewed here, warfare can be characterized as an individual, or "personal," pursuit (Johnson and Earle 1987:120). Spurred by blood revenge and the desire to kill, the objectives include taking human trophies, looting, and abducting women. Upon the successful conclusion of a raid, each warrior keeps for himself all the booty he can lay his hands on. Moreover, through his war exploits, each warrior accumulates personal power and gains the respect of his fellow tribesmen (Chagnon 1988:986–988; Hendricks 1988:219).

In the Circum-Caribbean chiefdoms, by contrast, revenge motives can provoke warfare, but they appear to be overshadowed by the acquisitive pursuits of chiefs. The purpose of chiefly warfare is expansionist; the seizing of land, resources, and captives takes precedence over avenging dead kinsmen (Oviedo y Valdés 1853:129; Morey and Marwitt 1975:441).

## *Organization*

Tribal and chiefly war parties are organized according to different time frames, degrees of organization, and available fighting power. The revenge raids conducted by the Jívaro and Yanomamö are organized on the local level by aggrieved individuals with the support of the village headman or of a renowned warrior. Several months before the raid, the designated leader of the raid will begin canvassing households as well as allied villages to recruit warriors for the raiding party. Arduous at times, the recruitment of a war party involves the art of persuasion, the declaration of formal war challenges and the lure of rewards, including the promise of wives. The resulting war party can consist of as few as five or ten men from a single village, to allied war parties of 50 to 100 warriors (and as many as 500 warriors at the turn of the century). But since participation in a raid is not mandatory, it is common for some of the raiders to cite a variety of reasons for deserting the raiding party before it reaches enemy territory. The achievement of intervillage and intertribal war alliances between autonomous villages is reaffirmed with a public feast, and often sealed with a mourning ceremony by the Yanomamö for the kinsman whose death they wish to avenge.

The warfare waged by the sixteenth-century chiefdoms was organized by regional chiefs and conducted on a society-wide, interpolity basis. As supreme military commanders, paramount chiefs had the authority to declare war and to mobilize local and regional fighting forces expeditiously, sometimes by simply blowing a conch-shell trumpet or sounding a drum. They also dispatched emissaries to summon neighboring chiefs on short notice to chiefly war councils in order to formalize their military alliances and to plot their common war stratagems in the privacy of the chief's sanctuary. Consequently, these paramount chiefs could mobilize large war parties almost immediately, whose size estimates range from as few as 100–500 warriors to as many as 10,000–20,000 men. I should add that women often participated as well in their "guerra de todos contra todos" (Trimborn 1949:284).

The preparation period for a tribal raid is longer, not only because warriors must be recruited, but also because new gardens—and sometimes new settlements—must be established (in the case of the Yanomamö, these may be some distance away). They must fortify settlements or upgrade the existing fortifications. The Jívaro erect special structures for the post-war victory feasts. Enough food and firewood are stockpiled to weather the expected counterraid. Upon the departure of a Yanomamö raiding party, for example, the village headman warned the women to "go now and get wood, because in three days' time none of you will be allowed to go out of the *shapuno* any more. In three days the Pishaanseteri, who will come from the rear, will have attacked. I want no one then, woman, child or man, to leave the *shapuno*" (Biocca 1970:265).

Yet, tribal raids can be totally ad hoc, embarked upon the day after an enemy attack. In the heat of revenge, there is virtually no time for such preparations. Individual warriors supply their own armament and their wives prepare their bundle of provisions for the raid.

In contrast, advance planning and considerable war preparations characterized the chiefdoms we have considered. Armaments and provisions were stockpiled in special storehouses at the chief's center, in quantities large enough to arm an entire chiefdom. Unlike the self-provisioning by individual warriors for a tribal raid, chiefs oversaw the stockpiling of military equipment and food in their storehouses and supplied the arms and provisions for their military campaigns. In fact, the Panamanian paramount chief of Tumanama had special long houses at his center to shelter warriors from allied villages in times of war (Anghera 1912:309). Fields were cultivated collectively by the members of military alliances, and enough food and water were stored at fortified centers to withstand a prolonged attack. In the Cauca Valley, one such fortified center endured a Spanish siege for 39 days (Trimborn 1949:344; Castellanos 1850:557–559; Simón 1892b:276). The chiefly storehouses at the Panamanian center of Natá were equally well stocked, for they provided Gaspar de Espinosa's army with more than a four months' supply of provisions, including maize, dried fish, three hundred deer, geese and turkeys (Espinosa 1864:488).

There are fundamental differences in the command structures of the South American tribal and chiefly war parties reviewed above. Tribal raiding parties exhibit, at most, a single tier of command above the individual warrior: the leader of the raiding party. There might be more than one such leader in the case of large, allied war parties, yet the single tier of command prevails. The leaders of raiding parties are usually renowned warriors or headmen, whom Chagnon characterizes as being "greaters among equals" (Chagnon 1983:6). They do not acquire any formal title of "war leader" and their leadership is temporary or episodic; the leader of a raiding party "leads only by example and the others follow if it pleases them to do so" (Chagnon 1983:124). Accordingly, although the members of a raid are theoretically expected to obey the leader during the raiding party's venture in enemy territory, "obedience, even on a war expedition, is often not as rigorous in practice as it is in theory" (Harner 1972:185).

Hence, there is no social differentiation among the participating warriors of tribal war parties other than by age and by tribe in the case of allied raiding parties. This is reflected in their homogeneous war attire. No special insignia, and no distinctive body painting distinguish the leaders of war parties from their fellow warriors. The war paint with which they anoint themselves is for camouflage, courage, and for common recognition by other members of the attacking party. As they line up in the village clearing "they form a straight line of naked, black-smeared bodies, of proud, impassive faces" (Lizot 1985:181–182). They stride off to war in single file, with the shortest warriors at the head of the line and the novices in the rear. The leader of the raiding party will file out in the middle or toward the rear of the line. The warriors of an allied raiding party will be intentionally interdigitated in the line of departing warriors, making it difficult to distinguish the allied components of the war party.

Chiefly war parties exhibited a two- or three-tiered military command hierarchy composed of: (1) the supreme war leader or paramount chief; (2) lesser chiefs (*sacos*) and military captains (*cabras*) who commanded troops of warriors; and (3) special war leaders, usually brothers or affines of the paramount chief, who were designated to lead some large, allied war parties, or one arm of an even larger allied fighting force (Oviedo y Valdés 1853:47–48; Espinosa 1864:494, 496, 508; Cieza de León 1853:364; Castellanos 1850:394–395; Trimborn 1949:256–257, 337–338). Paramount chiefs often led their forces to battle, as the great Panamanian chief Parita did in one of his attacks against Espinosa's forces, fighting, throwing lances, inciting his men, and clubbing any who retreated (Espinosa 1864:497–498).

This ranking of chiefly war parties was vividly apparent in the gold and feather insignia, armor, hairdress, and body-painting styles that member chiefs, military captains, and warriors donned for war. According to Oviedo y Valdés (1853:118, 130), war provided a public arena for individual warriors, and particularly for their chiefs and military captains, to flaunt the badges of their superior social and military status. In the aforementioned attack against Espinosa's men, for example, Chief Parita was easily distinguished by the many gold disks, plates, and bracelets he was wearing over his cotton tunic (Espinosa 1864:497). Moreover, large allied war parties displayed the distinctive war dress and standards of the multiple polities involved. The heterogeneous war attire of chiefly war parties, therefore, denoted both their internally ranked or vertical structure as well as their allied or horizontal components (Trimborn 1949:324; Oviedo y Valdés 1853:118; Wobst 1977: 327–328).

### *Pre-War Rituals*

On the eve of the planned raid the participants of Jívaro and Yanomamö raiding parties attend a public feast at the sponsor's village. The warriors gather in the village clearing for the pre-raid rituals, which include mock attacks, mourning ceremonies, piercing dialogues, and "weapon-waving" warrior lineups (Johnson 1982:405). The leader of the raid directs these pre-war rituals, signaling their start, supervising the lineup, and conducting the verbal exhortations. By means of these convivial, public acts the participating warriors reaffirm their alliance and their common purpose in war.

Among the chiefdoms considered here, however, such camaraderie was limited to the chiefly elite, who alone performed the pre-war rituals in the privacy of the paramount chief's precinct.

Here the chiefs of a military alliance and other members of the chiefly elite, with the help of their *tequinas* ("diviners"), invoked the divinatory powers of supernatural forces to counsel them about the impending campaign, by means of ritual invocations and acts of sacrificial bloodletting. Upon receiving the supernatural's call to arms, the assembled chiefs celebrated a feast, during which the objectives of their military alliance were set forth in song and performed, along with dancing, to the accompaniment of drums. At the inebriated conclusion of some feasts between allies, the chiefs and their men competed in war games, complete with duels and jousts. These pre-war rituals were a chiefly institution: they legitimized the chief's position of authority over his domain and expedited his call to arms; they also promoted the formation of military alliances between chiefs in order to defeat a common enemy.

### Offensive Tactics

There are some differences in the scale of warfare conducted by the tribes and chiefdoms we have examined. The revenge raids of tribes are directed against enemy villages that can be located up to ten days' travel away, sometimes far beyond their tribal boundaries. The target is an individual enemy settlement that can be located some distance away. This means that raiding parties must set out with suitable provisions for the expedition and stop to pitch a series of overnight camps along the way both going to and returning from war. A Jívaro raiding party of twenty-five warriors whose target village lay three days' walk away was accompanied by a retinue of twelve women and four boys bearing baskets of food and manioc beer (Cotlow 1953:144).

By contrast, the expansionist warfare waged by the Circum-Caribbean chiefdoms, is directed against adjacent political regions at the boundaries of a chief's territory (Trimborn 1949:280–282; Reichel-Dolmatoff 1951:91; see also Gibson 1974:132). A chief's war party will attack multiple settlements during its sweep through neighboring, enemy territory. Although the sixteenth-century sources do not provide us with precise size estimates of their territories, it has been suggested elsewhere that the distance to the boundaries of a chief's territory probably ranges from a half-day's travel to at most a day's travel (Helms 1979:33, 53; Spencer 1982:6–7, 23). Perhaps it is for this reason that the accounts of chiefly warfare make no mention of overnight camps or war-party provisions. We know that during the eight-day war between the neighboring Panamanian chiefs of Escoria and Parita, Parita's forces were able to retire from the battlefield each day and be replenished with fresh troops on successive days (Andagoya 1945:404).

A further difference in the scale of warfare of these tribes and chiefdoms stems from the tenfold size difference in their minimal fighting parties. Because of this, their offensive tactics differ. The hit-and-run raids of tribal war parties owe their success to the surreptitious ambushes of target settlements by attacking units of four to six warriors, who silently await the right moment to strike. But they will not wait for long, in view of their lust for blood revenge, as well as their war leader's tenuous authority over them (Cotlow 1953:145). The principal tactic is to ambush one or more male inhabitants—especially the headman or another renowned warrior—as they emerge from the village. The difficulty of keeping the raiding party in pursuit of their objective is illustrated in the Shuara Jívaro Tukup's account of the long wait for the intended enemy victim, Kayáp, to emerge. After a half-day wait, a member of Tukup's raiding party remarked of Kayáp: "Is he so important? Let's quit waiting for him" (Hendricks 1993:62, 229). And the raiding party disbanded.

At the moment of attack, the raiders fire their poison-tipped arrows and then retreat hastily. Lizot points out that Yanomamö raiders rarely confront the enemy in face-to-face combat during their hit-and-run raids (Lizot 1988:559–561). Generally it is only after a victorious raid that the raiders emit war cries, as they make their swift retreat from the enemy settlement (Biocca 1970:59–60; Cocco 1972:390). Any overnight camps and trophy-processing camps are pitched outside enemy territory along the route home.

Chiefly war parties also practiced surprise ambushes, but their significantly larger fighting forces enabled them to launch all-out attacks against enemy settlements. They surrounded a target settlement and descended upon it together, flinging spears and darts, setting its roofs on fire with firebrands, uttering war cries, and sounding noisemakers. The din produced by these noisemakers was characterized by Castellanos as "the fury of hell" and was enough to instill terror in even the strongest soul (Castellanos 1850:270, 293–294, 322). To intimidate the inhabitants further, some Panamanian raiding parties flung spears or darts with hollow balls attached to their points that whistled as they hurtled through the air (Oviedo y Valdés 1853:127; Lothrop 1937:20–21).

The group-warfare tactics practiced by chiefly war parties included open attacks in broad daylight. Their fighting forces advanced and fought in orderly formation, in troops, that assembled to confront the opposing force in face-to-face combat with broadswords and lances. The precision and intensity with which their troops fought impressed their Spanish adversaries (Espinosa 1864:516; Las Casas 1951:393). During a battle near Popayán in the Cauca Valley, Andagoya's men found it difficult to break through Apirama's front lines; between every two warriors armed with thrusting lances were warriors with *macanas*, who stepped forward to wield these broadswords and then retreated behind the picket of interlaced lances (Andagoya 1945:439). Moreover, when the front lines suffered casualties, reinforcement troops were sent forward tenfold (Espinosa 1864:497, 488).

Due to their strength in numbers and organization, chiefly war parties were capable of waging day-long battles. They also conducted repeated attacks, such as the battles that were fought on eight successive days between the chiefs of Parita and Escoria in central Panama (Andagoya 1865:30–31). And they could wage repeated attacks in one day, as Benalcázar's troops experienced during their passage through the Cauca Valley (Trimborn 1949:363).

These differences in the scale of tribal and chiefly warfare are reflected in the available mortality figures. Most tribal raids, if successful, will result in the killing of one or two of the enemy (Chagnon 1979:92). The organization and outcome of these hit-and-run raids are also borne out by Chagnon's data on the relationship between the number of Yanomamö victims and their killers: "while a few individuals have extremely large numbers of 'killers,' most victims were dispatched by relatively few. More than half (52%) had a single killer, 76% had either one or two killers, and 82% had three or fewer killers" (Chagnon 1990:50). In the case of a large allied raid such as the one launched by the Aguaruna and Antipas Jívaro against the Huambisa Jívaro, a total of eleven Huambisa Jívaro were killed and beheaded (Up de Graff 1923:275). The larger, confrontational military operations mounted by the sixteenth-century chiefdoms resulted in significantly higher death tolls. For example, a single raid conducted by the Paucura against the Pozo in the Cauca Valley concluded with the slaughter of no fewer than 200 victims (Trimborn 1949:388). And whereas tribesmen like the Yanomamö avoid killing women and children during their hit-and-run raids, the all-out attacks by chiefly war parties against enemy settlements produced victims of all ages and sexes (Cieza de León 1853:373; Trimborn 1949:388, 390, 392).

The looting and other intentionally destructive activities carried out by victorious Jívaro and Yanomamö war parties are of a sportive, capricious kind. Victorious raiders might or might not ransack and ravage the enemy village before retreating. Moreover, the taking of war captives is not a general practice among these tribes. Jívaro warriors who occasionally abduct the younger wives of their enemies consider it a way to acquire additional wives (Cotlow 1953:119, 144, 147, 243). The Yanomamö, when they do "steal women" (Biocca 1970:142), also take them as wives. In a list of the post-marital residence patterns of 350 Yanomamö marriages in 1975, however, only 0.8% of the wives had been abducted from their natal villages during a raid (Lizot 1988:540–541). Although Chagnon's figure of 17% for the minimal amount of wife abduction among the villages in his study region is significantly higher, he points out that most of these abductions do not occur in the aftermath of a raid (Chagnon 1990:51). Besides, few raids are expressly designed for this purpose (Chagnon 1983:175–176). Finally, any children abducted from a raided village are hardly considered prizes; they are persecuted by their captors, and more often than not, are killed (Chagnon 1983:175; Chagnon, Flinn, and Melancon 1979:304; Valero 1984:48–49, 487).

In the all-out warfare conducted by the Circum-Caribbean chiefdoms, their looting and destructive activities formed part of a larger, logistical plan of military expansion. War parties looted and set target villages on fire routinely, according to an overall plan of attack and intentional destruction. For example, when the Panamanian chiefs of Parita and Escoria raided Gonzalo de Badajoz's camp in 1516, their plan of attack involved overwhelming the defenders, seizing Badajoz's hoard of gold, and setting fire to the structures (Andagoya 1865:26; Oviedo y Valdés 1853:48). Furthermore, the men, women, and children taken captive in chiefly warfare were prized booty; they would serve their captors as slaves, concubines, sacrificial victims, and burial retainers.

## Defensive Tactics

The tribes considered here appear to practice a greater range of general defensive precautions than the chiefdoms (although we shall see how this difference may have more to do with the limitations of the ethnohistoric accounts of these chiefdoms and their focus on chiefly centers than with their actual practices). Defensive considerations govern the locations of all tribal villages. Tribesmen space their villages with respect to their neighbors and enemies. They also favor certain defensible positions for the location of their villages. Uninhabited buffer zones are established between hostile villages, sometimes by means of topographic barriers. Northern South American tribesmen defend their villages by erecting a variety of fortifications, including single and double wooden palisades, piles of firewood and additional wooden partitions inside their houses, and watchtowers. The Jívaro dig foxholes and tunnels inside their houses for further protection and escape during a raid.

Finally, there is a lower limit to the sizes of tribal villages, below which they become likely raiding targets. Yanomamö villages generally have no fewer than approximately 45 inhabitants, "for the population must be at least that large to field a raiding party of ten men and still permit a few men to remain home to protect the women" (Chagnon 1968a:138). The anticipation of enemy raids will prompt the inhabitants of smaller, vulnerable villages to pick up and relocate their villages, often in conjunction with allied villages. To a large extent then, warfare is responsible for the high degree of settlement mobility and settlement nucleation among tribal villages. Indeed, the intensive intertribal warfare waged by the Jívaro 150 years ago encouraged them to live in fewer larger villages, similar to the multihousehold *shabono* of the Yanomamö today (Ross 1980:54–56; Hendricks 1993:54).

Because the Spaniards journeyed from one chiefly center to another during their campaigns of conquest in the sixteenth century, our best descriptions of settlements, including their defensive facilities, pertain to the chiefly centers (Helms 1979:9). The ethnohistoric accounts of chiefly warfare in the Cauca Valley, Sierra Nevada de Santa Marta, and Panama do not specify whether all the villages and hamlets within a chief's territory were located in defensible locations and fortified with palisades. The numerous abandoned villages that the Spaniards encountered in these regions make it clear that many villages were simply abandoned in times of war. If there was enough time, their inhabitants hid their valuables, harvested their crops, and occasionally set fire to their own houses and fields to prevent the enemy forces from seizing their provisions.

The chiefly centers were generally located on high ground or in other defensible positions. They were outfitted with imposing external and internal palisades built of thick tree trunks, stone slabs, and columnar cactus that were difficult to scale and penetrate. Some fortified centers featured elaborate ramparts and watchtowers atop their defensive walls. Others were ringed by another line of defense in the form of an outer moat. The Spaniards referred to many of them as mountain fortresses, where the paramount chief's subjects took refuge in times of war (Castellanos 1850:458; Cieza de León 1853:368; Oviedo y Valdés 1852:457; Las Casas 1951:394–398). The chiefly centers were thus the foci of most defensive measures and were designed to accommodate an influx of fleeing villagers.

The descriptions of warfare among the sixteenth-century chiefdoms suggest that they used defensive warfare tactics more often than tribesmen, who rarely pursue or attempt to cut off the raiders' escape from the site of the ambush (Lizot 1988:559–561). The defense of their chiefly centers and territory and the desire to repel the enemy were incentives for the chiefs to quickly mobilize their forces to take up defensible positions and hurl missiles at the attackers. Led by their chiefs, the defending forces would also come out and confront the enemy force in face-to-face combat, and pursue them if they retreated. Another defensive tactic involved circumventing the enemy force and ambushing them in narrow passes, where the defenders could cut off the enemy's retreat and pounce on them in larger numbers like "fierce lions" (Las Casas 1951:393–394, 396).

## Post-War Rituals

Although the warring tribes and chiefdoms of northern South America both secure human war trophies and practice ritual endocannibalism, there are a number of differences in their post-raid practices and rituals. Following a tribal headhunting raid, the victors sever the victims' heads, sling them over their shoulders by their long hair or by stringing them on bark strips, and retreat immediately from enemy territory. They stop along the return trip to prepare the shrunken heads at trophy-processing camps, and continue preparing the head trophies back home as part of the subsequent victory celebrations.

The aftermath of a chiefly raid, however, included the decapitation and dismemberment of victims on a large scale on the battlefield. So many war victims suffered this fate during a battle between the Panamanian chief of Careta and a neighboring province that from then on the place became known as Acla, which "in the language of that land, means 'the bones of men,' and the province retained that name because of the quantity of bones strewn on the battle field" (Andagoya 1865:9). Similarly, when the Spaniards visited the battlefield where the eight-day war between the chiefs of Escoria and Parita had been waged, they "found a great street entirely paved with the heads of the dead, and at the end of it a tower of heads which was such that a man on horseback could not see over it" (Andagoya 1865:31).

Certain human body parts were consumed by the members of the victorious chiefly war party on the spot, either raw or sometimes cooked over battleground fires. The remaining "loads" of human flesh were sent home. Many of the bound war captives soon suffered a similar fate, by being clubbed to death, dismembered, and consumed at the scene of combat. After their allied victory over the Pozo, the war parties of Carrapa and Picara consumed more than 300 Pozo captives and sent more than 200 loads of human flesh to their settlements in the Cauca Valley. In turn, when the Pozo defeated the Carrapa, Picara, and Paucura, the Pozo chief and his retinue alone consumed 100 victims in one day (Cieza de León 1881:30, 1853:372–374). Other prisoners of war were taken to the chief's center where they were reserved in cages for large-scale sacrificial rituals celebrated later in the chief's plaza.

Those tribesmen who have killed during a raid begin a period of ritual observances on the way home from war. During this period, which can last from two weeks to more than two years after the raid, they must take special baths, and practice various forms of physical isolation and abstinence from certain foods, drugs, personal adornment, weapons, and sex. By means of these ritual observances the killers cleanse themselves and seek protection from the revengeful spirits of their dead victims. It is only at the conclusion of these purification rituals, marked by a great victory feast among the Jívaro, that the killers receive haircuts and body painting, don their personal trophies and other insignia, and enjoy the status of distinguished warriors. After the last victory feast, however, the trophies themselves lose much of their value. Cotlow remarked how the Jívaro do not treasure or hoard their trophy heads; "Jívaros don't treasure their *tsantsas*. After they have shrunk the heads and gone through the long and complicated feast celebrating it, the *tsantsa* holds little meaning for them. It is not really a trophy, like the mounted moosehead of the sports hunter" (Cotlow 1953:40, 230). So too did Up de Graff, who observed how easily the *tsantsa* could be discarded after the final *tsantsa* feast; "it is curious that the fanatical jealousy with which they are guarded up to the time of the festival should give place to that complete indifference which allows them to be thrown to the children as playthings and finally lost in river or swamp" (Up de Graff 1923:283).

No such purification rituals are described in the accounts of chiefly post-war rituals. Mention is made only of warriors cutting their hair and wearing black body paint after having killed, as tokens of their victory in war. Also, Andagoya (1945:404) reported that Panamanian warriors were distinguished from other members of society by their practice of not eating the meat of deer and tapir, only fish and iguanas.

By further killing, trophy taking, and hosting victory feasts, individual warriors pursue their quest for recognition as great warriors, leaders of war parties, and ultimately, as general leaders or "big men." Their acquisition of human trophies and fighting scars attest to their achievements; the top of an accomplished Yanomamö man's head, for example, "looks like a road map, for it is criss-crossed by as many as 20 large scars," which are further enhanced by rubbing red pigment on the tonsure (Chagnon 1983:171–172).

Overshadowing the individual warrior's celebration of his war deeds and his personal acquisition of human trophies and other war insignia was the hoarding and large-scale sacrifice of war captives and subsequent public display of their skulls, long bones, hands, feet, and flayed skins on the part of the paramount chief and other members of the chiefly elite. By virtue of their exalted status, the chief and his retinue hoarded and sacrificed the largest number of war captives, consumed the greatest amount of human flesh—over 100 victims in one day—and displayed the most war trophies—"an incredible quantity"—outside their residences in the chiefly precinct (Cieza de León 1853:372–373, 378).

This association between human war trophies and the office of the chief was evident in several ways. The chief erected special storehouses or charnels in his plaza where he displayed these symbols of his military victories, sometimes hundreds of them. Dominating the paramount chief of Lile's center in the Cauca Valley was his imposing charnel, where he displayed the desiccated, stuffed bodies of some 400 enemy warriors in lifelike poses, as well as a "great quantity of hands and feet"; next door stood another storehouse full of more remains of sacrificed war captives (Andagoya 1945:436; Cieza de León 1853:379–380). In response to the Spaniards' questions about this practice, they were told that a Cauca Valley chief's greatness was measured in part by the number of war trophies he possessed, which substantiated his military successes (Cieza de León 1853:380; Oviedo y Valdés 1851:218; Trimborn 1949:374–376). Moreover, these symbols of a chief's military might were regarded forever as prestige items, in contrast to their loss in value and potential for being discarded after the final victory feasts of tribal warriors. Consequently, the chief doled out human war trophies as rewards to his followers and as gifts to neighboring chiefs (Castellanos 1850:332, 334; Cieza de León 1918:26).

### *Funerary Treatment of Warriors*

There are differences in the mortuary treatment of warriors in the tribal and chiefly societies we have examined, both for those killed in action as well as for those who die a natural death. The bodies of raiders killed during a tribal raid are either lugged by members of the war party and buried hastily at an opportune moment along the route home, or claimed later by older kinswomen and carried home in hammocks. There is a definite concern among tribesmen for retrieving the bodies of dead or dying warriors and for administering their funerary rites at home (Karsten 1935:292–293; Drown and Drown 1961:98; Cotlow 1953:141; Cocco 1972:386, 388–390; Valero 1984:261, 355, 358). By contrast, the practice of retrieving the bodies of dead warriors does not seem to have been accorded to most warriors killed in the battles between the sixteenth-century chiefdoms. There are no descriptions of bringing the ordinary war dead home from war, only of battlegrounds strewn with the bones of war victims, from which we can infer that the bodies of most warriors killed in action were left behind. As for the severely wounded, we have only one report of their bodies being retrieved; after the war between the Panamanian chiefs of Escoria and Parita, so many of Parita's warriors died during the retreat that they stopped to bury them in mass graves along the way home (Andagoya 1945:390, 404; Trimborn 1949:368).

Distinguished warriors in tribal societies usually receive more elaborate funerary ceremonies, and repeated mourning rites, than other males their age. Their mourning ceremonies are designed to bestow the avengers of their death with some of the very qualities that they had achieved during their lifetime. Yet their final resting place is no different from that of their fellow tribesmen, be it in subfloor or scaffold burials (Jívaro) or as ashes in small gourds (Yanomamö). In the case of the Yanomamö, the final consequence of an individual's death involves the complete obliteration of his body, possessions—even his personal name. On the occasion of the final mourning ceremony for their deceased relative, some grieving Mahekotho-teri sadly acknowledged that "it is the last time; nothing of him must remain" (Biocca 1970:181). There is no place that is marked by the deceased's resting place, much less considered sacred (Lizot 1988:572).

Warring chiefdoms evidently endeavored to recover the bodies of their distinguished warriors who had become military captains or war leaders, and who were thus members of the chiefdom's elite. For example, when the paramount chief of Guaca's brother was killed while leading a battle against Francisco de César's men in the Cauca Valley, his warriors surrounded his body in order to prevent the enemy from seizing it, and lifted it on to his brother's (the chief's) litter for transport home (Castellanos 1850:395; Simón 1892b:86). Distinguished warriors were entitled to elaborate mourning ceremonies that included vigils, kettledrum sounding, epic songs, drinking, and dancing. The mourning ceremonies of certain illustrious warriors among the Pijao and Tairona included acts of ritual endocannibalism by fellow warriors who sought their bravery (Simón 1882:7; Castellanos 1850:342). In general, however, the funerary treatment of renowned warriors included the preservation of their bodies, a privilege reserved for the chiefly elite. In contrast to commoners, their bodies were considered worth recovering and preserving, either above ground in special funerary chambers or in stone-lined tombs. Of course, paramount chiefs received the most elaborate mourning ceremonies and their bodies were stored or buried in the chiefly precinct with rich funerary accompaniments, including burial retainers. So important was it to mark their resting place that in those instances when a Panamanian chief perished in battle and his body couldn't be recovered, the space that he was to have occupied in the chiefly funerary chamber was left vacant in his memory (Oviedo y Valdés 1853:155).

# Chapter 5

# The Archaeology of Tribal Warfare

If warfare is indeed a major factor in the internal dynamics of the tribes and chiefdoms of northern South America, then we archaeologists who investigate the aboriginal antecedents of these societies should address warfare in our research and in our discussions about prehistoric developments in the Intermediate area. Such an endeavor could also prove to be useful elsewhere, seeing how "most ethnographically reported chiefdoms seem to be involved in constant warfare" (Wright 1977:382; Carneiro 1990). Indeed, although warfare is often mentioned as an important factor in the development of chiefdoms and states, archaeologists have usually left it at that, preferring to concentrate on other variables that are more readily detectable archaeologically.

### *Investigating Warfare Archaeologically*

But how should we go about addressing warfare in our research and in our discussions of prehistoric developments? First of all, we need to set up a framework of archaeological expectations of warfare that relates directly to the cultural system(s) being studied. Such an approach circumvents the problems, for example, with the following list of expectations offered by Mackey and Green (1979:145) to determine the presence of warfare in northwestern New Mexico: (1) random burning of sites; (2) evidence of violent death in skeletal material; (3) defensive location of villages; and (4) other defensive features. From what body of ethnographic or ethnohistoric data do these expectations stem? Why have these expectations been singled out and not others? The archaeological expectations that we will examine in this chapter derive specifically from the information recorded about warring tribes and chiefdoms of northern South America and presented in the preceding chapters.

In the process of examining and comparing warfare among the tribes and chiefdoms of northern South America, I have discovered that warfare begins the moment a kinsman is killed in a raid. This killing precipitates a desire for revenge and sets the warfare cycle in motion: preparations for the revenge raid, the actual attack, the victory celebrations, and the warriors' funerary rituals, which often trigger another cycle of war. Accordingly, in the previous chapters we have considered the organizational, technological, and tactical aspects of offensive and defensive warfare and its sociopolitical and ideological components as well. I propose then that we begin by considering the archaeological manifestations of South American warfare in its totality, rather than by pointing to an odd assortment of traits—weapons, walls, wounds, and warriors' graves (Vencl 1984:125–129)—as has been the general practice. Similarly, Upham and Reed have suggested that archaeologists broaden the context for discussing prehistoric warfare by looking at more than just defensive sites and fractured burials (Upham and Reed 1989:154). This means that for the archaeological study of warfare among northern South American tribes and chiefdoms, we would consider, as I have in the preceding chapters, the preparations and organization for war, the pre-war rituals, the offensive and defensive strategies and their corresponding military tactics, and the post-war rituals, including the mortuary treatment of warriors.

Furthermore, if warfare is "a phenomenon that affects all aspects of their social organization, settlement pattern, and daily routines" (Chagnon 1983:5), then I propose that we should attempt to monitor its effects upon archaeologically known tribes and chiefdoms in a holistic, systemic way. The archaeological framework that I have in mind attempts to measure the effects of warfare upon individuals, households, communities, regions, and between neighboring regions, in keeping with the comprehensive research design outlined by Flannery (1976). It amounts to a research design that is aimed at examining the effects of warfare in its totality upon one or more dynamic prehistoric cultural systems being investigated (Figure 20).

Unfortunately, the current state of the art of investigating warfare among prehistoric societies is such that I am not able to present examples of archaeological manifestations for all these aspects of warfare on every observable unit of analysis. I would be the first to admit that the resulting matrix of warfare elements (preparations for warfare, warfare tactics, post-war activities) and observable units of analysis (region, community, household, feature) (Figure 20) probably would be characterized by more "sites unseen" (McManamon 1984) and "things unfound" (Vencl 1984:122) than by observable archaeological evidence. Nevertheless, the proposed research design can help establish certain

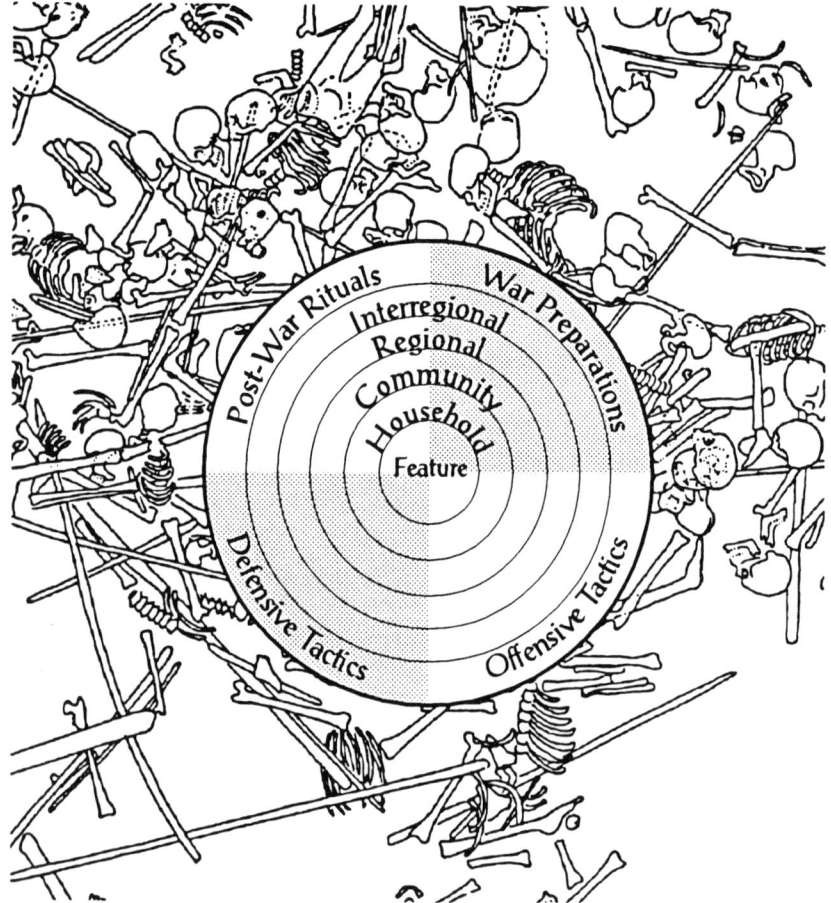

*Figure 20.* An ideal framework for the archaeological investigation of warfare. It attempts to examine warfare in all its stages (from the preparations for warfare to the offensive tactics, the defensive tactics, and the post-war rituals) on multiple units of analysis (from the smallest feature, to the household, the community, the region, and the interregional level).

guidelines for the archaeological investigation of warfare. Such a systematic appraisal of warfare and of its effects upon complete cultural systems can do more than simply establish the existence of warfare in an area under study. It might help us look harder for archaeological evidence of prehistoric warfare (Topic 1989:215) by considering additional aspects of warfare and their expected archaeological manifestations on various levels of analysis. In this way, we might overcome Cordell's warning, for example, that "village size, settlement patterns, village layout, enclosed plazas, and burned houses, are, by themselves, inconclusive" evidence of warfare (Cordell 1989:176).

With this kind of comprehensive framework we could attempt to measure the varying intensity of warfare in the societies being studied and examine differences or changes in their warfare strategies. On the regional level of analysis, for example, the degree of settlement nucleation and settlement relocation might reflect the intensity of warfare in a region. Community-level indicators of warfare would include the omnipresence of fortifications and other signs of preparedness for war, as well as the degree of settlement destruction and subsequent abandonment. The intensity of warfare should also be measurable on the level of individual households and features as well, in the form of the degree of household preparedness for warfare, the size of the resident household in times of war, varying mortality rates, and the relative abundance of dismembered human skeletons. Subsistence data on the community and household levels also may measure the intensity of warfare by revealing its impact upon the inhabitants' subsistence practices and diet (Milner et al. 1991:591). Such an archaeological assessment of warfare should make it possible to consider how warfare relates to other critical factors in the socioenvironment and to address the role that warfare plays in the dynamics of prehistoric tribes and chiefdoms, for "warfare, if it is to be considered a significant factor prehistorically, must be causally related to other processes of economic, political, and social change" (Upham and Reed 1989:154). We might then be in the position to address the question of the role played by warfare in the evolution of prehistoric centralized societies of greater complexity.

It was by means of such a comprehensive research design, for example, that David Wilson (1987, 1988) investigated the role of irrigation agriculture, population growth, and warfare in the evolution of prehistoric complex society in the Lower Santa Valley on the coast of Peru. His regional survey of this 750 km$^2$ area retrieved data on the location, size, density, and dating of some

1,020 archaeological sites. Pertaining to some ten prehistoric periods extending from before 1800 B.C. to A.D. 1532, they include habitation sites, fortresses, civic-ceremonial centers and cemeteries, as well as irrigation canals, field systems, roads and extensive walls. Individual site maps were prepared for a large number of these sites in order to document the architectural details of settlements of all types and sizes; they provided important information about the size and organization of communities and the nature of fortifications throughout the Lower Santa Valley's prehistory. Wilson's complete regional data on the number and distribution of fortress sites and their relation to overall settlement patterns and canal irrigation systems enabled him to monitor warfare in the Lower Santa Valley during much of its prehistoric sequence and to examine its relationship to irrigation agriculture, population growth, and developments in neighboring regions (Wilson 1987, 1988). These are precisely the kinds of archaeological data that we need in order to begin to examine the timing of warfare among prehistoric cultural systems, but also its dynamics, and its overall consequences. Let me turn now to the archaeological study of tribal and chiefly warfare per se.

## Archaeology of Tribal Warfare

In answer to Carneiro's question concerning the archaeology of tribal warfare discussed at the beginning of this book, let me review some of the possible archaeological manifestations of Jívaro and Yanomamö warfare. The generally poor archaeological preservation characteristic of the humid tropical forests and savanna grasslands in which these militant groups live has long been noted by ethnographers and archaeologists alike. Smole, for example, has said of studying the Yanomamö's past: "their very limited material culture is composed largely of perishable objects. Consequently, virtually no archaeological record exists, and very few tangible remains are left when a settlement is abandoned" (Smole 1976:214). Although I would expect the archaeological record associated with these lowland South American societies to be thin for these reasons, in an ideal world of limitless research funds and fieldwork permits I would look for the following kinds of archaeological evidence of their warfare. I should point out that some of the following examples come from outside northern South America, from places as far away as the southern coast of Peru and the North American Southwest. They are merely examples of the kinds of archaeological data bearing on warfare that I expect we too will recover someday in northern South America.

### Preparations for war

Beginning with their preparations for war, we would expect to find region-wide evidence of a variety of measures taken by individual communities in anticipation of raids. This kind of village-level preparedness for warfare is evident at the Preceramic site of Ostra (ca. 5400–5200 B.P.) on an ancient beach ridge north of the Santa River on the Peruvian coast. Here, John Topic mapped 53 piles of possible slingstones spaced 2–3 m apart in two lines that coincide with the village's outer boundaries (Figure 21). Topic has indicated that the closest natural source for these stones lay several kilometers away, and that these stones were selected from the available range of river cobbles for their particular properties. Accordingly, he suggests that the village inhabitants undertook considerable preparations for the village's defense. That they are slingstones is inferred from the spacing between the piles, which is consistent with the diameter of the slinging arc of known Andean slings and with the spacing of slingstone piles at later, fortified sites (Topic and Topic 1987:48). Also, the precise measurements of the stones in two of the piles compare to those of slingstones stockpiled at the Middle Horizon period site of Galindo in the Moche Valley (Topic 1989:217–222, 226–227). Finally, actual slings made of twined-reed stems have been found at several Preceramic sites on the coast of Peru, as were other weapons that I will describe in a later section (Engel 1963:57, 85–86).

Since warriors prepare their own armament and provisions for tribal war parties, this practice should be reflected in the widespread evidence of the manufacture and storage of nonperishable weapons such as bone or stone projectile points within communities, and specifically, within individual houses. As part of his ethnoarchaeological investigation of an Achuara Jívaro household on the Makuma River of Ecuador in 1977, James Zeidler recorded the individual activity areas assigned to its male inhabitants. The male head of household, Tsamirku, and his sons spent most of their time in the men's half of the house (*tankamash*) at the front and this is where they manufactured, repaired, and stored their personal possessions, including their weapons (Figure 22). Two communal activity areas at this end of the house were reserved for the sharpening of machetes and the manufacture of blowguns. The men's blowguns, lances, axes, and quivers of darts, containers of *curare* poison, and shotguns were either placed on their wooden platforms, lashed to posts, or hung from the rafters. Here too each man hung the net bag or basket that contained his personal ornaments, including archaeologically recoverable bone necklaces and ear ornaments, and *Bixa* seeds that he used for body-painting (Zeidler 1983:169–171, 174–175; Karsten 1935:97–98; Kelekna 1981:46–48). It is here that we should expect to find any nonperishable projectile points and axes, and any debitage relating to their manufacture. For Kelekna learned that it is here in the *tankamash* that men file their arrows and coat their tips with *curare* poison (Kelekna 1981:48). Accordingly, the remains of miniature ceramic pots with rim diameters no wider than 7 cm, like the ones the Jívaro use to store their dart poison, might be found here (Figure 23) (Stirling 1938:84, Plate 36c, 91). Clay cylinder seals for applying body paint might occur also, like the ones traditionally used for body painting by Jívaro warriors (Figure 24) (Karsten 1935:310–311). Individual activity areas within houses should feature the same set of tools, features, and refuse associated with the male inhabitants of the house (Zeidler 1984:373).

Zeidler recovered archaeological evidence of such male activ-

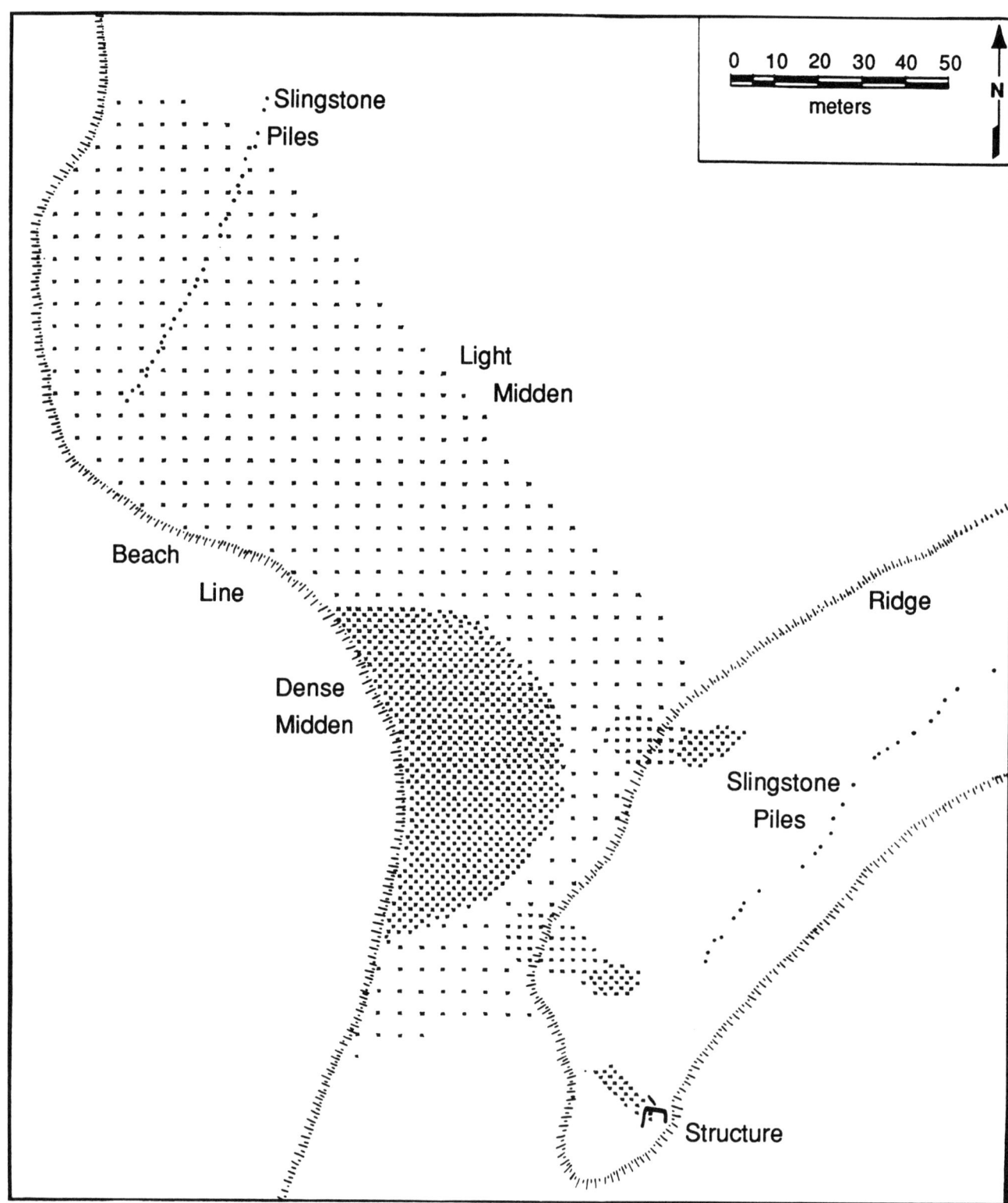

*Figure 21.* The Peruvian Preceramic site of Ostra, with the extent of the midden scatter and the locations of the piles of slingstones. [Reprinted by permission, from Topic 1989: Fig. 2.]

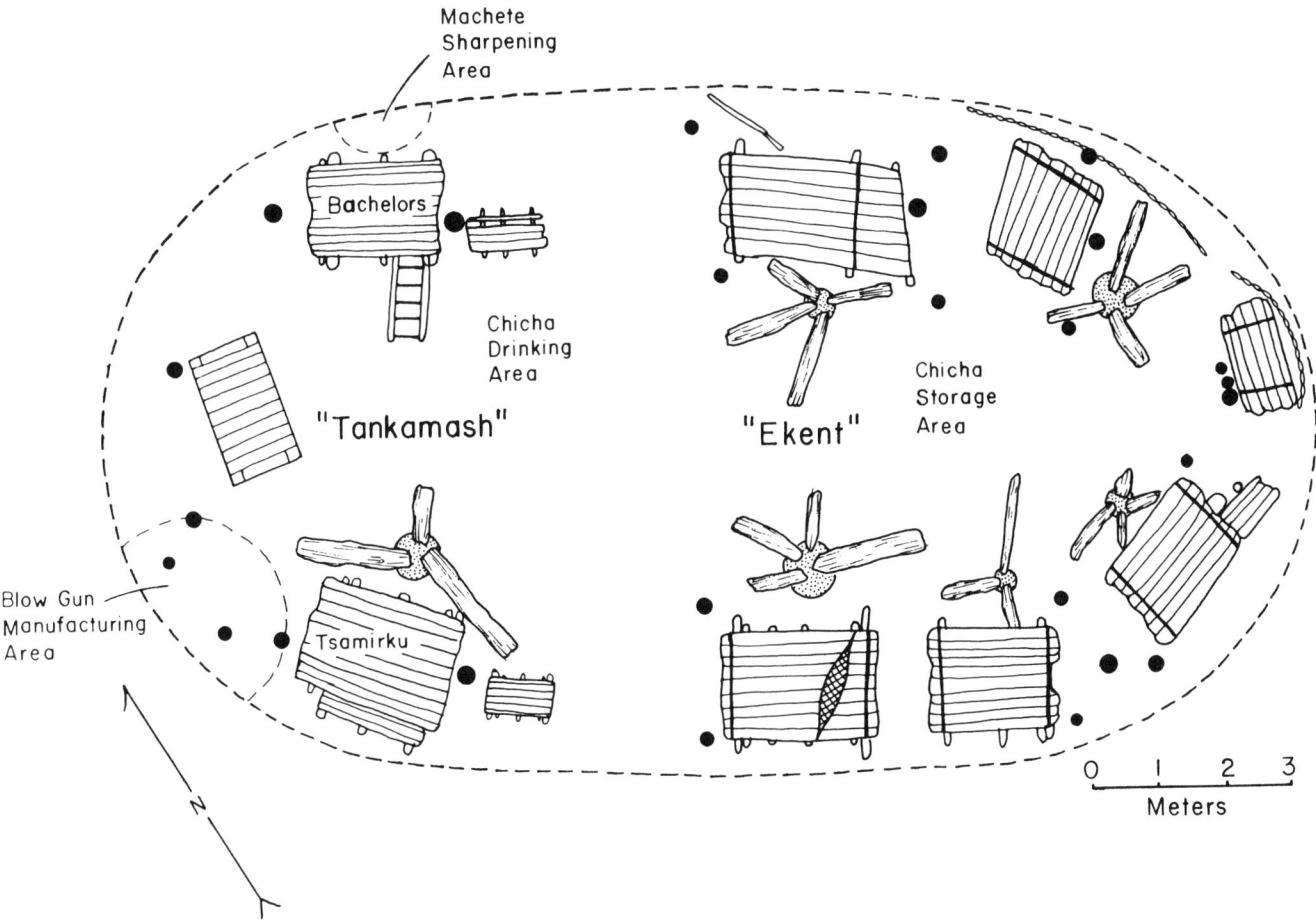

*Figure 22.* A plan of Tsamirku's house at Pumpuentsa, Ecuador, showing the male (*tankamash*) and female (*ekent*) sections, and several male and female activity areas therein. [Redrawn from Zeidler 1984: Maps 51, 52.]

ity areas on Valdivia III (2794–2668 B.C.) housefloors at Real Alto on the coast of Ecuador. Away from the centrally located food-preparation area inside the elliptical Structure 1, for example, lay peripheral male work areas, where the highest densities of lithic debris and chipped stone tools were obtained, and where shell working seems to have been practiced. Zeidler interprets two specific areas in this peripheral sector where shell and the pigment hematite co-occur as individual male activity areas (Zeidler 1984:447–448, 482–483). A similar pattern of female and male household sectors and work areas was obtained on the floor of the smaller Structure 20 (Zeidler 1984:564–567).

At the heart of any tribal war preparations are the intervillage alliances and the recruitment of allied war parties. What archaeological data can we expect to recover of the alliances formed by tribes for mounting a raid against a common enemy or for withstanding an anticipated enemy attack? On a regional scale, Haas (1989:503–505) offers the possibility that in the Long House Valley of northeastern Arizona in the mid-thirteenth century A.D., intervillage alliances existed between sites that were within view of each other. That the neighboring Kayenta Valley to the north was part of this alliance is suggested by the recent discovery that the similarly patterned clusters of sites and satellite villages there were within view of the Long House Valley. Accordingly, Haas suggests that the Kayenta Anasazi maintained local and intervalley defensive alliances at A.D. 1250. The same can not be said of the neighboring Klethla Valley to the south and west, for there is more than a 15 km-wide gap or empty zone between the nearest sites in the neighboring Long House and Klethla Valleys, which I will return to discuss later. Moreover, these nearest sites in the adjacent valleys are not visually interconnected. It appears then, that villages in the Klethla Valley did not participate in the Kayenta-Long House alliance system; they might even have been enemies, along with other groups like the Cibola to the south (Haas 1990:189).

In northern South America, rapid intervillage communication was probably achieved through drum signaling rather than by visual forms of communication in view of the forested and often rugged terrain. Jívaro villages traditionally communicated with their neighbors and allies by means of the wooden signal drum, which they used to sound the signal for someone's death, for

*Figure 23.* Tiny ceramic vessel used by the Jívaro to store *curare* poison for darts, from west of the Río Pastaza, Ecuador (M. Harner 1956–1957). The vessel is 3.2 cm tall and has a rim diameter of 6.8 cm. It has a blackened, burnished interior and a brown, wiped exterior. [AMNH 40.0/9798. Courtesy of the American Museum of Natural History.]

summoning help during an attack, and for mobilizing warriors for a planned raid (Karsten 1935:111–112; Cotlow 1953:142–143). The log signal drum is still slung from a post at the entrance to the men's half of the house and used by the Achuara Jívaro to sound the alarm (Kelekna 1981:46, 95).

*Pre-war rituals*

Since tribes mark their alliances with feasts, and with special pre-war feasts and rituals in the case of alliances for war, we should search for corresponding manifestations of their alliances at individual communities. Remains of their pre-raid rituals should occur in the village clearing, in the men's half of the host's house, or in a large structure, such as those built by the members of Jívaro war parties for their victory feasts. It is here that large manioc-beer jars (Figure 25), for example, should be found in relative abundance, and especially drinking bowls and cups like the *pinínga* that the Jívaro use to consume manioc beer and *natéma* (Figure 26) (Karsten 1935:286, 318, 335, 345).

In the aforementioned Achuara house of Tsamirku, for example, Zeidler noted the abundance of manioc-beer jars in the center of the women's half of the house (*ekent*), where each woman stores her manioc-beer jar (Figure 22). Also, each woman has a small basket suspended over this *chicha*-storage area that contains her drinking bowls or *pinínga*. By recording the movement of these two Achuara ceramic vessel categories within the house, Zeidler discovered that while the manioc-beer jars are restricted to the *chicha*-storage area in the women's *ekent*, the drinking bowls are frequently used by the men and any visitors to consume manioc beer in the men's *tankamash*. During large gatherings on ritual occasions, the entire *tankamash* is used for *chicha* drinking (Figure 22) (Zeidler 1984:340–341, 358–359; Kelekna 1981:49–51, 55–56).

At the Valdivia III phase site of Real Alto, evidence of ritual feasting and drinking was found not so much within individual houses, as in large refuse pits atop the Fiesta House Mound bordering the site's inner plaza, which Marcos (1978:15) suggests might have functioned as a men's house. These large refuse pits contained many complete or nearly complete drinking bowls that were most likely the remains of single events (Lathrap et al. 1977:9). They probably represented single and prolonged communal drinking bouts, for "the size of the carinated Valdivia drinking bowl found at the Fiesta House Mound refuse pits, with a diameter greater than 30 cm, indicates a communal drinking practice" (Marcos 1978:47). Incidentally, this is precisely the size of the drinking bowl (*pinínga*) used by Jívaro war leaders for their role as hosts of pre-war gatherings and victory celebrations (Stirling 1938:90). The pits atop the Fiesta House Mound also contained food remains—deer and other mammal bones, razor clams, rock-crab claws, chiton plates, sea turtle, "and other delicacies not commonly found elsewhere" (Marcos 1978:82; Lathrap et al. 1977:8–9). It is in the context of such all-male gatherings, drinking bouts, and feasts that the members of a war party celebrate their alliance and rouse their courage and bloodthirstiness before their departure to war.

*Warfare tactics*

The practice of pitching overnight camps on the way to and from war should show up in a region's settlement pattern, made up of village sites and subsidiary camps of various kinds (Figure 27). The overnight camps pitched by an all-male war party should differ archaeologically from other hunting and collecting camps. In the case of the Yanomamö, hunting camps can be occupied by 30–40 males and, periodically, females (Chagnon 1983:56). Not only will the war-party camps be of simpler construction, but they will also be occupied for a shorter period of time than other temporary camps—from nightfall until dawn generally (Valero 1984:51). A much narrower range of activities will be performed there by the male members of a war party; there should be much less evidence of hunting and primary butchering there, for example, than at hunting camps. Since target practice and body painting are performed at these overnight camps, discarded nonperishable projectiles and ceramic cylinder seals used for body painting might be recovered.

The size of such overnight camp sites and the number of constituent hearths will reflect the size and composition of the war party. For example, a recently abandoned Shama-tari camp consisted of "many" lean-tos, some with bark-strip hammocks still hanging inside, smoldering logs, and food remains (Valero

*Figure 24.* Ceramic cylinder seals (*payánga*) used by Jívaro warriors to adorn their bodies with black (*Genipa*) rolled-out designs. From Macas, Ecuador. [Redrawn from Karsten 1935: Fig. 9.]

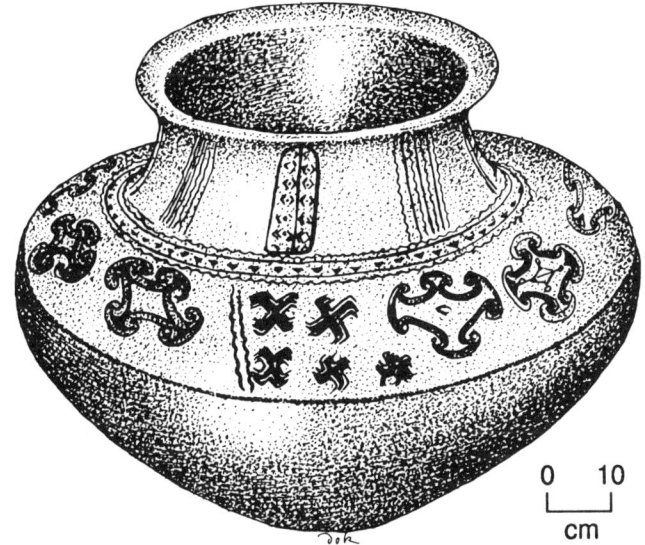

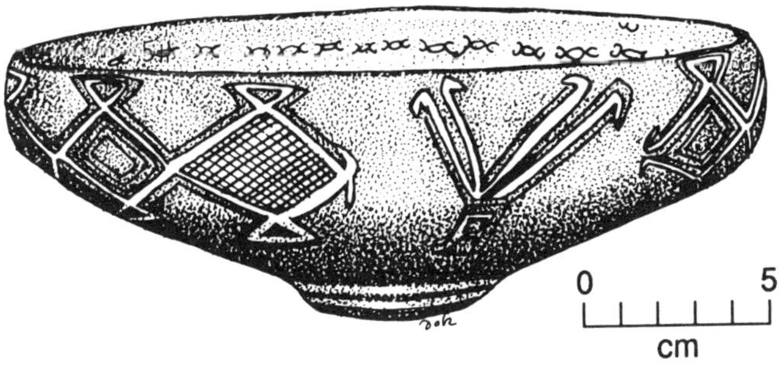

*Figure 26.* Shallow drinking dish (*pinínga*) used by the Canelos Indians on the Bobonaza River, Ecuador, to drink manioc beer and *natéma*. [Redrawn from Karsten 1935: Plate xx:2.]

*Figure 25.* Large ceramic conical jar used by the Canelos Indians on the Bobonaza River, Ecuador, to store manioc beer. Manioc-beer jars can hold up to 10 gallons. [Redrawn from Karsten 1935: Plate xx:1.]

*Figure 27.* Baniva camp on the Río Jsana, Brazil. [By L. Weiss and H. Schmidt (1907–1909), Neg. #2A13866. Courtesy of the American Museum of Natural History.]

1984:241). The camps of allied war parties will be larger, and like those of the Jívaro, might consist of separate clusters of shelters and hearths, more than 25 m apart (Up de Graff 1923:263; Cotlow 1953:226–227, 233). Finally, the presence of hearths at these overnight camps might be limited to camps that are pitched at a certain distance from enemy territory, since we know that the Yanomamö avoid lighting fires at those overnight camps closest to the enemy village (Chagnon 1983:184; Smole 1976:86; Valero 1984:340–341, 433).

Since the hit-and-run raids of most tribal war parties involve five to ten warriors striking singled-out members of the enemy village from a distance with lances, spears, or arrows made out of palm wood or cane and then hastily retreating into the forest, they are unlikely to produce significant spatial concentrations of archaeological remains per se (Vencl 1984:123). As Ranere (1980:33) reminds us, "from the ethnographic examples of the material culture of modern and historical tropical forest groups we are well aware that projectile points are made of hardwoods, chisels are made from rodent incisors, gouges from shell, and knives from bamboo." The long-distance hurling of missiles would seem to be represented at the Peruvian Preceramic site of Ostra, where piles of slingstones point to "a long-distance exchange of projectiles rather than close hand-to-hand fighting. The defenders had the advantage of ample ammunition; the attackers would have relied on retrieving and returning projectiles thrown by the defenders. All in all, the picture is one of a lot of bluffing, name calling, provocation, and rushing about on both sides, resulting in few casualties" (Topic 1989:222). Actual weapons that could have been used in this long-distance combat have been recovered at other Preceramic sites on the coast of Peru, in refuse and burial deposits at Paracas 514 and Asia; they include twined-reed slings, wooden spears and spearthrowers, and wooden and chipped-stone projectile points (Engel 1963:56–58, 79, 85, Table 14, 88; Engel 1981:32, 38; Quilter 1989:85; Quilter 1991:403, 405). Significantly, few weapons of the kind that would have been used in face-to-face combat have been recovered. The shark-teeth-studded wooden club recovered in a refuse layer at Asia is one of the only examples of such weapons, yet the fact that it was decorated with red-dyed wool and feathers casts doubt on its use in combat (Engel 1963:57).

The destruction and violence wrought by raiding parties should leave discernible archaeological evidence at target settlements. The offensive tactic of setting target settlements on fire will produce widespread evidence of burning, in the form of an ashy stratum throughout the settlement and unusually dense carbonized remains, usually accompanied by signs of the settlement's subsequent abandonment (Roper 1975:301). Such archaeological manifestations of a settlement's destruction by enemy forces will differ from the intentional burning of an infested Yanomamö settlement by its inhabitants, because in the latter case the inhabitants generally rebuild the settlement on the same spot or nearby (Chagnon 1983:52–53). The same will be true in the aftermath of accidental fires. Following the destruction by fire of two storage rooms at a small mid-thirteenth-century pueblo near Zuni, New Mexico, its inhabitants chose to remain there. They simply sealed off the burned rooms, hurriedly added two new storage rooms, and only later abandoned the pueblo "methodically, rather than as a consequence of disaster" (Zier 1976:22, 17)

Also different from the natural abandonment of a community will be the remains of abundant material possessions and agricultural produce at a community destroyed by fire. The two burned storage rooms at the aforementioned mid-thirteenth-century pueblo near Zuni, New Mexico, contained abundant unshelled and shelled corn. The fill of these rooms consisted of a 40–50 cm layer of burned, unshelled corn lying on the reddened clay floor, with shelled corn above it interspersed with ground-stone artifacts and burned clay and wood roofing material. It contrasts with the thin and unburned fill of the pueblo's other rooms and living surfaces, which contained few portable items (Zier 1976:19, 22).

Mackey and Green (1979) have also outlined some of the differences between naturally abandoned settlements and those destroyed by fire. Approximately 34% of all surveyed Largo-Gallina phase (A.D. 1100–1300) sites of northwestern New Mexico were burned. Burned sites were recognized by their bright red fired clay roofs, refired and oxidized ceramics, and carbonized roof beams and corn. Moreover, some sites that were recorded as "unburned" on the surface were found upon excavation to have been burned, a fact that makes that 34% figure a conservative estimate of all the burned sites. Excavations at the burned sites exposed a wealth of artifacts and storage bins full of corn, while the unburned sites, which were presumably naturally abandoned, had sparse remains. Mackey and Green suggest that "it is unlikely that occupants burning a structure they were abandoning would destroy all their agricultural produce and material possessions. The presence of large amounts of corn and artifacts in an excavated site, is, therefore, a strong indication that the occupants of the site were forced out and the structure burned in the process" (Mackey and Green 1979:145–146).

Burned settlements are just one of several indicators of inter-community warfare in the upper San Juan Basin in New Mexico and Colorado in post A.D. 800 times. Not only were some 80% of all pit houses and surface houses destroyed by fire, their clay roofs baked bright orange-red, but also inhabitants of at least two pit house villages suffered violent deaths. On the floor of Pit House 3 at Bancos Village lay the charred and calcined remains of four adults, and a group of three individuals were found in Pit House 5, all of whom were evidently trapped in these structures at the time they burned (Eddy 1966:299). At Sambrito Village, the slaughtered remains of three and twelve individuals were recovered on the floor of Pit House 6 and Pit House 25 respectively. Although I will be describing their remains in more detail later, their scattered position and fractured condition leave no doubt that they were the victims of an attack, after which the burning roofs collapsed upon them (Eddy 1966:248; Eddy 1974:81).

Inhabitants of five excavated Largo-Gallina phase (A.D. 1100–1300) villages in the Llaves Quadrangle of New Mexico experienced similar attacks and violent deaths. The bodies of five, nine, ten, eleven, and sixteen individuals were found on housefloors, lying in heaps or in random positions. Many of them exhibited pre-mortem fractures, crushed skulls, and embedded arrowpoints (Mackey and Green 1979:146–147). To take the pit house village of Rattlesnake Point as an example, the skeletons of ten adults were found in a heap on the floor of a pit house. Their skulls displayed pre-mortem fractures and four contained arrowpoints. Indeed, of the seven stone arrowpoints recovered in the pit house, five were associated with the skeletons, and a shark-tooth point was found embedded in the right ilium of one of the skeletons. Six flint chips were also found in close association with the skeletons; one was embedded below the left eye of one of the skulls (Bahti 1949:55).

Finally, excavations at the late thirteenth-century Sand Canyon Pueblo in southwest Colorado have revealed that this large aggregated community was enclosed by a massive masonry wall, studded with masonry towers, that was erected in a single construction effort early in the community's occupation (A.D. 1262–1274). Sand Canyon Pueblo's abandonment around A.D. 1285 was marked by the burning of many of its rooms, kivas, and towers, and by the hasty departure on the part of its inhabitants; on the floors lay smashed whole vessels and an array of bone tools, chipped stone, as well as certain valuables (Bradley 1992; Haas 1990:187).

Furthermore, over half of the 22 human skeletons recovered in the rooms of Sand Canyon Pueblo were not intentional burials, but rather lay exposed on floors and lacked any funerary offerings. Three bodies lay in a heap in Structure 1005, for example; Bradley suggests that they had perhaps been unceremoniously flung from the roof of an adjacent tower, and abandoned (Bradley 1992). Moreover, many of these abandoned bodies exhibited evidence of pre-mortem trauma, both before and near the time of death, as Anne Katzenberg's osteological analysis will demonstrate (Bradley, pers. comm.). In Bradley's words, "the high percentage of abandonment context human remains and evidence of trauma may indicate a violent demise for at least some of the site" (Bradley, pers. comm.). In sum, these burned villages with dead bodies lying on floors and vandalized property are textbook archaeological examples of what target villages might look like as a consequence of tribal warfare. The contextual data they offer are as close to the fleeting attacks of villages by enemy war parties and to the death and destruction they inflict as we can expect to get.

Village burial populations will also reveal information about tribal war tactics and the toll they take. We have seen how the war parties of South American tribesmen consist of males between the ages of 15 and 40 (Cocco 1972:385; Stirling 1938:51; Karsten 1935:237–242; Harner 1972:93; Cotlow 1953:238). Furthermore, the most sought-after victims of their revenge raids are males, and prominent adult males at that (Chagnon 1983:23, 180, 184–185, 189; Valero 1984:50, 70, 329, 353, 382, 417; Harner 1972:112–114; Cotlow 1953:144, 239, 242). For these reasons, the resulting number of war victims in a village burial population should be skewed in favor of males 15 years and older. More specifically, available mortality profiles by sex and age for a target settlement's population should represent a higher rate of death for adult males than other members of the population, possibly with additional signs of their having suffered a violent death.

This is precisely the kind of evidence that James Chase recovered in his analysis of a sample of Gallina Anasazi burials from the Llaves area of New Mexico (Chase 1976). To begin with, Chase reported that approximately 70% of the population died by the age of 30 from all causes (Chase 1976:88, 1978:18, 31). If we examine the mortality distribution by sex, we can observe certain differences in the death rate for males and females of different age groups. Figure 28 presents the mortality distribution for those Gallina individuals who could be aged and sexed, drawn from Chase's data (1976:89). This mortality profile reveals that death was more pronounced for men between the ages of 20 and 50 than for other members of the population; it is also evident that women outlived men. The fact that numerous individuals in this population show signs of having suffered violent injuries underscores warfare as the principal factor responsible for the skewed mortality profile. The skulls of at least six individuals exhibited pre-mortem fractures caused by blows with a blunt, clublike instrument, and undoubtedly with an ax in one case. Also, two males had projectile points embedded in their bodies. One serrated projectile point was recovered in a 25-year-old man's pelvic cavity, and another adult male had been struck at short range in his left knee with a small, side-notched projectile point from his left side and at a slightly superior position (Chase 1976:79, 85, 1978:18, 30). Finally, one-third of the Gallina burials were multiple burials, which suggests that the constituent pairs of individuals died at the same time, and in some instances, as victims of the same raid. One such multiple burial contained the remains of a female 20–28 years of age who had suffered a severe blow to the left side of her head, and the aforementioned adult male with the side-notched projectile point in his knee as well as other possible mutilations that I will describe later. They had been buried together under the foundation of a tall circular structure of the sort that functioned as defensive towers (Chase 1976:71–72). Chase reports on the extent of violence in the Gallina population:

> Violence was evident in 38% of the total population studied and 60% of the adults. Of those definitely sexed as male (five), three exhibit evidence of violence for a 60 percentile. Two identifiable females were killed by severe blows to the head. Violence was the way of life for this population in the Gallina. [Chase 1976:79–80, cf. 1978:19]

A similarly skewed age distribution exists among a subset of Oneota burials from the Norris Farms #36 cemetery (ca. A.D. 1300) in the central Illinois River valley, which offers a wonderfully complete picture of the nature of tribal warfare and its impact upon this prehistoric village (Milner et al. 1991). Out of a total of 264 burials in the village cemetery, which as a whole, match mortality profiles of traditional indigenous populations, 43 skeletons exhibited signs of having suffered a violent death. These individuals variously displayed arrowpoints embedded in their bones, massive injuries resulting from blows to the back of the head and to the upper limbs and trunk with ground-stone celts, and other signs of mutilation that I will discuss later. Of these 43 victims who died violently, 41 were over 15 years of age. In view of the fact that juveniles are well represented in the larger burial population (55% of all individuals buried in the cemetery were less than 15 years old), this skewed violent-death mortality distribution is significant. Not only did a sizable portion of the community die violently, but adults were much more likely to experience violent deaths than juveniles (Milner et al. 1991:589). And as we would expect, among the war victims were 35% of all the adult males buried in the cemetery; the authors conclude that "the high level of mortality from violence experienced by the men of this Oneota community approximates the proportions of males killed in several ethnographically recorded bellicose societies" (Milner et al. 1991:594).

Furthermore, the Oneota cemetery reveals abundant information about enemy raiding tactics and the casualties incurred by the village inhabitants. Although a handful of individuals buried at the Norris Farm cemetery showed signs of having survived the wounds they received in war, it seems that most victims were killed by the force of chert-tipped arrows flung at them, or by direct, multiple blows to their heads and upper bodies with hafted celt axes. The resulting jagged, radiating fracture patterns on their skulls, trunks, and limbs indicate that they occurred near the time of death (Milner et al. 1991:583–584). It is clear, however, that the 43 war victims met their deaths at different times throughout the cemetery's long duration. Their graves were found dispersed throughout the cemetery. Most of them contain a single victim. As a matter of fact, no mass burials were recovered at the Norris Farm cemetery, and the few multiple graves that were exposed contained two to five victims. It seems that one to five individuals were killed in any single raid. These casualty figures match those of most South American hit-and-run raids against villages or of ambushes of individuals or of work parties away from the village. Out of the six multiple graves that contained unambiguous war victims, five apparently represented single-sex work parties (Milner et al. 1991:587–588).

The pattern of warfare revealed by the victims buried at the Norris Farm cemetery suggests that it was a pervasive element in everyday life, that it included both long-range archery and face-to-face combat, and that it resulted in the killing of few

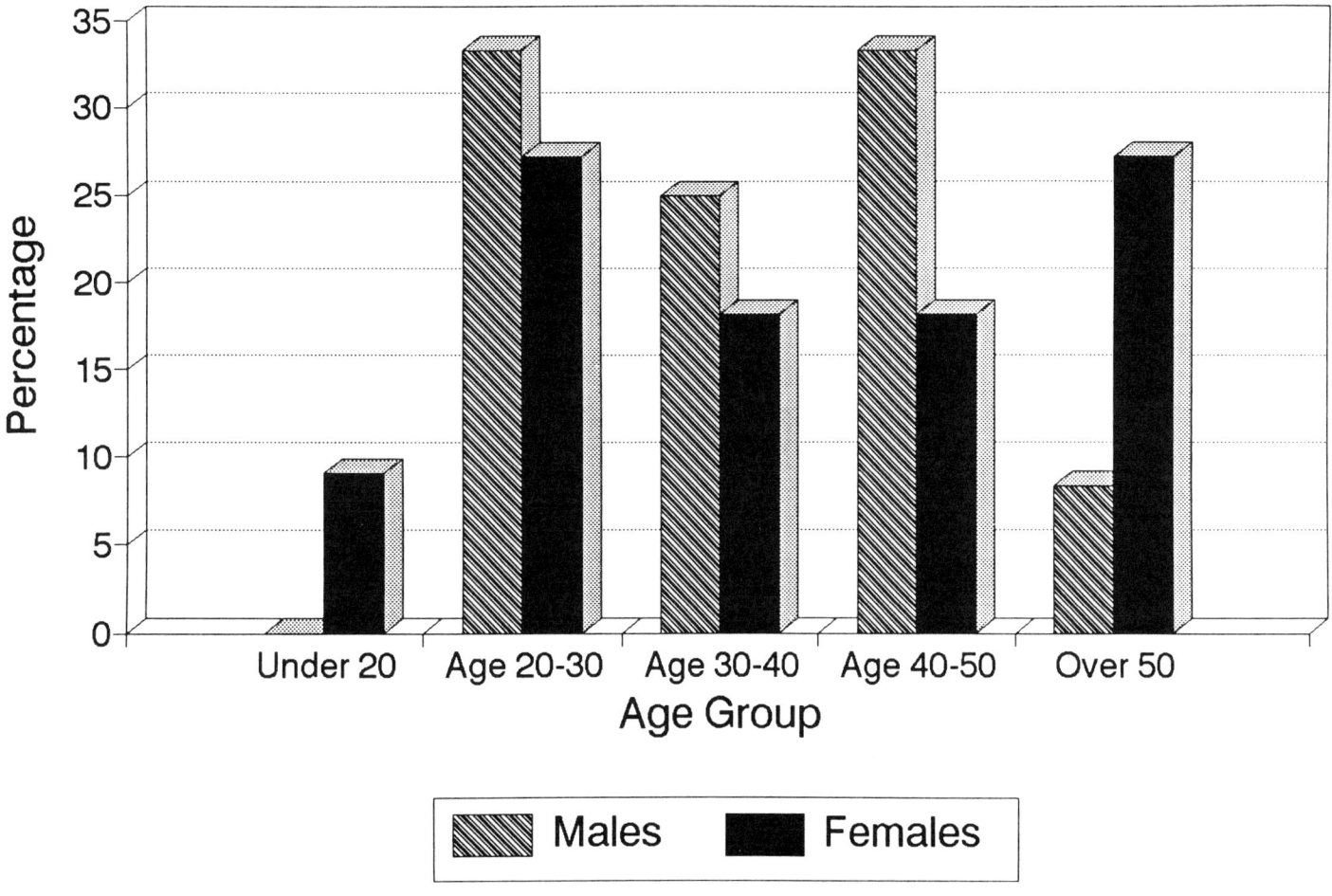

*Figure 28.* Distribution of age at death for a sample of male and female Gallina Anasazi burials from the Llaves area of New Mexico. [Source: Chase 1976:89.]

individuals at any single attack, usually by ambushing individuals or work parties caught by surprise far from the village (Milner et al. 1991:594). Finally, the severely carnivore-damaged remains of some victims suggest that they were killed in remote locations and that their bodies were recovered and buried much later (Milner et al. 1991:585–590). This concern for retrieving the bodies of those killed in war and carrying them home for proper funerary treatment is shared by South American tribesmen (Valero 1984:261, 366).

Multiple burials account for 72% of the burials at the large pit house Sambrito Village in the upper San Juan River basin of New Mexico and Colorado, along with other manifestations of endemic warfare, some of which we have already described. The multiple burials at Sambrito Village occur in groups of two, three, or four individuals, "indicating that village deaths often took place several at a time" (Eddy 1974:81). Frequently their bodies were stacked one on top of the other in pits. Although both sexes and mixed age groups are represented in these simultaneous death lots, it is clear that adult males often died several at a time, possibly by violent means (Eddy 1974:81; Eddy 1966:243–246, 527). Thus, multiple burials, and especially multiple burials of adult males who display signs of having suffered a violent death, is an expected outcome of tribal raids. And an increase in the occurrence of multiple burials and in the number of burials with pre-mortem fractures might signal increasing tribal hostilities in a study region (Upham and Reed 1989:156).

Tribal raiding parties, and especially allied raiding parties, are capable on occasion of mounting large-scale attacks upon enemy settlements and of massacring their inhabitants. Let me quickly note that massacres like the treacherous feast waged by the Shama-tari and their allies against the Pishaasi-teri in 1951, or the allied attack mounted by the Pishaasi-teri against the village of Tayari-teri in 1980, or for that matter, like the Jívaro's allied attack against the Spanish settlements of Logroño and Sevilla del Oro in 1599, are extraordinary events that loom in the oral histories of the participants, the survivors, and their descendants. Furthermore, the available casualty figures suggest that adult males are the principal victims, while young women are frequently abducted (Chagnon 1983:3, 175; Valero 1984:432; Chagnon 1988: note 24, 1990:100; Lizot 1989:28–29; Stirling 1938:17–18).

An archaeological consequence of such massacres might be

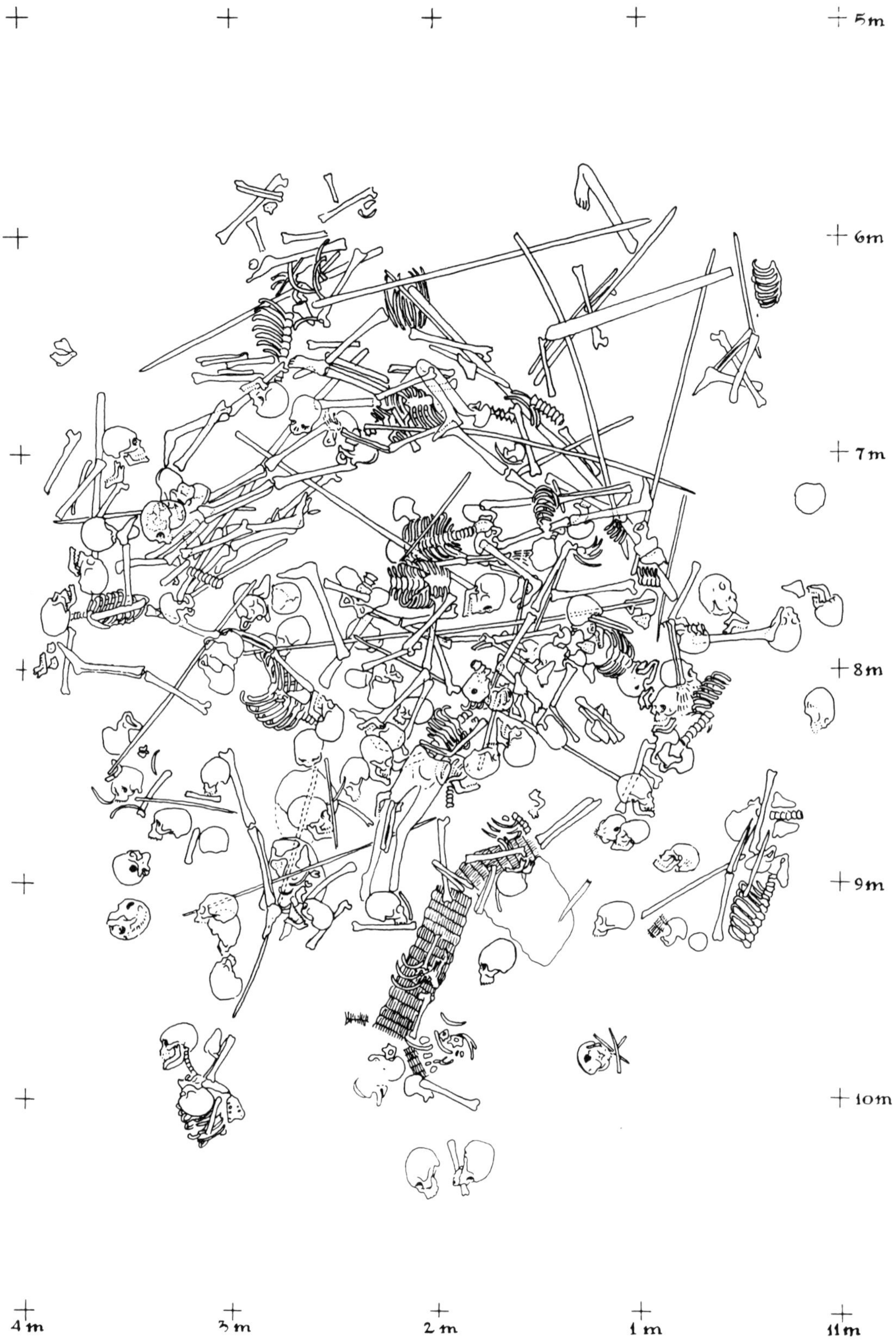

*Figure 29.* Plan of the mass grave at the Preceramic period ossuary site of Cabezas Largas, Paracas Bay, Peru. [Redrawn from Engel 1966: Fig. 20.]

the occurrence of mass graves, like the Preceramic (ca. 5000 B.P.) period ossuary of Cabezas Largas on Paracas Bay on the south coast of Peru (Figure 29). Unlike other broadly contemporaneous Preceramic ossuary sites such as those of Las Vegas and Real Alto in Ecuador, which are directly associated with habitation sites, the ossuary of Cabezas Largas is apparently an isolated burial ground, located at least 3 km from the nearest village site. Moreover, the Cabezas Largas skeletal population is unlike other Preceramic period cemeteries, including the above ossuaries, whose skeletal populations reveal mortality profiles that are typical of natural populations, including young children and infants (Klepinger 1979; Stothert 1985:625; Quilter 1989:82). At Cabezas Largas, only the remains of some 56 adult bodies were present, many of which were partly to fully disarticulated, and associated with slender wooden stakes 2 m long. Many wore fabrics of reed or cactus fibers and some skeletons had been wrapped in fine, fringed mantles. Although the sexes of the Cabezas Largas dead are not available, Engel refers to the "men buried in the ossuary" (Engel 1981:32). Moreover, Engel reports that "the majority of the corpses had been simply thrown in, as if one had in mind getting rid of them quickly. It looked as if a complete group had been exterminated" (Engel 1981:31; Quilter 1989:71–74). For the time being we can only guess as to the circumstances surrounding the death of these individuals. Were they members of a war party, killed in action and buried hastily with the mantles and posts they were borne on? Were they members of an all-male work party ambushed by a raiding party? Whatever the circumstances leading to the deaths of these 56 or more individuals, their mass grave on the uninhabited windward side of the Paracas Peninsula denotes what must have been an extraordinary event, and possibly a massacre, in Preceramic times (Quilter 1989:74).

Lastly, tribal war parties frequently loot the raided settlement before departing, a practice that might result in the absence of the utilitarian and exotic items. The acts of intentional destruction that raiding parties may carry out in the aftermath of a successful attack should be evident at the target settlement in the form of intentionally smashed ceramic containers and other signs of vandalism (Cocco 1972:388). At Sand Canyon Pueblo in southwest Colorado, which as we saw earlier was evidently attacked and burned in the late thirteenth century, there was no evidence of looting, yet artifacts in the rooms where dead bodies lay had been deliberately smashed (Bradley 1987, cited by Haas 1990:187; Bradley, pers. comm.).

*Defensive tactics*

Yanomamö and Jívaro villagers who live under the threat of enemy raids respond in a number of ways to actual or anticipated raids. The most immediate response practiced by the inhabitants of a village under attack is to flee into the surrounding forest, especially if the war party sets fire to the village. Under these circumstances the inhabitants have precious little time for removing their belongings from the village. Accordingly, we should expect to find the remains of burned villages laden with the material possessions of their evicted inhabitants. We have seen how Largo-Gallina phase villages in northwestern New Mexico that were burned during enemy raids still contained abundant food and material remains, which indicated that the occupants of the site were forced out, leaving their material possessions behind in the burning village. Not only did burned structures contain storage bins full of corn, but also they had a significantly larger number of potsherds and reconstructible pots than did structures at sites that were abandoned methodically (Mackey and Green 1979:145–146).

The presence or absence of dead bodies on village housefloors will also reveal the frequency with which (or the success with which) the defensive tactic of fleeing the village under attack was practiced. During the Piedra phase (A.D. 875–950) at Bancos Village in the upper San Juan River of northwestern New Mexico, only two out of fourteen pit houses in the village contained the bodies of trapped victims of enemy attacks. Accordingly, Eddy suggests that during most attacks the inhabitants escaped from their burning houses (Eddy 1966:290, 299, 302, 1974:82). High on a second-level Pleistocene terrace stood the stockaded village of Mascarenas, one of five such stockaded villages in the region that might have served as wartime refuges for the inhabitants of surrounding villages (Eddy 1966:255, 266, 1974:81–82, Fig.2), which I will describe shortly (see Figure 32).

As warfare escalates, South American tribesmen will find it necessary to relocate their villages, resulting in a high degree of settlement mobility. Archaeologically, then, tribal warfare will produce village sites that have short occupations. They may be characterized by relatively shallow archaeological deposits, or by the relative accumulation of material refuse, such as ceramic densities. Of the four tropical forest phases that Meggers and Evans defined archaeologically on Marajó Island, for example, the first three were characterized by 100-year-long village occupations. Village durations were estimated by the depth of the accumulated site refuse and by the density of accumulated potsherds. According to Meggers and Evans, this archaeological evidence points to "a quiet, peaceful existence, uninterrupted either by exhaustion of the food supply or by raids from belligerent neighboring tribes" (Meggers and Evans 1957:257). In the final Aruã phase, by contrast, estimated village occupations ranged from 1 to 19.2 years (Meggers and Evans 1957:253–254, 258). The much higher degree of settlement mobility at this time could in part reflect an increasing amount of intervillage raiding.

We have seen how even anticipated attacks will prompt South American tribesmen to pick up and move, sometimes in conjunction with allied villages. They will observe a series of defensive strategies in their choice of settlement locations, settlement sizes, and settlement spacings that should be readily detectable in a region's settlement pattern. Archaeologists working in the American Southwest have demonstrated how several Anasazi regions exhibited similar settlement pattern changes around A.D. 1250, along with other archaeological manifestations of intervillage raiding (Haas 1989, 1990; Upham and Reed 1989). In con-

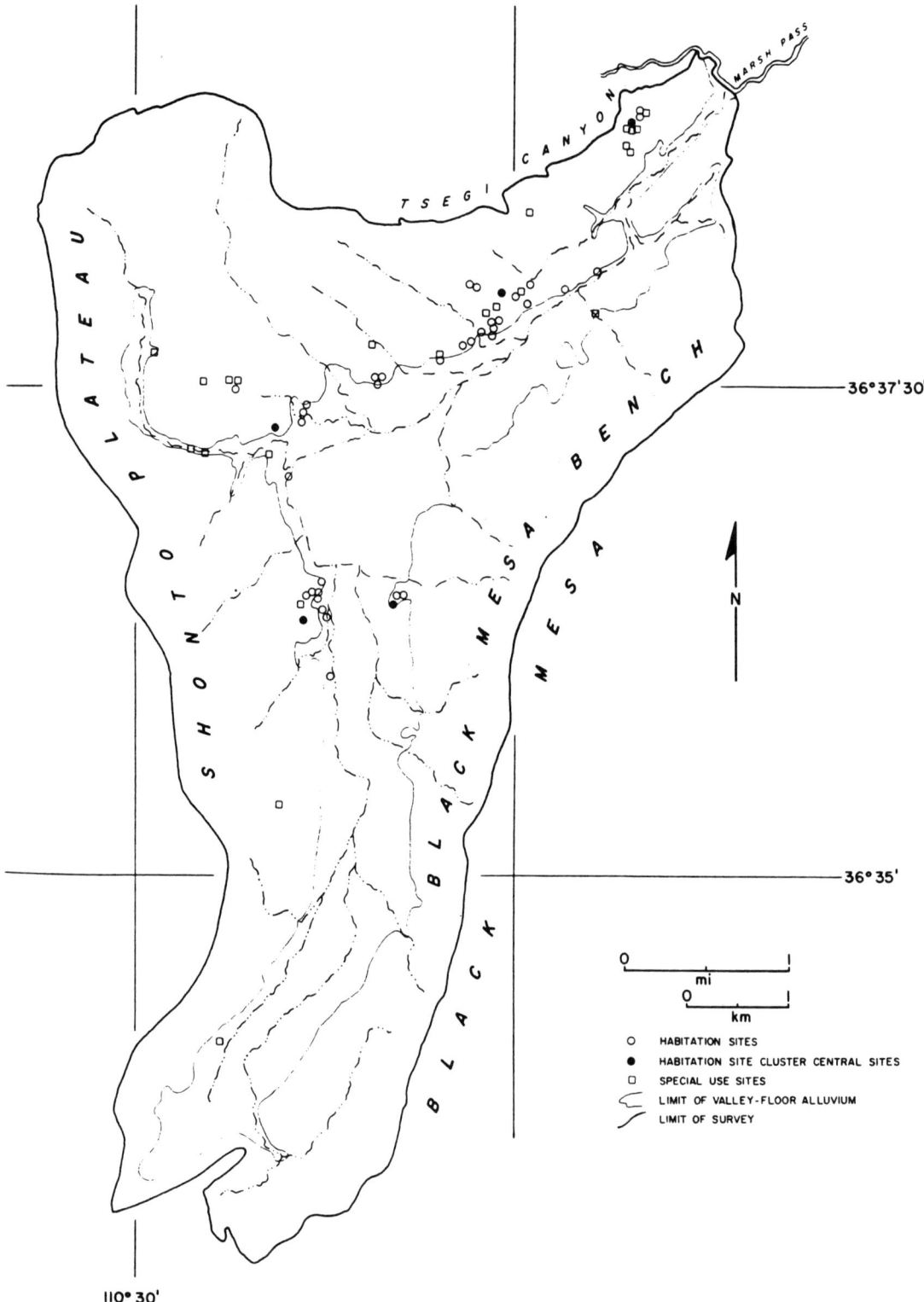

*Figure 30.* Regional settlement pattern in Long House Valley, northeastern Arizona in A.D. 1250–1300. Settlements are grouped into clusters centered on focal sites, which are shown as darkened circles. [Reprinted from Dean et al. 1978: Fig. 3. Courtesy of the Museum of Northern Arizona.]

trast to previous periods, settlements became grouped into discrete settlement clusters with clear boundaries. Kayenta Anasazi settlements in the Long House Valley in northeastern Arizona were concentrated in the northern half of the valley and grouped into one of five settlement clusters, spaced .5 to 1 km apart. Each settlement cluster consisted of two to twelve habitation sites surrounding a central, or focal, site (Dean et al. 1978:33; Haas 1989:502) (Figure 30). All of these focal sites were located on defensible hilltops or mesas, very often with direct view of each other. We saw earlier how these visually interconnected focal settlements might have participated in wartime alliances. Focal sites in the Gallina Anasazi region in northwestern New Mexico often featured tall, circular masonry towers, which were probably used for such intervillage communication as well as for storage and for defense (Mackey and Green 1979:148–151; Upham and Reed 1989:155–156). A similar pattern of five settlement clusters appeared in the Klethla Valley at this time, with focal sites either located in defensible, isolated positions or else enclosed by defensive walls (Haas 1990:185; Upham and Reed 1989:157).

I should point out, however, that these focal sites were not the only settlements to assume defensible hilltop positions and to feature defensive fortifications. In the Gallina Anasazi area, some 69% of all habitation sites were located on hilltops, ridges, or clifftops, and many habitation sites featured defensive walls, palisades, or stockades (Mackey and Green 1979:147–149). And all the sites making up one Kayenta Anasazi settlement cluster—focal site and satellite villages alike—were perched atop an isolated cliff at the mouth of Tsegi Canyon, which I will describe in more detail later (Haas 1990:184–185). We have seen how South American tribes routinely fortify their villages, and even their satellite camps, in response to warfare. I will describe some archaeological examples of village fortifications later.

The regional settlement pattern of these thirteenth-century Southwestern tribal polities, as Haas (1989:506) refers to them, suggests "that the people were concerned with attack and took major steps to defend themselves and their stored resources" (Haas 1990:185). Their common settlement pattern reflected their readiness and response to escalating warfare. I have described it here because it is a lot like the Jívaro's regional settlement pattern. Individual Jívaro settlements, or households, tend to be clustered along the upper reaches of a river or of a tributary stream, making up what anthropologists have referred to as neighborhoods, and leaving vast surrounding empty zones across the forested landscape. Jívaro neighborhoods can consist of six or seven (Stirling 1938:39), five or six (Meggers 1971:62), or two or three households (Zeidler 1983:160), spaced a half-mile (.804 km) or more apart (Harner 1972:78) (Figure 31). Like some of the fortified hilltop refuges in the Anasazi area, we have seen how the Jívaro always select defensible hilltops for their households, and further fortify them with external palisades, as well as with watchtowers in the past. Moreover, in response to intensive warfare, neighboring households will seek refuge at large, fortified Jívaro settlements, not unlike the larger, nucleated, and defensible focal settlements of the Anasazi, which might have served as wartime refuges (Haas 1989:503).

The settlement nucleation produced by the fusion of tribal villages in wartime might also produce large villages with populations of several hundred people or more, like the large communal *shabono* of the warring Shama-tari Yanomamö that can grow to have populations of up to 400 in response to the pressures of intervillage warfare (Chagnon 1983:79). Significantly, Ross points out that individual Jívaro villages of 150 years ago were larger, more like those of the Yanomamö (Ross 1980:49, 54–57; see also Hendricks 1993:54). A size estimate for such an archaeological nucleated settlement could be made using Smole's ratio of the total site area to site population for a representative highland Yanomamö *shabono*: a mean of about 100 square feet (9.29 m$^2$) of space per person (Smole 1976:66).

Archaeological examples of large, nucleated villages might include the large late Prehistoric western pueblos (A.D. 1275–1600), which could have housed several hundred people to over a thousand people (Adams 1989:106–107). The layout adopted by these large, aggregated pueblos of the late Prehistoric period also has certain defensive characteristics in common with the *shabono* of the Yanomamö:

> The new layout consists of enclosed, plaza-oriented villages. No outward doorways are visible; all are inward-focused toward the plaza. Access into the village from the outside is usually only through a narrow (1–2 m wide) break in the plaza enclosure, almost always on the east side. [Adams 1989:107]

In contrast to the temporary nucleation of Yanomamö and Jívaro villages, which rarely lasts longer than three or four years (Descola 1981:638), it seems that these large, enclosed pueblos, together with their satellite villages, were occupied for several centuries. Some pueblos that were established in the fourteenth or early fifteenth century were still occupied in the Protohistoric period and into the period of the establishment of Spanish missions after A.D. 1600 (Adams 1989:108). The relative stability of this settlement pattern can probably be explained by the fewer options available to Southwestern populations under conditions of population growth, environmental degradation, and warfare. Similar to the Kayenta Anasazi in the late thirteenth century, "the population was, then, 'pinned down' by its defensive posture and was unable to pursue a strategy of site movement every 15 or 20 years" (Haas 1989:507).

Warring tribesmen not only select defensive positions for relocating their villages, often in conjunction with allies, but they also space themselves with respect to their potential enemies. The clusters of villages making up a Jívaro neighborhood are spaced more than 20 km from other such neighborhoods, a day's walk or more apart (Figure 31). According to Ross, warfare results in the redistribution of these clusters of communities and in the creation of uninhabited territory between them. These unoccupied buffer zones, frequently about three days' travel in breadth, have been a common outcome of Jívaro warfare since

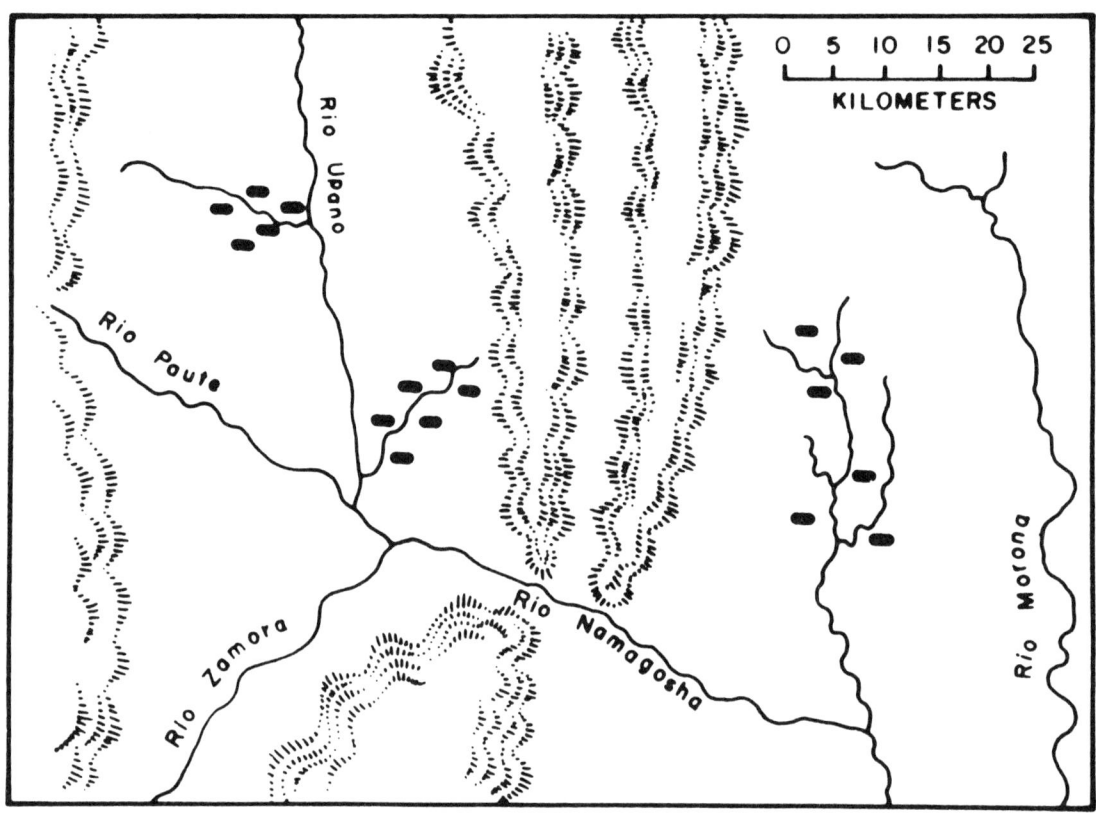

*Figure 31.* Regional distribution of three Jívaro neighborhoods in 1946 on the Namangosa River and its tributaries, Ecuador. [Reprinted by permission, from Meggers 1971: Fig. 11.]

at least the nineteenth century (Ross 1980:47, 53). Intervening mountain ranges or other natural barriers between some clusters of Jívaro villages help to further reduce contact—principally of a hostile nature—between them (Danielsson 1949:86). Yanomamö villages are generally a three or four days' walk apart; in those cases when villages are spaced more closely, the rugged terrain that separates them hinders intervillage travel (Chagnon 1979:93–94).

We have archaeological examples of such settlement spacings between the villages of neighboring tribesmen. While neighboring clusters of Tsegi phase (A.D. 1250) villages in the Long House Valley of northeast Arizona were located between approximately .5 and 1 km apart (Figure 30), a 15-km-wide stretch of unoccupied territory separated them from the nearest village in the Klethla Valley to the south and west. The development of this no-man's-land for the first time in the Tsegi phase, together with the evident lack of any visual communication across it, suggest that a strategic boundary was being observed by the inhabitants of the neighboring valleys at this time of heightened defensive considerations (Haas 1989:505, 1990:188–189; Upham and Reed 1989:157). A similar distance lay between the Peruvian Preceramic site of Ostra, whose defensive safeguards we saw earlier, and contemporaneous settlements. The closest contemporaneous settlements were located more than 12 km to the north in the Chao River valley, the source of any "likely attackers" (Topic 1989:222).

Vast buffer zones have been identified by archaeologists investigating prehistoric tribal societies in lower Central America and Amazonia. Warren DeBoer has outlined the sequence of unoccupied buffer zones, more than one hundred kilometers wide, that separated competing prehistoric groups, associated with their own ceramic complexes, who lived along the central and upper Ucayali River in eastern Peru from approximately the ninth century A.D. to the historic period (DeBoer 1981:373–375). Similarly, a clear ceramic boundary marked a likely buffer zone between the villages on the Gulf of Nicoya and competing societies in the Guanacaste region to the north on the Pacific Coast of Costa Rica during the period from A.D. 1200–1550, a time of apparent population immigration and territorial conflicts (Creamer and Haas 1985:748–749).

Finally, Jívaro and Yanomamö tribesmen often fortify their villages in anticipation of enemy raids. The external palisades erected by the inhabitants of Jívaro households and by other warring tribal villagers should leave detectable posthole patterns, like the pattern of closely-set upright posts that enclosed single-house sites, multiple-house sites, and parts of larger villages in

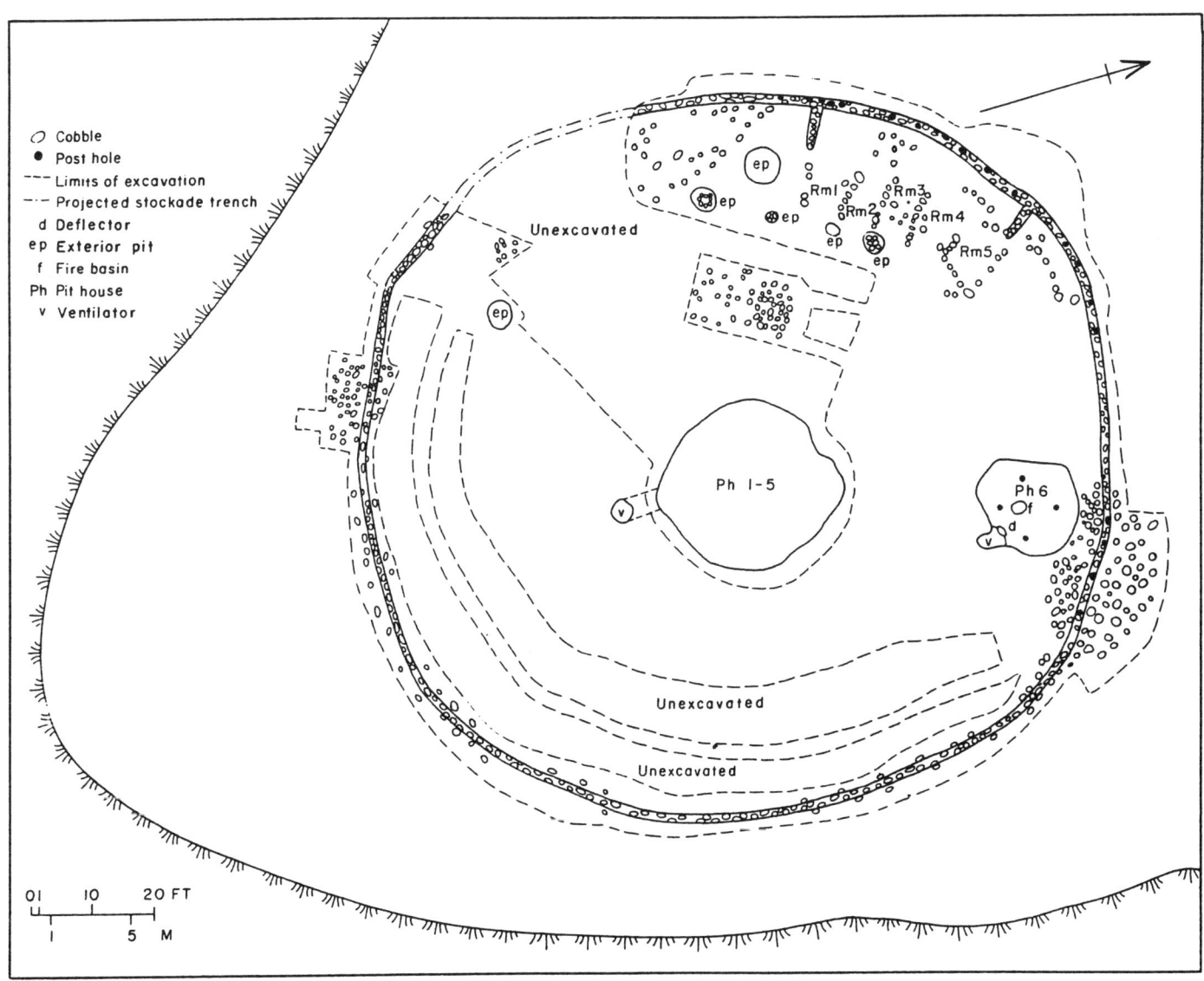

*Figure 32.* Plan of the fortified pit house site of Mascarenas (LA 4198) in the upper San Juan Basin of northwestern New Mexico, A.D. 900–1000. The oval-shaped ring of cobbles braced a stockade of wooden posts. [Redrawn from Eddy 1966: Fig. 33.]

the upper San Juan Basin of northwestern New Mexico between A.D. 900 and A.D. 1000, a time of peak warfare there (Eddy 1974:81). The single pit house site of Mascarenas, for example, was completely enclosed by an oval-shaped ring of cobbles, which upon excavation revealed a stockade of rotting wooden posts set into a one-foot-wide and one-foot-deep foundation trench braced with river cobbles (Figure 32). We have seen how this site also happened to be located on an elevated, second-level Pleistocene terrace overlooking the San Juan River and how it might have acted as a wartime refuge (Eddy 1966:255–257, 262).

Other kinds of archaeological defensive fortifications and community-level restrictions of access have been recognized in the American Southwest. Thirteenth-century Sand Canyon Pueblo in southwestern Colorado is perched at the head of a small canyon that drains into upper Sand Canyon, yet it was further fortified by a massive masonry wall into which masonry towers 4 to 5 meters tall had been appended at certain points along its length (Bradley 1992; Haas 1990:187). At least one Largo-Gallina phase tower site, situated on the isolated spur of a mesa in northwestern New Mexico, was sealed off by a thick masonry wall topped by a wooden stockade. This defensive wall incorporated outcrops, unit houses, and a tower in its construction (Mackey and Green 1979: Fig.2, 148–149). The focal site of Long House Pueblo in Long House Valley, northeast Arizona, featured a defensive wall across its only natural access, together with additional cross walls that served as "check points" along the two entry corridors. The focal site of Organ Rock Ruin, which as we saw earlier was defensively perched atop a cliff at the mouth of the Tsegi Canyon, can only be reached by a nearly vertical 10 m hand-and-toe climb through a narrow crack in the cliff face (Haas 1989:502, 1990:184).

A fortified settlement's bounded periphery should be further revealed by a change in the nature or in the distribution of utilitarian artifact densities that correspond to the different activities performed inside and outside the village palisade. The cleared strips surrounding some highland Yanomamö *shabono* are generally clear of village refuse except for a series of trash heaps, which are deposited in a few specific locations immediately outside the palisade (Smole 1976:68). This was precisely the pattern of trash disposal at the stockaded pit house village of Sandoval in the San Juan Basin, where three large mounds of trash were located outside the stockade and downwind to the southeast (Figure 33) (Eddy 1966:200).

Within villages, some housefloors might include evidence of additional defensive features such as the postmold patterns of interior walls and house towers (also associated with concentrations of rocks and other missiles), and subfloor tunnels and foxholes. Remains of such a partition were recovered inside a Valdivia 3 phase (2794–2668 B.C.) house at the site of Real Alto on the coast of Ecuador. A line of 14 postmolds in the front half of the house would have formed a screen between the doorway and the rest of the house (Zeidler 1984:282, Map 37). And excavations at the Largo-Gallina tower site of Bg 88, for example, revealed subfloor tunnels that connected pit houses to the centrally located defensive tower (Figure 34) (Mackey and Green 1979:149, Fig. 3). Should anyone question the defensive nature of such tunnels, I should add that on the floor of Bg 88B pit house lay the bodies of eleven victims, as I mentioned earlier, which supports the notion that warfare was prevalent here (Mackey and Green 1979:146–147).

*Post-war rituals*

The post-war rituals of tribes center upon the acquisition of head trophies and the public celebration of their victory. There are some obvious archaeological consequences of the head hunting practiced by the Jívaro, in the form of decapitated and/or scalped human remains. In keeping with their practice of killing and beheading as many of the inhabitants of the raided settlement as possible, we should recover headless burials, possibly of all ages and sexes (Karsten 1935:291). Such discrete, headless, but otherwise undisturbed burials were recovered at the late Preceramic (1400 B.C.) site of Asia on the central coast of Peru (Engel 1963). The bundle burial in Grave 23 in the center of the walled compound (Unit 1) was that of a strong, adult (probably male), whose flesh, skin, and hair were well preserved, and who lay in a flexed position, undisturbed, were it not for the fact that its head was missing. The body was accompanied by an animal-tooth pendant, two wooden spears, and a twined-reed sling tied around its abdomen (Figure 35). So too lay the adult in Grave 42, with the bones all in their normal position, but with the skull missing (Figure 36) (Engel 1963:69, 100–101, 110). That they represent beheaded individuals, as Engel (1963:69) referred to them, is supported by the contents of Grave 48, which consisted of an adult's skull with three additional vertebrae (Figure 37) (Engel 1963:115). The presence of the vertebrae is significant, for this is precisely the kind of evidence we would expect from the Jívaro headhunters' practice of cutting the heads of their victims as close to the trunk or the base of the neck as possible, which would include the cervical vertebrae (Karsten 1935:294; Up de Graff 1923:274, 277; Stirling 1938:55; Cotlow 1953:127, 147; Drown and Drown 1961:97; Zikmund and Hanzelka 1963:269). It is significant too, that other than the couple of headless burials and head trophies recovered at Asia, "no charred, split, or broken human bones were found" (Engel 1963:67), in keeping with the limited dismemberment of war victims practiced by South American tribesmen.

Among the burials in the Oneota cemetery in the central Illinois River were eleven decapitated skeletons. They lacked crania, and they had cutmarks on one or more of the upper cervical vertebrae, which constitute another unmistakable sign of head taking (Milner 1991:584, Fig.3). Similarly, the occurrence of cutmarks on cervical vertebrae at the mass burial site of Polacca Wash (A.D. 1580) in northeastern Arizona, which I will be describing in more detail, suggests that many if not most of the victims buried there were beheaded (Turner and Morris 1970:323). It is also possible that the multiple skull caps recovered in an exterior pit at the stockaded Sánchez site (A.D. 900–950) in New Mexico, a pit house village where an unusually large quantity of axes were found, represent decapitated raiding victims (Eddy 1966:173, 175). A final indication of decapitation is present in the human bone assemblage at the twelfth-century A.D. pueblo site of Mancos, where cutmarks produced by sawing, hacking, and slicing motions on the superior and anterior surface of clavicles were probably related to the removal of the platysma, sternocleidomastoid, and deltoid muscles during decapitation, which involved removing the head and the upper cervical vertebrae as a unit (White 1992:230–233, 236).

That males were more likely to be targeted and beheaded by a raiding party than other members of the population is suggested by the corresponding burial population. For example, Haas (1990) reports that of four burials excavated in Long House Valley of northeastern Arizona, two were females with no unusual features. The other two burials were males; "one had his head removed and placed beside him on the bedrock, while the second was missing his head altogether" (Haas 1990:186).

Taking the victims' scalps will also leave discernible marks on the victims' skulls. Grave 10 at the Peruvian Preceramic site

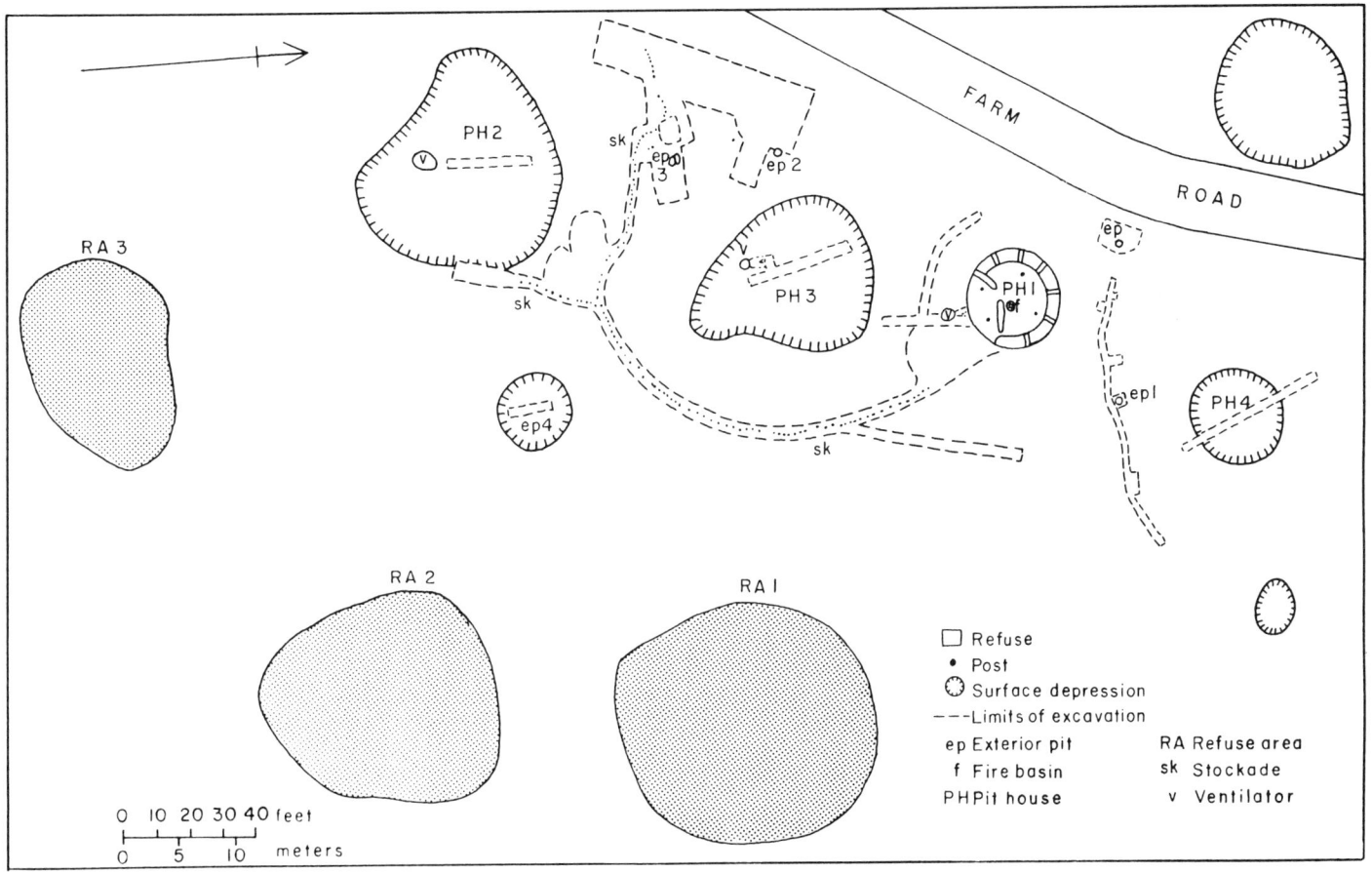

*Figure 33.* Plan of Sandoval pit house village site (LA 4131) in the upper San Juan Basin of northwestern New Mexico, A.D. 900–1000. The three large refuse areas were located outside the stockade and downwind. [Redrawn from Eddy 1966: Fig. 25.]

of Asia contained four skulls wrapped in mats and bound with braided rope and twisted-hair string (Figure 38). One skull, of an adult, featured the lateral cutmark across its forehead from having had the skin of the face removed (Engel 1963:47–48, 69, 94–95). The unmistakable marks of scalping are present on fourteen crania at the Norris Farm cemetery in the central Illinois River valley. These scalped crania have

> multiple more-or-less parallel transverse and oblique cut marks on the anterior, lateral, and posterior sides of the cranial vault. Usually the cuts are concentrated on the frontal bone (Figure 2). The typical scalping procedure apparently involved cuts across the forehead near the hairline followed by incisions along the side and across the back of the head above the ears. [Milner et al. 1991:584]

A number of mass burials in the American Southwest, including the slaughtered remains of victims recovered in two pit houses at the site of Sambrito Village in New Mexico, have skulls that exhibit cutmarks in the appropriate locations for scalping (Turner 1983:234, Table 2; Flinn et al. 1976:313). Of course, the Jívaro's practice of removing the entire headskin with a bamboo knife is likely to produce a different configuration of cutmarks on the victims' crania.

Since the taking of captives is limited to the occasional abduction of women and children, any evidence of captives in the archaeological record of tribes should center accordingly on the treatment of women and children. The mass burial site of Polacca Wash (A.D. 1580 ± 95) in northeastern Arizona has been interpreted as a place where a Hopi war party stopped on its way home from a raid on Awatobi to kill and dismember its captives. The site is located on the left bank of the Polacca Wash, some ten miles from the nearest habitation site. In keeping with a Hopi legend, which described the killing of an untold number of women and children taken captive in the attack against Awatobi in A.D. 1700, nearly half of the 30 mutilated individuals were subadults, and of the three adults whose sex is certain, at least two were females. The age and sex composition of the mass burial is not characteristic of any known Hopi special-purpose work party, and together with its isolated location, it is best explained by the legendary aftermath of the raid on Awatobi (Turner and Morris 1970:320–321, 329–330; Olson 1967:825). A similar age and sex composition is evident in the slaughtered remains of eleven individuals recovered on the floor of Pit House 1 at Burnt Mesa (A.D. 900–950) in northwestern New Mexico (Flinn et al. 1976:310). Although there is no sign that Pit House

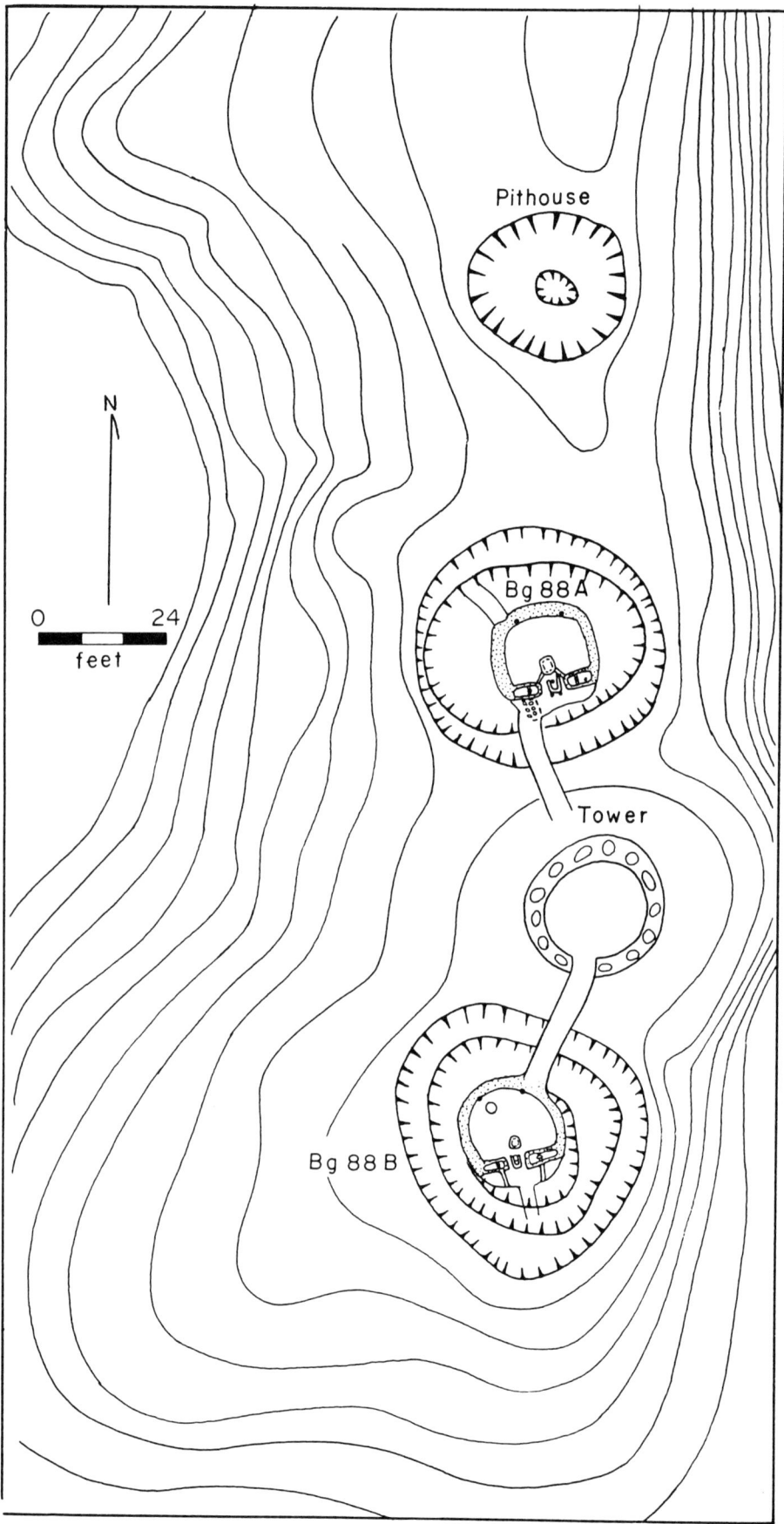

*Figure 34.* Plan of Largo-Gallina phase (A.D. 1100–1300) tower site of Bg 88, in the Llaves Quadrangle area of northwestern New Mexico. Subterranean tunnels connected pit houses Bg 88A and Bg 88B to the defensive tower in the center. [Redrawn from Mackey and Green 1979: Fig. 3.]

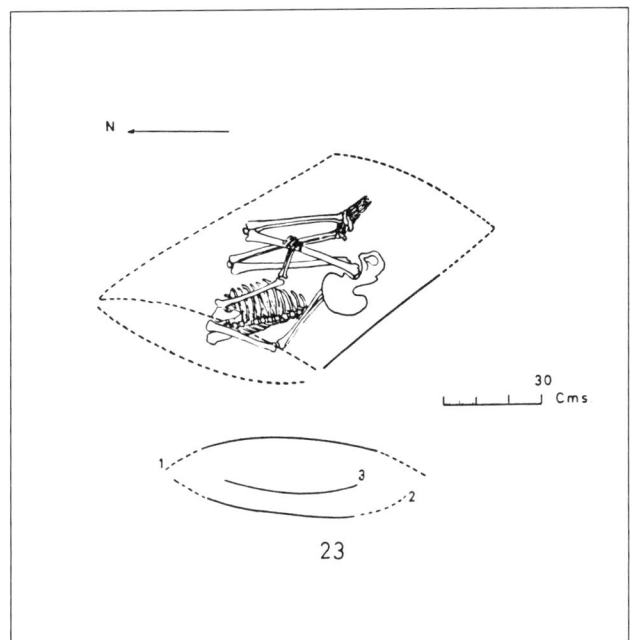

*Figure 35.* The adult individual buried in Grave 23 at the late Preceramic site of Asia, Peru, lay undisturbed in a flexed position, accompanied by offerings. Only the skull was missing. [Reprinted by permission, from Engel 1963: Fig. 222.]

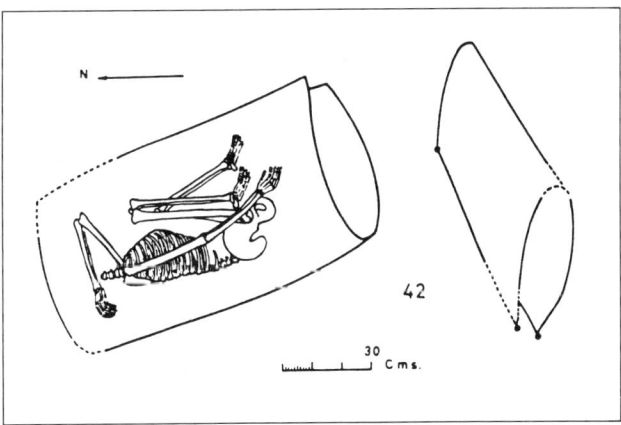

*Figure 36.* The adult individual buried in a flexed position in Grave 42 at the late Preceramic site of Asia, Peru, like the individual in Grave 23, lacked a skull and had been beheaded. [Reprinted by permission, from Engel 1963: Fig. 245.]

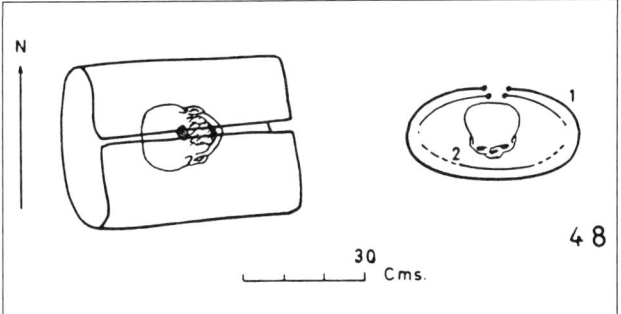

*Figure 37.* Grave 48 at the site of Asia, Peru, consisted of one adult skull to which three cervical vertebrae were still attached. This would be in keeping with the Jívaro practice of beheading war victims as close to the base of the neck as possible. [Reprinted by permission, from Engel 1963: Fig. 257.]

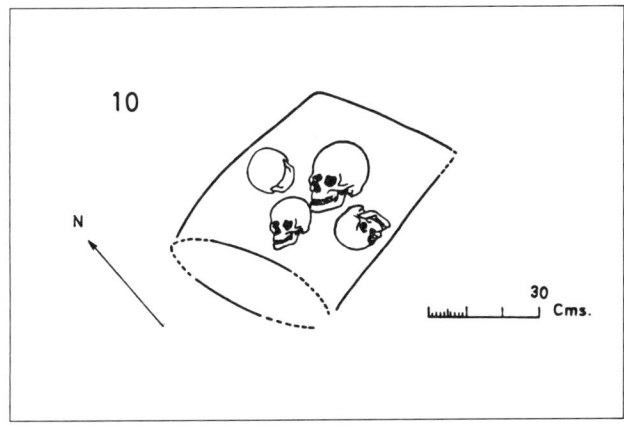

*Figure 38.* One of the four skulls wrapped in mats tied with string made from twisted human hair in Grave 10 at the site of Asia, Peru, featured unmistakable signs of having been scalped. [Reprinted by permission, from Engel 1963: Fig. 213.]

1 was burned or intentionally destroyed, its striking similarities with the mutilated human remains at Sambrito Village and at Polacca Wash suggest that it too represents the post-war slaughter of victims, and possibly, of captives (Flinn et al. 1976:309–310, 315, 317).

The trophy-processing camps pitched by victorious Jívaro war parties along watercourses on their way home from war should, like the site of Polacca Wash, be located on a watercourse, near but not on the trail home from enemy territory. Such a location would be in keeping with the need for water and the need to remain out of sight (Turner and Morris 1970:330). Trophy-processing camps should exhibit large hearths, and the clam-shell knives, stone axes, conical cooking jars, heated stones, and charcoal that are used to skin and prepare the head trophies (Figures 9, 39). The use of clam shells for severing heads is clearly depicted on a Nasca 7 vessel in the Amano Museum in Lima (Proulx 1989: Fig. 9). These special-purpose camps might also yield the victims' skulls, since after being skinned, the skulls are often discarded at the trophy-processing camp (Up de Graff 1923:280, 287; Cotlow 1953:147).

Back home, signs of their victory feasts—similar in many ways to those of their pre-war feasts—should be recovered in the village clearing or special victory house. We would expect to recover lots of jars for manioc beer and *natéma,* and lots of drinking cups (like the Jívaro's *pinínga* bowls), which generally contain one liter. However, tiny elaborately painted *pinínga* cups, which hold less than one liter, are used by the principals

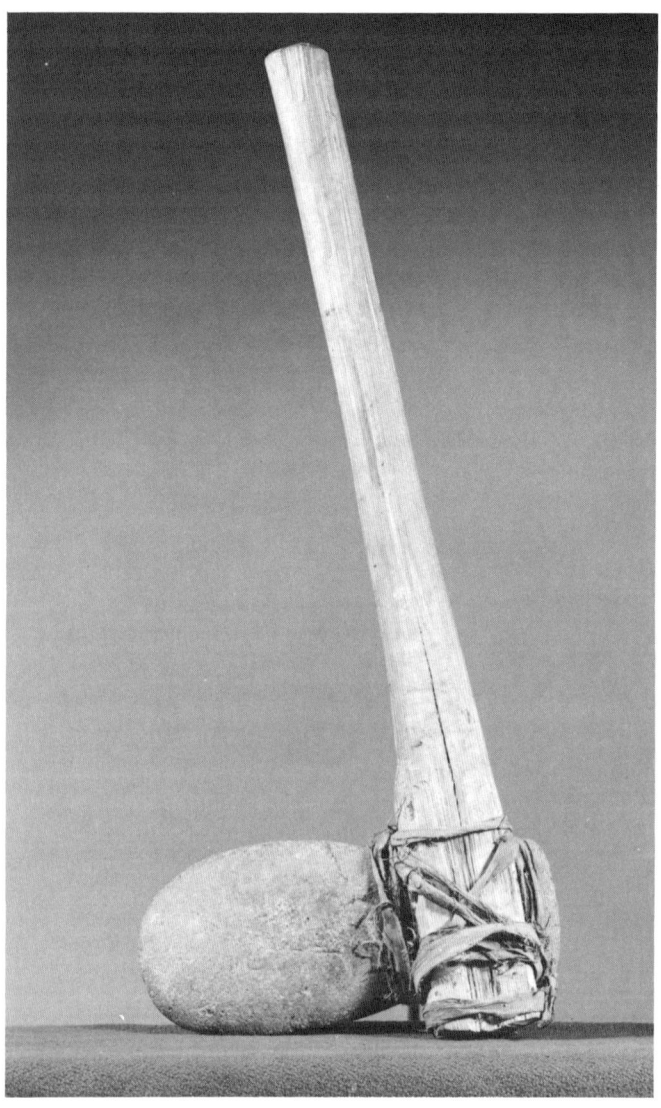

Figure 39. Hafted stone ax from Muratos, Río Pastaza, eastern Peru. [By Rota (1956), Neg. #124791. Courtesy of the American Museum of Natural History.]

at these feasts for drinking manioc beer and *natéma* (Karsten 1935:100, 103, 318, 345, Plate XX 3–4; Stirling 1938:95). We should also recover the remains of the meat and fish consumed at these feasts (Karsten 1935:319).

The victory feasts center on the final preparation of the trophy heads and the killer's emergence from a period of ritual observances. Accordingly, we should recover the clay cylinder seals like those that are used by the Jívaro to paint the killer's body with *Genipa* paint, and the special vessels like the tiny composite silhouette pots that contain the green tobacco water, the *Ilex* tea, and the hallucinogenic *Datura* juice that the killer takes throughout the victory feasts (Karsten 1935:100–101, 103, 243, 310, 318, 344, Plate XVIII 1–2). These special-purpose composite silhouette vessels were the least common vessel type in Tsamirku's house and their use was restricted to the

hearth in the men's half of the house (Zeidler 1984:356–359; Harner 1972:66).

Finally, can we expect to recover the human trophies that are prepared and paraded by their takers at the victory celebrations? In addition to the headless skeletons excavated at the Peruvian Preceramic site of Asia, four graves consisted only of skulls, adding up to three skulls of adults and three skulls of children, and constituting the earliest evidence of trophy heads (Engel 1963:67; Quilter 1991:414). Such possible trophy heads have been recovered at other Preceramic sites (Quilter 1989:85, 140). Moreover, one of the skulls in the cache of skulls that was Grave 10 had a hole suitable for being suspended by a rope, in the manner of mummified trophy heads from the Nasca, Acarí, and Ica valleys dating to the Early Horizon period (Engel 1969:69; Proulx 1971:16–18, 1989; Lumbreras 1974:47; Quilter 1989:78).

The individuals buried in cemeteries at the early farming villages of Cerro Mangote and Sitio Sierra (250–25 B.C.) in the Santa María River basin in Central Panama exhibited little status differentiation. The few funerary accompaniments that could be considered exotic included a set of stingray spines and a human skull or head trophy, both of which most likely attest to their possessors' participation in warfare and headhunting (Cooke 1984:285, 287; Cooke and Ranere 1989:310; Hansell 1987:120).

The North American tribesmen whose warfare I have considered also produced human war trophies. We have seen how the decapitated skeletons at the Norris Farm cemetery leave no doubt as to the practice of headtaking among the Oneota (Milner et al. 1991:584). The skull of an adult female from Polacca Wash featured a 25 mm diameter hole on the coronal suture, as did another skull fragment, the function of which is not clear. Olson's remark that the holes appear to be mechanical, and that they were probably made after death, suggests that they may have been intended for carrying or hanging the individuals' heads by a rope (Turner and Morris 1970:326–327). A bone pendant recovered in a midden at the stockaded pit house Sandoval village on the San Juan River in New Mexico was a human phalange that had been drilled through one end for suspension but otherwise unmodified. It was found near a burial, and may have been a funerary offering (Eddy 1966:207). The practice of headhunting clearly has a long prehistoric tradition and a widespread distribution among tribal societies. The archaeological picture of Oneota warfare is representative of tribal warfare, including the taking of human trophies:

> internecine conflict resulting in a gradual attrition of community members was a pervasive element of everyday life. Few individuals were killed in any single action, and these people were often vulnerable to surprise attacks because they were physically disabled or were exposed in locations far from the main settlement. Bodies were often mutilated to obtain status-enhancing trophies. [Milner et al. 1991:594]

Those warriors who achieve the status of great warriors by means of their reputation as killers, headtakers, and victory feast hosts, should be archaeologically discernible in two ways: (1) as hosts, their houses would serve as the loci of the victory feasts, and should be associated with the attendant archaeological remains; and (2) they would be accorded special funerary rites, which we will turn to next.

*Mortuary treatment*

Tribes show a tremendous concern for returning wounded and dead warriors home from war, and for the most part, the victims of a raid will be accorded the same funerary treatment as others of their age and sex. Nevertheless, I would not expect the funerary treatment of Jívaro and Yanomamö warriors to be easily detectable in the archaeological record. We have seen how dead Yanomamö warriors—and other members of the tribe—are cremated on rectangular funeral pyres of split logs erected in the village clearing and how their charred bones are pulverized and ritually consumed, a practice which bodes ill for archaeologists and human osteologists (Smole 1976:214). As a matter of fact, the absence of burials at some prehistoric sites in lowland South America has been attributed occasionally to the aboriginal practice of cremation. For example, Evans and Meggers attribute the lack of any burial remains at Taruma phase sites of the contact period along the upper Essequibo River in Guyana to the ethnographically documented practice of cremation among the Taruma Indians (Evans and Meggers 1960:244). Similarly, the absence of burial remains at Santarém along the lower Amazon River has been attributed to the known practice of ritual endocannibalism among the Tapajós Indians of this area; according to Willey (1971:416), the ornately modeled, pedestaled ceramic vessels of the Santarém style were probably intended for use in such mourning ceremonies.

In the case of the Jívaro, however, the mortuary treatment accorded to dead tribesmen, including warriors, will produce discrete burials, including some headless burials like those at the Peruvian site of Asia, and some burials with a human trophy or two. In general, warriors and raiding victims will be granted a subfloor or scaffold burial according to their age and sex, with little evidence of status differentiation. For the most part, we would expect to find relatively complete (with the exception of some decapitated) primary burials. We would not expect to find the fragmentary, disarticulated remains of butchered or cannibalized victims, an expectation supported by the discrete burials at Asia (Engel 1963:67).

While the chronic nature of tribal warfare will contribute a steady supply of war victims to the burial population, the low casualty rate that is characteristic of tribal raids will produce relatively few victims buried at any given time. Consequently, we would expect to recover a range of burials in houses throughout a village, or dispersed throughout a village cemetery. We would expect to recover multiple burials of related victims killed in a single raid, be they of the same sex, of both sexes, or of different ages. However, we would not expect to find mass burials. At the Oneota cemetery, for example, where war victims were buried throughout the village cemetery, and where each burial pit contained the remains of usually one, and up to five individuals, "there were no instances of mass burials in single features indicative of the expedient interment of numerous people who died simultaneously" (Milner et al. 1991:588).

In tribal societies, all males are warriors, hence their archaeological identification in a burial population should be relatively straightforward. In accordance with the Jívaro saying "I was born to die fighting" (Harner 1972:170), we saw earlier how males in tribal societies tend to die young (Chase 1976, 1978). Due to the possibility that the bodies of warriors can not always be retrieved and brought home for burial, however, or that they might be accorded special burial treatment elsewhere, there may be lower frequencies of males of fighting age in the corresponding burial population (Chase 1978:31; Haas 1990:178). The 50 burials recovered by the Rainbow Bridge Monument Valley Expedition at a mid-thirteenth-century defensive focal village (RB 568) near Kayenta, Arizona, in the 1930s make up the largest scientifically excavated burial population from the Kayenta region (Crotty 1983:26; Haas 1990:186). Of 42 whole or partial skeletons were the remains of one possible young adult male (17–30 years) and five older adult males (over 30 years) (Berry 1983: Fig. 57, 68). The near absence of young males of fighting age in this large burial population is a likely consequence of their participation in war parties. Moreover, it is a phenomenon that occurs in the burial populations associated with other contemporaneous large pueblos in the Southwest as well (Berry 1983:67). The Oneota cemetery at Norris Farm in the central Illinois Valley also contained more adult females than males (Milner et al. 1991:583, 594).

Dead warriors will also exhibit additional signs of violent injuries more often than other members of the population. They will often be buried with their weapons. The funerary accompaniments of a number of the interments at Asia included weapons: wooden spears and spearthrowers, cane quivers, quartzite and obsidian projectile points (Engel 1963:55–58, 79). Moreover, a cache of weapons had been dug into the grave of an adult (male?) with short hair, who was buried with a quartzite point (Engel 1963:90, Fig. 203, 98). This cache (Pit 16) contained one wooden spear, two spearthrowers, two harpoon foreshafts, a cane quiver with wooden implements and three sticks, eight additional wooden tools, and an obsidian projectile point (Engel 1963:118) (Figure 40).

The only likely archaeological differentiation among dead warriors will be the aforementioned great warriors, who in Jívaro society are accorded protracted above-ground mourning ceremonies before being buried in a central position of their house, after which their houses are abandoned. Thus, distinguished warriors will be reinterred as secondary burials in a central position of their houses after a temporary period of seated burial above ground. Moreover, their burial will coincide with the abandonment of their houses. Such a practice seems to be evident at the Preceramic village site of Paloma (5000–2500 B.C.) in the Chilca Valley on the Peruvian coast. Most of the burials recovered at Paloma were interred in houses, and in all cases the burial in the center of the house was that of an adult male. The best-preserved

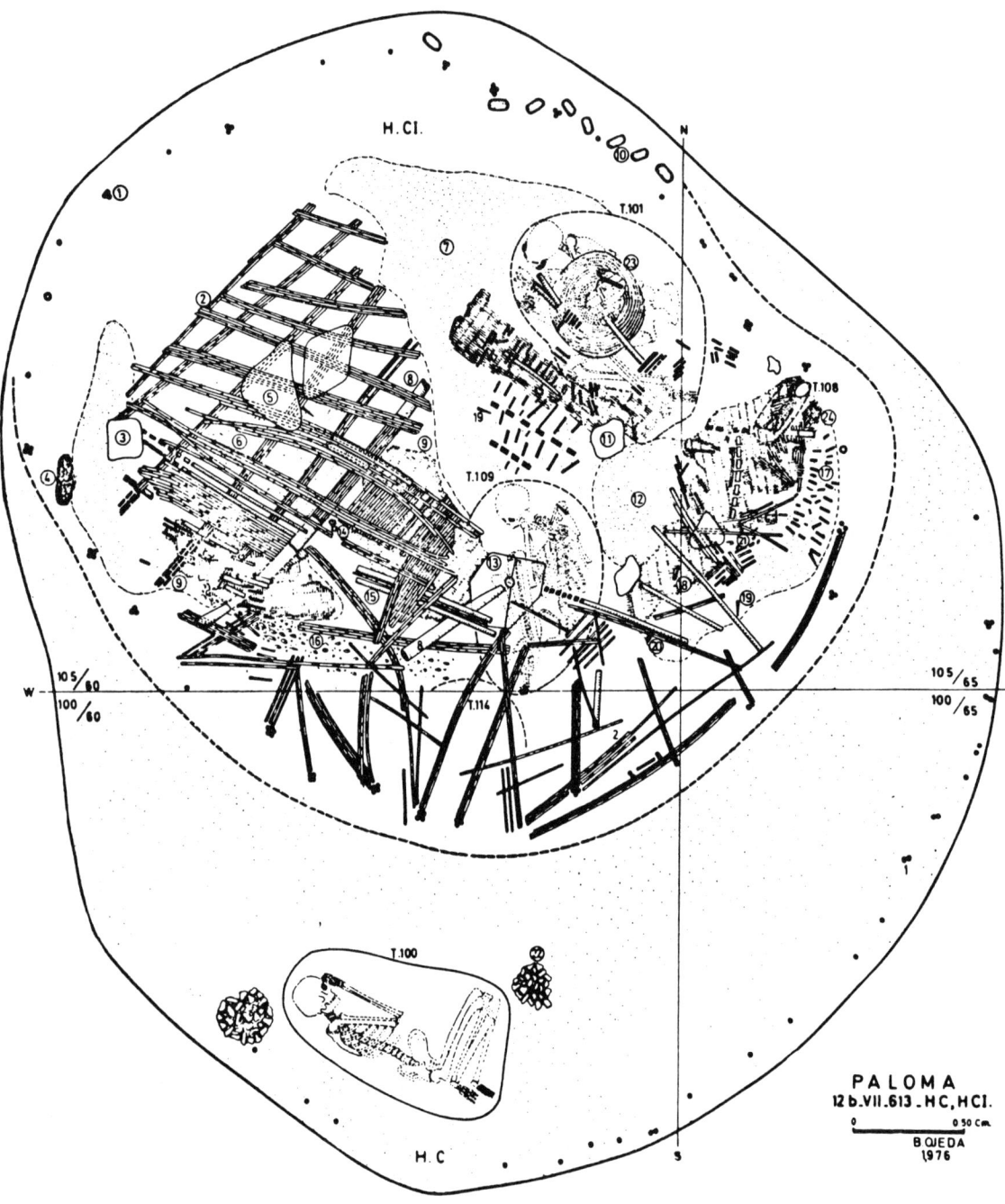

*Figure 41.* Plan of House C1 at the Preceramic village site (5000–2500 B.C.) of Paloma in the Chilca Valley, Peru. Three burials were interred below the floor of the house, including adult male Burial 109 in the center, and an adult male in Burial 101, whose skull lay just below the floor of the house. House C1 was deliberately burned down at the time of abandonment. [Reprinted by permission, from Engel 1980: Fig. 25.]

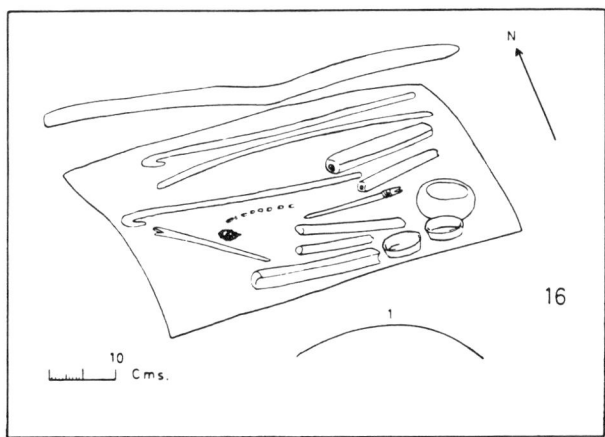

*Figure 40.* A cache of weapons, including spearthrowers, foreshafts, a spear, a quiver containing wooden implements, and an obsidian projectile point were recovered in Pit 16, an intrusive pit in the grave of an adult at the Preceramic site of Asia, Peru. [Reprinted by permission, from Engel 1963: Fig. 264.]

house at Paloma was House C1 (100/101) (Figure 41). Several individuals were buried here, including Burial 109 (an adult male) in its center and Burial 101 (an adult male, whose skull was found almost poking out above the floor). The fact that Burial 101 had been forced into a flexed position and jammed into this shallow pit may have resulted from its reinterment after a formal lying-in-state period, in the manner of distinguished Jívaro warriors. After his burial the house was deliberately burned and abandoned. The house's posts had been set on fire at their bases, the walls deliberately collapsed, and a large grinding stone placed on top of the rubble (Engel 1980:110; Quilter 1989: x, 26–27, 54–56).

# Chapter 6

# The Archaeology of Chiefly Warfare

The expansionist warfare waged by militaristic chiefdoms like those of the Cauca Valley, the Sierra Nevada de Santa Marta, and Panama should be manifested regionally by the growth of chiefly polities and their territories. Over time, the regional settlement pattern should witness changes in the settlement-size hierarchy and in the boundaries of expanding chiefly polities as they seize territory and exert their dominion therein (Renfrew 1973, 1982:3–4; Peebles and Kus 1977:431–432, 440–441). The consequent changes in regional and interregional alliances among neighboring chiefdoms should be evident in the regional distribution of chiefly items or prestige goods, which as we saw earlier are used by chiefs to cement alliances (Spencer 1982:59–60, 152–154, 184–187, 194–195; Redmond 1983:74–81; Roosevelt 1987:155).

### Preparations for War

Since chiefs oversee the mobilization and provisioning of their warriors, we would expect to find remains of storehouses at the chiefly centers, where provisions and armament are stockpiled. Located in the chiefly precinct, such storehouses should include facilities and containers for storing food and water, weapons, and the remains of other war provisions. There are several kinds of structures that have been identified as storehouses at the protohistoric Tairona regional center of Buritaca 200 (or Ciudad Perdida) in the upper Buritaca River valley of the Sierra Nevada de Santa Marta, Colombia. These structures tend to be associated with elite residences and temples, and the ones that have been excavated have produced abundant ceramic containers and stone tools (Castaño 1987:238–239). There are at least four such storehouses at Buritaca 200, according to Serje (1987:93). Moreover, at least two large rectangular structures in the center's hub that have sunken floors might have served as storehouses for food (Castaño 1987:238; Serje 1987:93).

Other archaeological examples of chiefly storehouses come from regional centers in other areas of the New World. Late in the occupation of Real Alto, Ecuador (ca. 2000–1500 B.C.), by which time the site became a regional chiefly center, a series of small circular structures and regularly spaced bell-shaped storage pits were in use on ridges overlooking the center's northern plaza. Zeidler (1984:53, 635–636) has suggested that the circular structures served a special function as communal storage facilities, and that others like them might be found on a similarly shaped ridge at the plaza's southern end. The thirteenth and fourteenth century (A.D.) paramount center of Casas Grandes, in Chihuahua, Mexico, where many indicators of warfare occur, was equipped with a centrally located well. Designed to tap the region's water table at more than 14 m below the ground surface, this well supplied the inhabitants of Casas Grandes with a permanent and defensible supply of water (Minnis 1989; Ravesloot 1988:76; Di Peso 1974:356–359).

What specific evidence of a war chief's arsenal might we expect to recover? Another Tairona center that has been investigated in the Sierra Nevada de Santa Marta region is one known as El Pueblito. Practically all the monolithic stone axes and batons recovered by Mason excavations at this regional center were concentrated in three of the site's largest structures, along with axe heads, stone clubs, and sounding plaques (Mason 1931:66–67, 87, 97–98, 104, 171). Moreover, the material excavated from the large settlement of Gairaca in Santa Marta included a serrated stingray spine, which we know the Tairona used as arrowpoints (Mason 1931:232). Another archaeological stingray spine might be the one stylized on a Tairona gold lip plug, 5.6 cm long, which was probably worn by a warrior (Bray 1978:167[285]). Stingray spines and shark teeth were among the funerary accompaniments of burials at the site of Sitio Sierra (300 B.C.–A.D. 1520) in the Santa María River basin on the Pacific coast of Panama (Cooke and Ranere 1989:310). And as we shall see, stingray spines were found in bundles in many of the burials at Sitio Conte in the Coclé province of Panama, along with points made of stone, bone, shark teeth and sawfish spikes (Figure 64) (Lothrop 1937:97–99).

The most striking examples of amassed weapons, however, come from looted tombs in the Quimbaya area of the Central Cordillera of Colombia, including the Cauca Valley, which were described by Luis Arango C. in his memoirs (Arango C. 1924). Table 1 is a compilation of inventories of the perishable weapons, for the most part of palm wood, encountered by professional

TABLE 1
Inventories of Weapons Encountered in Tombs Looted in Hoya del Quindío, Colombia

| Source | Location | Contents | Bodies |
| --- | --- | --- | --- |
| I:43 | Cauca valley, a few leagues from Cartago. | More than 600 *lanzas de macana* | —* |
| I:160-161 | near El Espejo | Bundle of 30 *flechas de macana*, points | — |
| I:161 | La Cuchilla, above El Sabanzo | 320 *armas de macana*: lances, darts (*puñales*) | — |
| I:161 | near R. Pijao | More than 100 *lanzas de macana* | — |
| I:163 | Portugal (Hoya del Quindío) | More than 100 lances | 7 |
| I:168 | near Sevilla | Upright canoe containing 50 *lanzas de macana* | — |
| I:194 | near Caicedonia | Upright drum, 2 m long, containing 4 carved batons and many *lanzas de macana* | — |
| II:51 | Floodplains of Barragán R. | 180 *armas de macana*: lances, darts (*puñales*), and small palmwood ladders | 3 |
| II:52 | Barragán region | 2 canoes containing 300 *lanzas de macana* | 2 |
| II:155 | Hacienda de la Honda, a few km from El Zarzal, Cauca Valley | Pits with knives and daggers (*puñales*) of bone and marine shell, with holes for suspension | — |
| II:211 | Caicedonia region, near Pijao R. | More than 200 palmwood lances and 100 palmwood darts (*dardos*) | 1 |
| II:307 | at head of Buga | more than 400 *lanzas de macana*, many in good condition | 4 |

SOURCE: Arango C. 1924
*Number of individuals not known.

*guaqueros* in tombs in the Hoya del Quindío area of the Cauca Valley in the first quarter of this century. Although I do not mean to suggest that the hundreds of wooden spears, darts, and *macanas* associated with the dead buried in these shaft tombs represent stockpiled weapons, there are several points worth making about them here. First of all, the quantities of weapons recorded in these tombs are staggering, especially if we consider those cases where we have information about the number of individuals buried in the tomb, which range from one to, at most, seven. To take the tomb at Buga as an example, four bodies were encountered in the tomb, along with piles of more than 400 *lanzas de macana* in all (Table 1). Moreover, many of the weapons found in tombs like this one were in good condition, well polished and sharpened (Arango C. 1924, I:161, 163; II:51, 155, 307), and I would venture to add, unused. The ability to dispense 600 weapons on the occasion of an individual's burial certainly reflects the general availability of such weapons, and by extension, the practice of stockpiling armament.

### Arrow Poisons

This brings me to the arrow poisons known to have been used by some of the sixteenth-century chiefdoms of the Circum-Caribbean area, and to consider the archaeological correlates that might be associated with them. We have seen how chiefdoms in the northern Cauca Valley, in the Sierra Nevada de Santa Marta, and in eastern Panama and the Gulf of Urabá used poisoned arrows. The precise plant and animal components of this *mala hierba*, as the Spanish chroniclers repeatedly referred to it, its preparation, and its properties are examined here.

We saw earlier that poisoned arrows were reportedly used by some groups in the northern Cauca Valley. Presumably this was the same poison used to the north on the coast in the province of Cartagena, where Chief Macuriz of Bahaire gave Cieza de León the following information about this *mala yerba*:

Y díjome que por la costa del mar, junto á los árboles que llamamos manzanillos, cavaban debajo la tierra, y de las raíces de aquel pestífero árbol sacaban aquellas: las cuales queman en unas cazuelas de barro y hacen dellas una pasta, y buscan unas hormigas tan grandes como un escarabajo de los que se crían en España, negrísimas y muy malas. . . . Tambien buscan para hacer esta mala cosa unas arañas muy grandes, y asimismo le echan unos gusanos peludos, delgados, complidos como medio dedo. . . . Hácenla también con las alas del murciélago y la cabeza y cola de un pescado pequeño que hay en el mar, que ha por nombre peje tamborino, de muy gran ponzoña; y con sapos y colas de culebras, y unas manzanillas que parecen en el color y olor naturales de España. . . . Otras yerbas y raíces también le echan á esta yerba; y cuando la quieren hacer aderezan mucha lumbre en un llano desviado de sus casas ó aposentos, poniendo unas ollas; buscan alguna esclava ó india que ellos tengan en poco, y aquella india la cuece. [Cieza de León 1853:361–362]

It seems that this poison consisted principally of manchineel (*Hippomane mancinella*) roots that were cooked in large ceramic jars. Ants, spiders, and caterpillars were added to this poisonous brew. It could also be made with bat wings, parts of the *tamborino* fish, as well as with toads, snake tails and manchineel apples. Other plants and roots could also be added. The job of cooking this noxious brew and reducing it to a paste took place away from their settlements, over large fires, and was relegated to female slaves or other women of low status.

Some Panamanian chiefdoms were also reported to use poisoned arrows, most notably those in eastern Panama along the Caribbean coast. According to Oviedo y Valdés, it was a plant poison, derived from the many "mançanillos de aquellos, con que se haçe la hierva de los caribes flecheros, assi en el golpho de Urabá como en la costa del Darien é de Acla, y en muchas isletas de por allí" (Oviedo y Valdés 1853:143), probably the manchineel tree. Antonio de Herrera described a poison used by Indians in the Gulf of Urabá that was virtually identical to the poison reported above by Cieza de León; it was a concoction of cooked manchineel roots, toxic animal remains, including toads, and *mançanillas* (Herrera cited by Wassén 1934b:617–618). Finally, a 1607 *Relación* from Panama reported the use of large toads for their poison: "Hay muchos y muy grandes sapos; no muerden pero golpeados sudan por cima el cuero un çumo blanco como leche, que veuido o comido es mortal" (Descripción de Panamá 1908:158–159; Wassén 1934b:617). This source goes on to describe the poisonous fruit of the *mançanilla* and other deadly but unnamed *yervas*. There is no mention of using poisoned arrows in hunting; arrows and lances are listed instead as the principal weapons used by the Indians of Chepo, east of Panama City (Descripción de Panamá 1908:151, 216–217).

The Cuna Indians are known to have used poisoned darts. The precise poison they used is not known, but seeing how the range of dart-poison frogs, including members of the toxic *Phyllobates* genus, extends today into areas formerly occupied by the Cuna in Panama, it is possible that the Cuna used anuran poisons along with plant poisons. Moreover, the fact that anuran exudates are mentioned as the source of a snake's venom in Cuna Indian songs and picture writings makes it clear that the Cuna were aware of anuran poisons (Myers et al. 1978:341; Myers and Daly 1983; Stout 1948:260; Wassén 1934b:619).

The Tairona and neighboring groups in the Sierra Nevada de Santa Marta, who were great bowmen, also used a deadly arrow poison or *yerba*, which the earliest Spaniards to penetrate the region, beginning with Rodrigo de Colmenares in 1510, greatly feared (Simón 1891:7; Oviedo y Valdés 1852:353; Aguado 1916:57, 98, 102, 153–155). We have the eyewitness account of Oviedo y Valdés, who in 1514 ventured some three leagues inland from Santa Marta, and reported seeing many balls of pitch-black poison the consistency of wax ("muchas pelotas de hierba de color de çera pez") in a chief's storehouse, along with many bows and countless bundles of arrows (Oviedo y Valdés 1852:354). As often as Fray Pedro Simón mentioned poisoned arrows in his accounts of Spanish incursions into Tairona territory, he did not list any of the poison's ingredients; although he often mentioned the *hierba's* potency, he remarked that the poison used by the Tairona of the higher sierra, up the Don Diego River, was not as toxic (Simón 1892a:357, 1892b:206; see also Castellanos 1850:322).

Directly contradicting Simón was his fellow Franciscan, Fray Pedro de Aguado, who argued that the *hierba* produced by groups inland was no less poisonous than that used by warriors in the Santa Marta area (Aguado 1916:102, 154). Indeed, García de Lerma was warned by the inhabitants of the lower Buritaca River valley not to proceed inland to the territories of Posigueica and Buritaca for fear of the extremely poisonous, high-quality arrow poison used by their warlike inhabitants (Aguado 1916:97–98). Aguado stated that the arrow poison was prepared in different ways in the various provinces of the Nuevo Reino de Granada, and moreover, he stated with confidence that some of these native groups had developed another kind of *hierva* so strong that it caused the victim's flesh to rot, to turn blue and purple, to the point of exposing his bones (Aguado 1916:155; Aguado 1917:189).

Aguado's most detailed description of the arrow poison used by the sixteenth-century groups of Santa Marta and other provinces of the Nuevo Reino de Granada is found in his informative account of the Palenques or Patangoros, who inhabited the eastern slopes of the Cordillera Central, some nine leagues above the Magdalena River, where the Spanish settlement of Vitoria was founded (1557–1561) (see Kirchhoff 1948:339; Simón 1892b:123). Aguado cautioned that the arrow poison had been improperly designated *yerva* by the *conquistadores,* who mistook it for an herbal poison used by hunters in Spain, but that in reality the native arrow poison lacked any herbal ingredients at all (Aguado 1917:188–189, see also 492). The Patangoran arrow poison was prepared much like the "*mala yerba*" reported by Cieza de León (given earlier)—it also consisted of a blend of poisonous snakes, red ants, scorpions, caterpillars, large spiders, to which any available male testicles and female menstrual blood were added, and left to rot. Then, toads were gathered and left in a jar for several days, after which time they were taken one by one and spreadeagled over a jar. They were rubbed with sticks in order to trigger their poisonous exudate, which dripped into the jar. When enough toad poison had been collected in this fashion, it was added to the putrid blend, as was the milky sap of thorny, fruit-bearing trees or ceibas (Bombacaceae family). If the poison weakened over time, more of this milky ceiba or manchineel sap was added:

> En vn vaso o tinajuela hechan las culebras ponçoñosas que pueden aver y muy gran cantidad de unas hormigas bermejas que por su ponçoñosa picada son llamadas caribes, y muchos alacranes y gusanos ponçoñosos de los arriba referidos, y todas las arañas que pueden aver de vn genero que ay que son tan grandes como huevos y muy vellosas y bien ponçoñosas, y si tienen algunos conpañones de hombre los hechan alli con la sangre que a las mugeres les baxa en tiempos acostumbrados, y todo junto lo tienen en aquel vaso hasta que lo viuo se muere y todo junto se pudre y corrompe, y despues desto toman algunos sapos y tienenlos çiertos dias ençerrados en alguna vasija sin que coman cosa alguna, despues de los quales los sacan, y vno a vno los ponen ençima de una caçuela o tiesto, atado con quatro cordeles, de cada pierna el suyo, tirantes a quatro estacas, de suerte quel sapo quede en medio de la caçuela tirante sin que se pueda

menear de vna parte a otra, y alli una vieja le açota con vnas varillas hasta que le haze sudar, de suerte quel sudor cayga en la caçuela, y por esta orden van pasando todos los sapos que para este efeto tienen rrecogidos, y desque sea recogido el sudor de los sapos que les pareçio bastantes, juntanlo o hechanlo en el vaso, donde estan ya podridas las culebras y las demas savandijas, y alli le hechan la leche de vnas ceybas o arboles que ay espinosas, que llevan çierta frutilla de purgar, y lo rebuelven y menean todo junto, y con esta liga vntan las flechas y puyas causadoras de tanto daño. Y quando por el discurso del tiempo açierta esta yerva a estar feble hechanle vn poco de la leche de çeyvas e de mançanillas, y con aquesta solamente cobra su fuerça y vigor. [Aguado 1917:189–190]

Another similarity between the arrow poisons described by Cieza de León and Aguado, above, is the fact that the job of preparing the arrow poison was left to women, in the latter case to old women, the majority of whom were likely to succumb to the noxious fumes of the pitch-colored poison. Finally, Aguado reported ways to identify those arrows anointed with poison; telltale signs included stripes, grooves, or scaly surfaces near the point, as well the sizzling noise and smoke that escaped from the poisoned arrows when they were exposed to fire (Aguado 1917:51).

The Panamanian *Relación* and Aguado's account stand out for their mention of anuran poisons, a subject worthy of further discussion here because the use of anurans for their poisonous exudate might have some archaeological implications. Both sources report the extraction of the poisonous exudate of toads (*sapos*), which probably refer to members of the poisonous *Bufo* genus, who are known to possess pharmacologically active compounds, including cardiotoxins (Daly and Myers 1967: Table 1). There are scattered references in the ethnographic literature on South American Indians about the use of *Bufo* poison, most notably the observations of M. Roulin, who witnessed the seasonal collection of toads by the inhabitants of the Orinoco River floodplain in 1825. The toads were impaled and placed over fires. The poisonous exudate that the toads secreted in response to being heated was collected in vessels, into which the arrowpoints were dipped directly and then left to dry (M. Roulin cited by Vivante and Homero Palma 1966:82–83). The poison of the large *Bufo ictericus* was also reported to have been used by certain Amazonian groups in the late nineteenth century for its arrow poison (L. Filho 1878:39, cited by Vivante and Homero Palma 1966:87).

The toxic qualities of *Bufo marinus* must have been widely recognized, for soon after the toad's post-Columbian introduction to Europe, its venom was extracted by poisoners. In the early eighteenth century the toad's poison was also adopted by European military arsenals. It was mixed with saltpeter to make gunpowder and added to explosive shells; "presumbably, the military commanders believed that if the cannon did not kill their enemies, the toad toxins would" (Davis and Weil 1992:52).

Otherwise, the ethnographic literature on anuran poisons centers on frog poisons, which are still used by the Chocó Indians of western Colombia. Although the Chocó Indians tip darts with poison for hunting with their blowgun, they are still capable of "turning it occasionally on man" in warfare as well (Myers et al. 1978:311, 362). The small dart-poison frogs, as they are commonly known, belong to the family Dendrobatidae, and they are found today in South America and southern Central America. The most toxic dendrobatids are three species of *Phyllobates* that today are found west of the Andes in the Pacific drainage of Colombia, whose poison is collected by the Chocó of the San Juan and Saija Rivers. Their poison is considered to be the most potent of all animal poisons, against which no effective antidote is known; victims suffer muscle contractions, burning skin sensations, gagging, violent convulsions, respiratory difficulties, and cardiac failure (Myers and Daly 1983; Myers et al. 1978:339–340).

To collect the poison, the Chocó catch the tiny frogs and confine them in lidded baskets or in hollow cane tubes. A frog is impaled on a pointed stick, its forelegs tied with string and outstretched, and then is beaten on its back with the dart points. Sometimes the impaled frog is held near a fire. In response to these extremely stressful conditions the frog secretes a white froth, especially from its dorsal glands, which contains the poison. The dart or arrowpoints are rubbed over the frog's frothy back and then left to dry. One frog secretes enough poison to anoint what various sources report as two to three, twenty, thirty, and up to fifty points. At the end of the poison-collecting process the frog is returned to the container, to be used again at some later time, or simply discarded. It might well die, or surprisingly, it might hop away from this ordeal (Wassén 1957:85–87; Myers et al. 1978:343–344).

The possibility that arrows tipped with frog poison were used in the past by western Colombian groups, including the inhabitants of the Hoya del Quindío, in the Cauca Valley, was raised by Arango C. (1924), although he neglected to give the name of the particular group or groups who used the frog poison, nor did he list the source of his information. According to Arango C., the poison used to tip arrows for warfare and hunting came from the skin of frogs:

Los indios acostumbraban sacarle el pellejo a algunas ranas, estando vivo el animal, sacándole la piel por encima de la garganta; después de esta operación tan bárbara largaban el pobre animal para que se fuera a echar nueva piel para luego volverlo a desollar o para que procreara.... El pedazo de piel de la rana lo depositaban en un tarro donde quedaba el veneno, y quién sabe qué otro veneno le echaban; luego introducían las puntas de las flechas y éstas se envenenaban. [Arango C. 1924, I:160–161]

Accordingly, the use of anuran poisons by warring Circum–Caribbean chiefdoms in the sixteenth century and their modern descendants has some possible archaeological correlates for the prehistoric record of warring chiefdoms here. We might expect to find unusually high densities of anurans in the faunal assemblages of sites, and especially, in middens and storehouses at chiefly centers, where war provisions would have been stockpiled. The faunal remains recovered by Cooke at Period IV Sitio Sierra (300 B.C.–A.D. 1520) in central Panama included abundant anuran remains from housefloors and middens, the majority of which belonged to the toad *Bufo marinus*. Over 34% of the *Bufo* remains at Sitio Sierra came from a single refuse dump (ca. A.D. 65–500) that accumulated over a short period of time, perhaps from some short-lived event (Cooke 1989:130). Although Cooke argues convincingly that the breakage patterns exhibited by some of the *Bufo* bones represent the butchering of *Bufo* for food, we cannot rule out the possibility that they might have been procured for their poison as well (Linares 1977:25–27). Skinning of the toad and removing its poisonous exudate also renders it useful as food (Cooke 1989:127, 129). Anuran remains also appear in small quantities in the faunal assemblage of the ridgetop site of Cerro Brujo, in Bocas del Toro, Panama (A.D. 900), where as we shall see other possible war provisions were recovered, as well as at other central Panamanian sites (Wing 1980:199; Cooke and Ranere 1989:300–301). *Bufo marinus* remains are also among the faunal remains from Herramientas (A.D. 1200–1500) on Chira Island in the Gulf of Nicoya, Costa Rica (Creamer 1983:400–401).

The disarticulated remains of *Bufo marinus* turned up in surprising quantities in the faunal assemblage at the Olmec center of San Lorenzo, Mexico, and constituted almost 10% of the site's total faunal remains. The high incidence of skull and pelvic remains of *Bufo* recovered in San Lorenzo phase (1150–900 B.C.) deposits supports Cooke's analysis of the likely butchering units produced by decapitating and skinning the animal, and compares with the body parts recovered at the Panamanian site of Sitio Sierra. Unlike the other faunal species that were abundant at San Lorenzo, which were distributed more or less uniformly throughout the site, the disarticulated *Bufo* remains were concentrated in only eight stratigraphic levels at San Lorenzo. This distribution pattern is also reminiscent of the stratigraphic context of *Bufo* remains at Sitio Sierra, where *Bufo* seem to have been processed in large numbers quickly, over a short period of time (Cooke 1989:130–132). Coe and Diehl suggest that toads were periodically used at San Lorenzo in large quantities, most likely for their pharmacological properties, including their poison (Coe and Diehl 1980:378–379, 383, 390). *Bufo marinus*'s toxic properties have been reviewed recently (Davis and Weil 1992), including the violent physiological effects of bufotenine, which produces nausea, cardiovascular dysfunction, and a purpling of the victim's skin color. On this basis Davis and Weil rule out its use as a ritual hallucinogen by the Olmec (Davis and Weil 1992:53–54). Other archaeological indicators of chiefly warfare were recovered at San Lorenzo, and they will be discussed later.

In addition to the discarded remains of poisonous anurans, we would expect to recover the ceramic containers that held their poison, which would have been amassed in storehouses along with other war provisions. Peter Furst mentions small effigy bowls from the Maya area that represent toads with prominent poison glands, which he suggests could have been used to hold toad poison (Furst 1974:154). He is referring, no doubt, to the small effigy "toad" bowls from Preclassic contexts at Kaminaljuyú and Chalchuapa (Dobkin de Rios 1974:149–150; Shook and Kidder 1952:91, Figs. 35, 70b-d; Sharer 1978:34, Fig. 15h6–8). Their modeled appliqué representations of anurans feature prominent bosses that are considered to represent the poison glands of a common Middle American species of toad. They are shallow bowls with rim diameters of between 15 and 41 cm, with average rim diameters of 25 cm and 34.8 cm from Chalchuapa and Kaminaljuyú respectively (Shook and Kidder 1952:9; Sharer 1978:34). We would expect to find large numbers of such containers of poison in storehouses at chiefly centers, as part of a warring chief's arsenal.

Finally, the use of anurans by northern South American societies might also be rendered iconographically in other forms. For example, gold ornaments from this area frequently portray batrachian figures, with more frog attributes than toad attributes (Bray 1978:168–169, 195, 209; Cooke and Bray 1985:37–38). The metallurgical depiction of frogs is a subject treated at length by Wassén (1934a). In the case of the seven such ornaments recovered by Mason in his excavations at the sites of Gairaca and Pueblito in the Tairona area, however, he presumed that they represented the toad rather than the frog, "for the former is common in this region, grows to a large size and is venerated to some extent by the modern Arhuaco Indians" (Mason 1931:259). My own hopes of identifying the gold anurans zoologically were dashed by Charles Myers, who thinks the gold portrayals are only stylized renditions of frogs, and not identifiable taxonomically (Myers, pers. comm.).

## Pre-War Rituals

In contrast to the public pre-war rituals celebrated by warring tribesmen, the pre-war rituals of the Circum-Caribbean chiefdoms were performed by the chiefs of a military alliance and other members of the chiefly elite in the inner sanctum of the paramount chief's precinct. Here they planned their common war stratagems with the help of sacrificial bloodletting acts and divinations before cult figures. Consequently, any archaeological evidence of their rituals, feasts, and associated activities, including war games, should occur in chiefly precincts and sanctuaries.

Lothrop (1937:296) and Cooke (1984:289) have suggested that the basalt-column-enclosed ceremonial precincts at the Period V (A.D. 500–700) Panamanian sites of El Caño and Sitio Conte, with their associated stone human and animal idols, and stone altars or stools (Figure 42), could have been the site of chiefly war councils and pre-war rituals. Rows of stone columns, some up to six meters long, and many of them bearing carved human and animal figures, may have lined a 150,000-square-foot (13,950 m$^2$) area. The columns were paired with flat-topped "altar" stones, which may have been sitting places for those who gathered here (Cooke 1984:289; Verrill 1927:54–56; Lothrop 1937:31, 295–296). While Lothrop based his suggestion as to the function of the ceremonial precinct at Sitio Conte on ethnographic analogy of outdoor meeting grounds throughout the Americas, Cooke's point of departure for this interpretation is the scenes of ceremonial life that appear on certain Period IV (300 B.C.–A.D. 500) Tonosí trichrome ceramic vessels from central Pan-

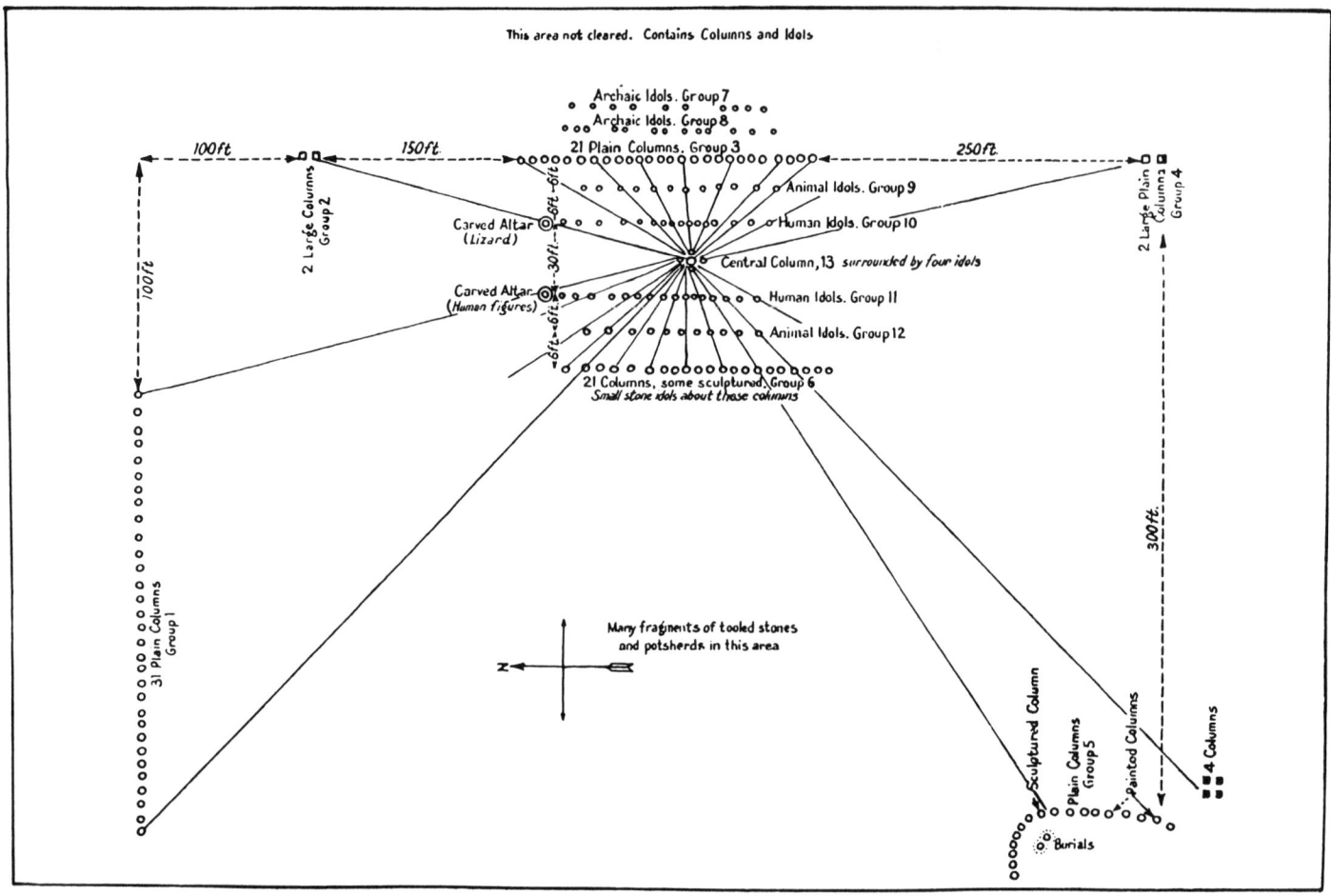

*Figure 42.* Plan of the ceremonial precinct at the Period V (A.D. 500–700) site of El Caño, Coclé, Panama. The precinct was lined with basalt columns, some of which had been carved in the form of human and animal figures. [Reprinted by permission, from *Coclé: An Archaeological Study of Central Panama* (Lothrop 1937: Fig. 16). Peabody Museum.]

ama. Several vessels depict teams of two to four men lugging heavy columns, possibly to erect such a ceremonial precinct, and perhaps like the collective work parties still convened by the Guaymí, which involve opposing teams who assemble to carry out some communal project and to drink *chicha* (Young and Bort 1976:81–83, 87). Some of these trunk-lugging scenes include secondary figures who hold bowls of *chicha,* clubs, and lances or digging sticks. Then there are scenes of men wielding sticks or spears, perhaps warriors playing a game not unlike the *balsería* or *krun* (stick-throwing) game played by the traditional Guaymí (Cooke 1984:289, 1985:34–37; Ichon 1980: 138–140, Fig. 41, Pl. XXVIII, XXIX, LXV).

Since one of the ritual activities celebrated at chiefly feasts in sixteenth-century Panama was a game that Gaspar de Espinosa (1864:470) described as "se jugaron á las cañas," which could mean "playing with sticks," or "aiming at shinbones," or "bluffing," it is worth describing the traditional stick-throwing game of the Guaymí. Until the 1960s, the *balsería* game formed the centerpiece of four-day-long feasts that drew thousands of Guaymí from large regions, up to four days of travel away. The game involved teams of eight men throwing sticks five to six feet long—the earlier sources say pointed sticks, while more recent descriptions of the game say the players threw sticks with rounded or leaf-wrapped ends—at their opponents. Four opposing pairs of players stood approximately ten feet apart on either side of the rack that held the *balsa* sticks. Each player took a turn throwing four sticks at his paired opponent's lower legs, who with his back turned to his opponent, had to bravely anticipate and dodge the sticks thrown at him. With breaks for drinking *chicha,* which the Guaymí claim gives them strength, the *balsería* game would last all day, followed by more feasting (Johnson 1948:250–251, Pl. 46–47; Young 1971:204–208, 1976:44–46, 50, Young and Bort 1976:82).

Although Espinosa did not describe the *cañas* game played at a Panamanian chiefly feast in any detail, Pascual de Andagoya and Cieza de León provided some details on the *cañas* game played after the feasting and much drinking at chiefly feasts in the Cauca Valley, which Andagoya noted were similar to those celebrated by the Cueva Indians (Andagoya 1865:75, 1945:436; Cieza de León 1853:375). Much like the *balsería* game of the traditional Guaymí, the sixteenth-century *cañas* game involved teams of thirty or more men who took their places and in turn rushed at their opponents with spearthrowers and darts (*varas*) and shields, "darting at each other like enemies, and in this way they continued skirmishing, sallying forth and retreating in skirmishing order, during the whole afternoon" (Andagoya 1865:75). It is possible, therefore, that some of the Tonosí trichrome vessels depict this jousting game that was played at chiefly feasts. The rectangular enclosure or building with its upright poles or columns that appears at the center of the scenes of two to four men lugging trunks on some Tonosí trichrome vessels might represent the rectangular rack of *balsas* that presides over the *balsería* court (Cooke 1984:289, 1985:34–37; Johnson 1948:250–251, Pl. 46–47). While the traditional Guaymí played the *balsería* game on a large, flat grassy field or *llano* of unspecified dimensions, the game could certainly have been played in the column-lined precincts at El Caño and Sitio Conte. In the wake of a traditional four-day *balsería*, the field was littered with corn husks, food scraps, and animal bones (Young 1971:207).

Stirling described a similarly enclosed ceremonial plaza at the site of Barriles (A.D. 400–800) in the Volcán Barú region of Chiriquí province in western Panama. It was a raised area, about 50 yards long and 30 yards wide, paved with massive stone slabs. This 1,254.19 m² plaza was delimited at its eastern end by a large boulder with carved petroglyphs and at its western end by a row of life-size stone statues on pedestals whose war-related attributes will be described later. The meter-high lidded urns recovered in some number here might have contained *chicha,* for consumption in the ritual feasts and games held here (Stirling 1950:234–243; Linares et al. 1975:141). Similarly, the two large rectangular structures located in the Tairona ceremonial center of Buritaca 200 might have been the site of chiefly war councils and pre-war rituals; numerous and elaborate offerings have been found in them (Serje 1987:93).

In the patio group of the highest-ranking individual at the Middle Formative village of La Coyotera, in Oaxaca, Mexico, Charles Spencer and I recovered evidence of chiefly rituals and associated activities. In this patio group that comprised the village chief's residence, ceremonial platform, and tomb, we recovered numerous obsidian blades (probably used for sacrificial bloodletting), figurines, a deer antler (for making music), red pigment and a paint palette (for body painting), and a lime-filled basin (for taking lime with tobacco) (Spencer 1982:112–114, 140–143; Spencer and Redmond 1983:71–72).

Evidence of feasting has also been recovered recently by Roosevelt at the Marajoara mound site of Teso dos Bichos, on Marajó Island, Brazil (A.D. 730–1110). Roosevelt excavated several pits and caches associated with earthen platforms that consisted of large fish bones, reconstructible, decorated ceramic vessels, and chipped stone. The massive specimens of baked or smoked fish included the 3-m long *pirarucu (Arapaima gigas)* and the *aruana (Osteoglossum bicirrhosum),* which today are fished by men with harpoons for special occasions. Remains of these large fish were not found in domestic contexts at the site. There the remains of small fish, which are caught in communal fish-kills today, predominated. The elaborately decorated ceramics included wide-rimmed (.5 to 1 m) vessels with large holding capacities for cooking and serving food for large numbers of people at one time. This Marajoara decorated pottery included pigment pots, snuffers and small drinking cups like those used by Amazonian Indians today for taking hallucinogenic infusions. Roosevelt suggests that these feasts were held for male work groups or on the occasion of male initiation rituals, to which I would add that they were probably also celebrated in preparation for warfare, which was apparently a regular phenomenon in Marajoara society (Roosevelt 1991:273–276, 325, 339, 370–372, 380, 401).

Finally, the sounding of conch-shell trumpets and drums was an important element in the war councils and associated pre-war rituals celebrated by the Circum-Caribbean chiefdoms. Therefore, we should expect to find remains of these musical instruments in association with chiefly precincts and storehouses, like the conch-shell trumpets recovered in the principal midden at the Bocas phase (A.D. 900) ridgetop hamlet of Cerro Brujo in western Panama (Figure 43) (Linares 1980a: Table 3, 144–145; Linares 1980b:63–64, 1980c:293). Conch-shell trumpets were used until recently by the Guaymí to summon players to the *balsería* or *krun* game and to dance and be merry at various events of the four-day gathering:

> people sang the old songs and danced around and stomped their feet on the *llano.* As they filled themselves with *chicha,* the din increased. The deep blasts of conch shells and cow horns mingled with the high-pitched tones of flutes of bone and wood and the clatter of gourd rattles. When the *krun* was held at Hato Culantro, the noise could be heard in Cascabel (a linear distance of only about three miles, but with intervening hills and valleys). [Young 1971:207, 1976:43–45]

The *Strombus* shell trumpet recovered at the base of the earliest mound erected in the ceremonial precinct of Real Alto (2900 B.C.) is another example; its association with the wattle-and-daub structure atop the mound, which served as a place for ceremonial gatherings, makes it the earliest example of a ceremonial "signifier" in South America (Marcos 1978:33, 531–532; Zeidler 1984:644). Actual shell trumpets and wooden drums have been reported from tombs looted in the Cauca Valley, which I shall discuss in a later section. The association of these musical instruments with the conduct of chiefly warfare is illustrated by the contents of a tomb in the vicinity of Caicedonia. Along with the many wooden lances (see Table 1), was a 2-m-long wooden drum, standing upright. Inside the drum was a crystal rock and four wooden batons, each 20 inches (50.8 cm) long with their heads encircled by incised lines, which were probably used to sound the drum (Arango C. 1924, I:194).

### Organization of War Parties

In the militaristic chiefdoms of the Intermediate Area, all able-bodied men were warriors. As part of Roosevelt's archaeological project on Marajó Island, David Greene examined Marajoara skeletal material in museum collections. His analysis of fifteen to seventeen individuals from Marajoara urn burials revealed that the majority were exceptionally robust males. Their average stature was 172 cm, and their bones had the well-developed muscle attachments characteristic of wrestlers on their upper arm and skull, suggesting that they were strong and athletic. Moreover, they did not show any of the pathologies such as osteoarthritis that are generally associated with a life of heavy agricultural labor (Roosevelt 1991:57–58, 388–395). Using Greene's results, Roosevelt suggests that males in Marajoara society participated

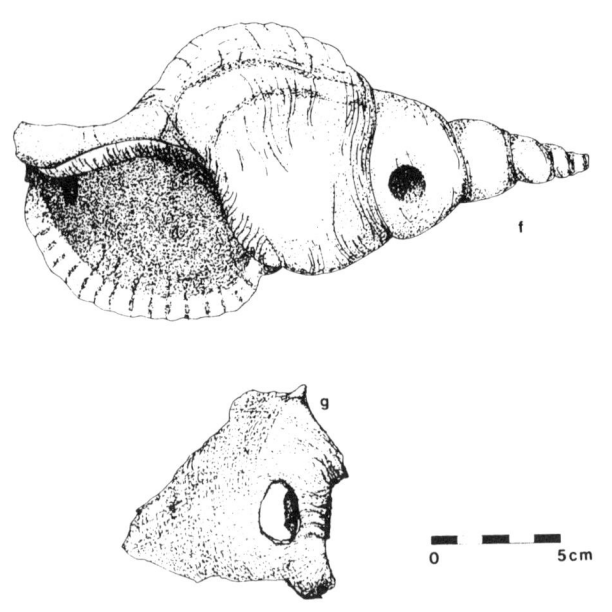

*Figure 43.* Conch-shell trumpets recovered at the site of Cerro Brujo (A.D. 900) in western Panama. [Reprinted by permission, from *Adaptive Radiations in Prehistoric Panama* (Linares and Ranere 1980: Fig. 9.0–3). Peabody Museum.]

in warfare on a regular basis, and that they were primarily warriors. Their athletic build and robustness might have been the result of their training for warfare, which today among Amazonian Indians includes wrestling, racing, and other war games and athletic contests. In view of the fact that these males were buried in large and elaborately decorated urns, they may represent an elite sector of Marajoara society, a "warrior elite" suggests Roosevelt (1991:406–407).

All men in the Circum-Caribbean chiefdoms sought the glory of dying as warriors in war (Castellanos 1850:342). Yet we have seen how warriors in the Circum-Caribbean chiefdoms were organized into a military hierarchy composed of fighting units led by military captains and their chiefly commanders. A warrior's rank was reflected in the accoutrements he donned for war: his haircut, face and body painting, and his array of gold and feather ornaments.

Their red (*Bixa*) and black (*Genipa,* charcoal, pitch) war-painting styles are depicted on human effigy vessels, like the effigy polychrome jars recovered in Graves 5, 24, and 26 at Sitio Conte in central Panama (Figures 44, 45, 46). The Panamanian warriors' practice of painting their faces and bodies with red and black for war and tattooing their faces and bodies—and those of their captives—obviously varied according to their social and military rank. Perhaps that variation is displayed on these human effigy polychrome vessels, of which no two are exactly alike. Many are painted in the manner specified by Oviedo y Valdés (1853:130, 138–139) with distinctive Conte-style designs (Lothrop 1942:110–111; Linares 1976:15–17; 1977:61–62). Evidently some of the individuals buried at Sitio Conte were associated with actual pottery stamps or seals used for body painting, which constitute tangible evidence of the role that body painting assumed in signaling an individual's social and military rank (Linares 1976:17).

Looted tombs in the Hoya del Quindío area of the Cauca Valley, Colombia, have also yielded ceramic figures of warriors, up to twenty in one tomb, with striped face and body-painting patterns, along with other warrior attributes (Arango C. 1924, I:43–44, II:321). And nearly all the human effigy vessels from Casas Grandes, in Chihuahua, Mexico, feature face painting; some of the human effigies also wear helmets, nose ornaments and other military attributes. Actual paint-grinding stones and palettes have been recovered at Casas Grandes too (Di Peso 1974:479–485). Finally, the possibility of recovering more direct evidence of the face and body paint prepared by the warring chiefdoms of northern South America is strengthened by the recovery of a *Bixa orellana* seed at the Ilama phase (720–160 B.C.) habitation site of El Topacio, on the upper Calima River, just west of the Cauca Valley (Bray et al. 1988:6).

We do not have to go far afield in the archaeological literature to find examples of the expected kinds of non-perishable insignia worn by sixteenth-century warring chiefs and their warriors. The corpus of gold objects from northern South America and lower Central America includes gold helmets, diadems, earrings, nose plugs, lip plugs, necklaces, breastplates, arm bands, leg bands, clubs, staffs, and double-spiraled badges that made up their heterogeneous war dress (Bray 1978:51, 163–168, 174–175, 189, 193–197, 209; Restrepo Tirado 1929:72–74). Some helmets from the Quimbaya area of the Cauca Valley (A.D. 400–1000) have a diameter of about 20 cm and two holes on each side for the attachment of a chin strap, attesting to their likely use (Bray 1978:127, 189; Falchetti 1987:6). The principal male individual buried in Grave 5 at Sitio Conte was wearing an elaborately decorated gold helmet along with a full array of gold ornaments (Lothrop 1937:133–135, 230–234). The additional military accoutrements recovered to date include the small gold disks, buttons, and star-shaped ornaments that studded the cloth standards carried to war, and actual litters, some consisting of palm-wood lances, and some sheathed in copper and gold plates like the ones that we know bore chiefs to and from battle (Bray 1978:127; Restrepo Tirado 1929:76; Arango C. 1924, II:22, 96, 106).

The goldwork of Colombia and Panama includes representations of warrior figures on pendants, helmets, and staffs. There are pendants of male figures wearing the accoutrements of war listed above, carrying spearthrowers, lances, clubs, and bows and arrows, ropes, and the heads of their victims (Bray 1978: 138, 162, 228) (Figures 47, 48, 49, 50, 51). Figures 47–49 are gold pendants of male figures from the Tairona area (A.D. 800–1500), whose regalia include fanlike headdresses, helmets, earrings, nose ornaments, lip plugs, and necklaces; all three carry a baton, or rope, with double spirals, which was evidently an insignia or accoutrement of widespread use (Dussán de Reichel-Dolmatoff 1979:44–45; Falchetti 1987:4, 7, 13). Figures 50 and 51

*Figure 44.* Polychrome jars with human effigy covers from Grave 24, Sitio Conte, Panama. Scale 1:3. They display some of the red and black face and body-painting styles and tattoos worn by warriors. [Reprinted by permission, from *Coclé: An Archaeological Study of Central Panama* (Lothrop 1942: Fig. 205). Peabody Museum.]

are *tumbaga tunjos* or anthropomorphic plaques from the Muisca area. These two warrior figures, with their weapons, ropes, and trophy heads, illustrate the Muisca practice of rendering human figures in a stylized and stereotyped fashion while displaying their accoutrements and insignia in detail (Dussán de Reichel-Dolmatoff 1979:43).

In keeping with the group warfare practiced by the sixteenth-century chiefdoms, there are examples of double-warrior figures, bedecked for war, armed with clubs, spearthrowers, and darts, and carrying trophy heads. One of the best examples of these double-warrior pendants is the *tumbaga* pendant associated with the high-ranking male buried in Grave 5 at Sitio Conte, Panama (Figure 52):

> It consists of twin human figures standing side by side with their toes encircling a metal wire. On their heads are conical caps and around their necks are necklaces of several strands. Across the body of each runs a braided bandolier which supports on the hip a tiny bird [parrot]. Both wear belts and small aprons in two folds. At one side of the belts are two projecting nail-like objects. There are bandages around the calves and ankles. In one hand each carries a paddle-shaped club and in the other a bundle of spears. The twin figures are joined at the shoulders by three small buttons from which, suspended by a braided cord, hangs a human head. Two other heads hang from the club handles. . . . The subject portrayed by this specimen evidently is the return of the victorious warriors, who carry as a trophy the heads of their slain enemies. [Lothrop 1937:166]

Another *tumbaga* double-warrior pendant was recovered in the grave of a single individual along with a *tumbaga* disk and Period VII (A.D. 1100–1500) polychrome pottery vessels at the site of El Hatillo on the Azuero Peninsula (Dade 1972:36–38; Cooke and Bray 1985:44). A *tumbaga* figure of two male twins (or warriors?) was also reported from the tomb of a single individual looted in Nápoles, in the Cauca Valley, along with other fine gold pieces (Arango C. 1924, II:218).

Other double-warrior figures, such as an example from Chiriquí province, Panama (Figure 53), represent two male humans, similarly dressed and equipped with clubs and spearthrowers (Bray 1992: 45–46, Fig. 3.11). Yet these apparent warriors feature the erect ears, the nose-leaf, and open mouth with pointed teeth characteristic of leaf-nosed bats of Central America and South America. Traditionally, these nocturnal bats have been considered blood-sucking vampires, for which they can be readily associated with the nocturnal, blood-seeking aspects of chiefly warfare (Cooke and Bray 1985:39; Willey 1971:331).

Finally, the head of a *tumbaga* staff or baton recovered in a tomb, containing one individual, that was looted in El Espejo, in the Hoya del Quindío region of the Cauca Valley, featured the fine rendering of a male figure, who held a spear in one hand and a cup in the other (Arango C. 1924, II:84). It is fitting that this symbol of leadership should in all likelihood display a warring chief with the symbols of his authority.

We know from the ethnohistoric sources that the gold ornaments and accoutrements marked their possessor's social status and military rank (Oviedo y Valdés 1853:74; Cieza de León 1853:371, 375). These gold insignia communicated visually a

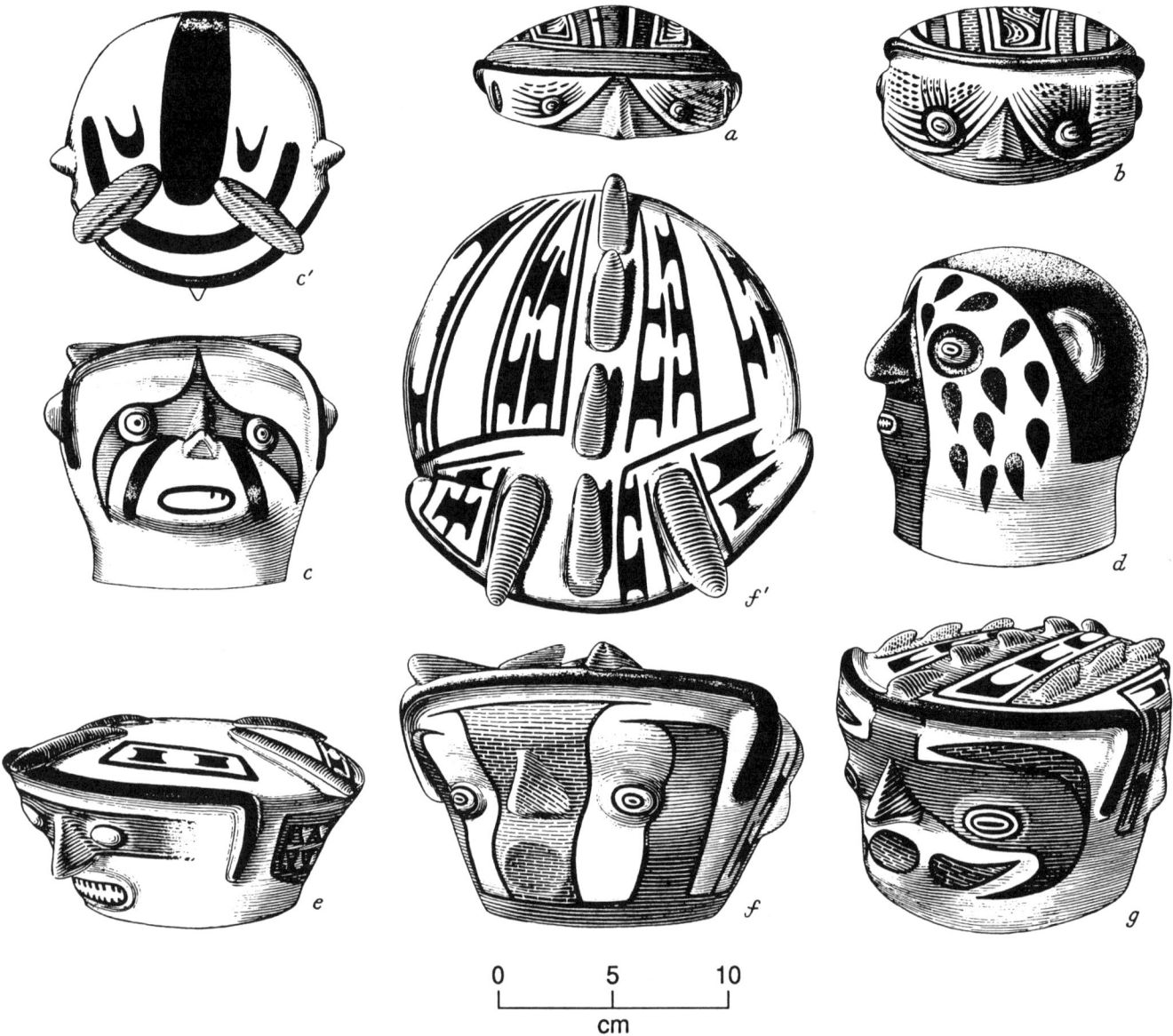

*Figure 45.* Polychrome human effigy covers from Grave 5 (*a, b*) and Grave 24 (*c-g*) at Sitio Conte, Panama. They display some of the face-painting styles and tattoos worn by warriors. [Reprinted by permission, from *Coclé: An Archaeological Study of Central Panama* (Lothrop 1942: Fig. 206). Peabody Museum.]

warrior's rank, both in life on the battlefield, and in death, especially in the case of military captains and their chiefs. As Cooke and Ranere (1992:286) have posited, therefore, "if metalwork served qualitatively to identify who was the leader, it is logical that it should have been linked quantitatively to degrees of leadership." If the day comes when such gold insignia might be spared from the hands of looters and be recovered from known contexts and proveniences, we might really be able to examine the social and military hierarchy of the Circum-Caribbean chiefdoms in some detail. For the time being, however, we must make do with the existing corpus of largely unprovenienced gold objects. We might suggest, for example, that the rank of the thirty individuals recovered in a tomb in the Hoya del Quindío must have been the same, for each one wore a gold-plated copper nose ornament and an additional gold or copper ornament of comparable "value" (Arango C. 1924, I:27). At the end of the spectrum were the chiefly elite, represented by six graves at Sitio Conte, Panama, whose insignia—gold plaques, disks, pendants (including the double-warrior pendant in Grave 5), arm and leg bands, and helmets—were confined to them (Briggs 1986:166–168). I will return to describe the Sitio Conte burials in a later section dealing with the mortuary treatment of warriors.

Finally, the central role of warfare in chiefly leadership is revealed on large stone sculptures of male figures lining the ceremonial plaza at Barriles in Chiriquí, Panama, prior to the eruption of Volcán Barú in A.D. 600. These Atlantean statues of males

*Figure 47.* A Tairona gold pendant of a male figure wearing a semicircular headdress, helmet, ear plugs, nose plug, and lip plug, and carrying a double-spiraled baton or rope, which may have been a military accoutrement or insignia. The figure is 2.6 cm tall, 3.7 cm in total height including the headdress. [AMNH 41.2/7090. Courtesy of the American Museum of Natural History.]

warriors and chiefs reveal the important role that warfare served in the maintenance of chiefly authority. Many San Agustín sculptures from the upper Magdalena River of Colombia (pre-700 A.D. in date) are also of warriors, who wear helmets and "who in menacing gesture grasp huge clubs in their upheld hands" (Reichel-Dolmatoff 1972:42). Very often these larger-than-life-size warriors flank ferocious stone figures, in threatening, combat-ready array. These San Agustín sculptures are associated with large stone-slab tomb chambers inside earthen mounds or barrows; they were probably intended to serve as eternal defenders of the chiefly elite buried there (Reichel-Dolmatoff 1972:41–45, 63; Drennan 1991:275–277).

### Warfare Tactics

When large-scale raids against enemy settlements were launched at night or before dawn, they must have been a terrifying spectacle, complete with torches, noisemakers, and deafening war cries. Open attacks were also waged in broad daylight by opposing forces. The group-warfare tactics practiced by the Circum-Caribbean chiefdoms (whose allied war parties could number up to 4,000 warriors, and in a few instances as many as 10,000 and 20,000 warriors) are revealed archaeologically in a number of ways. We have already discussed the amassed weapons and the iconographic representations of armed warriors, sometimes multiple warriors in warlike poses. Aside from conch-shell trumpets, blown to mobilize warriors and sound the alarm,

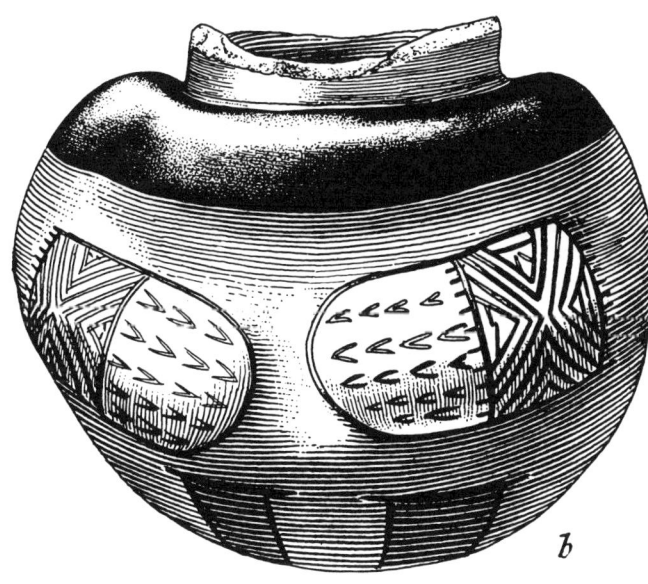

*Figure 46.* Polychrome effigy jars from Grave 26 and Trench I, Sitio Conte, Panama. Scale 1:2. [Reprinted by permission, from *Coclé: An Archaeological Study of Central Panama* (Lothrop 1942: Fig. 204). Peabody Museum.]

wearing helmets and other (gold) ornaments, and bearing trophy heads, had originally been mounted on pedestals and lined up at one end of the ceremonial plaza. Other figures of males wielding axes are carved on the large tripod supports of giant metates or seats from the site (Stirling 1950:227, 241, 243; Linares et al. 1975:141, Figs. 5–7; Linares 1980:242–243). By their sheer size and location in the ceremonial precinct, these stone renditions of

*Figure 48.* A Tairona gold pendant of a male figure wearing a fantastic bird headdress, helmet, earrings, nose plug, and lip plug, and carrying a double-spiraled baton or rope. The pendant's total height is 10.6 cm. It originated from San Pedro de la Sierra, Ciénaga, Magdalena, Colombia, and is now in the Museo del Oro, Bogotá. [Redrawn from Bray 1979.]

which have been recovered archaeologically in middens and burials (see Figure 43), other noisemakers known to have been sounded by chiefly war parties have been recovered. Wooden drums, long-bone flutes, and gold horns have been recovered in tombs in the Cauca Valley (Arango C. 1924, I:190, 194; II:22, 180, 314; Restrepo Tirado 1929:74; Rodríguez 1985:50). Among the chief's "ceremonial trove" recovered in a single structure at Casas Grandes, in Chihuahua, Mexico, which I will describe later, were two shell trumpets and a deer-bone rasp; and bone rasps fashioned from human long bones were recovered in the fill of other rooms and burial vaults at the site (Ravesloot 1988:36–39, 71–72; Di Peso 1974 et al., 51–52).

Scenes of the face-to-face combat characteristic of chiefly warfare are available in the iconography of South American chiefdoms. Some gold helmets from Samarraya in the Cauca Valley depict in relief two warriors fighting with *macanas*. Others portray two figures, possibly warriors or war captives, "con los brazos en cruz, de fisonomía apacible, como en actitud de esperar estoicamente la muerte que iban a afrontar" (Restrepo Tirado 1929:72, Lámina 32, 33). Similar scenes of face-to-face combat between opposing forces and its aftermath are found on two vessels from the Moche Valley of Peru, presented by David Wilson (1988:338–340) as a way of assessing the context of expansionist chiefly warfare in which the Moche state arose (Figures 54, 55). The first depicts a battle waged between Moche warriors who wear their distinctive and heterogeneous war dress with clubs, spears, and shields (shown on the right of each pair of fighting figures on the upper panel, and on the left in the lower panel) and enemy warriors (Figure 54). Many of the non-Moche warriors, who wear little more than hair knots and loincloths, are shown enduring spear thrusts and bleeding, and some are shown being grabbed by their topknots, bound with ropes around their necks, disrobed, and thus, vanquished. The second vessel (Figure 55) depicts victorious Moche warriors in the aftermath of battle, dragging their bound, bleeding, weaponless, naked, and unwilling captives home. Since none of the defeated warriors are shown dead, it seems that they were taken home alive and reserved for sacrifice later (Wilson 1988:338–339; Benson 1972:45–46).

We would expect to find evidence of the widespread destruction that chiefly war parties brought upon target settlements, principally their destruction by fire. Some of the clearest archaeological evidence of this warfare tactic is found at the regional center of Casas Grandes in Chihuahua, Mexico, which was attacked in A.D. 1340 by an enemy war party who set fire to the first floor master beams, causing the center's densely packed, multi-

*Figure 49.* A Tairona gold pendant of a male figure wearing a helmet, ear ornaments, a nose plug, and a lip plug, and carrying a double-spiraled baton or rope. The figure is 2.8 cm tall, and it appears likely to have once had a flat headdress affixed to the back of the head. [AMNH 41.2/7020. Courtesy of the American Museum of Natural History.]

storied architectural units to collapse like a house of cards. The bodies of 126 men, women, and children, whose unburied bodies constitute nearly one-fourth of all the burials at Casas Grandes, lay strewn throughout the burned settlement, as were the bodies of breeding macaws and turkeys, left trapped in their pens. Moreover, the attackers ransacked the community's sanctuaries and intentionally destroyed their stone altars, figures, and high-status burial urns. In one unroofed chamber of a sanctuary atop the Mound of the Offerings, which borders the central plaza, lay the unburied bodies of two adult males, who were probably guarding the sanctuary at the time of the attack (Di Peso 1974, Vol. 2:320–321, 419, Fig. 19–2, 577–578, 639; Di Peso et al. 1974:372; Ravesloot 1988:21, 24–25, 54, 76; Ravesloot and Spoerl 1989:131, 134–135).

Evidence of destruction by fire has been recovered at the Tairona center of Buritaca 200, where dense ash deposits coincide with the center's destruction and abandonment in the sixteenth century (Cadavid and Groot 1987:80). Similarly, the first-order center of Gaván on the Canaguá River of Barinas, Venezuela, was abandoned at around A.D. 1000–1100 following a conflagration, marked by the burning of the community's defensive palisade and widespread burning throughout the center (Spencer and Redmond 1992:144, 153).

Other regional centers such as the Olmec center of San Lorenzo and Sitio Conte in central Panama have also exhibited signs of the intentional destruction of their stone monuments prior to their abandonment. At San Lorenzo, statues of human

*Figure 50.* A Muisca *tumbaga tunjo* figure of a warrior armed with a *macana* and rope. In his right hand he holds a human head trophy. The figure is 10.6 cm in height and is in the Museo del Oro, Bogotá. [Redrawn from Bray 1979.]

figures were intentionally decapitated and mutilated, and other stone monuments were subjected to intentional blows, before being removed and buried in dumps around 900 B.C. (Coe and Diehl 1980:297–298). Similarly, many of the columns enclosing the ceremonial precinct at Sitio Conte had been overturned and shattered, possibly by fire, leading Lothrop (1937:296) to suggest that perhaps Sitio Conte too "was sacked and fired" and abandoned for a time. The story was probably much the same at the column-enclosed ceremonial precinct of Río Caño, where similar signs of intentional destruction have been recovered (Verrill 1927:56–61).

The "kill-all"—or as Oviedo y Valdés (1853:129) put it, "a los que pueden matar matan"—strategy pursued by chiefly war parties should be reflected in the mortality profiles of target populations. In contrast to the skewed mortality distributions of warring tribesmen, who as we have seen are selective in their pursuit of prominent male victims, the mortality profiles produced by chiefly warfare should be less skewed and more representative of the population as a whole, with both sexes and all ages likely to be among the victims.

The mortality profile of war victims at the regional center of Casas Grandes in Chihuahua, Mexico, is precisely what we would expect to find in a target population, especially one not

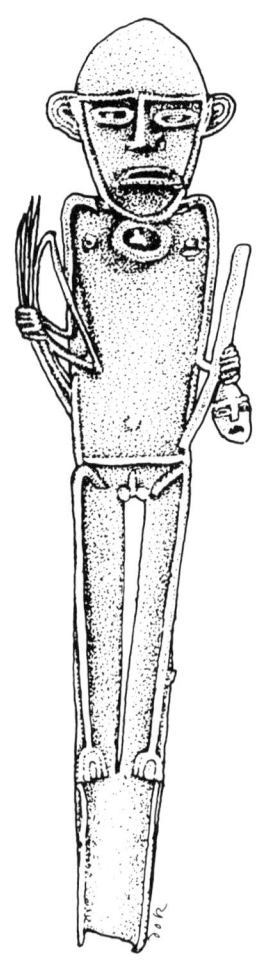

*Figure 51.* A Muisca *tumbaga tunjo* figure of a warrior armed with a bow and arrows, and a club. In his left hand he holds a human head trophy. The figure is 12.4 cm in height and is in the Museo del Oro, Bogotá. [Redrawn from Willey 1971: Fig. 5.88.]

poised for an enemy attack. The 126 unburied bodies encountered on floors of rooms and plazas there, who presumably represent those individuals trapped or killed on the day when Casas Grandes came under its final enemy attack, included the remains of individuals of all ages. They ranged from infants to adults over 50 years of age, although the bulk of the victims were adults between 18 and 35 years of age. Furthermore, of the 92 adult victims, 17 (18.5%) were males, 36 (39.1%) were females, and 39 (42.39%) were of indeterminate sex (Ravesloot 1988:54). By Di Peso's calculations, the majority (82.5%) of the 86 victims whose remains could be identified to their age and sex were women, children, and old men, compared to the 12 (14%) men of fighting age and three (3.5%) men of indeterminate age (Di Peso 1974:639, 751). Di Peso also pointed out that the percentiles of sexed males and females among these unburied victims were comparable to the percentiles of adult males (19.3%) and adult females (30.7%) in the site's burial population (Di Peso et al. 1974:337). Lest anyone think that these victims were merely trapped in the burning buildings and that they died accidentally, the two young adult males guarding the sanctuary atop the Mound of the Offerings showed signs of having suffered a violent death; the disarticulated bones of individual 1-4 lay on the floor along with the smashed contents of the room, while individual 5-4 lay on his right side in an alcove with his legs drawn up behind him. So too had an adult female, who had received a fatal blow to the head, which fractured her right frontal and parietal bones. According to Di Peso, "it can be surmised that many of these persons met their deaths in a like manner" (Di Peso et al. 1974:337). Another young adult male had suffered parry fractures on his right arm during the attack. Two adult males over 50 years of age in the site's burial population had suffered massive blows to the head, which had shown signs of having healed (Ravesloot 1988:76; Ravesloot and Spoerl 1989:134; Di Peso 1974:419, 643, 681, 751; Di Peso et al. 1974:337, 372).

The loss of life resulting from attacks against chiefly centers was always great. At Casas Grandes, for example, 16.7% of the site's total body count consisted of victims who perished in the final attack that destroyed the center (Di Peso et al. 1974:337). Accordingly, we would also expect to find the mass graves of war victims in the archaeological record of chiefdoms. Some of the mass graves recovered at the early Period V (A.D. 500–700) site of Venado Beach in Panama might represent the victims of such an attack. Here up to 50 bodies had been buried together in mass graves. A good third of the 369 recorded individuals buried at Venado Beach were tightly flexed on their backs, indeed so tightly compressed that their bodies might have been bound with ropes or sewn in sacks (Lothrop 1954:232). And unlike the large graves at Sitio Conte, where, as we shall see, a distinction could be made between the principal occupant of the grave and his burial retainers, this was not generally the case in the mass graves at Venado Beach (Lothrop 1954:226). Furthermore, 71 (19%) of the bodies recovered in the cemetery had been mutilated in ways which I will describe in a later section dealing with post-war ritual practices. The mass graves at Venado Beach have been variously interpreted as containing the bodies of warriors killed in a raid and returned home for burial, or sacrificed prisoners of war (Lothrop 1954; Linares 1977:72; Cooke 1984:287).

## Defensive Tactics

As chiefly warfare escalated, the inhabitants of villages sought refuge at regional centers, which were fortified and readied for war. If there was time, villagers took provisions and hid their valuables by burying them before fleeing their homes. This practice may account for some of the buried caches associated with residences in the archaeological record of chiefdoms. It appears that villagers at La Coyotera in the Cuicatlán Cañada hastily buried spectacular shell ornaments, a polished onyx bowl, an obsidian blade, incense burners, and red pigment in an intrusive,

*Figure 52.* A *tumbaga* pendant from Grave 5, Sitio Conte, Coclé, Panama. The two figures are warriors armed with clubs, spearthrowers, darts, and ropes, who carry human head trophies (actual size). [Reprinted by permission, from *Coclé: An Archaeological Study of Central Panama* (Lothrop 1937: Fig. 150). Peabody Museum.]

*Figure 53.* **Tumbaga** pendant from Chiriquí, Panama, of two warriors armed with clubs and spears, who feature the ears, leaf-nose, mouth and pointed teeth of Central and South American leaf-nosed bats (7.5 cm tall). [Redrawn from Willey 1971: Fig. 5–91.]

*Figure 54.* Scene of battle from a Moche ceramic vessel from Trujillo, Moche Valley, Peru. [Reproduced by permission of the Smithsonian Institution Press from *Prehispanic Settlement Patterns in the Lower Santa Valley, Peru.* David J. Wilson. Copyright Smithsonian Institution, Washington, D.C. 1988. Fig. 185.]

*Figure 55.* Scene from a Moche ceramic vessel from Chimbote, Santa Valley, Peru, showing victorious warriors leading their captives home from war. [Reproduced by permission of the Smithsonian Institution Press from *Prehispanic Settlement Patterns in the Lower Santa Valley, Peru.* David J. Wilson. Copyright Smithsonian Institution, Washington, D.C. 1988. Fig. 186.]

shallow pit inside a residence, probably to hide these valuables from the Valley of Oaxaca Zapotec, who attacked and burned down the community in the Late Formative period (Spencer 1982:216–220, 241–242). Similarly, the nine marked caches of ceremonial stone objects—including fine greenstone winged pendants, monolithic axes, and batons—buried inside the largest circular structure at the Tairona center of El Pueblito might also represent caches of this nature (Mason 1931–1936:97–98, 170–171).

Because the inhabitants of satellite villages and hamlets sought refuge at fortified centers in times of war, the number or sizes of these centers should reflect the intensity of warfare in the region. For example, the pervasive threat of warfare to the inhabitants of the Santa Valley on the northern Peruvian coast in prestate times was responsible for the twenty Early Horizon (1000–350 B.C.) hilltop citadels and ridgetop sites that were located up to 700 m above the valley (and a one or two hour's climb) that overlooked some 24 habitation sites throughout the uppermost and middle stretches of the valley. These hilltop citadels featured massive rock walls, 2 m wide and 2–4 m high, bastions, ramparts, and restricted entryways. They were ringed by bulwarks and moats. Wilson estimates that an average of 130 persons occupied these hilltop fortresses, although his population estimates range up to 375 persons. A number of them include elite residences and ceremonial architecture (Wilson 1987:58–61, 1988:104–108).

In the Circum-Caribbean area, chiefly centers were particularly large, which reflects the degree of settlement nucleation, and indirectly, the intensity of warfare experienced in the region. They also were in prominent and often defensible locations, and displayed defensive fortifications, as did so many of the archaeologically known Tairona centers. The regional center known as Buritaca 200, for example, is located in the upper Buritaca River valley in the Sierra Nevada de Santa Marta on a nearly inaccessible ridgetop at an elevation of 1,200 m, flanked by the river on one side and by a steep gorge on the other. By the fourteenth century A.D., the center extended over approximately 2 km², and its population is estimated to have exceeded 5,000 people. It could be reached only by means of a single stone-slab staircase that ascends the steep slope in a series of zigzag turns and penetrates tall stone-slab retaining walls (Cadavid and Groot 1987:65–67; Castaño 1987:233–234; Oyuela 1987:220–221). One of the best preserved staircases is one at Pueblo Bernardo that, in 48 steps, ascends a steep ridge bordered by gullies at an angle of 30 degrees (Figure 56) (Mason 1931:116).

Chiefly centers occupying flat terrain would most certainly have been fortified with palisades of thick trunks, which should leave discernible post-mold patterns. The thirteenth-century A.D. Mississippian center of Moundville in Alabama was enclosed by an extensive wooden palisade, which was evidently rebuilt at least five times during the center's heyday.

The evidence for this exists as scars left in the ground by the trenches dug to receive the upright posts. Using stone, shell, and wooden hoes, the Indians excavated long narrow trenches as much as two meters into the ground. Pine logs about 20 centimeters in diameter were used. They were placed quite close together and the earth returned to chock them in place. They probably extended three meters or more above the surface. [Vogel and Allan 1985:63]

Rectangular bastions projected at 35–40 m intervals along the palisade, from which the defenders could launch missiles at the enemy. Narrow openings in the palisade afforded limited access to the center.

The sixth-century A.D. regional center of Gaván in Barinas, Venezuela, also seems to have been encircled by a palisade of thick posts that was erected atop the oval earthwork, or *calzada,* one meter tall, that rings the settlement (Figure 57). Charles Spencer and I exposed an alignment of carbonized postmolds along the centerline of the *calzada* for a distance of 11 meters, which we suggest formed a stretch of the center's external palisade, before it was burned in the settlement's final conflagration at around A.D. 1000–1100 (Spencer and Redmond 1992:144, 153). The 3-m-tall and 10-m-wide earthwork encountered at certain points along the periphery of the Teso dos Bichos 7-m-high mound site on Marajó Island may have served a similar defensive function. Like the defensive fortifications at Moundville and Gaván, the peripheral earthwork at Teso dos Bichos was built of sterile clay and was virtually devoid of artifacts (ceramics), reflecting its special, non-habitational function (Roosevelt 1991:310–320, 333–334, 337, 401, 422–423).

The thirteenth- and fourteenth-century A.D. regional center of Casas Grandes, in Chihuahua, Mexico, displayed an array of defensive measures. The center was located on a prominent river terrace that provided wide-ranging views of the Casas Grandes River valley. Its architectural layout was highly aggregated and enclosed, with restricted entry points, bastions, and beveled exterior windows that may have functioned for defense as well as for sighting. Casas Grandes had a direct line-of-sight to a stone-masonry tower (*atalaya*) atop the Cerro de Moctezuma, probably for rapid communication by means of smoke or fire signals. Indeed, some 75 of these hilltop *atalayas* and trails linked the regional polity centered at Casas Grandes with its secondary centers and outlying communities within a 130 km radius (Ravesloot 1988:75–76; Di Peso 1974, Vol. 2:360–375, 449–451; Minnis 1989:292, 296–297).

The creation of buffer zones was another defensive strategy practiced by chiefdoms. Buffer zones have turned up in the regional settlement patterns of thirteenth and fourteenth century regional polities in the American Southwest that manifest a three-tiered settlement hierarchy based on site size, architecture, and ceramics. Empty buffer zones measuring 15 to 20 miles wide have been reported for the Hohokam in central and southern Arizona, at a time when settlements became nucleated and when fortified hill sites (*trincheras*) might have functioned as defensive refuges (Wilcox 1989:164–165; Fish and Fish 1989:119–122). The unoccupied zone between two clusters of settlements in the Volcán Barú region of highland Panama prior to the eruption of

*Figure 56.* Long stone-slab staircase at the Tairona center of Pueblo Bernardo, Colombia. So restricted and steep were the Tairona's staircases, like this one which ascended at an angle of 30 degrees, that the Spaniards' horses could not ascend them. [Redrawn from Mason 1931: Plate XXIV.]

Volcán Barú in A.D. 600 was smaller in scale but it probably served a similarly defensive function. One settlement cluster, which was centered on the regional center of Barriles, was separated by an intervening stretch of cultivable land more than 5 km wide that was nevertheless unoccupied from the other cluster of settlements in the Cerro Punta region. This boundary between the distribution of settlements in the two adjacent regions is also marked by differences in ceramics; Olga Linares and Payson Sheets (1980:53, 272) have suggested that it served as a buffer zone between neighboring polities.

The defenders of a fortified settlement hurled missiles—spears, darts, arrows, stones, and rocks—at the attackers from behind fortifications. Unless the defenders were taken completely by surprise, they evacuated women, children, and elderly men to a safe refuge. Accordingly, defensive warfare was a form of long-distance combat that was generally pursued only by males of fighting age. This defensive strategy should be reflected archaeologically at fortified centers that successfully withstood enemy attacks. Long-distance missiles should predominate in their arsenals. And in contrast to the final attack against Casas Gran-

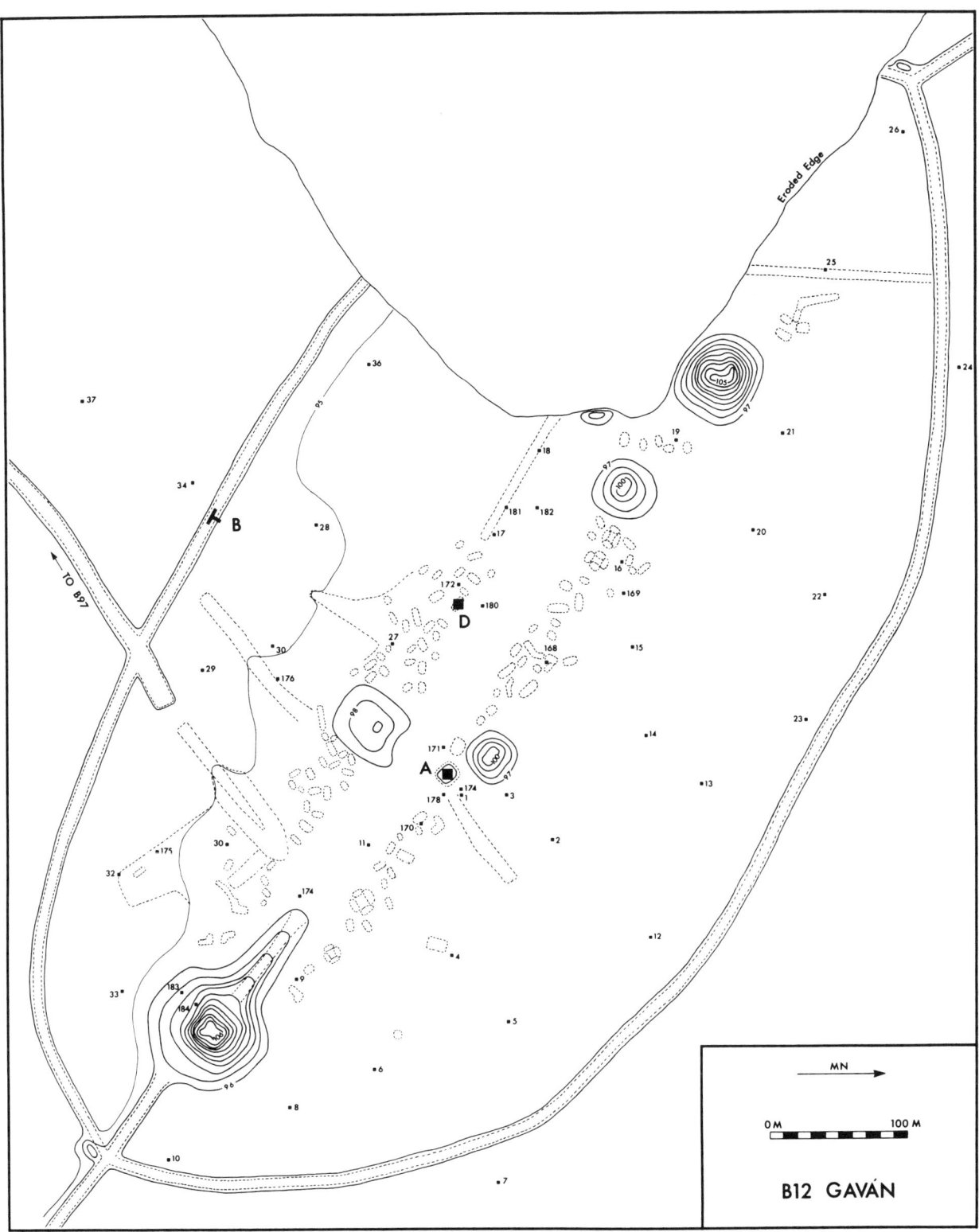

*Figure 57.* Map of regional center of Gaván, Barinas, Venezuela. This center was encircled by an oval earthwork a meter or more high on top of which stood a palisade of wooden posts. [Reproduced with permission, from *World Archaeology* (Spencer and Redmond 1992).]

des, where as we have seen the majority of the victims were women, children, and old men, men of fighting age should be the principal victims of defensive warfare.

So impregnable and well defended were some sixteenth-century fortified centers that they endured prolonged sieges, for up to 39 days in the case of the defense of the fortress of Nobobarco in the Cauca Valley (Simón 1892a:276–278). The impact of such prolonged or chronic warfare should be reflected in the subsistence practices of a community. The disruption of seasonal cultivation tasks for a period of thirty days and the loss of crops to intentional destruction by fire would have had serious consequences for the diet and general health of these agriculturalists. The hardship endured by the defenders of a fortified center should be reflected in the disruption of subsistence practices and in the consequent restriction of available resources to consume. Accordingly, the diversity of plants and animals consumed might deviate from those consumed in normal times. The consequences for the long-term health of the inhabitants of such a community might include nutritional deficiencies and other debilitating diseases, evidence of which will be reflected in the associated skeletal population (Milner et al. 1991:590–592; Powell 1988:66–79).

## Post-War Rituals

For the members of a victorious raiding party, the post-war rituals began right on the battlefield with the slaughter and dismemberment of victims. Live victims were bound with rope and clubbed to death, before being decapitated and dismembered with cane and flint knives. We have descriptions of sixteenth-century battlefields strewn with dead bodies in the Cauca Valley and the Sierra Nevada de Santa Marta. The battlefields of neighboring chiefs in Panama were similarly strewn with the bones of victims, including the battlefield named Acla ("bones of men") in the territory of Chief Careta. Accordingly, the archaeological record of chiefly battles should, in spite of Vencl's warning that "this kind of behavior deposits archaeological remains neither in great depths in the ground nor in significant spatial concentrations" (Vencl 1984:123), include battlefields strewn with disarticulated bodies, or bone fields.

The taking of war captives was also practiced, probably as rendered on the Moche vessel scene of bound, naked, and bleeding captives being dragged home (Figure 55). The fact that the bound captives on this vessel are all bleeding from their noses suggests that this maltreatment was uniformly suffered by captives. In interpreting the Huaca de la Luna mural scene of prisoners being sacrificed, Lyon (1989:64) mentions a figure holding a cup to receive the blood dripping from the nose of a prisoner, in the latter's role as a sacrificial victim. Lyon also raises the possibility that captives of the Moche were branded with special nose ornaments, in view of a Moche stirrup-spouted bottle that depicts fully bedecked warriors dragging by their hair small warriors with captive nose ornaments (Lyon 1989: Fig.1, 66–67; Benson 1972:151). If Moche captives were branded with special nose ornaments, the way prisoners of Panamanian chiefs were branded with the indelible tattoo of their new chiefly overlord, then we would expect to recover this tangible insignia of their enslavement archaeologically.

We know that Panamanian chiefs also branded war captives by knocking out one of their incisors (Oviedo y Valdés 1853:129), a form of mutilation that should be manifested in the dentition of captives. The possibility that the cemetery at the Panamanian site of Venado Beach included the remains of war captives is supported by the 71 mutilated bodies recovered there, of which 10 individuals had had one or two of their front teeth extracted. Among them were otherwise complete bodies with only some teeth extracted, an act which Lothrop suggests was performed while the individuals were alive (Lothrop 1954:229–232, 234). War victims or captives taken during the Pueblo II–IV periods in the American Southwest also seem to have had their front teeth intentionally extracted (Figure 58). One of the features shared by the mutilated human remains that were deposited in ten mass burial sites in the Four Corners area is the perimortem damage to the front teeth. Christy Turner reported that:

> Anterior tooth sockets are "blown out" by high velocity blows, such as might be expected by impact with a club or large cobble. Because the posterior teeth are seldom affected, protective muscle and flesh had to have been present. [Turner 1983:233, Fig.3]

Since this portion of the skull lacks nutritional value, the act of knocking out the victims' front teeth may perhaps be attributed to the intentional disfigurement of war captives and coincidentally, to the seizure of their teeth as war trophies (White 1992:195–196, 201–207).

Bound war captives were taken home by the victorious war chief for use as slaves, for exchange, and for sacrifice. A number of chiefly centers feature iconographic evidence of the taking and sacrifice of war captives. Among the corpus of Olmec stone monuments at San Lorenzo, for example, are portrayals of rulers with bound captives in submissive poses (Coe and Diehl 1980:392, 320–321, 370–372). I would venture to suggest that the stone statues of naked male figures with grim expressions and arms-across-the-chest poses lined up in the ceremonial precinct of El Caño, in the Panamanian province of Coclé, also represent war captives (Figure 59) (Lothrop 1937:31, Fig.17; Verrill 1927:49–56). At the regional center of Barriles in the Volcán Barú region of Panama, Matthew Stirling (1950) described a similarly enclosed ceremonial plaza, paved with massive stone slabs, and delimited at one end by a row of stone statues on pedestals. These large human figures, male and female, wear conical helmets, human effigy pendants, and they hold human head trophies in their hands (see Haberland 1984: Fig.9.4; Linares, Sheets, Rosenthal 1975: Fig. 5–6). A similar theme is portrayed on enormous (2.20 m wide) ceremonial metates from Barriles, as well as upon 1-m-tall stone "drums" for which the site is named. The stone sculpture at Barriles clearly portrays high-status individuals with symbols of war, including stone

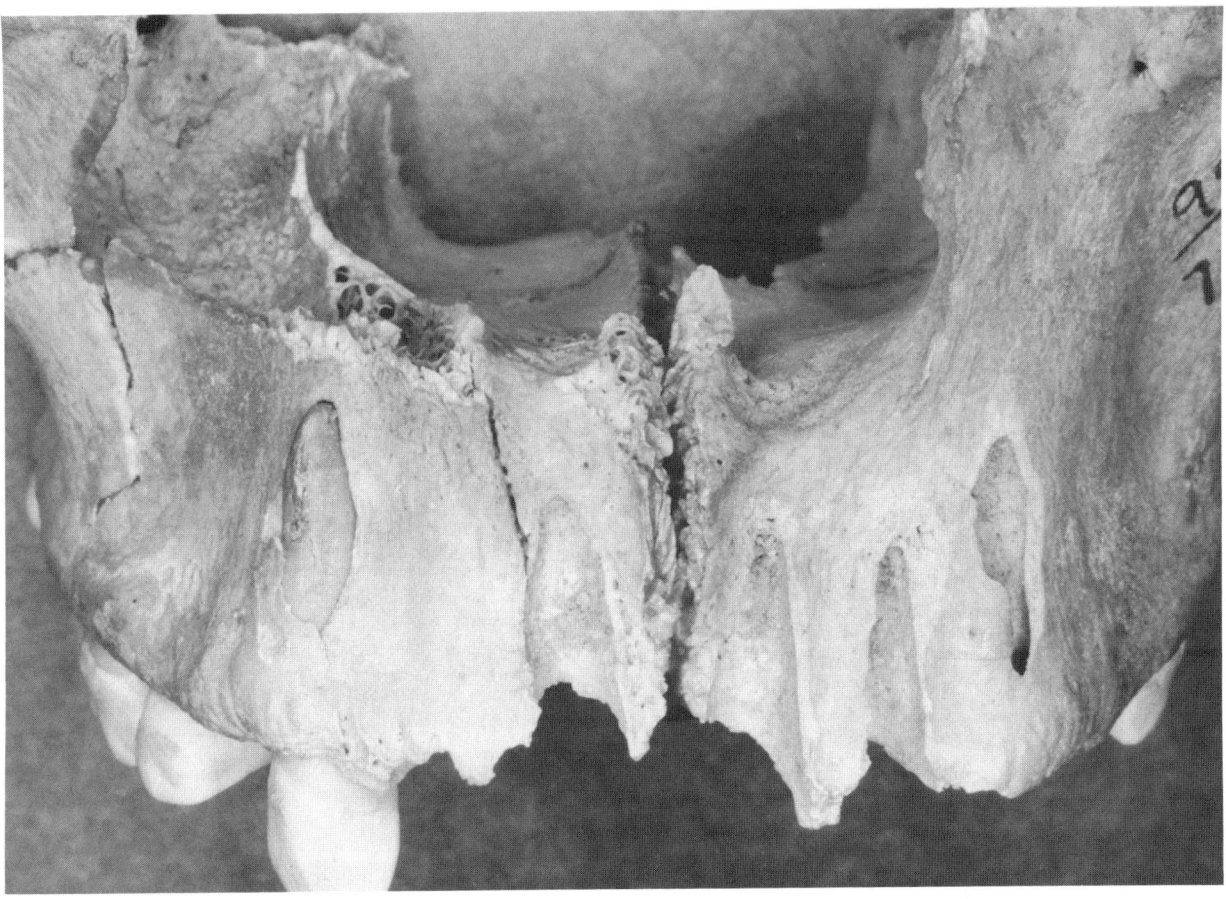

*Figure 58.* Human maxilla from Cave 7, Cottonwood Wash, Utah, with "blown out" front teeth. [AMNH 99/7375, CGT neg. 15:S5 1978.]

axes, and human head trophies (Linares, Sheets, Rosenthal 1975:141–143).

## Ritual Cannibalism

The post-war rituals of militaristic chiefdoms centered on the sacrifice, dismemberment, and sometimes the consumption of victims and war captives on a large scale. In view of the controversy that any mention of cannibalistic practices elicits, and the contention by some anthropologists that there are no reliable ethnohistoric and ethnographic descriptions—no reliable firsthand witnesses—of this practice (Arens 1979; Kolata 1986:1497), let me review some specific reports of post-war ritual cannibalism in northern South America. The earliest precise report is by Oviedo y Valdés, who on arrival on the coast of Santa Marta with Pedrarias Dávila in 1514, claimed:

> Son estos indios caribes, flecheros y comen carne humana; y esto se supo, porque en algunas casas se hallaron aquel dia tasajos é miembros de hombres ó de mugeres, assi como braços y piernas y una mano puesta y salada y enjairada, y collares engastados en ellos dientes humanos, que los indios se ponen por bien paresçer, y calaveras de otros puestas delante de las puertas de las casas en palos hincados á manera de tropheos y acuerdo de triunfo de los enemigos que han muerto ó de los que han comido. [Oviedo y Valdés 1852:355]

Fray Tomás Ortiz also referred to the cannibalistic practices of the groups in the area of Santa Marta, in an account dating to 1525, after having spent many years there (Simón 1882:7).

The most complete reports of cannibalism come from the Cauca Valley, and specifically from the pen of Cieza de León, who was a member of Juan de Vadillo's expedition through the Cauca Valley in 1537, and who personally witnessed the decapitation, dismemberment, and consumption of indigenous war captives taken by some of the chiefdoms that Juan de Vadillo and his contemporaries, Sebastián de Benalcázar and Jorge Robledo, encountered in the Cauca Valley. His eyewitness accounts excerpted below all refer to exocannibalism, or to the consumption of outsiders or enemies. Only in one instance did Cieza de León allude to the endocannibalistic practice of survival cannibalism, when he reported that the defenders of Popayán responded to a famine by engaging in human cannibalism (Cieza de León 1853:383; White 1992:12).

Cieza de León documented the scale on which ritual cannibalism was practiced by warring chiefs in the Cauca Valley. Cieza de León reported how victorious Pozo warriors, who had joined Sebastián de Benalcázar's military campaign into the neighboring provinces of Picara and Paucura, consumed the bodies of those they had killed or taken captive:

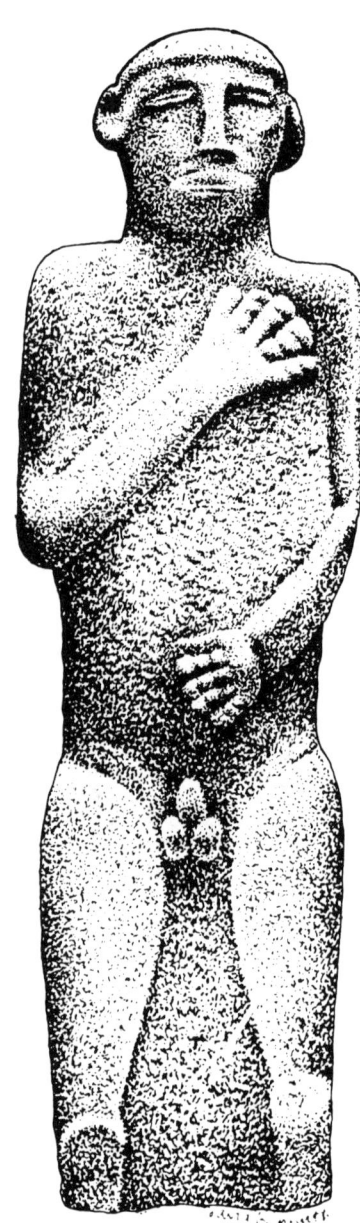

*Figure 59.* Carved stone column from the ceremonial precinct at the site of El Caño, Coclé, Panama. This naked male figure probably represents a captive in a gesture of submission. [Redrawn from Lothrop 1937: Fig. 17.]

cuando quieren matar algunos de aquellos malaventurados para comerlos, los hacen hincar de rodillas en tierra, y abajando la cabeza, le dan junto al colodrillo un golpe, del cual queda atordido y no habla ni se queja. . . . Yo he visto lo que digo hartas veces. [Cieza de León 1853:372]

Cieza de León witnessed the execution and sacrifice of a female war captive there, who kneeled resignedly and awaited her death. She was clubbed to death by one individual and beheaded with a flint knife by another. Her executioners

luego se bebieron la sangre y se comieron crudo el corazon con las entrañas, llevándose los cuartos y la cabeza para comer la noche siguiente. [Cieza de León 1853:373]

Captives were also held in pens and fattened up for later sacrifice and consumption, as Cieza de León recorded both in Arma and in Paucura:

Dentro de las casas de los señores tienen de las cañas gordas que de suso he dicho, las cuales, después de secas, en extremo son recias, y hacen un cercado como jaula, ancha y corta y no muy alta, tan reciamente atadas, que por ninguna manera los que meten dentro se pueden salir; cuando van á la guerra, los que prenden pónenlos allí y mándanles dar muy bien de comer, y de que están gordos, sácanlos á sus plazas, que están juntos á las casas, y en los dias que hacen fiesta los matan con gran crueldad y los comen; yo vi algunas destas jaulas ó cárceles en la provincia de Arma. [Cieza de León 1853:372]

Cieza de León described where such ritual sacrifices were conducted at fortified hilltop centers in the province of Arma:

en mitad desta fuerza tienen, ó tenian cuando yo los vi, un tablado alto y bien labrado de las mismas cañas, con su escalera, para hacer sus sacrificios. [Cieza de León 1853:371]

From these sacrificial platforms they tied their victims by their shoulders with long ropes, leaving them hanging,

y á algunos dellos les sacaban los corazones y los ofrecian á sus dioses, al demonio, á honra de quien se hacian aquellos sacrificios, y luego, sin tardar mucho, comian los cuerpos de los que ansí mataban. [Cieza de León 1853:371]

That the victors cooked their victims' body parts is evident in Cieza de León's description of what some of Juan de Vadillo's hungry men, who were searching for food in Anserma, pulled out of a cooking jar and gorged on:

hallaron una olla grande llena de carne cocida; y tanta hambre llevaban, que no miraron en mas de comer, . . . mas ya que estaban todos bien hartos, un cristiano sacó de la olla una mano con sus dedos y uñas; sin lo cual, vieron luego pedazos de piés, dos ó tres cuartos de hombres que en ella estaban. [Cieza de León 1853:368–369]

These body parts were smoked sometimes, as Cieza de León noted when he described the Gorrones' display of their victims' body parts at the doors of their houses, hanging like sausages:

yo les vi un dia comer mas de cien indios y indias de los que habian muerto y preso en la guerra. [Cieza de León 1853:373]

Furthermore, when some 4,000 or more Picara warriors joined Jorge Robledo's expeditionary force, Cieza de León witnessed their killing and consuming more than 300 individuals (Cieza de León 1853:373–374).

Cieza de León described precisely how victims were clubbed to death on the back of the neck in the province of Paucura:

Junto á las puertas de sus casas, por grandeza, tienen de dentro de la portada muchos piés de los indios que han muerto, y muchas manos; sin lo cual, de las tripas, porque no se les pierda nada, las hinchan de carne ó de ceniza, unas á manera de morcillas y otras de longanizas, desto mucha cantidad; las cabezas, por consiguiente, tienen puestas, y muchos cuartos enteros. [Cieza de León 1853:378]

As a matter of fact, one member of Juan de Vadillo's expedition mistook the hanging innards for long pork sausages and rushed forward to seize them! Cieza de León added, with some prescience:

Y si yo no hubiera visto lo que escribo, y supiera que en España hay tantos que lo saben y lo vieron muchas veces, cierto no contara que estos hombres hacían tan grandes carnecerías de otros hombres solo para comer; y así, sabemos que estos gorrones son grandes carniceros de comer carne humana. [Cieza de León 1853:378]

Finally, it is clear that Cieza de León personally entered chiefly charnel houses in Pozo and in Lile, where he saw the stuffed flayed skins of war captives who had been killed and whose flesh had been consumed. Inside Chief Petecuy of Lile's charnel:

así como entraban dentro, estaba en alto una larga tabla, la cual la atravesaba de una parte á otra, y encima della estaban puestas por órden muchos cuerpos de hombres muertos de los que habian vencido y preso en las guerras, todos abiertos; y abríanlos con cuchillos de pedernal y los desollaban, y después de haber comido la carne, henchian los cueros de ceniza y hacíanles rostros de cera con sus propias cabezas, poníanlos en la tabla de tal manera, que parescian hombres vivos. [Cieza de León 1853:380]

Cieza de León also saw great numbers of hands and feet hanging in the charnel. An adjoining structure contained a great number of dead bodies as well as the skulls and bones of many cannibalized war victims (Cieza de León 1853:380).

Cieza de León's accounts of post-war ritual cannibalism are supported by those of Fray Pedro Simón, who recounted the fate of Spanish victims seized by Cauca Valley forces during attacks against Spanish settlements there in 1574 and 1577. During a successful dawn attack by five allied Nutabae and Tahamí chiefs with 500 warriors against Governor Andrés de Valdivia's fortified settlement near Cáceres, Valdivia was wounded by an arrow and seized by the chiefly war leaders, as was his brother-in-law, Loaiza. At a clifftop retreat, chief Quime informed Valdivia that he would now eat him in retaliation for Valdivia's mistreatment of him and his people. An elderly *mohán* ("diviner") approached Valdivia, raised his *macana* and delivered a blow that succeeded in smashing Valdivia's head and spraying his brains over the clifftop (Simón 1892c:18–21). Following Valdivia's execution:

Al punto arremetieron cuatro, y desnudándolo, le cortaron la cabeza, y se bebían la sangre á cual más podía, como perros en el matadero. Hiciéronle en un punto cuartos y le comieron los hígados allí luégo, sin llegarlos al fuego, repartiendo la carne entre los más principales. [Simón 1892c:21]

Loaiza and three others met the same fate, including Gaspar Jalofo, who had died of numerous poisoned arrows, but whose flesh was nevertheless carefully processed by an elderly man and consumed (Simón 1892c:22).

Valdivia's successor, Gaspar de Rodas, founded the Spanish settlement of Cáceres very near this site in 1576. In his absence, however, Chief Omaga led an attack against Spanish farmsteads in the vicinity, and his warriors killed, butchered, and ate many Spanish soldiers and their servants (Simón 1892c:66).

Elsewhere, Simón reported that the Guazuzues in the goldmining area of Buritaca sacrificed slaves and extracted their body fat to make small oil lamps for the mines:

Aquí era la gran carnicería de carne humana de estos naturales, que mataban los esclavos tendiéndolos sobre una piedra á propósito para eso, donde vivos los abrían desde los pechos, sacábanles el unto para hacer candilejas para los socavones de las minas, y de la carne vendían y comían. [Simón 1892c:173]

Aside from the reports of cannibalism by Oviedo y Valdés on the coast of Santa Marta in 1514, and the 1525 account by Fray Tomás Ortiz, there are no eyewitness accounts of exocannibalism among the Tairona. While Simón alluded to the practice there late in 1535 or in 1536, when an unfortunate Capitán Salazar met his death with a poisoned arrow during an entry into Tairona territory and "fue sabroso almuerzo su desgraciado cuerpo" (1891:37), in 1570 Simón (1892a:356) maintained that the Indians of Santa Marta did not eat human flesh. That they did decapitate, dismember, and flay their victims is clear, however, from the accounts of Simón (1892a:366, 1892c:27, 46, 48) and Castellanos (1850:273, 277, 332, 334, 354).

So too did victorious Panamanian war parties, who as far as the ethnohistoric sources report, stopped short of consuming their victims. Indeed, Pascual de Andagoya learned in 1516 and 1522, respectively, that the Panamanian chiefdoms dreaded bellicose groups to the north and south who consumed human flesh (Andagoya 1865:40, 44). Their forms of ritual sacrifice included dismembering and mutilating victims bit by bit. Espinosa learned firsthand of this practice on his return to Chiniá in 1517, after having left two sick men in the care of chiefs Chiribuque and Queracombe in 1516. No sooner had Espinosa departed than:

los dichos caciques é indios hizieron sus areytos, é tajada á tajada, é poco á poco les fueron cortadas las manos é brazos, hasta que los mataron. [Espinosa 1864:474]

To this can be added the reports of Oviedo y Valdés, who arrived in Darien with Pedrarias in 1514, and who wrote about the Panamanian chiefdoms with the authority of an eyewitness (Lothrop 1937:10). Oviedo y Valdés described how some prisoners had their front teeth knocked out, and how captured spies were tortured by being cut to pieces (Oviedo y Valdés 1853:129–130).

These ethnohistoric accounts of ritual sacrifice are supported by the archaeological record. Various forms of ritual sacrifice were practiced on the 71 mutilated bodies recovered at the Venado Beach cemetery, which constitute 19% of all the bodies excavated there. These individuals had been decapitated, and their bodies hacked to varying degrees: fingers, hands, arms, legs, feet (Lothrop 1954: Table 8, 229–232). This is in keeping with Espinosa's (1864:474) description of how two of his men had been ritually sacrificed, bit by bit, by their chiefly captors. In the Cauca Valley, Arango C. reported looted tombs that contained only skulls, or only disarticulated bodies, or only loose long bones, or the burned bones "from floor to ceiling" of several hundred individuals (Arango C. 1924, I:28, 152; 1924, II:15). Some nonperishable knives of bone and marine shell for use in such human sacrifice have turned up in pits inside tombs here as well; they are well-sharpened and have holes at their ends for suspension (Arango C. 1924, II:155, see Table 1).

There is widespread evidence of headhunting in the archaeological record of South and Central American chiefdoms. In addition to Early Horizon period Paracas ceramics, textiles, and gourds that depict masked, armed human figures holding trophy heads by their hair, are actual caches of trophy heads, one with thirteen heads from the Ica Valley on the south coast of Peru. These Paracas trophy heads had been prepared in the following way:

> After the head had been severed from the body, the cervical vertebrae and remainder of the neck were removed. Next the foramen magnum was enlarged, sometimes being expanded up to the occipital protuberance. The brain and soft tissue of the skull was then removed through this aperture. A hole was pierced through the frontal bone at the center of the forehead, and a cotton cord was extended through the hole for use as a carrying rope. The eye orbits were either left empty or filled with a black resinous substance. Often rags were placed in the cranial cavity, and these often can be seen protruding from the eye sockets. Finally the lips were pinned shut with one or two thorns, perhaps for ritualistic purposes. The hair was often ornamented, and sometimes a warrior's head was wrapped with a sling. [Proulx 1971:17–18]

Indeed, human skulls—and perforated, decorated skulls at that—will be far more likely to turn up in the archaeological record of warring chiefdoms than in the archaeological record of tribal headhunters, who as we have seen simply string the severed heads by passing cords through the mouth and out the neck. Moreover, after tribesmen have skinned the trophy heads, the skulls are discarded (Up de Graff 1923:274, 287; Cotlow 1953:147).

Trophy heads have been recovered throughout northern South America and Central America, with burials at the village sites of Caño Caroní and Punto Fijo in Barinas, Venezuela (Zucchi 1975:58, 60–61; Zucchi and Denevan 1979:59), as well as at Sitio Sierra in Panama (Cooke 1979:952; Cooke and Ranere 1989:310; Hansell 1987:120). Actual perforated human skulls have been recovered in many tombs in the Quimbaya region of the Cauca Valley (Arango C. 1924, II:325). These will be discussed further in another section that deals with mortuary practices. Finally, there are iconographic depictions of trophy heads, like Ilama phase vessels from the Cauca Valley that represent human heads, resting on bowls, some with downturned, half-opened mouths, and with tears streaming from the eyes (Bray et al. 1985:6).

The accompanying sacrificial practices of dismembering and ritually consuming the butchered remains of war captives on a large scale are evident in the fragmentary, disarticulated, and reportedly "cannibalized" human remains that have been recovered principally in midden deposits at a host of South and Central American sites. Let me review some of the specific deposits and the interpretations of the archaeologists who excavated them. Alberta Zucchi and William Denevan reported the following human remains, together with other animal bone remains, at the small gallery-forest settlement (ca. A.D. 1400) of Copa de Oro in Barinas, Venezuela:

> Mezclados con los restos de comida y el material, se encontraron una mandíbula quebrada, así como algunos fragmentos de cráneo y de huesos largos. Es probable que la gente del complejo Copa de Oro practicara el canibalismo, ya que a estos huesos al igual que a los de los animales les fue extraída la médula. [Zucchi and Denevan 1979:68, 69]

Two secondary urn burials at the similar and contemporaneous site of Caño Caroní (A.D. 1200–1400) also contained fragmentary, burned human bones from which the marrow had been extracted; in one urn they were mixed together with the bones of fish, birds, and small mammals (Zucchi 1975:57–61). Zucchi proposes that ritual cannibalism was practiced on the occasion of an individual's secondary burial:

> A título explicativo, si se considera que las prácticas canibalísticas estaban generalmente asociadas con actividades guerreras, se puede deducir que el individuo enterrado en la urna pudo haber fallecido en una de estas contiendas; mientras que, los huesos quemados, pertenecían a algún prisionero tomado en la misma contienda y sacrificado posteriormente, en ocasión de la ceremonia del entierro secundario, del fallecido miembro del grupo. [Zucchi 1975:62]

The occurrence of scattered, disarticulated human long bones in Momil Ib-Ic refuse deposits at the 2 ha Formative site of Momil on the lower Sinú River in northern Colombia has also been attributed to the practice of ritual cannibalism (Reichel-Dolmatoff 1965:77). Specifically,

> En los Niveles 11, 9 y 8 se hallaron dispersamente algunos huesos humanos. Se trata de fragmentos muy deteriorados de hueso largos, mezclados con la tierra y los vestigios culturales. Estos restos óseos se encontraron distanciados el uno del otro y no parece tratarse de entierros. Es de observar sin embargo que en los Niveles 9 y 8 los huesos estaban asociados a pequeñas manchas de ceniza y mínimas partículas de carbón. [Reichel-Dolmatoff 1956:253]

Cutmarks are reported on some of the long bones in an urn burial from a shaft tomb (A.D. 710) at Hacienda La Amapola in La Cumbre, west of the Cauca Valley:

> the urn contained four individuals. Some of the bones display a network of irregular shallow marks 6–10 mm long. The marks occur on long bone shafts such as tibia (Fig. 59) and femur, and os coxae. The origin of those marks remain enigmatic. [Gähwiler-Walder 1988:52]

Archaeological evidence of cannibalism is present in lower Central America as well, perhaps as early as the Late Preceramic at Aguadulce Shelter, central Panama (Cooke and Ranere 1992:291). The human bones recovered in middens at the .5 ha ridgetop hamlet of Cerro Brujo (ca. A.D. 600–930) on the Aguacate Peninsula of the Atlantic Bocas del Toro coast included disarticulated and/or mutilated bones, "facts that suggest they were considered 'trash' and treated as such" (Linares 1980c:303–304, 1980b:63–64). Similarly, "miscellaneous body parts" were recovered in two household trash pits at the 65 ha Period III (1000–200 B.C.) Panamanian center of La Mula-Sarigua (Hansell 1987:131, 128–129).

The only human remains recovered at the Olmec center of San Lorenzo were fragments of skulls and long bones that turned up, along with other faunal remains, in Chicharras and San Lorenzo phase (1250–900 B.C.) midden deposits on the Northwest Ridge of the San Lorenzo plateau and in the Cañada del Macaya barranca some 23 m below (Coe and Diehl 1980:84, 91, 375–377, 386). Coe interprets these deposits as "kitchen debris" and associates the "cannibalized" human remains with Olmec warfare (Coe and Diehl 1980:386, 392).

Taken together, these archaeological examples of ritual cannibalism meet many of the criteria outlined by a number of archaeologists who have analyzed cannibalized bone assemblages (Turner and Morris 1970; Turner 1983; Turner and Turner 1992; Flinn et al. 1976; Villa et al. 1986; White 1992). Villa et al. (1986:431) proposed the following four lines of evidence for recognizing cannibalism in the archaeological record: (1) similar butchering techniques in human and animal remains; (2) similar patterns of long bone breakage that might facilitate marrow extraction (Figure 60); (3) identical patterns of postprocessing discard of human and animal remains; (4) evidence of cooking. At least 25 human bone assemblages from the American Southwest can now be considered cannibalized, including the human bodies reported as having met a violent death at the aforementioned sites of Bancos Village, Sambrito Village, Largo Gallina, Polacca Wash, and Burnt Mesa (Turner 1983: Table 1; White 1992:34–36, Fig. 3.1–3.2, 350–355, Appendix 1).

White's rigorous examination of the 29 cannibalized MNI from the pueblo site of Mancos (A.D. 1100–1150), Colorado, can be considered a benchmark. His element-by-element consideration of the Mancos assemblage in its maximally conjoined state, from the perspective of a physical anthropologist, was complemented by his analysis of the unconjoined assemblage from the perspective of an archaeological faunal analyst. White discovered that the patterns of skeletal representation and the patterns of bone modification in the Mancos human bone assemblage were similar to those of nonhuman faunal assemblages in the Southwest. The heads were removed and heated before being cracked open with hammerstones on anvils to remove brain tissue. The trunk was completely disarticulated and the limb bones were differentially heated and cracked, crushed, and reduced to splinters by bending and by percussion with hammerstones on an anvil in order to extract the marrow (Figure 60). The hands and feet were removed and their spongy bone portions were crushed with hammerstones and anvils. The ribs were snapped off and the clavicles, scapulae, vertebrae, and pelvic bones were heated and their spongy bone portions were crushed.

In addition to cutmarks produced by stone blades and wedge-shaped chopmarks produced by hammerstones, White identified scraping marks related to the removal of tissue from the surface of bones and percussion scratches (White 1992:146–152). White also identified and documented experimentally the existence of pot polish especially on the tips of humerus, femur, and tibia splinters and broken ribs, produced through contact with the interior walls of ceramic vessels during cooking by boiling, a characteristic of other cannibalized assemblages as well (White 1992:121–124, 324–325, 344; Turner and Turner 1992:679). The bone representation and modification patterns of the Mancos victims point to the extraction and direct consumption of fatty marrow tissue, and the production of bone grease by boiling.

Should anyone doubt the nutritional motivation that underlay the intensive processing of 17 adults and 12 children at Mancos, which occurred simultaneously sometime before A.D. 1150, a few metapodials and phalanges showed the characteristic punctures and crushing on their ends produced by human chewing, similar to those seen in nonhuman faunal assemblages (White 1992:334–335). Supporting evidence for the direct consumption of spongy bone tissue in the Southwest comes from coprolites, which have been discovered to contain tiny charred bone fragments (White 1992:345–346). The only pattern of processing seen in the Mancos remains that does not seem to have been nutritionally oriented is the incidence of cutmarks on the vault of the skull, which may have been related to scalping, a form of trophy taking already noted at other sites in the Southwest (White 1992:206–207; Flinn et al. 1976:313; Turner 1983:234; Turner and Turner 1992:675).

The examples of ritual cannibalism from the Circum-Caribbean area, while tantalizingly incomplete when compared to the cannibalized remains from the American Southwest, manifest similar patterns of skeletal representation and bone modification. The disarticulated human remains consist principally of skulls and long bones that are fragmentary, and sometimes burned or associated with ash and charcoal. Some long bones bear broad, wedge-shaped chopmarks (White 1992:146–148) and the characteristic signatures of marrow extraction (Figure 60). These modified human bones occur in middens, trash pits, or general refuse deposits; the only exception to this rule of context would appear to be the human remains associated with urn burials at the site of Caño Caroní, but here they are mixed with other faunal remains (Zucchi 1975:59). As a group, then, they meet the conditions for inferring cannibalism in archaeological contexts:

> when archaeologists find *faunal* remains whose context, element representation, and damage patterns are in accordance with exploitation for nutritional benefit, the faunal remains may be interpreted to represent evidence of human consumption. When *human* remains are found in similar contexts, with similar patterns of exploitation, they are best interpreted as evidence of conspecific consumption, or cannibalism. [White 1992:339]

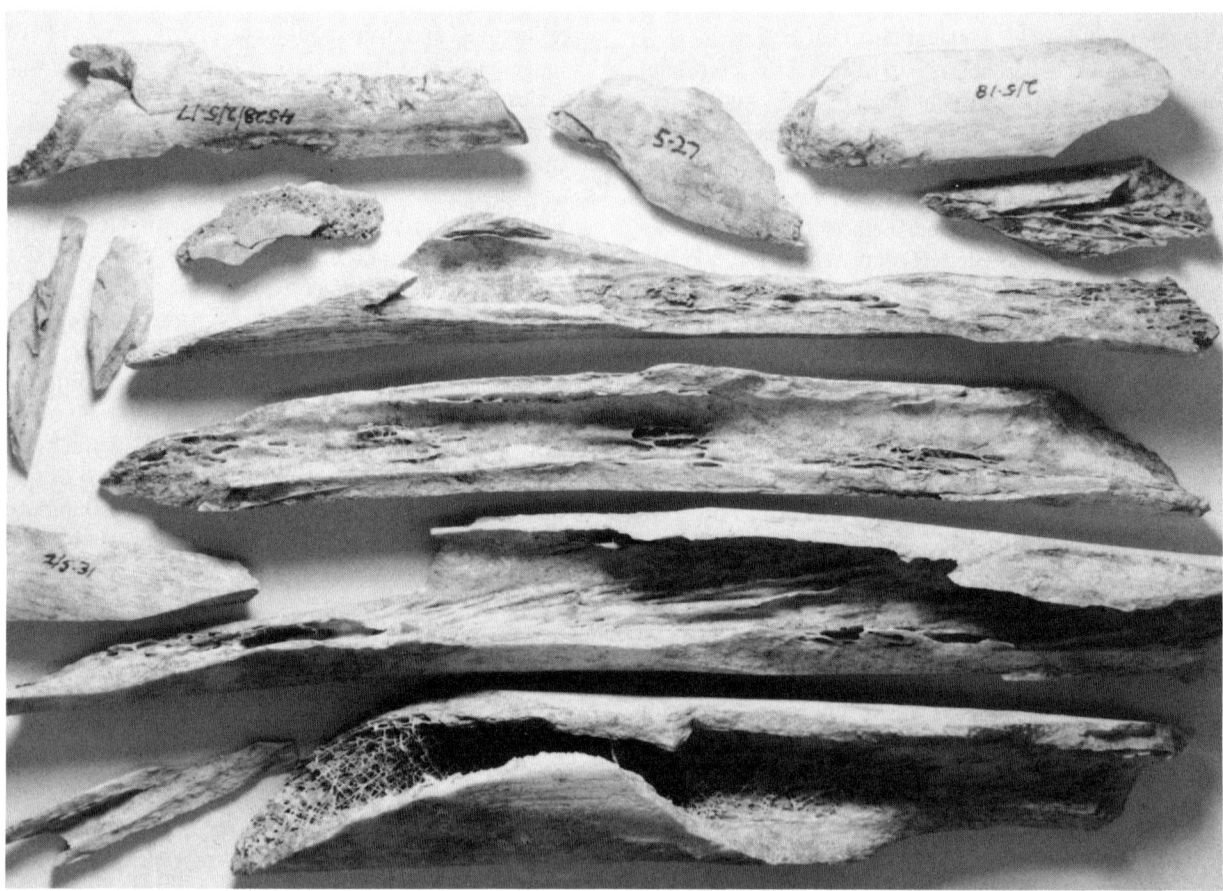

*Figure 60.* Splintered long-bone shafts from Burnt Mesa, New Mexico. They are a diagnostic feature of a pattern of bone modification associated with the extraction of marrow. [CGT neg. 1–12–83:22.]

## *Display of Human War Trophies*

The heads, limbs, hands, and feet of their victims became trophies, to be displayed in public at the doors of their residences, and on the posts of palisades and enclosures. Although these post-war practices were not limited to the chiefly elite, we know that chiefs presided over the large-scale sacrifice of captives in their precincts and that they displayed and hoarded human war trophies in their precincts and in special charnels, as symbols of their military victories and hence, of their greatness. We would therefore expect to recover disarticulated human skeletons of both sexes and of all ages at chiefly centers, associated with residences, but with the highest densities occurring in the chiefly precinct. In keeping with the Cauca Valley and Tairona chiefs' practice of storing human war trophies in special storehouses, structures within the chiefly enclosure might contain large quantities of skulls, long bones, and other skeletal remains.

It is true that the disarticulated human remains reported at a host of South and Central American sites (and described above) largely consist of skulls, skull fragments, long bones, and phalanges. They represent precisely the kinds of human body parts that victorious chiefs and their followers hung or impaled at the doors of their houses, which would have wound up as household refuse. At the chiefly center of Gaván in Barinas, Venezuela, Charles Spencer and I recovered the fragmentary remains of at least four disarticulated human skeletons, which differed in their context and disposition to the articulated skeletons buried in extended positions beneath housefloors at the center. These disarticulated, partial skeletons, which could not be considered "burials" in the ordinary sense of the term (and which are currently being examined by a physical anthropologist at the Museo de Ciencias Naturales in Caracas), were recovered in public or ceremonial contexts, underlying earthen mounds on the plaza, including the main mound (Spencer and Redmond 1992:148–149). It is possible that the piles of human bones reportedly excavated in stone mounds at the ridgetop site of Cerro Banco de Natá, near Olá, Panama, represent the same practice of displaying or storing human war trophies:

> there are a number of stone mounds consisting of boulders piled up in a ring. The diameter of the circles is about ten meters and the width of the rings is a meter. A Colombian named Cárdenas dug to a great depth in

several of these rings. He found only human bones but piled up in great quantity, in one case to a depth of two meters. [Lothrop 1942:211]

Some of the clearest archaeological evidence of the chief's right to possess human war trophies, is found at the regional center of Casas Grandes, in Chihuahua, Mexico. A cruciform-shaped room in the centrally located House of Skulls contained six skulls, all of which lacked mandibles and four of which had been perforated with drill holes, probably for suspension; the four skulls that could be aged and sexed were adult males, whose physical characteristics differed from the skulls of other burials at Casas Grandes. The possibility that this cruciform-shaped room served as a charnel house is strengthened by the collection of worked and unworked human bones that were also found here, which included long bones, long-bone wands, bone nose ornaments, bone rasps, and the drilled mandible of an adult male decorated with turquoise mosaic and red pigment. This "ceremonial trove" also contained four stone axes and two shell trumpets (Di Peso et al. 1974:53–64; Ravesloot 1988:36–39, 71–72).

Other artifacts fashioned from human remains have been recovered at Casas Grandes, among them a skullcap dish, a necklace of hand and foot phalanges, and rasps made from notched long bones (Di Peso et al. 1974:51, 63–65). Because of the material from which they are made, they convey important symbolic meaning; Ravesloot (1988:71) proposes that "these artifacts probably represent personal trophies taken in battle and suggest that military force and organized warfare played an important part in the emergence of a hierarchical social structure at Casas Grandes."

Artifacts fashioned from human bone have turned up at many northern South American and Central American sites, like the incised astralagus from the site of Gairaca, east of Santa Marta, Colombia (Mason 1931:231) (Figure 61), and the humerus whittled into a spatula and stained with grease that was recovered in a grave at the cemetery of Venado Beach, Panama (Lothrop 1954:232). I will describe additional examples of human war trophies associated with burials in the following section that deals with mortuary treatment.

## Mortuary Treatment

The accounts we have of chiefly warfare suggest that the bodies of warriors who met their death on the battlefield were left behind to the whims of the victors and the elements. And the warriors who were taken captive by the enemy wound up in their burial population or faunal assemblage. For these reasons, warriors will be underrepresented in the burial populations of chiefdoms. At Casas Grandes, for example, over 60% of the adult burials whose sex could be determined were females. It is likely that many adult males, as warriors, met their death away in war and that their bodies were buried or deposited elsewhere (Di Peso 1974:640–641).

We know that the bodies of renowned warriors and war leaders in the Circum-Caribbean chiefdoms were returned home. As members of the chiefly elite, they were entitled to having their bodies preserved and often buried in tombs. The Period V (A.D. 500–700) cemetery at Venado Beach, Panama, may represent such an elite burial ground, where renowned warriors and other members of the elite—including children bedecked with gold breastplates and other gold and shell ornaments—may have been buried, together with many sacrificial victims and retainers (Lothrop 1954, 1956; Linares 1977:72; Cooke 1984:287).

The possibility that the Period V cemetery at Sitio Conte, in Coclé, served as an elite burial ground (Linares 1977:76–77) is supported by Briggs's (1986) examination of the sex and age of the individuals interred in more than 100 graves there, which were excavated principally by the Harvard Peabody Museum (1930–1933) and the University Museum of the University of Pennsylvania (1940). Approximately 75% of the individuals buried there (whose remains could be aged and sexed) were adult males. Only two children (or 1%) were among the 201 individuals buried there, and all but one of the females found in the graves were buried with an adult male (Briggs 1986:101–104, 156–157). Briggs concludes that "if the Sitio Conte cemetery is a specialized burial facility for individuals who have achieved a unique status entitling them to interment in this necropolis, such special treatment centered on adult males" (Briggs 1986:157). The adult males buried in Graves 13 and 19 are likely examples of renowned warriors or *cabras* (Figures 62, 63). They are extended burials, lying face down in an east to west orientation, wearing agate winged pendants, metal disks and nose ornaments, and bone and stone beads. Their funerary accompaniments feature bundles of stingray spines, bone awls, shark teeth, chipped-stone blades, chips, and arrowpoints, and other possible weapons and accoutrements (Figure 64) (Lothrop 1937:58, 64, 245–249, 255–256).

A similar burial pattern occurs at the Mississippian center of Moundville (A.D. 1200–1500), where burial in mounds and nearby burial grounds was reserved principally for adult males (Peebles and Kus 1977:438–439). Not only do adult males far outnumber adult females and children in what appear to be restricted burial grounds and have richer, more exotic funerary accompaniments, but they are also taller and they exhibit more healed fractures and piercing wounds, a pattern that is repeated at other Mississippian communities (Powell 1988:144–145, Table 47, 193–196). The fractures probably represent wounds suffered in combat, and suggest that distinguished warriors in Mississippian society were also entitled to sumptuary privileges, including a special burial: "given that demonstrated prowess in warfare enhanced male ranked status in Mississippian society . . . the observed pattern of tall males bearing skeletal evidence of successful (healed) past combats and buried in restricted burial locations (mounds, perimound cemeteries) with grave goods denoting high status does not seem surprising" (Powell 1988:196).

An analogous pattern exists among Marajoara urn burials, which were placed in individual pits in spatially discrete cemeteries located in mounds. There are differences between the individuals buried in plain urns and those buried in urns decorated

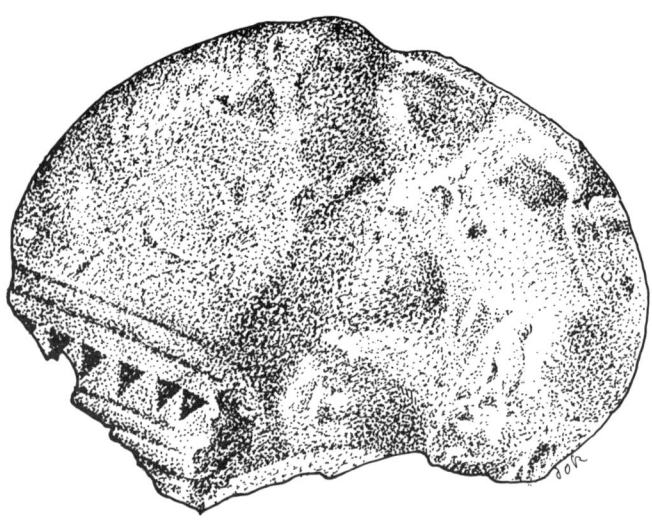

*Figure 61.* Incised human astralagus from Nahuange, Santa Marta, Colombia. Scale 2:1. [Redrawn from Mason 1936: Plate CXXIV:3.]

with elaborately painted, incised, excised, and modeled designs and motifs: "most of the skeletons from decorated urns are tall, robust men with strong dense bones and few or no pathologies" (Roosevelt 1991:55). In view of their different physique, the implications of which I examined earlier, and their special burial context, Roosevelt (1991:407) suggests that the tall, muscular individuals accorded burial in decorated urns represented a warrior elite in Marajoara society.

Be they primary burials or secondary burials, including urn burials, the burial context and the nature and number of funerary accompaniments will reflect the individual's social persona, including his military rank (Peebles and Kus 1977:431, 435–440). There will be a fundamental difference between those warriors interred in simple graves and distinguished warriors and other members of the chiefly elite, who are buried in stone-lined shaft tombs with numerous, elaborate offerings. Individuals of high rank must have been accorded burial in the stone-slab tombs inside earthen mounds in the San Agustín area of the upper Magdalena River during the first few centuries A.D. Moreover, they were accompanied by Atlantean stone sculptures over 2.50 m tall of men wearing helmets and bearing weapons, "warriors or guardians perhaps—who in menacing gesture grasp huge clubs in their upheld hands" (Reichel-Dolmatoff 1972:42, Figs.16, 17, 33; Drennan 1991:275–277). Likewise, the funerary accompaniments in a shaft tomb excavated at Hacienda de la Marquesa, near Timbío, on the upper Cauca River included gold nose ornaments and other spiraled ornaments, necklaces made up of tiny gold frogs, an anthropomorphic gold plaque, as well as three ceramic male figurines shown sitting on benches, wearing headdresses, body paint, necklaces and leg bands, and bearing round shields (Lehmann 1953:206–212, Plates II, III; Reichel-Dolmatoff 1965:133).

Moreover, there is considerable status differentiation among the individuals buried in shaft tombs, as represented by the kind and quantity of their funerary accompaniments. Looters in the Quimbaya region of the Cauca Valley claim that in most cases the only gold objects are the deceased's personal ornaments—ear ornaments, nose ornaments, and bracelets—and that it is mainly very large tombs with multiple burials that contain gold ornaments and other gold accoutrements in any quantity (Bruhns 1972:142). Helms has argued convincingly that the quantity, the diversity, and the iconography of the goldwork found in the largest and richest tombs in neighboring Panama symbolized the deceased's supernatural energy and sacred chiefly authority and power, which derived largely from the acquisition of esoteric knowledge about foreign and supernatural domains (Helms 1979:77–92, 160–171). The iconographically rich golden helmets, breastplates, earrings, nose rings, pendants, and other "ornaments" remain as glittering material emblems of the sacred power of pre-Columbian chiefly elites, "whose travels have long been over, but whose material emblems of chiefly journeys, esoteric knowledge, and rivalrous power remain to us" (Helms 1979:142–143).

In addition to personal ornaments and insignia, the tombs of distinguished warriors and of other members of the chiefly elite also contain, as we noted earlier, weapons and other military accoutrements. Among the more than twenty shaft tombs that Stirling excavated at Hacienda La Pita, in Veraguas, Panama, was Tomb 15, which contained an animal ornament, nose ornament, beads, and a solid human figure of gold, as well as a necklace of polished carnelian beads and a large carnelian pendant, 50 ceramic vessels, six ceramic effigy whistles, and two carved stone metates. But the most abundant funerary accompaniments in Tomb 15 were weapons: 26 flint arrowheads, and 76 polished stone axes (Stirling 1950:246). Enormous quantities of weapons have been reported from tombs looted in the Cauca Valley (see Table 1). In the Calima Valley to the west, a Sonso period (A.D. 1200–1290) shaft tomb with a trough-shaped wooden coffin contained two ceramic vessels, and a spearthrower and five wooden darts made of *chonta* palm wood, which "may have been the personal weapons of the occupant" (von Schuler-Schömig 1981:25–27).

A variety of musical instruments that we know were used by warring chiefs to sound the alarm and summon warriors as well as to intimidate the enemy and to intone pre-war and post-war rituals have been recovered in tombs and graves. Tombs in the Cauca Valley have been reported to contain conch-shell trumpets, wooden drums, flutes, horns, and rattles (Arango C. 1924, I:163–164, 169, 190, 194; II:22, 180, 217, 314; Rodríguez 1985:50). In northwestern Panama, a Bocas phase (A.D. 900) burial recovered at Cerro Brujo was accompanied by two large *Strombus* shell trumpets (Linares 1980c:299). Finally, one of the richest tombs dating to Monte Albán's founding (Period I) is Tomb 43, which featured 18 conch-shell effigy vessels among its 70 or more ceramic vessels. The occurrence of so many conch-shell effigies in this tomb may indicate that the individual buried

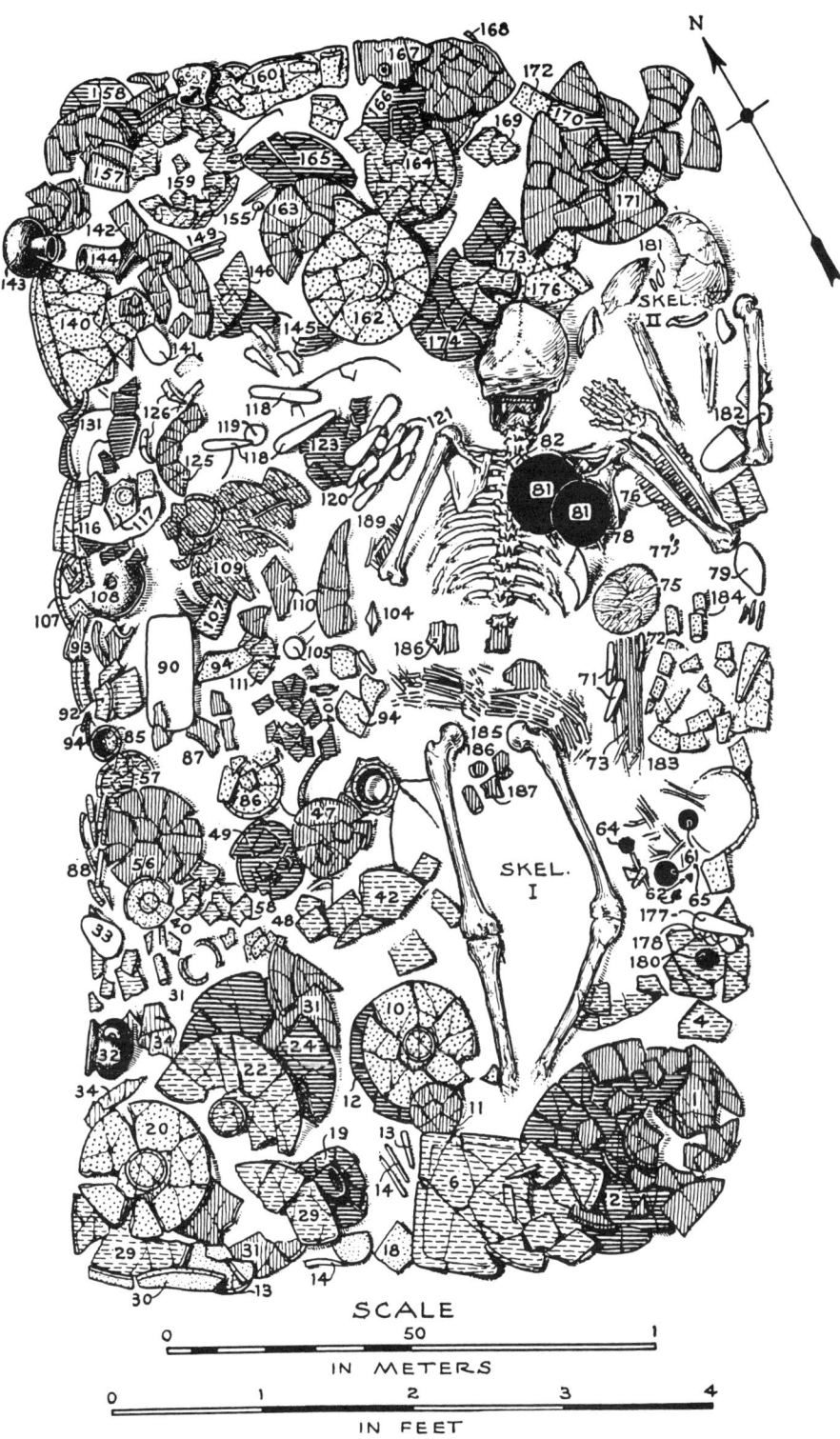

*Figure 62.* Plan of Grave 13, Sitio Conte, Coclé, Panama. The principal occupant was an adult male, who was buried in an extended, face-down position. His funerary accompaniments included stingray spines (66), a bundle of stingray spines (73), stone arrowpoints (69, 71), bone arrowpoints (26, 72), and shark teeth (74, 151). On his back lay two gold disks (81) and an agate winged pendant (82). [Reprinted by permission, from *Coclé: An Archaeological Study of Central Panama* (Lothrop 1937: Fig. 229). Peabody Museum.]

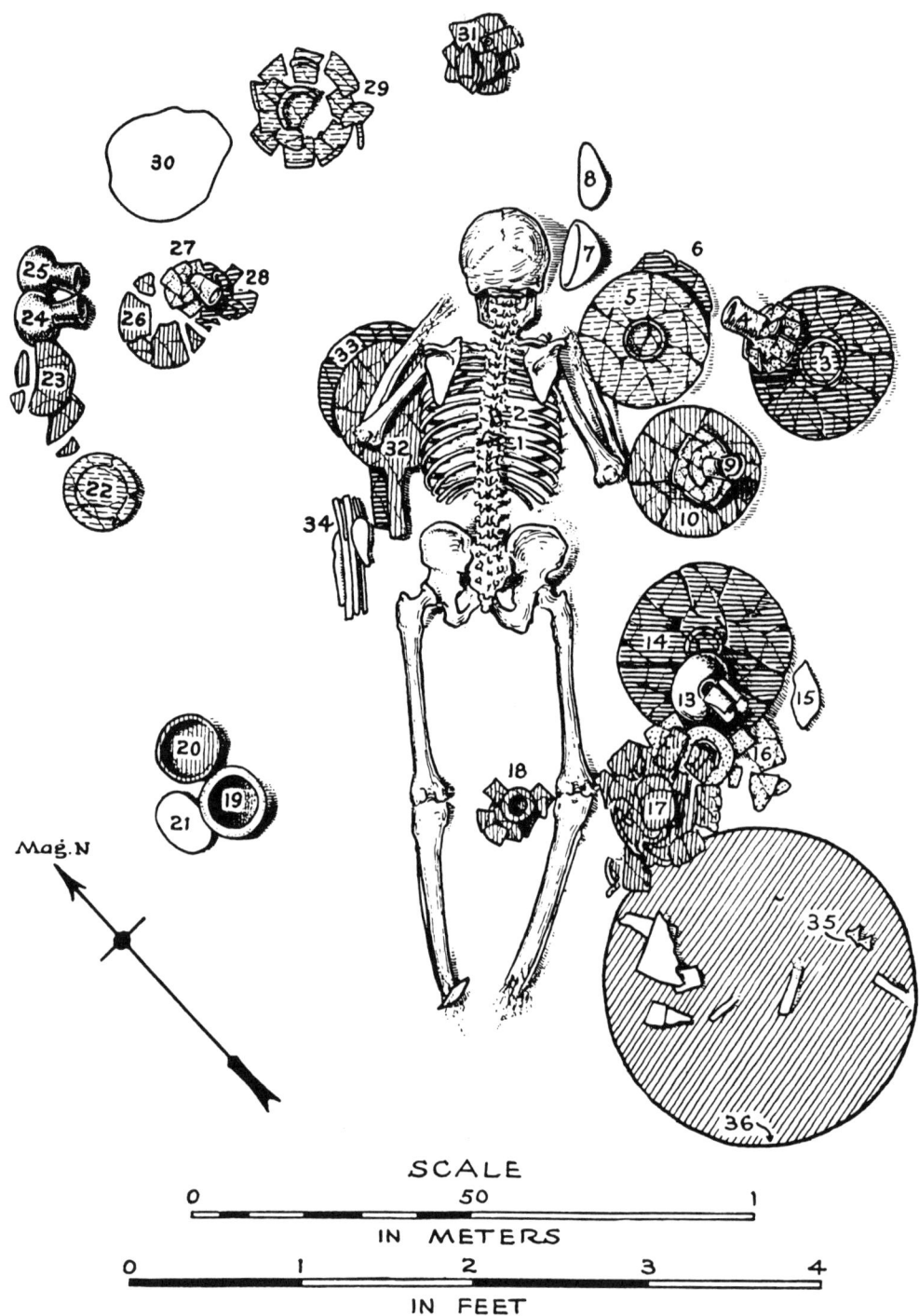

*Figure 63.* Plan of Grave 19, Sitio Conte, Coclé, Panama. A single adult (male?) skeleton lay in an extended, face-down position. By the left hip lay a bundle of stingray spines, chipped-stone knives, chisels, and a shark tooth (34). Other offerings included two shark teeth (35) and a polychrome human effigy jar (29). On the back lay an agate winged pendant (1) and two stone beads (2). [Reprinted by permission, from *Coclé: An Archaeological Study of Central Panama* (Lothrop 1937: Fig. 233). Peabody Museum.]

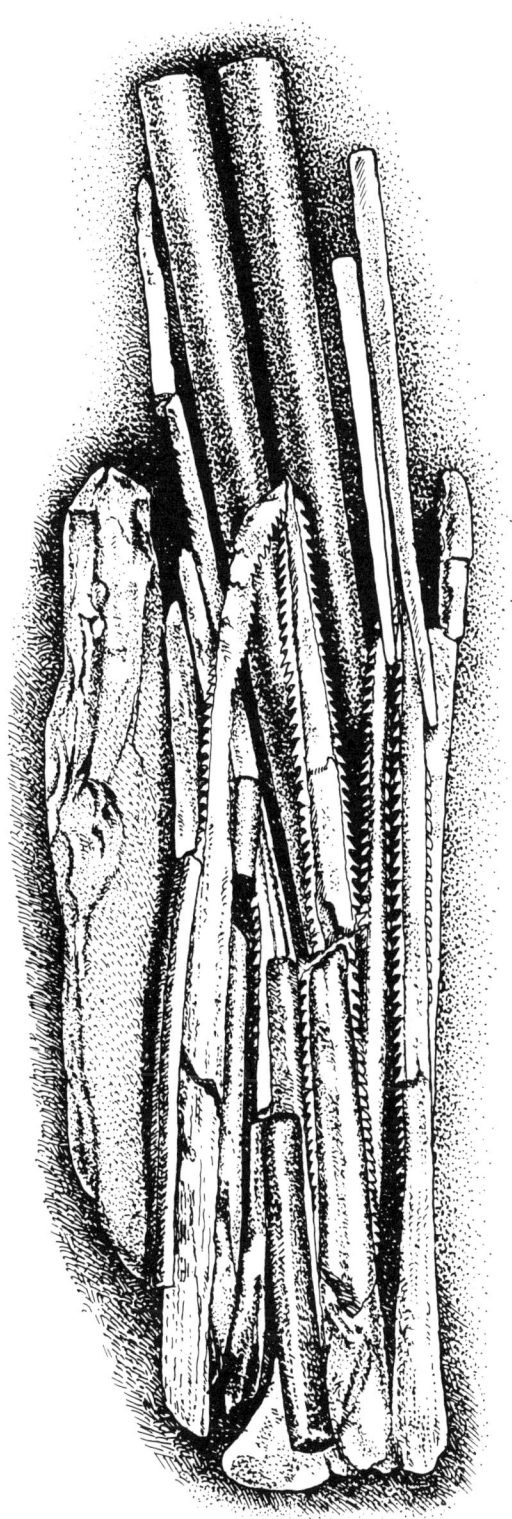

Figure 64. Bundle of stingray spines, two gold chisels, two stone rods, two chipped-stone knives, and a shark tooth that lay by the left hip of the adult skeleton buried in Grave 19, Sitio Conte. [Redrawn from Lothrop 1937: Fig. 32.]

there was a member of the ruling elite (Flannery and Marcus 1983:90).

Another sign of the deceased's status in life would be the presence of human war trophies buried with him. As early as 240–25 B.C., certain subfloor flexed skeletons at Sitio Sierra, in central Panama, were buried with stingray spines and a trophy head (Cooke 1979:952; Cooke 1984:287; Cooke and Ranere 1989:310). Extended Burial 6 in the main mound at La Pitahaya, in western Panama (A.D. 600), had two skulls by its side (Linares 1980d:312, Fig.7/4). Many tombs in the Quimbaya region of the Cauca Valley are reported to have contained perforated human skulls (Arango C. 1924, II:325). The possibility that other human body parts could wind up as funerary accompaniments is raised by the contents of one of the ceramic vessels recovered in the shaft tomb from Calima described above; a 23 cm-tall utilitarian jar with a sooty exterior surface contained a high animal fat content, probably from a dismembered body part with skin and hair (von Schuler-Schömig 1981:27).

In addition to actual human war trophies, there are iconographic renditions of human war trophies in many high-status tombs. For example, the most elaborate shaft tombs excavated at the Panamanian center of Barriles (A.D. 400–800) contained only carved ground-stone metates or stools with three or four legs, 1.50 to 2.20 m in length and about 100 pounds in weight, and therefore "too large for practical use" (Stirling 1950:244). Their carved supports portray helmeted males bearing multiple head trophies that line the rim of the metate's basin (Stirling 1950:243–244; Linares, Sheets, Rosenthal 1975:141, Figs. 5–6).

Artifacts fashioned from human bone, which can be considered war trophies as well due to the material from which they derive, also occur as funerary accompaniments. In addition to the incised human astralagus recovered in a burial at the Tairona site of Nahuange, Colombia (Mason 1931–1939:37, 231, Plate CXXIV:3) (Figure 61), and the whittled, grease-stained humerus associated with a burial at Venado Beach, Panama, several carved bone staff heads were recovered in Tairona burial urns at Gairaca, Colombia, including one in the shape of a male figure wearing headgear and sitting on a curved seat with his hands outstretched (Mason 1931–1939:29, 229, Plates CXXV–CXXVI) (Figure 65).

There are burials wearing human trophies in the form of necklaces and other ornaments made of human bone, as a further and personal display of their prowess and victory in warfare. The two clusters of human teeth recovered in Grave 32 at Sitio Conte, one of which consisted of 53 teeth, may have been originally strung together on a necklace (Lothrop 1937:288). A bead gorget recovered in a grave at Venado Beach had been strung on strands of human hair (Lothrop 1956:36). While strands of human hair are arguably questionable war trophies, they do point to the opportunistic use of various human body elements as raw materials, whose intrinsic value might have stemmed from their very source. As it is, looted tombs on the mountain ridge of El Capitolio in the Cauca Valley are reported to have contained bone tubes made from long bones to be worn as a pendant or necklace:

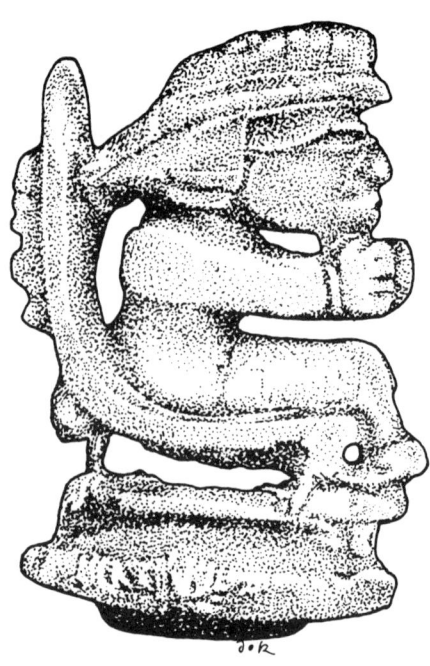

*Figure 65.* Carved bone staff head from an urn burial at Gairaca, Colombia, shows a seated male figure wearing a helmet, with his hands outstretched. Scale 2:1. [Redrawn from Mason 1936: Plate CXXV.]

"varios huesos hasta de 10 pulgadas de longitud y 2 pulgadas de diámetro, en forma de canutillo, perforados a lo largo con un orificio circular para pasarle un hilo y colgarlos al cuello" (Arango C. 1924, I:190).

Of course, warring chiefs were accorded the most elaborate mourning ceremonies and funerary treatment. Their tombs should be located within the chiefly precinct, and should have the richest offerings, including human war trophies and sacrificed burial retainers. As in the mortuary practices of chiefdoms in other areas, we have seen how the "nonpersons" (Peebles and Kus 1977:439), sacrificed in order to serve as burial retainers for dead chiefs in northern South America and lower Central America, included captives seized in warfare. The sacrifice of captives to serve as burial retainers on the occasion of a chief's burial can be considered an extension of the chiefly practice of hoarding the remains of war victims in charnels and of burying human war trophies with the deceased. Only it involves the seizing and sacrificing of entire bodies, sometimes on a large scale, depending on the deceased chief's greatness (Cieza de León 1853:380; Espinosa 1873:27). These "nonpersons" became funerary accompaniments, whose purpose was to serve their lord forever, and to rest in mute testimony of his power and authority (Espinosa 1873:27; Oviedo y Valdés 1853:154–156).

The most high-ranking individuals buried at Casas Grandes, for example, were buried in special locations and featured human war trophies and burial retainers. Ravesloot's investigation of social ranking at Casas Grandes on the basis of mortuary practices revealed that the three highest-ranking individuals buried at Casas Grandes were laid to rest in Ramos polychrome urns in special chambers or vaults in a sanctuary atop the Mound of the Offerings on the western edge of the central plaza. Two of them were a middle-aged male (Burial 4–4) and female (Burial 3–4), who were laid to rest together in one vault (Vault 2) along with human war trophies: a musical rasp made from a long bone, a necklace of human phalanges, and two unworked long bones (Ravesloot 1988:25). Another location where members of the Casas Grandes elite were buried was the House of the Dead on the southern edge of the central plaza. Two adult males (13–13, 44E-13) were buried in elaborate subfloor tombs here, together with a large number and diversity of funerary accompaniments, including ceramic effigies, hand drums, copper pendants, stone and shell beads, and burial retainers (Ravesloot 1988:32–34; Di Peso et al. 1974:390, 392–393). The latter middle-aged male (44E-13) in particular had the remains of one male and five females stacked below and above him; the fragmentary, disarticulated remains of four adolescents and one adult of undetermined sex were found scattered above in the top level of the tomb (Ravesloot 1988:3234; Di Peso et al. 1974:387–389, 392–393).

The burial of high-status individuals with rich offerings and multiple burial retainers is well documented throughout northern South America and the Intermediate area. In the principal Guajará mound at the site of Monte Carmelo on the upper Anajás River on Marajó Island, Meggers and Evans excavated a cluster of Marajoara funerary urns. Among them was an elaborate Joanes Painted anthropomorphic urn burial (Jar L) that was flanked by two Inajá Plain urns containing the remains of at least three young adults of both sexes (Meggers and Evans 1957:259–261, 271–275). Meggers and Evans suggested that "the elaborateness of the central jar makes it probable that it contained an important personage whose comfort in the next world needed to be assured" (Meggers and Evans 1957:273). To their interpretation Roosevelt has added that "this was a high-status burial with low-ranking attendants, perhaps killed for the occasion" (Roosevelt 1991:54).

Village cemeteries of the Middle Cauca complex (A.D. 1000–1200) in the Quimbaya region of the Cauca Valley, Colombia, feature shaft tombs with multiple chambers, "the largest and richest tombs often containing several bodies stretched out on the floor of the funerary chamber—perhaps those of a chief and his retainers, as described by Cieza" (Bray 1978:49). Arango C.'s memoir of looted tombs in the Cauca Valley includes many descriptions of tombs containing multiple burials. Tombs could contain up to 80 individuals, Arango C. said in his general remarks about mortuary practices (Chapter III), most of whom, he suggested, represented burial retainers (Arango C. 1924, I:27). His description of two tombs is illustrative of the use of many burial retainers in high-status tombs. A tomb in La Argentina that contained the cremated remains of a single individual was accompanied on either side by ten and nine extended burials, respectively, along with ceramic offerings. Arango C. interpreted the sequence of burial in the tomb as follows:

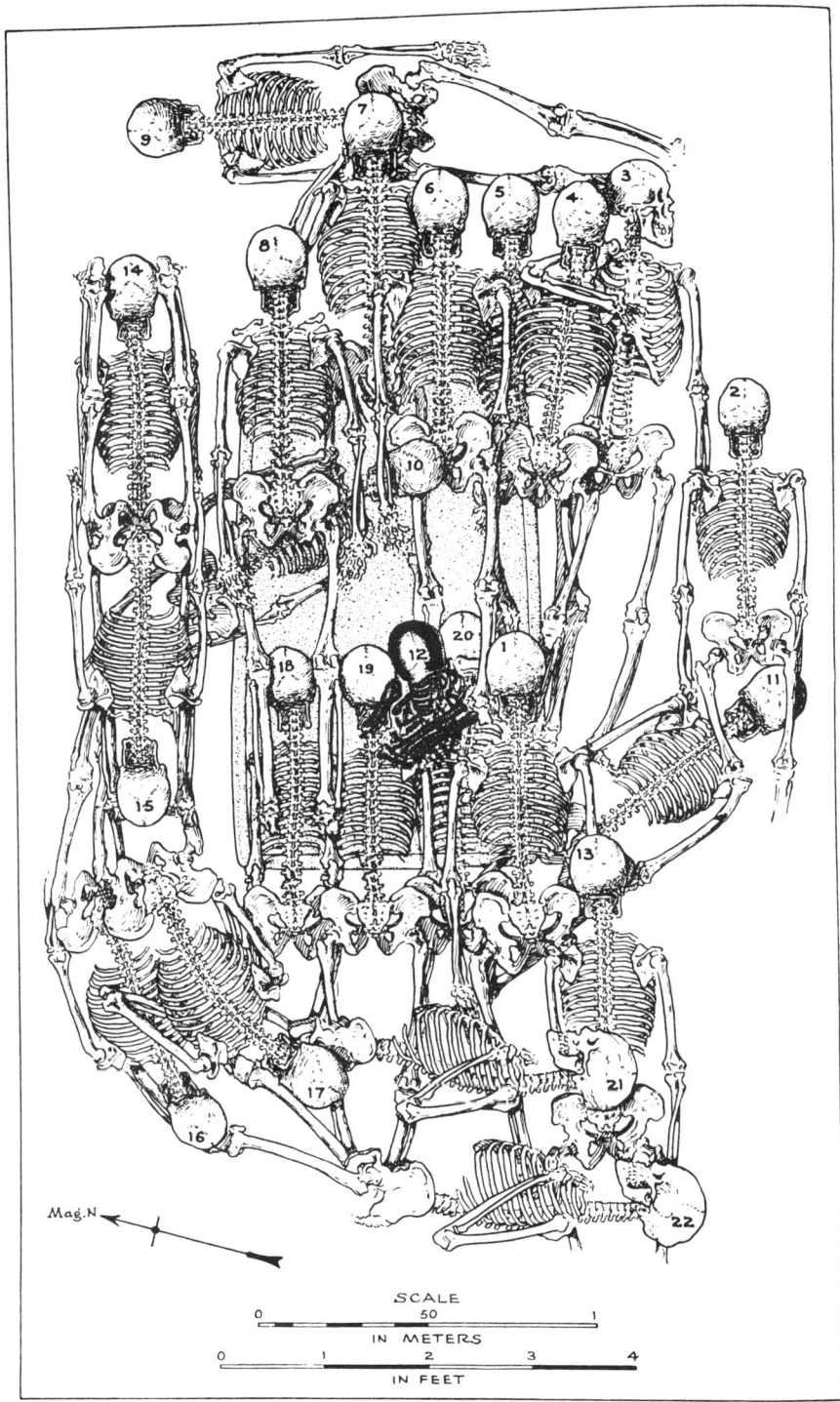

*Figure 66.* Plan of skeletons in Grave 26, Sitio Conte, Coclé, Panama. The principal occupant of the grave was an adult male (12), who was laid to rest in a seated position in the center. Stacked in rows around him lay the extended bodies of 21 male and female burial retainers. [Reprinted by permission, from *Coclé: An Archaeological Study of Central Panama* (Lothrop 1937: Fig. 31). Peabody Museum.]

el del centro lo habían quemado los indios allí mismo, así: fue el primero que acostaron, sin tendido, con el cuerpo rígido; luego le pusieron encima combustible y lo quemaron; los sobrevivientes respetaron esas cenizas, pues se hallaron tal como habían sido dejadas por el fuego. Después dieron sepultura a sus compañeros mortecinos. [Arango C. 1924, II:161–162]

Each of the burial retainers possessed a copper ring and a gold-plated nose ornament. Near the ridge of El Maizal, south of Tolima, Arango C. reported a six-chambered tomb. Each of the four smaller chambers flanking the two central chambers contained one or two skeletons; the two central chambers were full of skeletons. Finally, more than 300 skulls and a considerable number of skeletons were recovered in the shaft of the tomb, evidently burned, crushed, and thrown into the tomb in disorder and without offerings (Arango C. 1924, II:182).

To date, some of the best-documented burials of high-ranking individuals in the Circum-Caribbean area are the handful of large graves from Sito Conte (A.D. 700–900) in central Panama, which have been attributed to deceased paramount chiefs or *quevís*, on the basis of their similarities to the burials of sixteenth-century Panamanian chiefs (Lothrop 1937:64; Mason 1942:104). They are "truly great undertakings, elaborately constructed" (Lothrop 1937:49) with stone-slab floors, and are distinguished by their size and depth, their concave floors and flaring walls, their orientation to the cardinal points, as well as by the hundreds of ceramic vessels, metal ornaments, bone tubes, whale teeth, and the twenty or more burial retainers they contain (Lothrop 1937:48; Briggs 1986:111–112, 129–130, 167–168). The largest and the richest are Grave 26, excavated by Lothrop (1937) and Burial 11, which lay nearby but which was excavated by Mason (Briggs 1986:123–130; Hearne 1992:7).

Grave 26 was that of an adult male (Skeleton XII), whose desiccated body had been interred, seated on a stool in a perishable shelter on a stone slab lined with textiles in a concave or bowl-shaped grave, whose floor measured 2.1 m by 3.1 m and lay some 3 m under the ground. His funerary accompaniments consisted of stone, bone, gold and feather regalia and weapons, hundreds of polychrome ceramic vessels, baskets, and the extended bodies of 21 other adults, carefully stacked in rows around the principal male personage (Figure 66). Of the nine accompanying skeletons whose age and sex could be determined, two were adult females, one of which was old. The remainder were males: one old adult male, five adult males, and one young adult male (Lothrop 1937:62–63, 269). They were no doubt the wives and war captives who were sacrificed in order to serve as chiefly burial retainers (Lothrop 1937:49–52, 269–277).

Burial 11 was the grave of one or two principal adult individuals, who lay in extended, face-down positions in the center of the bowl-shaped grave, one lying on top of the other, and were associated with a staggering amount of gold ornaments and other fine ornaments of resin and bone, a cache of projectile points, and a fine stone celt (Briggs 1986:126–127). Mason noted in his expedition diary that he assumed that the bottom one of the pair was the grave's principal occupant, whose funerary regalia has been reconstructed:

> On and near the skull were numerous small embossed gold discs that once must have been affixed to a headdress. A pair of gold ear rods were found on either side of the skull. Quantities of both round and tubular beads were found in the neck and chest area, and pelvic region, indicating gold necklaces and a beaded girdle at the waist. Below each elbow were embossed gold cuffs with smaller plain cuffs underneath. Since the narrow ends of the cuffs were pointing toward the skull, it seems likely that the arms of the deceased originally had been crossed over his chest. Smaller plain gold cuffs were found near the ankles. Five large gold embossed plaques with anthropomorphic designs were found on or near the skeleton. This same individual was also associated with the most famous object from Mason's excavations at Sitio Conte, a unique animal effigy pendant with an emerald set in its back, found on the skeleton's chest. [Hearne 1992:11]

The primary occupant (or occupants) of the grave was sandwiched between 21 or 22 additional interments. They include adults of both sexes and ages, who had been laid to rest in extended, face-down positions in three layers. Below the primary occupant lay three individuals of unknown sex, who rested on a bed of ceramic vessels, and who were associated with wooden implements, quartz projectile points, and stone celts. Flanking the primary occupant in the middle layer of the grave, on a bed of ceramic vessels and bark cloth, were ten or eleven individuals, including an individual identified as a female (Skeleton IX) and an individual identified as a young male (Skeleton XII), many of whom were associated with gold ornaments (Briggs 1986:128; Hearne 1992:10–11, 21). Above the primary occupant lay eight individuals in extended, face-down positions, six of whom were identified as adult (mature) males. They were variously associated with stone ornaments, a few gold ornaments and chisels, stingray spines, shark teeth, stone and bone projectile points, and stone celts. With at least 23 individuals buried in three layers and over 7,500 funerary objects, Burial 11 is the richest grave at Sitio Conte (Briggs 1986:123, 129; Hearne 1992:7).

It seems that not only was a great value attached to the number of burial retainers interred with the primary occupants of Burial 11 and Grave 26, but also, as Briggs suggests, the additional burial retainers in these large graves at Sitio Conte were intended as "human bedding" for the primary occupants, along with the stone slabs, ceramic vessels, and turtle carapaces that were used as flooring and filler for the graves (Briggs 1986:106, 113, 125). They leave little doubt as to the chiefly status of the primary occupants, who were accorded such elaborate burial treatment, and who were accompanied by members of their retinue in the middle layer of Burial 11, and consequently, the low status of those "nonpersons" seized in warfare, who were sacrificed, stacked and stuffed in the tombs, as if to counter some *horror vacuus*.

# Chapter 7

# Conclusion

The warfare strategies of uncentralized tribes and centralized chiefdoms in northern South America and the Intermediate area differ in some fundamental ways. There are differences in the objectives that are sought through warfare, and in the scale, organization, tactics, and intensity with which tribes and chiefdoms wage warfare. There are differences in the sociopolitical and ideological components of warfare as well. In tribes, an aggrieved individual and his kinsmen will wage war in order to seek personal revenge and prestige. These goals are supplanted in chiefdoms by the military pursuits of the chief, through which he enlarges his authority over his regional domain—in the absence of internal administrative specialization. Warfare is directed by the chief, who oversees the preparations, leads large, allied fighting forces in frequent and devastating all-out attacks against enemy settlements, and reaps a variety of foreign resources therefrom, including captives and trophies, which reinforce his military might.

Moreover, the differing warfare strategies of northern South American tribes and chiefdoms can be monitored archaeologically and documented fully in the case of their prehistoric antecedents. With the framework that I have presented for examining warfare among prehistoric tribes and chiefdoms we have the chance of doing more than simply establishing the existence of warfare in a study region at a given time period. With this kind of systematic appraisal of prehistoric warfare we might be able to measure the varying intensity of warfare among the societies being studied and examine differences or changes in their warfare strategies. We might then be in the position to address the role that warfare plays in the dynamics of prehistoric tribes and chiefdoms, and to consider the role that warfare assumes in the emergence of centralized chiefly societies.

## *The Authority of Tribal War Leaders and Warring Chiefs*

Having reviewed and compared the conduct of warfare by uncentralized tribesmen to the military pursuits of centralized chiefs, it is easy to spot the limitations of tribal authority, which is characterized by consensual decision-making. Jívaro and Yanomamö war leaders face the long and arduous task of recruiting warriors from allied villages for each raid. And even after the raid is finally mounted, the war leader leads only by example; his authority can be challenged and even ignored by the members of the allied war party.

In keeping with the sequential decision-making of tribesmen, the authority or influence of war leaders is specific and temporary. Their authority over the members of a war party lasts only for the duration of the expedition. The intervillage alliances they forge in wartime do not necessarily persist in peacetime:

> certain groups may ally for a time and a purpose, as for a military venture, but the collective spirit is episodic. When the objective for which it was called into being is accomplished, the alliance lapses and the tribe returns to its normal state of disunity. [Sahlins 1968:21]

The leadership they achieve in warfare does not necessarily carry over into leadership in other tribal activities; as Spencer puts it, "different aspiring leaders may be prominent in differing contexts, some excelling in warfare, others in diplomacy, exchange, religion, adjudication, and so forth" (Spencer 1993:41–42). And no matter how distinguished war leaders become during their lifetime, other warriors will emerge and challenge their authority as they grow older and less able to lead war parties. Finally, the leaders of victorious Jívaro war parties host a series of large victory feasts, from which they derive enormous prestige, but which virtually exhaust their family's resources (Harner 1972:191). Thus, the tribal ethic not only makes the mounting and carrying out of a raid difficult, but also makes it difficult for distinguished warriors to emerge as general leaders and to amass power and wealth.

By contrast, chiefly and military authority were vested in the office of the chief among the Colombian and Panamanian chiefdoms, in keeping with the simultaneous hierarchies characteristic of chiefdoms (Johnson 1982:407–410). Sixteenth-century chiefs were chiefs first and foremost, who realized their chiefly powers in their war exploits. Chiefs were the supreme military leaders, who presided over the stockpiling of armament and provisions at chiefly centers, declared war, and convened war councils with neighboring chiefs in order to mobilize large, allied fighting forces. They were capable of summoning fighting forces that could number up to 20,000 men, a figure forty times greater than that generally recorded for the allied war parties of tribes (Harner 1972:204). Indeed, one measure of a chief's authority was the size of the fighting force he could raise (Trimborn 1949:335–338; Lothrop 1937:9–10). Compared to the protracted recruitment of warriors for a tribal war party, warring chiefs had the capacity to mobilize large, allied war parties expeditiously, as quickly as at the sound of a conch-shell trumpet or wooden drum, and in a day or two at the latest, by one account (Espinosa 1873:25). The interpolity scale at which these chiefdoms waged war was great and the organization for war was centralized and hierarchical. Paramount chiefs led multi-tiered war parties composed of troops of warriors under the command of lesser chiefs and military captains. With their greater manpower and organization, chiefly war parties could sweep through enemy territory in open advances and attack multiple settlements. They could reinforce their front lines tenfold with fresh troops during their day-long battles, and launch repeated attacks, as many as five in one day (Trimborn 1949:363).

In times of war, the chief's subjects took refuge at his fortified center, where they could either withstand a prolonged siege for up to several months, or take up arms and launch a counterattack in defense of their chief's center and territory. If we view chiefly warfare from the perspective of uncentralized tribesmen, the military readiness of chiefs and their efficient mobilization of large, hierarchically organized allied war parties is a testimony to the advantages of centralized chiefly decision-making in the conduct of warfare. With their centralized, hierarchical, decision-making organization, chiefdoms "can respond to system-endangering changes in the environment with much more sensitivity, speed, precision, and flexibility" (Rappaport 1971:66) than can uncentralized tribesmen.

Through their military victories, warring chiefs enlarged their authority over their regional domain. They expanded the boundaries of their territories and acquired land, natural resources, captives, and other spoils of war, including human war trophies, which substantiated their military might. Through warfare, warring chiefs accumulated foreign resources, which they could manipulate in self-serving ways to host feasts, build alliances, and reward followers. The wealth they garnered in warfare served to further enlarge and legitimize their authority. Chiefly authority, therefore, was closely linked to the conduct and consequences of warfare; citing passages in the accounts of Cieza de León (1853:361) and Oviedo y Valdés (1853:129), Trimborn concluded that "en realidad, los señores del valle del Cauca, como los caciques cueva, ejercían un gobierno despótico, que especialmente en guerra o, mejor dicho, a consecuencia del continuo estado de guerra, aumentaba hasta un poder ilimitado" (Trimborn 1949:241).

### The Ideological Motives of Warfare

I would like to consider the ideological motives of warfare in the tribes and chiefdoms reviewed here, and particularly their relationship to the emergence of centralized chiefly decision-making. The Jívaro saying—"I was born to die fighting" (Harner 1972:170)—eloquently illustrates the strong ideological character of tribal headhunting raids. Warfare provides tribesmen with opportunites to acquire prestige and certain supernatural powers, such as the quest for *arutam* soul power among the Jívaro and the *waiteri* qualities sought by Yanomamö warriors. Acquiring and accumulating personal power through warfare is an individualistic endeavor, pursued by all warriors (Hendricks 1988:219). The *arutam* power that a Jívaro warrior captures from his dead victim increases his personal power (*kakárma*) both physically and mentally.

According to Karsten, when a Jívaro warrior speaks of wanting to kill an enemy, he speaks of eating him: "Yuotahei" ("I will eat him") (Karsten 1935:317). This belief in consuming the dead enemy was enacted in the past during the final victory feast, just before the victorious warrior donned his head trophy, when he consumed a small piece of the skin of the head trophy (Karsten 1935:361). At the conclusion of the victory feasts the Jívaro headtaker feels a sudden power surge into his body, which fuels his self-confidence and assertiveness and results in certain detectable changes in his personality, including a forcefulness in his speech. He is seized with a tremendous desire to kill, and will soon kill and capture another victim's *arutam* power, thereby accumulating greater personal power. At the same time, however, the acquisition of *arutam* power provides the killer with protection from death by any physical or supernatural harm, which as Harner (1972:140) points out, "is therefore a matter of life or death" (Harner 1972:139–142). Acquiring *arutam* power through killing and augmenting one's personal power is a vital endeavor, central to an individual's image of himself and of others, and necessary for survival (Hendricks 1988:219). Not only is the killer accorded a certain measure of personal security, but he can offer protection to others, and as his reputation for being powerful (*kakáram*) increases, he can actually deter the revenge raids of his enemies (Harner 1972:142, 224; Karsten 1935:366–367). The term *arutam* means "ancient" or "old one," and refers to the first ancestors of the Jívaro, who were great warriors (Harner 1972:135; Karsten 1935:448), and worthy of emulation.

Likewise, a Yanomamö creation myth tells of how the moon was shot in the belly and its drops of blood fell to earth and changed into men, "but men who were inherently *waiteri*: fierce. Where the blood was 'thickest,' the men who were created there were very ferocious and they nearly exterminated each other in their wars. Where the droplets fell or where the blood 'thinned out' by mixing with water, they fought less and did not exterminate each other.... Because of this, humans are *waiteri*" (Chagnon 1983:95). Through warfare Yanomamö men seek to become killers (*unokais*), and ultimately, to acquire the distinction of being *waiteri*, a highly valued status in the moral code of the Yanomamö.

To kill, among the Yanomamö, means to eat, to be hungry for meat (*Naiki a, Naiki a!*) (Valero 1984:230, 355–356, 476, 537). When Yanomamö warriors kill an enemy, and enter the period of *unokaimou*, they suffer the physical and spiritual ill effects of having supernaturally ingested the blood and flesh of the slain enemy: weakness, dizziness, loss of appetite, stomach ache, nausea, fetid breath, even the sensation of having worms emerge from their noses or mouths from the decaying flesh of the deceased whom they have consumed, whose body has not yet been cremated (Cocco 1972:391; Valero 1984:75, 78, 83, 239, 342; Albert 1989:638). During this same period prior to the deceased's cremation and the ritual consumption of the deceased's cremated remains, the killers also fear the deceased's spirit, will, or vital force (*no porep i*), which is liberated at death and which can haunt them at night and cause them to suffer physical ill effects, especially if the deceased was a brave warrior (Valero 1984:241, 416; Cocco 1972:407–408).

Upon the dead enemy's cremation and the completion of the *unokaimou* purification rituals and observances, however, Yanomamö killers receive the distinction of being *unokais* and are accorded supernatural protection from the revengeful spirits of those they have killed. As their reputation as *unokais* increases, they can deter retaliation by their enemies and offer protection to their relatives and followers (Chagnon 1988:987, 990). After a long career of killing and fulfilling the attendant purification observances, distinguished warriors gain the reputation of being *waiteri*. They are considered brave, fierce, daring, bold, and stoic. The animals who best personify the qualities of *waiteri* are the coatí, for its fighting spirit and its courage, and the sloth, for its stoicism (Lizot 1989:32–33). They are fearless, they are capable of confronting others, and they can endure great physical and spiritual suffering. And since their reputation is constantly challenged and tested by younger, *waiteri*-seeking warriors, they, like the Jívaro *kakáram*, must reassert themselves and undertake ever more daring revenge raids.

Sometimes, in fact, this system of values alone is responsible for instigating a new round of tribal raiding, as Chagnon observed when he dropped off a war leader, the brother of a slain Yanomamö headman, and his fellow raiders on a river bank to launch a revenge raid:

> He looked frightened, reluctant, anxious, but determined. . . . Even he was not enthusiastic about going on the raid, despite the fact that he lectured the younger members of the raiding party about their overt reluctance and cowardice. He was older, however, and had to display the ferocity that adult men are supposed to show. . . . Thus, the system worked against him and demanded that he be fierce. [Chagnon 1983:188]

The implacable logic of the system, as Lizot (1988:556) refers to it, compels distinguished warriors to carry out ever more dangerous exploits and consequently, to perpetuate warfare. This is why the Shuara Jívaro warrior Tukup' recounted how as a child an elder of his, a distinguished warrior, told him:

> Only when I die,
> when I am mortally wounded,
> will I stop fighting. [Hendricks 1993:39]

So strong are these ideological motives that in his review of South American tribal warfare, Métraux (1949:385) suggested:

> In certain groups the alleged reasons for hostilities and the enemies themselves were less important than the system of values connected with warfare. Warfare was the principal means of acquiring prestige and high social status; consequently, pretext[s] for wars were eagerly sought and expeditions and raids were part of the normal functioning of the society. *Tupinamba* men waged war in order to obtain victims for the ritual sacrifices and cannibalism by which they gained prestige in the community. Because of the magico-religious and social factors involved, it was necessary that warfare be maintained with some regularity. When Villegaignon forbade the *Tupinamba* to sacrifice war prisoners, they complained that war had lost its meaning.

Among the Circum-Caribbean chiefdoms examined here, similarly acquisitive ideological motives underlay their war pursuits, only they were primarily intended to benefit the institution of the chief, who sought the augury of supernatural forces before declaring war. Oviedo y Valdés learned of the decisive role their diviners (*tequinas*) played in seeking the counsel of the supernatural being (*tuyra*):

> Sus guacábaras ó peleas son muchas veces sin propóssito; pero no sin darles el diablo causa, porque son gente que aunque tienen diferençias é passiones un señor con otro, las menos veçes son movidos con raçon, é las mas voluntarias é induçidos por el tuyra é su tequina, dándoles á entender ques divinamente intentada la guerra que les conseja. [Oviedo y Valdés 1853:129]

Upon receiving the *tequina's* augury, the participating chiefs planned the military campaign and proclaimed it publicly in the form of songs (*areytos*), which were performed to the accompaniment of drums, amid dancing and drinking. By means of *areytos*, they recorded and transmitted any information that they did not want to forget, noted Oviedo y Valdés (1851:128): battles, marriage alliances, tributes to dead chiefs, and upcoming military stratagems. They were recited by a designated intoner and then repeated in step and sometimes to a beating drum by the participants (Oviedo y Valdés 1851:127–130). At a war council convened by Chief Sinago of Pequí in 1569, Sinago voiced his call to arms, the allied chiefs agreed, and then the participants "comenzaron luego a hacer bizarras demostraciones de palabras y acciones de sus cuerpos en prosecución de lo determinado" (Simón 1892b:331). A planned military undertaking, as decreed in an *areyto*, was considered inviolable; "é lo ponen por obra, como si quedassen obligados por un firme é bastante contracto ó juramento é pleytesia inviolable" (Oviedo y Valdés 1853:137). In this way, all military pursuits were supernaturally sanctioned and formally ordained. Nobody could challenge the chief's call to arms, and when the outcome did not match the one prognosticated by the *tequina*, it could be attributed to some anger or change of mind on the part of the *tuyra*, and not to a failure by the chief (Oviedo y Valdés 1853:127). Similarly, Formative period chiefs in Mesoamerica sought the divinatory counsel of a sacred ritual calendar before launching military campaigns, a practice which offered them some protection from blame should things go wrong (Marcus 1992:33, 111).

Through warfare, chiefs sought war captives, who served as slaves, as items of exchange, and as sacrificial victims. We have seen how captives were bound, sacrificed, dismembered, and sometimes ritually consumed in large numbers by the victors following a raid. By means of these ritual acts the victors appropriated the enemy's vital forces, including the victims' strength and valor. The enemy's skulls, limbs, and flayed skins became trophies, commemorating the victory over the enemy and the appropriation of his strength. Although these post-war rituals were not an exclusive chiefly privilege (Trimborn 1949:400–401, 426), we have seen how the chief presided over the large-scale sacrifice of war captives in his enclosure and publicly displayed hundreds of human war trophies therein, atop the posts of the chiefly enclosure, at the door of his residence and in special charnels. When Cieza de León asked a native informant why the paramount chief of Lile in the Cauca Valley hoarded so many human war trophies, he learned about the terrific supernatural power that they possessed, which accrued to the chief who hoarded them. Accordingly, a chief's greatness was measured by the number of war trophies he possessed (Cieza de León 1947:380; Oviedo y Valdés 1851:218). Finally, a chief's right to sacrifice war captives and to hoard human war trophies persisted into his afterlife, for they were included in his elaborate burial offerings.

In sum, warfare was declared by chiefs in consultation with the supernatural, and the chiefly pursuit of sacrificial victims and human trophies in warfare was intimately tied to the ritual sanctification of chiefly authority in these centralized societies. A chief's tally of sacrificial victims and human war trophies not only attested to his military victories but also to the special relationship that existed between the supernatural world and his centralized authority (Trimborn 1949:369, 374–375, 426). Through warfare, chiefs acquired the innate power imbued in the human flesh of the dead warriors that they consumed and in the human trophies that they stored and displayed on such a grand scale, a power which augmented and sanctified their chiefly authority. Warfare provided chiefs with opportunities to expand their centralized authority and at the same time to sanctify their chiefly power by means of their post-war rituals and war trophies. Given the material and immaterial benefits that chiefs stood to gain through warfare, it is not surprising that they waged warfare frequently and with such intensity. As Simón put it, chiefs were the richest and the bravest:

> los señores más principales, que eran los más ricos y valientes (porque entre ellos no hay otra soberanía de cabezas, ni que se funde más que en estas dos cosas). [Simón 1892b:331]

And their quest for the power and resources that could be acquired in war made for chronic warfare.

> Sus guerras eran sin cesar, unas provincias y pueblos con otros, porque el enemigo de la paz á quien servían no les dejaba descansar un punto sin que anduviesen derramando sangre humana, si bien esto los hacía más valientes. [Simón 1892a:371]

## The Alternating Roles of Warfare and Exchange

Warfare and exchange assume parallel roles in the internal sociopolitical dynamics of northern South American tribes and chiefdoms. Like warfare, most exchange between Yanomamö villages takes place during the dry season (Chagnon 1983:151). Both tribes and chiefdoms appear to alternate between these forms of external relations, perhaps because "exchanges are peacefully resolved wars and wars are the result of unsuccessful transactions" (Lévi-Strauss [1969:67] cited in Sahlins 1972:182). So tenuous is the dividing line between them that, for example, when a Namowei-teri Yanomamö war leader unexpectedly encountered a party of hunters from an enemy village, instead of shooting them on sight (as he had previously threatened to do), he exchanged arrows with them and fled (Chagnon 1983:123–124). Similarly, when a party of men from Namowei-teri failed to return from Wakawaka-teri, where they had gone to seek machetes in exchange, they were presumed killed in a treacherous attack. Immediately, the Namowei-teri headman blackened his face and mounted a revenge raid. The war party was on its way to avenge their deaths the next morning, only to run into the missing Namowei-teri on their return to the village, bearing loads of machetes, axes, aluminum pots, hammocks, balls of cotton, *mostacilla* seeds, and Western clothing (Valero 1984:246–247)!

The external relations of a Yanomamö village at any given moment will include warring enemy villages, villages with whom sporadic trading but also raiding goes on, and allied villages with whom trading and feasting occur regularly. Neighboring villages are usually on trading terms with one another and are not actively raiding each other—barring some provocation. Also, a village tends to avoid raiding those villages with which it trades and feasts—again barring some unprovoked incident such as the abduction of a woman. In fact, most abductions occur in the context of visits between allies, when the stronger hosts coerce the weaker visitors out of women, or simply take their women and threaten the outnumbered party, "and see what happens next" (Chagnon 1990:51).

Any visit between allies is an occasion for lengthy exchanges, which are conducted in such a heated manner that the participants appear close to confronting one another (Lizot 1988:554). Exchanges are conducted with formal rituals and dialogues in the village clearing. The participants don special body paint and feather ornaments and they assume squatting positions or form pairs of opposing men, their legs interlaced. The guests shout their demands for material goods from the hosts, and after having their demands met, to a greater or lesser extent, depart quickly (Valero 1984:233–234, 284). By means of "the long and difficult road of feasting and trading" (Chagnon 1983:148), the Yanomamö establish political and military alliances with other villages. For example, only after many feasts had been celebrated by the Pishaasi-teri and the Shama-tari, could it be said that "eran un poco amigos, pues" (Valero 1984:377). However, former enemies who initiate alliances by visiting and exchanging are granted safe-passage through enemy territory (Chagnon 1983:122). Exchange relationships constitute an important starting mechanism in the process of developing alliances between mutually suspicious Yanomamö villages (Chagnon 1983:149).

Their enthusiasm for intervillage exchange is so great that although traditional Yanomamö villages can be considered economically self-sufficient, each village produces special items for these exchanges with allies. The exchange items include hallucinogenic drugs, *curare* poison, arrowpoints, shafts, bows, hammocks, baskets, ceramic pots, and dogs. While most of these items are locally available, nonlocal species or varieties of these products are particularly sought after. In Lizot's words,

> although it is true that they are not lacking in anything essential for their livelihood, the Yanomamö always prefer that which comes from far away; an object is considered more valuable the more distant its source is. Any object that forms part of their personal belongings has its history, and when you ask where it comes from, you discover that many things come from other places, in spite of the fact that it could have been produced right there. These Indians are devoted to trade, to exchange for the sake of exchange. [Lizot 1988:554, my translation]

Today, Western manufactured goods such as steel machetes, axes, knives, fishhooks, nylon fishline, aluminum pots, and matches are also sought after and exchanged (Chagnon 1983:149, 46–52, 212; Lizot 1988:512; Cocco 1972:205–206; Valero 1984:315, 387, 455, 522; Ferguson 1992b).

The Yanomamö also gain information through exchange. During feasts, the men exchange information about existing hostilities between villages. On one occasion, a group of visiting Shama-tari revealed to their hosts that their headman had blown a curse on some Namowei-teri (Valero 1984:224). Also, at the conclusion of a feast held by the Namowei-teri, when the visiting Irota-teri asked the Namowei-teri for hammocks, cotton, axes, machetes, and arrows, the visiting Irota-teri promised them pots and dogs; the visitors also told them about the Shama-tari's desire to raid and kill their hosts, the Namowei-teri (Valero 1984:284). Thus, information is as worthy an item of exchange as are pots and dogs. What Gregor has said about the trade among the tribal groups that inhabit the Upper Xingú basin in central Brazil applies equally to the Yanomamö: "Trade means trust, since the items offered may not be reciprocated for several months or more . . . Trade is a social relationship that is valued in and of itself, and is a conscious reason for maintaining the monopolies" (Gregor 1990:111–112).

The Yanomamö also exchange esoteric lore with other groups. Each village or *teri* group possesses its own songs, which are sung and exchanged during feasts (Valero 1984:282–283). A Pishaasi-teri headman had accepted the invitation to a Shama-tari feast because in his words, "quiero oír el canto de las mujeres Shama-thari. Quiero que mis mujeres aprendan sus cantos" (Valero 1984:386). Singing, the Yanomamö believe, helps crops to ripen and gardens to be bountiful. Increasingly, they seek to learn the foreign ways of white men (*napë*), including their songs. At one feast, the headman implored Valero to sing Portuguese songs, which she had learned as a young girl in Brazil before being abducted by the Kōhōrōshi-tari in 1932, and which he wished the women to learn (Valero 1984:275–278). He believed that she sang beautifully because she came from the mythological place of the *amoa hi* tree, where she had learned to sing (Valero 1984:275–278, 282–283). As with material items of exchange, it seems that there is an added value attached to the esoteric lore that derives from distant places and groups, including white men today. So amazed were the Witokaya-teri by an Iyëwei-teri's eyewitness account of an airplane, which he now understood was not a bug, nor a harmful supernatural *pore,* but instead something that flew and that carried white men fully dressed with their feet sheathed in shiny black shells, that to them, "Osheoshewë, porque había visto el avión de cerca, era ya un *napë*" (Valero 1984:426). Osheoshewë's understanding of foreign *napë* ways was accorded a certain value, which distinguished him from others, who nicknamed him Napë thereafter. Similarly, those Iyëwei-teri Yanomamö who live in proximity to mission settlements along the Ocamo and Mavaca rivers are also considered to have become *napë* according to other Yanomamö (Cocco 1972:377).

For the Jívaro and other Amazonian tribes, the revenge raids of the kind still being conducted by the Yanomamö have declined and are being replaced by other forms of intertribal relations, beginning with an intensification of native trading partnerships at the end of the Amazonian rubber boom (1914–15). These trading partnerships are formal exchange relationships between two men or "friends" (*amigri*) who generally live one to two days' walk apart, and who visit each other several times a year in order to exchange goods that are scarce in their respective territories. The Achuara Jívaro produce blowguns, *curare* poison, beads, feather ornaments, cotton kilts, palm fiber, latex, cinnamon, monkeys, parrots, and pelts. The Shuara Jívaro, in turn, supply salt, machetes, shotguns, and ammunition to the long-distance chain of trading partnerships. Many of the items exchanged between trading partners today were formerly obtained through warfare, either by looting enemy villages after a successful raid, or by rewarding a renowned warrior who carried out a revenge killing for an aggrieved party (Harner 1972:116, 125–133, 187, 200, 207; Taylor 1981:656, 665–666; Descola 1981:635; Ross 1984:105). Moreover, the ties that bind *amigri* include the obligation to provide personal protection to the visiting trade partner, when he is traveling through enemy territory. In a very real sense, therefore, the *amigri's* right to safe-conduct through enemy territory makes possible the exchange of goods across Jívaro territory. A chain of trading partners facilitates the exchange of goods across the Jívaro territory, from the Achuara, to the Shuara, to the frontier Jívaro and back (Harner 1972:131–132). The growing number of trading partnerships form an important vehicle of intertribal exchange under conditions of declining warfare. The importance of these trading partnerships is illustrated by the dilemma that the Shuara war leader Tukup' faced when he encountered his trading partner at an enemy settlement during a raid; he promptly seized his trading partner's shotgun and sent him away before resuming the attack against the inhabitants (Hendricks 1993:40, 152).

These intertribal trading partnerships make possible not just the exchange of material goods, but also the exchange of information, ideas, and cultural practices. Trading partners exchange news regarding disputes, planned attacks, and assassinations in their respective regions, which enlarge their universe of information (Kelekna 1981:211). They also exchange cultural practices. For example, from the Achuara Jívaro, the Shuara Jívaro have learned and adopted a new ritual that is celebrated by *amigris*; they kneel on a cloth and embrace one another, thereby formalizing their partnership (Harner 1972:200; Kelekna 1981:89–90). Intertribal trading relationships also offer new social relationships with the "outside" (Kimura 1985:496–498), including frontier traders, missionaries, teachers, and other governmental agents today. Taylor (1981) has documented how such trading partnerships between the Shuara and Achuara led to the establishment of missions in Achuara territory in the 1960s and 1970s. Achuara big men had long maintained trading partnerships with the Shuara to the west, from whom they obtained Western manufactured goods—even during periods of intense intertribal warfare. They came to rely almost entirely upon the Shuara for these items in the 1940s and 1950s, by which time the latter had become missionized. Through their Shuara trading partners the Achuara big men initiated contact with the missionaries, who promised them continued access to these manufactured goods on the condition that they clear an airstrip and relocate their dispersed groups in a nucleated settlement around it (Taylor 1981:649–652, 674; Descola 1981:636). Although the Achuara initially viewed the missionaries as "merely another ethnic variety of purveyors of manufactured goods" (Taylor 1981:652), their contact with the missions effectively put an end to 400 years of resistance to penetration by the outside world.

Such contacts with foreigners are making it possible for certain tribesmen to accumulate Western manufactured valuables and to become acquainted with foreign ways. Both the material and informational aspects of these exchange relationships are having a decided effect upon the internal dynamics of tribal societies like the Yanomamö and Jívaro. Yanomamö headmen are the principal recipients of Western valuables from foreign visitors and missionaries, a privilege which they have at times tried to manipulate in self-serving ways (Ferguson 1992b:217–218, 221–222). The Achuara Jívaro big men who initiated contact with the missions were rewarded individually with cattle, which today constitute a principal source of wealth among the Achuara Jívaro. Their privileged access to such foreign commodities and their unprecedented accumulation of wealth have brought a new economic base to their power. They are also seeking new sources of power and prestige, by assuming formal offices (*cargos*) within the institutional organization of the mission settlements, and by offering their daughters in marriage to bilingual teachers, who are recognized as knowledgeable and successful participants in the white man's world. Some go so far as to adopt the public oratory of the missionaries in their quest for new sources of power. The Jívaro attach tremendous value to goods from the "outside," and the more distant the source of the item, the more valuable. This is the case not only with material goods, but also with foreign symbolic values, which today emanate principally from the "white world" (Taylor 1981:653–656, 660, 672; Hendricks 1988:224, 232, 235–236). Indeed, the greatest of all recorded Jívaro war leaders on the Upano River for a span of almost twenty years, Utitiaja, abandoned the pursuit of war after about 1949 and adopted the following Western customs: cultivating sugar cane, bananas, and papayas, wearing clothes, shaking hands with or embracing foreign visitors, and offering them food rather than manioc beer (Zikmund and Hanzelka 1963:186).

With the decline of intertribal warfare, another mechanism of intertribal exchange has been the growing number of partnerships between Jívaro shamans and shamans of the Canelos Quichua tribe to the north, from whom they acquire shamanistic knowledge and foreign trade goods. To the Jívaro, who attach enormous value to foreign material goods and foreign sources of symbolic power, Canelos Quichua shamans control superior supernatural powers, both traditional and, increasingly today, derived from the white man's world. They serve as "brokers" with the outside world, and thus, have access to cash and other Western valuables (Harner 1972:116–120; Taylor 1981:656, 666–667, 672–673; Whitten 1978:850–852; Hendricks 1988:222; Salazar 1981:610).

Not surprisingly, a growing number of Jívaro men are becoming shamans, in part to benefit from the material and esoteric advantages that accrue to the participants of these foreign partnerships. The great Shuara war leader, Tukup', was learning to become a shaman in 1971 and by 1982 was greatly respected as a shaman, as well as a warrior (Hendricks 1993:19–20). This recent development in the external relations of the Jívaro, Harner (1972:201–202) notes, is leading to an unprecedented increase in the power and wealth of Jívaro shamans within their neighborhoods, who today are organized into hierarchies, based on their acquisition of exotic shamanistic power and valuables from a widening "Chinese-box" series of enclosed domains as they move up the hierarchy of shamans (Taylor 1981:672, 675; Harner 1972:121–125; Kelekna 1981:91–92). Moreover, in the case of powerful Canelos Quichua shamans, their sons and sons-in-law are often chosen to serve as indigenous representatives for governmental and ecclesiastical agencies (Whitten 1978:850–851), thereby extending their sphere of power further. Similarly, in his study of the determinants of leadership among the Mekranoti-Kayapó of central Brazil, Werner (1980:290–292, 297–302; 1982) discovered that contact with outsiders is a principal factor in the inheritance of leadership positions in Mekranoti villages. By virtue of their family's dealings with missionaries and governmental agents, sons of the village headman have an advantage in becoming "culture-brokers" for the community, and therefore eventually titled village leaders—or village chiefs.

Turning to the external relations of chiefdoms, the interregional exchange relationships maintained by the Cauca Valley chiefdoms, for example, were so important that they were interrupted only by warfare, and in many cases traders were granted safe-passage rights through enemy territory (Trimborn 1949:276). For this reason, traders in the Sierra Nevada de Santa Marta were seldom armed (Simón 1892c:178). Similarly, Oviedo y Valdés (1853:133, 140) was careful to specify that the Cueva-speaking chiefs of northern Colombia and eastern Panama, when they were not at war, spent their time feasting and trading:

> Quando los indios no tienen guerra, todo su exerçiçio es tractar é trocar quanto tienen unos con otros; é assi de unas partes á otras los que viven en las costas de la mar ó por los rios, van en canoas á vender de lo que tienen complimiento é abundançia, é á comprar de lo que les falta. E assimesmo tractan por la tierra, é llevan sus cargas á cuestas de sus esclavos: unos llevan sal, otros mahiz, otros mantas, otros hamacas, otros algodon hilado ó por hilar, otros pescados salados; otros llevan oro.... En fin, aquello que les falta á los indios es lo que mas estiman. [Oviedo y Valdés 1853:140]

In these centralized societies, it was the chief and his retinue above all who reaped the material benefits from interregional exchange and warfare. We have seen how in the process of waging war, Circum-Caribbean chiefs acquired foreign resources, such as property, captives, and war trophies, which they disposed of in much the same way that they bestowed items obtained through interpolity exchange. While participating warriors received a share of the war spoils and distinguished warriors were further rewarded with property, women, and other sumptuary privileges, members of the chiefly elite were entitled to a large portion of the booty by virtue of their exalted status and genealogical relationship to the successful war chief. The paramount chief sent a share of the war spoils as gifts to village chiefs, as well as to the paramount chiefs of allied polities. Warfare placed foreign resources, "with all of [their] political ramifications, at the disposal of the chief, at precisely the same time as he has acquired heightened prestige and public support from successful war leadership" (Webster 1975:468). A paramount chief used the foreign goods that he acquired by means of either interregional exchange and warfare to honor his alliances with other paramount chiefs and reward the deeds and allegiance of village chiefs and other loyal subjects (Helms 1979:32). Oberg (1955:206) and Carneiro (1981:65) go so far as to suggest that the material benefits that accrued to chiefs and their followers through warfare enhanced their status as members of a separate social class.

Likewise, the external relationships maintained by these chiefdoms enlarged the chief's wealth of information. By participating in prestige-good exchange networks with distant chiefs, a chief acquired esoteric knowledge about foreign regions, which distinguished him from unknowing commoners (Helms 1979:129–140). Helms has proposed that the paramount chiefs of sixteenth-century Panama

> who presumably held the deepest understanding of the most esoteric sacred-secular lore and who were also involved in long-distance contacts, were most familiar with distant geographical regions that were *terra incognita* to the less educated elite and to the "unknowing" commoners. For such "ordinary" persons the "center of the world" was their own domain. Distant geographical realms were extraordinary "foreign" worlds that were as unknown and awesome as were the supernatural nether worlds above and below the earth. [Helms 1976:134]

A paramount chief also increased his knowledge about foreign regions through his participation in military campaigns with other paramount chiefs, I would maintain. In the process of holding private war councils and war-related rituals, the chiefs of a military alliance acquired a tremendous amount of information about distant regions and about the ways of both their allies and enemies. Moreover, a chief's leadership and success in raids against foreign polities honed his tactical expertise and enlarged his understanding of distant territories and foreign affairs. His mastery of military affairs and proven success in war enhanced his prestige and power before his subjects and further legitimized his chiefly authority. Warfare, like long-distance exchange, was a way for a chief to give "overt evidence of his personal ability to wield effective power" (Helms 1976:28), thereby reinforcing his authority at home and maintaining regional political cohesion in the absence of any internal administrative specialization.

The alternation of warfare and exchange in the external relations of chiefdoms was like the two faces of a coin that is tossed. At the death of a Panamanian chief, his heir and successor as the new chief dispatched messengers to neighboring chiefs, to announce the death of his predecessor, and to make overtures to his allies and enemies. There were two possible outcomes to these entreaties made on behalf of a new chief, much like the toss of a coin. Neighboring chiefs, including former enemies sometimes, might respond favorably by sending a delegation to make their offerings of exchange and to reaffirm their friendship and alliance with the new chief. But if they chose to remain enemies, they seized or killed the messengers, "para que sea mas fija é perpétua la guerra entrellos" (Oviedo y Valdés 1853:156–157). Whether raiding or trading, the resources, knowledge, and power that accrued to chiefs through their participation in both these far-flung activities played a vital role in the sociopolitical dynamics of Circum-Caribbean chiefdoms (Helms 1979:37).

## Warfare and the Development of Centralized Societies

I conclude, therefore, that the warfare pursued by the northern South American tribes and chiefdoms examined is an acquisitive pursuit—like long-distance exchange—that plays a central role in the integration and operation of these prestate societies. Among the uncentralized tribes, it is the quest for personal revenge, prestige, and power by individual warriors that largely motivates the launching of raids and the building of intervillage alliances for war. The war pursuits of the Colombian and Panamanian chiefdoms, by contrast, were a chiefly enterprise in the sense that the hundreds, if not thousands, of participating warriors carried out the chief's military stratagems, which were designed to enhance his prestige and authority above all. The different objectives of chiefly warfare were realized by the chief's leadership in the organization and conduct of war, and by his identification with the associated feasts and rituals. And as chief and supreme war leader, he had direct access to the spoils of war and to privileged information about foreign affairs, which he used to further augment his centralized regional authority.

In view of the advantages that centralized decision-making offered warring chiefs, I would like to consider some of the ways in which uncentralized, warring tribes might have taken the first steps towards political centralization. Specifically, I would like to examine the potential sources of power that could accrue to a successful tribal war leader through his frequent leadership of raiding parties. For under certain conditions, his leadership in warfare could provide him with the political leverage, or raw political power, to cast off the unwieldy yoke of collective decision-making and to exercise centralized decision-making on a regional level, much like a chief.

Should a renowned war leader gain prominence and power over the villages in his region, how then could he make his centralized authority fixed or permanent? I will consider the conditions under which a lineage of related war leaders might be favored, legitimized, and made permanent by the development of centralized, hereditary leadership. Named for its paramount chief, this sociopolitical institution is known as the chiefdom.

*Sources of power*

The leaders of tribal raiding parties are usually renowned warriors or village headmen. Although they look no different from their fellow warriors when they set off to war—and in fact, the leaders of Yanomamö war parties often file out of the village toward the rear of the line of departing warriors (Cocco 1972:385; Valero 1984:148–149)—they do assume a tier of command above the other members of the war party. They plan the raid, recruit warriors, oversee the pre-war rituals, and decide on the precise timing and tactics of the raid. Their leadership of war parties provides these distinguished warriors with opportunities to hone their skills in the art of leading, of persuading the other members of their war parties to follow, sometimes in the direst of circumstances. It is they who signal the attack, the retreat, and sometimes, who decide to abort the raid altogether (Karsten 1935:267–268; Drown and Drown 1961:79–80; Hendricks 1988:223; Chagnon 1983:186; Valero 1984:72, 149–151, 242; Johnson and Earle 1987:123).

However challenging the experience of leading war parties may be, commanding war parties—and especially allied war parties, which could number up to 500 Jívaro warriors at the turn of the century—offers these war leaders decided organizational and strategical advantages in terms of manpower and fighting power (Harner 1972:204). When the Jívaro gather to plan an allied raid, they must first elect a war leader, or a "common chief," as Karsten describes him:

> When a whole tribe, or perhaps several tribes together, prepare a war against one or more other tribes, the first thing is to elect a common chief.

> He should be an elderly, experienced man, who has taken part in several wars, killed many enemies, and celebrated at least one victory feast. The rest of the warriors, who are generally younger men, swear him unlimited obedience. [1935:282]

In theory, then, the war leader's word is "absolute law" (Cotlow 1953:144) during the raid. Of all the all-male task groups formed by the Jívaro—for establishing new gardens, erecting houses, hunting, and raiding—the raiding party is the most highly organized, under the leadership of a renowned warrior, who enjoys the allegiance of his fellow warriors and who commands a highly effective fighting unit (Kelekna 1981:213; Siverts 1972:13–14). The ability of certain tribal war leaders to command sizable fighting forces is illustrated by the success of the Jívaro's uprising against Spanish rule in 1599, when the great Jívaro war leader, Quirruba, organized a military alliance that drew some 20,000 Jívaro warriors from the Morona River, together with their allies, the Macas and Huamboyas. In spite of the Macas's failure to comply at the last moment, Quirruba's allied forces attacked two Spanish settlements spaced 25 leagues (137 km) apart in Jívaro territory and massacred some 30,000 Spaniards, which effectively eliminated Spanish rule in the area (Stirling 1938:16–18).

Not only could war leaders derive sheer power from organizing and commanding large fighting forces, but they could also gain experience, or wisdom, through their frequent participation in warfare. Most raids are waged against enemy settlements located several days' travel away, sometimes far beyond their tribal boundaries. The participating warriors' knowledge of the terrain, of the trails, settlements, and customs of their enemies would be repeatedly tested and enhanced through warfare. This wealth of information and power that warriors acquire throughout their careers, first as warriors, eventually as distinguished warriors, and ultimately as the leaders of war parties, is keenly sought and respected by tribesmen. The Jívaro talk of *kakárma,* a warrior's accumulated personal *arutam* power and wisdom that is acquired by warriors who have killed, which increases their physical strength and their intelligence (Harner 1972:139). The renowned Shuara war leader, Tukup', expressed his views on the knowledge gained through warfare in this way:

> Those who have not sought knowledge through visions are sure to die. Those who have not participated in wars know nothing. [Hendricks 1993:44]

As their reputation as *kakáram,* or "powerful ones," grows, these distinguished killers will be sought out to organize and lead war parties for others. In the process of conducting raids for other villages, successful war leaders accumulate further *kakárma,* including information about other regions and tribes, and become *ti kakáram,* or "very powerful ones" (Harner 1972:115). The more distant the foreign group encountered in warfare, the more valuable and highly prized their acquired knowledge, and hence, their personal power. Their accrued personal power enables war leaders to influence the actions of others (Hendricks 1988:221–224; Taylor 1981:656). Yanomamö warriors who participate in frequent raids and kill repeatedly earn the reputation of being *waiteri* or "fierce," and they too can influence others (Lizot 1985:183).

In the process of waging war for other villages and gaining renown in the region, a successful war leader also accumulates material forms of wealth: trophy heads, women, weapons, ammunition, *curare* poison, tools, ornaments, and other valuables. These foreign resources are offered as inducements or rewards to him by the individuals mounting a revenge raid (Harner 1972:116, 187, 207; Drown and Drown 1961:98–99; Valero 1984:398, 485, 532; Ross 1984:105). If not promised beforehand, the successful war leader obtains these foreign goods for himself during the looting spree that follows a successful raid. The war leader acts no differently from his fellow warriors, for we are told that each member of the raiding party keeps for himself all that he can lay his hands on in the process of ransacking the enemy settlement (Up de Graff 1923:274–275; Drown and Drown 1961:98). The booty includes the heads of their victims, a practice that can result in up to 50 or more trophy heads reportedly taken by distinguished warriors and war leaders (Table 2). Although captured women are divided among the warriors, the leader of the war party takes his choice first (Stirling 1938:56; Drown and Drown 1961:99). The Shuara war leader Tukup', who was known to have killed more than twenty men (and presumably to have taken their heads, although he doesn't say so), had five wives, including a woman captured during a raid (Hendricks 1993:15, 19, 293; Drown and Drown 1961:81). These are material benefits that accrue to a successful war leader, who stands to accumulate substantial wealth through his frequent participation in war. Moreover, a war leader can manipulate this wealth in self-serving ways. When a distinguished Achuara Jívaro warrior was invited to lead a revenge raid for some Huambisa in 1973, he gave the invitation serious consideration because it offered him not only the opportunity to strengthen his reputation as a killer, but also he received several highly valued machetes as a gift from the Huambisa, and he expected to collect much-needed shotgun shells from the Huambisa who had readier access to them (Ross 1984:105). A war leader can use the wealth he accumulates through his frequent participation in war to provision his war parties, host feasts, bestow gifts upon the members of his following, and build a network of alliances and obligations.

Along with their accumulation of power and wealth, distinguished warriors and war leaders achieve a superior social status, which is manifested in a number of ways. Yanomamö men who have killed tend to have more wives, which they have acquired either by abducting them from raided villages, or by the usual marriage alliances in which they are considered more attractive as mates. The same is true of Jívaro war leaders, who might have four to six wives; as a matter of fact, a great war leader on the Upano River in the 1930s by the name of Tuki or José Grande had eleven wives (Table 2; Stirling 1938:108; Cotlow 1953:117, 119; Hendricks 1993:15). Distinguished warriors also have more offspring, due mainly to their greater marital success. As of 1988, the *waiteri* headman of Bisaasi-teri had had eight wives and twenty-five children (Chagnon 1988:989–990, 1990:101).

There are other signs of the superior social status achieved by distinguished warriors. One Jívaro war leader in the 1940s boasted that "many people come to my victory dances, to my *tsantsa* feasts" (Cotlow 1953:123). Accordingly, distinguished Jívaro warriors tend to have large, well-built houses, where they can put up guests and host feasts and dances. By virtue of their status as killers, they will don a crown of multicolored feathers and other ornaments when they receive visitors. For his role as a host, the war leader will have an especially large drinking bowl, a foot in diameter (30.48 cm), for offering manioc beer to visitors (Harner 1972:45–46, 112–113; Cotlow 1953:14; Stirling 1938:90; Zikmund and Hanzelka 1963:187).

Distinguished warriors adopt a stylized manner of greeting others that is frank and forceful. A Jívaro war leader named Caneros on the upper Yaupe River in the 1930s received a party of four war leaders and some 60 men from the Upano River, sitting on his official stool in the middle of his house facing the entrance; he sat very straight and did not move or say a word as the visitors filed in and seated themselves in rows along the walls on each side of the door. After offering his visitors manioc beer, followed by food, the war leader initiated ceremonial greetings with the visiting dignitaries. Pairing off with individual guests, the ceremonial greeting consisted of a shouted dialogue emitted through clenched fists, which were placed against their mouths, accompanied by rhythmic foot stomping and arm waving, and punctuated by lip smacking, tongue clicking, and vigorous spitting (Stirling 1938:96–98). During another meeting of two war leaders in the 1940s, the host "spat through his fingers vigorously, looking quite fierce as he did so" (Cotlow 1953:24). In every aspect of their public personae, distinguished warriors and war leaders convey the impression of being invincible. They appear strong, dignified, defiant but under control, as they glare unblinkingly at their audience (Harner 1972:113; Cotlow 1953:24; Hendricks 1993:20).

At death, distinguished warriors will receive more elaborate and repeated mourning ceremonies than other males their age (see Chapter 2). In the case of the Jívaro, distinguished warriors are honored with a formal period of lying in state before burial (Harner 1972:168–169).

Tribal war leaders cap their careers as distinguished warriors and hosts when they are accorded the status of being "great" or "big" or "old" (*untä, patas*) and are recognized as overall leaders or village headmen. They are respected for their prowess and feared for their willingness to use force if necessary. Not surprisingly, all Yanomamö headmen are killers and most are *waiteri*; villagers will turn to them and carry out their orders in anticipation of an enemy attack or at other critical moments (Chagnon 1983:6, 124, 1988:988; Harner 1972:110–115; Karsten 1935:575, 267; Descola 1981:627; Valero 1984:342, 363, 370, 382–383).

By the time war leaders have achieved this status, they will have gained renown outside their villages, in the region at large.

TABLE 2
Tally of Trophy Heads and Wives Acquired by Jívaro Warriors and War Leaders

| Warrior | Age/Title | Heads | Wives |
|---|---|---|---|
| 1. Chumbika | 30, young *curaca* | 4 | |
| 2. older brother of **1** | dead, but would have become *curaca* | | 8 |
| 3. an Aguaruna | 55 | >2 | |
| 4. Peruche | 70, old *curaca* | >50 | 4 |
| 5. Juanga | 35, son of **4** | "numerous" | 4 |
| 6. several men | great *curacas* | 50-60 each | |
| 7. Utitiaja | 56 or 57 | 59 | >1 |
| 8. Juantinga | young, son-in-law of **7** | | |
| 9. Cucusha | *curaca* | >50 | |
| 10. Anguasha | *curaca* | >50 | |
| 11. Tuki (José Grande) | *curaca* | | 11 |

SOURCE: Cotlow 1953 and Stirling 1938

The invitations that a war leader accepts to lead raids for other aggrieved parties in other villages provide him with opportunities to build alliances and to enlarge his network of reciprocal obligations. The Shuara warrior, Tukup', recounted how the Shuara (in southeastern Ecuador) invited a renowned Huambisa "killer" by the name of Asap ("from far away, from the south, from Peru") to lead their raid against the Achuara; Asap in turn recruited his allies for the raid (Hendricks 1993:41–42, 155). In time, the leader of many Jívaro raiding parties who becomes a *ti kakáram* "may theoretically have on call almost all the men of several neighborhoods and some of the men of a number of other localities" (Harner 1972:115). Those local war leaders who emerge as regional war leaders are referred to today by the Quechua-derived designation *curaca*. Although their power is based solely on their personal reputation and influence over the members of their following, a strong *curaca*, through his war exploits, can augment his influence and power and become acknowledged as a leader over many villages in the region, and sometimes beyond. By agreeing to conduct war parties for other, weaker *curacas*, a strong *curaca* can dominate them and "have 8 or 10 curakas more or less under his control" (Stirling 1938:39; Cotlow 1953:46, 116, 125).

The renown of one *curaca*, Utitiaja, who gained prominence on the Upano River in the 1940s was such that another older *curaca*, Peruche, who lived several days' travel downriver clearly deferred to Utitiaja. Peruche, who was considered a head *curaca* in his own region, had this to say about Utitiaja's renown in 1945:

I am not the greatest warrior, although I have many heads. Today the greatest is Utitiaja, who lives there . . . many days' journey. I have traveled much but I have never been that far. But I have heard of Utitiaja. All Indians have heard of Utitiaja. [Cotlow 1953:128]

It seems that Peruche's brother, Tukup', however, did know and fight the great Utitiaja (Hendricks 1993:42, 79). It is highly likely that this war leader, Utitiaja, whom Cotlow met in 1949, is the same war leader as the renowned Utita referred to by Stirling as having gained prominence on the Upano River as early as 1930, and the Utita encountered by the Czechoslovakian filmmakers Miroslav Zikmund and Jirí Hanzelka at Chupientsa in 1949 (Zikmund and Hanzelka 1963:180–188).

The degree of regional prominence that can be achieved by ambitious *curacas* through warfare is illustrated by the ways in which the Jívaro refer to the supravillage alliances that they head. To begin with, there is little naming of alliances between villages in peacetime; "the Indians recognize a community of interest, but rarely name it" (Cotlow 1953:110). Most Jívaro groups that recognize a common war leader, or *curaca*, are made up of several villages along five or six miles of a small river, yet that group of villages does not designate itself by any name other than the name of the river on which it is located—as in the case of *Kapawi shuar*, or "people of the Capahuari river" (Stirling 1938:39; Descola 1981:626). In times of war, however, the Jívaro designate their war alliances by the name of the war leader or by the name of the river on which he resides. The Achuara Jívaro in Ecuador recognize such leaders in times of conflict for their prowess in warfare and for their capacity to mobilize vast supravillage alliances. Because the chosen war leader represents the unity of his group of allied villages, very often the territory of that leader's group will bear his name, as in *Mashient nunkari* ("the land of Mashient") (Descola 1981:627). Siverts has suggested that some of the tribal names recognized by the Jívaro began as designations for such war alliances under the leadership of a war leader. The Antipa, for example, "may well have been an Aguaruna group distinguished from other Jívaro on account of a powerful leader by the name of Antipa" (Siverts 1975:667). A similar practice might exist among the Yanomamö, for when the Pishaasi-teri raided the Iwahikoropë-teri, headed by Riokowë, they referred to their enemies as the Riokowë-teri ("the group of Riokowë") (Valero 1984:485–487).

*Legitimation of power*

With the organization, resources, information, status, and access to human labor that tribal war leaders acquire, it would seem easy for them to assume permanent positions of leadership. How can a tribal war leader exercise centralized authority permanently, in view of the fact that his war powers generally lapse once hostilities are over? The regional leadership achieved by Jívaro *curacas* is usually short-lived: "owing to the loose organization and lack of any real power on the part of the head curaka, the large group becomes unwieldy or develops diverse interests and it tends to split up again into independent units. Consequently, in as little as 2 or 3 years' time, the original head curaka may find that one or more of his former lieutenants are now stronger than he" (Stirling 1938:39).

Even if a *curaca* manages to retain his influence over his following, as he grows old and dies, so too will his authority. Harner points out that by the time a Jívaro war leader has achieved the regional prominence and power of a *curaca,* he tends to be elderly. He will reach an age when he no longer leads war parties himself, and eventually, other war leaders will supplant him (Harner 1972:116; Drown and Drown 1961:98–102). The career of one Jívaro war leader illustrates the rise and fall of a *curaca's* power:

> Four or five years ago there was a strong chief on the Upano River named Tuki, known to the Ecuadoreans as José Grande. In the manner previously described, all of the curakas from Macas on the Upano River to Mendez on the Paute River became subchiefs under him until he was generally recognized as the strongest of all of the Jívaro curakas. However, he was beginning to grow old by this time and some of his subcurakas were strong men in their own right. About 2 years ago, Ambusha, who had been gradually gaining in power and becoming famous for his head hunting activities, split off with his own group, taking several curakas and their men with him. A little later Utita did the same thing. At the time of the writer's visit (1931), although Tuki was recognized by the Government of Ecuador as being head chief of the Macas-Mendez region, actually he had lost all power excepting that over his own family group and was in reality no more than a *capito* [head of household]. [Stirling 1938:40]

An aging tribal war leader can overcome the above dilemma by encouraging his sons to distinguish themselves in warfare and to lead war parties for him, thereby being in a natural position to succeed him as he grows old and dies. The Jívaro's concern for nurturing future warriors is evident in their preference for having sons. Seventy-five percent of the Achuara men interviewed by Kelekna preferred having male chidren (Kelekna 1981:157). Boys receive their first instruction in warfare beginning at five years of age from their father in what amounts to a daily litany or war rally around the fire of the men's *tankamash*. They listen to their father's somber discourse on past hostilities and the killings of relatives by their enemies, and on the status of current hostilities. The daily peroration ends with the father's wish that his sons become brave warriors in order to avenge the deaths of their kinsmen, which the Jívaro consider to be their sacred duty (Cotlow 1953:130–131, 238–239; Kelekna 1981:93). This is why a seven-year-old Huambisa boy announced with conviction that "most of all I want to be a great warrior when I grow up so I can avenge my father's death and take many Aguaruna heads" (Cotlow 1953:49).

Between the ages of six and eight years most Jívaro boys are taken along on their first raids. The boys perform subsidiary tasks on these expeditions, such as carrying provisions, serving food, and collecting pebbles for the preparation of shrunken heads at the trophy-processing camps. Although young boys do not participate in the raid, they nevertheless have the opportunity to observe raiding tactics and to gain experience in war and bloodshed. To this end a father will have his accompanying son approach the corpse of a slain enemy and have him thrust his lance into it or fire at it with a shotgun (Harner 1972:113; Kelekna 1981:93, 135, 213; Cotlow 1953:129, 148, 239).

Jívaro boys also begin seeking *arutam* powers like their fathers by fasting, taking ritual baths, and drinking green tobacco water (Harner 1972:136). Their initiation rituals at the age of 15 or 16 years test some of their growing qualities as warriors. They must venture into the forest by themselves, build a lean-to, kill a tree sloth and prepare a trophy from its head, and then celebrate mock victory feasts, complete with fasting and the taking of the hallucinogenic juice squeezed from the bark of *maikua*. During this hallucinogenic experience the initiates endure visionary ordeals and encounter the supernatural *arutama* ("old ones"). The youths' initiation into the *arutam* cult is designed to fill them with the necessary power and resolve as they enter the adult world and begin to participate in warfare. It is only after they kill an enemy, take his head, prepare the shrunken trophy head, and celebrate the victory feasts that they become full-fledged warriors. Accordingly, the great war leader on the Upano River, Utitiaja, took his first head when he was seventeen years old (Harner 1972:90–91, 93; Karsten 1935:238–242; Kelekna 1981:125–127, 136, 208–209, 213; Cotlow 1953:238–241; Stirling 1938:51). The Shuara warrior, Tukup', who was approximately nineteen years old when he killed an Achuara enemy for the first time, remarked that "then, having killed, I, too, became an adult" (Hendricks 1993:41, 152).

As war leaders grow older, they encourage their sons to enter the limelight, to sound the log drum for them, and to fill in for them on ceremonial occasions. When they are no longer fit to lead war parties they will send their sons, who are achieving renown as warriors themselves, in their place (Cotlow 1953:124–125; Harner 1972:116; Drown and Drown 1961:98; Zikmund and Hanzelka 1963:271). Their desire to pass on their prowess in war to their sons culminates as they approach death. On their deathbed they inform their sons that they wish for them to acquire their *arutam* power when they die. Each night during the subsequent lying-in-state period, their sons will pay them ritual visits and take tobacco water in order to seek their *arutam* power (Harner 1972:168–169).

Theoretically, the eldest son of a *curaca* inherits his father's position of leadership in war "because he is, as it were, a direct continuation of his father, has received a careful education for the deeds of war, and has always had the good example of his great father before his eyes" (Karsten 1935:267). Nevertheless, he is entitled to receive his father's "chieftainship," according to Stirling (1938:40), only if he has pursued the art of warfare and gained renown as a distinguished warrior. At least three of the *curacas* whose tally of trophy heads is reported in Table 2—Chumbika, Juanga, and Utitiaja—inherited their fathers' positions of leadership through their own prowess in warfare (Cotlow 1953:13, 46–47, 119, 125, 242). Should the son of a great war leader be sickly or not adept, another aspiring warrior will succeed to the position of war leader or chief (Stirling 1938:40–41; Karsten 1935:267).

This is precisely the condition upon which the sons of distinguished warriors could inherit the title and elite status of *cabras* (military captains) in the Circum-Caribbean chiefdoms as outlined in Chapter 3. Andagoya and Oviedo y Valdés reported that common warriors who committed great feats on the battlefield, in spite of any wounds sustained, were rewarded with the noble title of *cabra*. A chief further rewarded these distinguished warriors with women, territory, and subjects to command. War was thus a vehicle for aspiring commoners to enter the elite sector of society; their wives became entitled as well, and henceforth, these distinguished warriors and their families were accorded all the sumptuary privileges generally associated with the chiefly elite. Oviedo y Valdés made it clear that sons of *cabras* could inherit their father's title provided that they, too, pursue the military art of warfare (Oviedo y Valdés 1853:129–130; Andagoya 1945:392). As a matter of fact, warfare was an important vehicle for social advancement in all sectors of chiefly society. When Chief Sinago of the Cauca Valley province of Pequí called a war council of allied chiefs in 1569, the participants included two nephews of his: "á donde entraron los más principales, dos sobrinos suyos llamados Yutengo y Arama, que aunque mancebos, tenían ya dadas muestras de sus valerosos ánimos en hechos heroicos de la milicia" (Simón 1892b:331). At this council, Chief Sinago appointed one of these young men (Yutengo) to serve as the messenger of his allied force. Yutengo was charged with the task of confronting General Gaspar de Rodas and issuing Sinago's ultimatum that the Spaniards withdraw immediately or else face the consequences—"á fuego y sangre cruel guerra" (Simón 1892b:332). Positions of military leadership were awarded to those warriors on the basis of their bravery and achievements in warfare. This strategy for military and social promotion ensured that warring chiefs always had a body of ambitious, combat-ready warriors who were eager for the opportunity to perform great feats in war (Lothrop 1937:22).

Those tribal war leaders hankering for ways to make their leadership positions more permanent can do so by investing a lot of time and effort in training their sons in the art of war, by giving them opportunities to lead war parties, and by passing on their special powers to them. By offering their sons the chance to inherit their position of leadership in times of war these tribal war leaders will sow the seeds of hereditary leadership. This advantage held by sons of tribal war leaders, when coupled with their own success in warfare, could lead under certain conditions to the establishment of a line of hereditary war leaders, like the sons of *curacas* whose accomplishments in warfare are listed in Table 2, and like the inherited *cabras* in the sixteenth-century chiefdoms.

*Favorable conditions*

We must consider some of the socioenvironmental conditions related to warfare that might promote centralized, hereditary leadership on the regional level, in which such a lineage of related war leaders might be institutionalized and made permanent. In particular, how might changes in the predictability, the frequency, and the scale of warfare (which are all prompted by external conditions as much as by the ambitious pursuits of war leaders) favor the development of centralized leadership?

South American tribesmen appear to have a preferred season for waging warfare. Since intervillage travel is difficult during the rainy season, the Yanomamö plan their raids for the dry season. They will go so far as to carry out a raid against an enemy village at the end of the dry season, in order to postpone the likelihood of withstanding an enemy counterraid until the following dry season (Chagnon 1983:5, 179; Smole 1976:186). So seasonal is Yanomamö warfare that when the leader of a victorious Shama-tari raiding party unexpectedly encountered some allies who happened to be visiting the target village when his raiding party raided it, he scolded them by saying: "Qué es lo que estaban ustedes haciendo en medio de esta gente? Ustedes sabían que este es el tiempo bueno para ir a hacer la guerra y que yo venía a matar a mis enemigos" (Valero 1984:70). Although there is no distinct dry season in the humid rainforests of Jívaro territory, it has been suggested that populations who inhabited the floodplains of the upper Amazon River in the past would have moved inland and encroached upon the Jívaro during the flooding season. The seasonal movements of many Amazonian populations were associated with increased warfare. The Cocama, who lived along the Ucayali River in the sixteenth century, embarked on war expeditions up and down the Huallaga and Marañon rivers during the flood season. At the beginning of the dry season, Cocama war parties returned home with their war spoils, including trophy heads (Ross 1980:41; Métraux 1948:688; Harner 1972:47–48, 222). Warfare tends to be a seasonal activity for these South American tribesmen, a fact which makes it somewhat predictable too.

Also, we have seen how all the planning and preparations for a raid, when considered along with the seasonal intervals, can make for relatively long lapses between raids. The frequency of tribal raids generally ranges from weeks or months apart to sometimes years apart (Harner 1972:204; Cotlow 1953:108–109; Chagnon 1983:71).

In addition to the relative predictability and frequency of tribal warfare, most tribal warfare consists of sporadic hit-and-run raids by parties of five, ten, or thirty warriors against enemy villages located up to ten days' travel away. Furthermore, the objectives of tribal warfare are largely to seek personal revenge and prestige, not to seize land or other resources. When women are abducted, they are taken as wives, not as slaves. Neither the scale on which tribal warfare is waged nor its objectives place any undue organizational and administrative demands on the warring groups. The consequences of tribal warfare usually involve a high degree of settlement mobility, a process of "fight and flight" (Carneiro 1970:735) whereby villages relocate for defensive reasons and remain dispersed and autonomous.

But as the frequency of tribal warfare increases, due to external stresses of population growth and environmental and social circumscription (Carneiro 1970:735–737; Chagnon 1968b:250–251, 1983:72), but also, to the pursuit of unrelenting warfare on the part of power-seeking war leaders, the limitations of uncentralized tribal authority will soon be felt. Take the case of the warfare pursued by two Jívaro *curacas* in the Canga and Yaupe rivers of eastern Ecuador in the first quarter of this century:

> In 1925 the region of the Canga River and upper Yaupe was very populous and prosperous. The Indians here were a warlike group confident of their own strength and much feared by all of the Indians in neighboring regions. The curaka of the Canga Jivaros was a well-known warrior called Cucusha. Anguasha, ... another warlike leader, was head of the Yaupe group. The two had always been close friends and companions. During a period of 10 or 15 years they compiled a notable war record, each being credited individually with more than 50 heads during this time. Their raids extended to all of the tribes in the district and some quite distant, until they became the terror of the region. However, these constant raids under two such aggressive leaders began to take their toll of men. Although many victories were registered, they were constantly losing warriors, until eventually their numbers were appreciably reduced. [Stirling 1938:40]

The informal and temporary authority of war leaders, who must recruit warriors from a dwindling pool of available warriors, and who then can lead them only by example (Chagnon 1983:124), will not be sufficient to meet the demands of escalating warfare. As tribal warfare approximates the intensity of warfare observed among chiefdoms, who are known to wage warfare year-round, in the form of monthly attacks, and even repeated, daily attacks against their enemies, warfare becomes more frequent and unpredictable, irrespective of the season of the year. Warfare was so frequent and unpredictable in the Cauca Valley, for example, that when laborers were out in their fields, in one hand they held a club to clear the fallow, and in the other they held a lance to fight (Cieza de León 1947:373). Moreover, as warfare intensifies, tribesmen have difficulty observing their post-war purification rituals, celebrating their victory feasts, and conducting their funerary practices and mourning ceremonies. Warriors who have killed are too engaged in warfare to observe a month-long period of seclusion, and the constant threat of counterraids interrupts the hosting of feasts and mourning ceremonies (Valero 1984:207, 343, 384; Karsten 1935:293; Cotlow 1953:242). Ironically, these ritual activities, which are the vehicle for a warrior's personal protection and power, must be postponed at the very times when they are most needed.

Under conditions of increasing warfare a new level of readiness for war might be called for by tribesmen. For both offensive and defensive purposes, warring villages will grow increasingly dependent upon the supravillage alliances through which they can mobilize large, allied war parties. Accordingly, they will turn to those war leaders who have proven experience in establishing and leading such intervillage alliances and who have achieved victory in war. As warfare becomes more frequent and unpredictable, the consensus-based authority of tribesmen will reach its breaking point and will give way to the development of permanent, centralized leadership. These conditions of unpredictable conflict in post-Contact times are the very ones that Whitehead claims led certain Amerindian groups in northeastern South America, who were accustomed to relatively predictable warfare, to militarize themselves (Whitehead 1992:138).

The first steps in this process have been documented by Chagnon in the interior of Yanomamö territory, where villages are surrounded on all sides by neighbors, where warfare is more frequent, and where the opportunities for settlement relocation are fewer than along the tribe's periphery. Here, for example, the Patanowä-teri were raided at least 25 times between November 1964 and February 1966, and they retaliated frequently (Chagnon 1968a:141, 1983:71–72, 180). In response to the more intense warfare that is waged in the tribal heartland, village headmen establish more offensive and defensive alliances with neighboring villages than do village headmen elsewhere. Settlements here are also larger, due in part to a higher degree of population nucleation that is produced by the fusion of allied villages (Chagnon 1983:79). Finally, village headmen are stronger here; in Chagnon's words, "another striking feature of the center is the considerable authority wielded by headmen during times of warfare, which is to say, much of the time" (Chagnon 1968b:251). They are called upon to lead repeated allied raiding parties and to anticipate and face enemy counterraids. As villagers turn to them more frequently for their leadership skills and their prowess in war, their authority increases in the village and beyond. Therefore, "while still at the autonomous village level of population organization," those Yanomamö subject to the pressures of population growth and circumscription "have clearly moved a step or two in the direction of higher political development" (Carneiro 1970:737).

The pursuit of frequent warfare by ambitious war leaders seeking power and prominence can also trigger this kind of political development, as the example of the constant raids waged by two Jívaro *curacas* over a fifteen-year period and culminating in 1925 made clear. Likewise, in a 1948 issue of the Quito newspaper, *El Comercio,* a Salesian missionary reported an increase in warfare along the Upano River. One of the chief factors responsible for the increase in the number of wars and revenge raids there was the pursuit of warfare by the great *curaca,* Utitiaja, who had already achieved renown in Jívaro territory back in 1945, and most likely a decade earlier (Cotlow 1953:128, 212; Table 2; Stirling 1931:40; Zikmund and Hanzelka 1963:133, 180). The Shuara war leader, Tukup', refers to this period of escalating warfare triggered by the *curaca* Utitiaja in his narrative:

So, because he did this, well, then, I raised it
again with that.
Then again, well, he,
indeed because he killed again,
indeed I killed again.
indeed I killed again.

So many people I killed.
so many we killed.
yes

And we killed so many.
And they killed so many of us.
yes [Hendricks 1993:280]

Thus, internal sociopolitical pressures posed by power-seeking war leaders can also accelerate this process of political development, independently of or even in the absence of external socioenvironmental stresses (Sillitoe 1978:268–269).

In the face of escalating warfare, there will be a continuing need for mobilizing allied war parties. Those distinguished war leaders who have built up a large network of supravillage alliances and obligations, who can mobilize large fighting forces on short notice, will be poised for positions of permanent leadership. Their readiness in the face of more frequent, year-round warfare, and their successful command of supravillage war parties will be recognized and endorsed by their followers, who will turn to them for protection and depend increasingly on their leadership (Sillitoe 1978:259). Their capacity for centralized leadership will enable them to respond quickly and effectively to frequent socioenvironmental stresses, in the manner of chiefs, and over time they and their designated successors will be sought out repeatedly as leaders (Harner 1972:115; Rappaport 1971:66; Chagnon 1983:124). Their authority will extend beyond their villages and become regional in scale. Their authority will persist in peacetime as well, like that of certain sixteenth-century Tupinambá war chiefs: "chiefs like Cunhambebe, Japi-açu, and Abati-Poçanga, who had successfully led the combined forces of several villages in war, gained a permanent renown that extended many miles beyond the borders of their own villages" (Carneiro 1979:88).

In time, the temporary grouping of allied villages under the authority of such a war leader would be made permanent and institutionalized in the form of a chiefdom, with the war leader's village as the chiefly center, and with a common territory to defend. This regional polity would probably be named for the war chief who spawned it or for the river on which his village lay (Descola 1981:627; Siverts 1975:667). Subsidiary villages that once maintained their own sovereignty would embrace the protective hegemony of the paramount chief, whose heirs would inherit that designation upon their succession to office.

*Conclusion*

In this way, the chiefdom constitutes the permanent institutionalization of a tribal military alliance into a single, centralized political unit with a common territory. Under conditions of increasingly frequent and unpredictable warfare, then, tribal war leaders can transcend their temporary leadership over allied war parties and assume the permanent leadership of chiefdoms. They can exercise centralized decision-making authority on a regional level and become titled, hereditary chiefs.

The centralized chiefdom has obvious military advantages over the temporary groupings of allied villages that form to conduct tribal raids. A paramount chief stockpiles weapons and provisions in his storehouses to arm his forces and withstand prolonged attacks. He can mobilize allied fighting forces of 10,000 men or more—at the sound of a conch-shell trumpet in the case of Tairona paramounts (Castellanos 1850:270, 273; Simón 1891:47)—that can sweep through enemy territory, waging repeated, all-out attacks and day-long battles.

Moreover, the inhabitants of the emergent chiefdom's component villages, who previously pursued their own revenge raids, will now heed the paramount chief's call to arms and carry out his expansionist agenda of seizing land, villages, and other resources, including captives. Given the military advantages of the centralized chiefdom, once the process of chiefdom formation is set in motion, we witness the rapid development of chiefdoms. Carneiro has demonstrated the rapid pace of chiefdom formation whereby "it will not be long before autonomous villages as such will cease to exist. Either they will be defeated by and incorporated into one of the existing chiefdoms or they will join forces with other such villages in a defensive alliance, which will itself tend to become a chiefdom" (Carneiro 1981:66).

But this scenario of the role of warfare in the emergence of centralized societies is based entirely upon ethnographic examples, whose usefulness for evolutionary interpretations is problematical. According to Service (1968), the impact of European colonial expansions upon societies like the Jívaro led to an increase in organized warfare, including the formation of unprecedented military confederacies. This line of argument has been taken up recently by some ethnographers and ethnohistorians, who question the occurrence of chronic warfare among South American tribesmen in pre-Contact times, and who argue that European contact transformed native intertribal relations by generating and intensifying warfare (Ferguson 1990b, 1992a; Whitehead 1990, 1992). Furthermore, the aboriginal chiefdoms that were flourishing in northern South America in the early sixteenth century disintegrated shortly after the Spanish Conquest, and have left no modern counterparts that can be reported on by ethnographers. And most of the remaining militant tribesmen of the upper Amazon and Orinoco River basins whose warfare can be investigated are conducting less intertribal raiding.

Consequently, if we wish to determine the importance of warfare in the dynamics of northern South American tribes and in the emergence of centralized chiefdoms here, we must undertake archaeological investigations of these societies and their warfare strategies in pre-Columbian times. To that end I have outlined archaeological manifestations of tribal and chiefly warfare that derive from what is known ethnographically and ethnohistorically about the warfare conducted by certain northern South American tribes and chiefdoms, an exercise which I hope will serve as a catalyst to the study of warfare and its role in the development of centralized societies elsewhere too.

# Bibliography

Adams, E. Charles
   1989  The case for conflict during the late prehistoric and protohistoric periods in the western Pueblo area of the American Southwest. In: Cultures in Conflict: Current Archaeological Perspectives, edited by D.C. Tkaczuk and B.C. Vivian, pp. 103–111. Proceedings of the Twentieth Annual Chacmool Conference, the Archaeological Association of the University of Calgary, Calgary.

Aguado, Fray Pedro de
   1916  Historia de Santa Marta y nuevo reino de Granada. I. Publicaciones de la Real Academia de la Historia, Establecimiento Tipográfico de Jaime Ratés, Madrid.
   1917  Historia de Santa Marta y nuevo reino de Granada. II. Publicaciones de la Real Academia de la Historia, Establecimiento Tipográfico de Jaime Ratés, Madrid.

Albert, Bruce
   1989  On Yanomamö "violence": inclusive fitness or ethnographer's representation? Current Anthropology 30:637–640.

Andagoya, Pascual de
   1865  Narrative of the proceedings of Pedrarias Davila in the provinces of Tierra Firme or Castilla del Oro, and of the discovery of the south sea and the coasts of Peru and Nicaragua, translated and edited by Clements R. Markham. Hakluyt Society 1st series no. 34. New York: Burt Franklin.
   1945  Relación de los sucesos de Pedrarias Dávila en las provincias de Tierra firme ó Castilla del oro, y de lo ocurrido en el descubrimiento de la mar del Sur y costas del Perú y Nicaragua, escrita por el Adelantado Pascual de Andagoya (1826). In: Colección de los viages y descubrimientos que hicieron por mar los españoles desde fínes del siglo XV, tomo III, edited by Martín Fernández de Navarrete, pp. 387–443. Buenos Aires: Editorial Guaranía.

Anghera, Peter Martyr d' (Pietro Martire d'Anghiera)
   1912  De Orbe Novo: The Eight Decades of Peter Martyr D'Anghera. Translated from the Latin by Francis Augustus MacNutt. vol. 1. G.P. New York: Putnam's Sons.

Arango C., Luis
   1924  Recuerdos de la Guaquería en el Quindío. Tomo I, II. Editorial de Cromos, Luis Tamayo & Co. Bogotá.

Arens, William
   1979  The Man-Eating Myth: Anthropology and Anthropophagy. Oxford: Oxford University Press.

Bennett, Wendell C.
   1944  Archaeological Regions of Colombia: A Ceramic Survey. Yale University Publications in Anthropology 30. New Haven.

Benson, Elizabeth P.
   1972  The Mochica: A Culture of Peru. New York: Praeger.

Berry, David R.
   1983  Appendix I: skeletal remains from RB 568. In: Honoring the Dead: Anasazi Ceramics from the Rainbow Bridge-Monument Valley Expedition, by Helen K. Crotty. Museum of Cultural History UCLA Monograph Series 22.

Biocca, Ettore
   1970  Yanoáma: The Narrative of a White Girl Kidnapped by Amazonian Indians. New York: E.P. Dutton.

Bradley, Bruce A.
   1992  Excavations at Sand Canyon Pueblo. In: Sand Canyon Archaeological Project: A Progress Report, edited by William D. Lipe. Occasional Paper No. 2, Crow Canyon Archaeological Center, Cortez, Colorado.

Braun, David P.
   1986  Midwestern Hopewellian exchange and supralocal interaction. In: Peer Polity Interaction and Socio-Political Change, edited by C. Renfrew and J.F. Cherry, pp. 117–126. Cambridge: Cambridge University Press.

Bray, Warwick
   1978  The Gold of El Dorado. London: Times Newspapers Limited.
   1979  Gold of El Dorado. New York: Harry N. Abrams.

Bray, Warwick, et al.
   1985  Report on the 1982 field season in Calima. Pro Calima 4:2–26.
   1988  Report on the 1984 field season in Calima. Pro Calima 5:2–42.
   1992  Sitio Conte metalwork in its Pan-American context. In: River of Gold, edited by P. Hearne and R.J. Sharer, pp. 32–46. The University Museum, University of Pennsylvania, Philadelphia.

Briggs, Peter S.
1986 Pre-Conquest Mortuary Arts and Status in the Central Region of Panama. Ph.D. dissertation, University of New Mexico, University Microfilms, Ann Arbor.

Brown, James A.
1975 Spiro art and its mortuary contexts. In: Death and the Afterlife in Pre-Columbian America, edited by E.P. Benson, pp. 1–32. Washington, D.C.: Dumbarton Oaks.

Bruhns, Karen O.
1972 Illicit tomb looting in Colombia. Archaeology 25(2): 140–143.

Cadavid Camargo, Gilberto, and Ana María Groot de Mahecha
1987 Buritaca 200: arqueología y conservación de una población precolombina (Sierra Nevada de Santa Marta, Colombia). Museo del Oro 19:57–81.

Carneiro, Robert L.
1970 A theory of the origin of the state. Science 169:733–738.
1979 Factors favoring the development of political leadership in Amazonia. El Dorado vol. IV(1): 86–94.
1981 The chiefdom: precursor of the state. In: The Transition to Statehood in the New World, edited by G.D. Jones and R.R. Kautz, pp. 37–79. Cambridge: Cambridge University Press.
1990 Chiefdom-level warfare as exemplified in Fiji and the Cauca Valley. In: The Anthropology of War, edited by J. Haas, pp. 190–211. Cambridge: Cambridge University Press.

Castaño Uribe, Carlos
1987 La vivienda y el enterramiento como unidades de interpretación: Anatomía de dos casos de transición del modelo de cacicazgo. In: Chiefdoms in the Americas, edited by R.D. Drennan and C. A. Uribe, pp. 231–249. Lanham, Maryland: University Press of America.

Castellanos, Juan de
1850 Elegías de varones ilustres de Indias. Biblioteca de Autores Españoles. D.M. Rivadeneyra, Madrid.

Chagnon, Napoleon A.
1968a Yanomamö social organization and warfare. In: War: The Anthropology of Armed Conflict and Aggression, edited by M. Fried, M. Harris, and R. Murphy, pp. 109–159. Garden City, NY: The Natural History Press.
1968b The culture-ecology of shifting (pioneering) cultivation among the Yanomamö Indians. Proceedings of the VIIIth International Congress of Anthropological and Ethnological Sciences, Vol. III:249–255. Tokyo.
1974 Studying the Yanomamö. New York: Holt, Rinehart and Winston.
1979 Mate competition, favoring close kin, and village fissioning among the Yanomamö Indians. In: Evolutionary Biology and Human Social Behavior: An Anthropological Perspective, edited by N.A. Chagnon and W. Irons, pp. 86–132. North Scituate, Mass.: Duxbury Press.
1983 Yanomamö: The Fierce People. New York: Holt, Rinehart and Winston.
1988 Life histories, blood revenge, and warfare in a tribal population. Science 239: 985–992.
1990 On Yanomamö violence: reply to Albert. Current Anthropology 31:49–53.

Chagnon, Napoleon A., and Paul E. Bugos, Jr.
1979 Kin selection and conflict: an analysis of a Yanomamö ax fight. In: Evolutionary Biology and Human Social Behavior: An Anthropological Perspective, edited by N.A. Chagnon and W. Irons, pp. 213–237. North Scituate, Mass.: Duxbury Press.

Chagnon, Napoleon A., Mark V. Flinn, and Thomas F. Melancon
1979 Sex-ratio variation among the Yanomamö Indians. In: Evolutionary Biology and Human Social Behavior: An Anthropological Perspective, edited by N.A. Chagnon and W. Irons, pp. 290–320. North Scituate, Mass.: Duxbury Press.

Chase, James E.
1976 Deviance in the Gallina: a report on a small series of Gallina human skeleton remains. Appendix in Archaeological Excavations in the Llaves area, Santa Fe National Forest, New Mexico, 1972–1974, edited by H.W. Dick. USDA Forest Service, Archaeological Report No. 13.
1978 North-Central New Mexico Gallina: Analysis and Comparative Study of Their Physical Remains. Master's thesis, Department of Anthropology, Colorado State University.

Cieza de León, Pedro de
1881 Guerras civiles del Perú (Segundo Libro): Guerra de Chupas. In: Colección de Documentos Inéditos para la Historia de España, Tomo 76, pp. 1–371. Imprenta de Miguel Ginesta, Madrid.
1947 La Crónica del Perú (1553). In: Biblioteca de Autores Españoles, Tomo 26, Historiadores Primitivos de Indias Tomo 2, comp. Don E. de Vedia, pp. 349–458. Ediciones Atlas, Madrid.

Cocco, P. Luis
1972 Iyëwei-teri: Quince Años entre los Yanomamös. Escuela Técnica Popular Don Bosco, Caracas.

Coe, Michael D., and Richard A. Diehl
1980 In the Land of the Olmec, vol. I: The Archaeology of San Lorenzo Tenochtitlán. Austin: University of Texas Press.

Cooke, Richard G.
1979 Los impactos de las comunidades sobre los ambientes del trópico estacional; datos del Panamá prehistórico. Actas del IV Simposio Internacional de Ecología Tropical 3:917–973.
1984 Archaeological research in central and eastern Panama: a review of some problems. In: The Archaeology of Lower Central America, edited by F.W. Lange and D.Z. Stone, pp. 263–302. Albuquerque: University of New Mexico Press.
1989 Anurans as human food in tropical America: ethnographic, ethnohistoric and archaeological evidence. ArchaeoZoologia Vol. III (1.2):123–142.

Cooke, Richard G., and W. Bray
1985 The goldwork of Panama: an iconographic and chronological perspective. In: The Art of Precolumbian Gold: The Jan Mitchell Collection, edited by J. Jones, pp. 35–49. London: Weidenfeld and Nicholson.

Cooke, Richard G., and Anthony J. Ranere
1989 Hunting in Pre-Columbian Panama: a diachronic perspective. In: The Walking Larder: Patterns of Domestication, Pastoralism and Predation, edited by J. Clutton-Brock, pp. 295–315. London: Unwin Hyman.
1992 The origin of wealth and hierarchy in the central region of Panama (12,000–2,000 BP), with observations on its relevance to the history and phylogeny of Chibchan-speaking polities in Panama and elsewhere. In: Wealth and Hierarchy in the Intermediate Area, edited by F.W. Lange, pp. 243–316. Dumbarton Oaks, Trustees for Harvard University, Washington, D.C.

Cordell, Linda S.
1989 Warfare: some issues from the prehistoric Southwest. In: Cultures in Conflict: Current Archaeological Perspectives, edited by D.C. Tkaczuk and B.C. Vivian, pp. 173–178. Proceedings of the Twentieth Annual Chacmool Conference, The Archaeological Association of the University of Calgary, Calgary, Alberta, Canada.

Cotlow, Lewis
1953 Amazon Head-Hunters. New York: Henry Holt and Company.

Creamer, Winifred
1983 Archaeological faunal remains as indicators of territory size and subsistence strategy. Brenesia 21:395–401.

Creamer, Winifred, and Jonathan Haas
1985 Tribe versus chiefdom in lower Central America. American Antiquity 50:738–754.

Crotty, Helen K.
1983 Honoring the Dead: Anasazi Ceramics from the Rainbow Bridge-Monument Valley Expedition. Museum of Cultural History, UCLA Monograph Series 22.

Dade, Philip, L.
1972 Bottles from Parita, Panama. Archaeology 25(1): 35–43.

Daly, John W., and Charles W. Myers
1967 Toxicity of Panamanian poison frogs (Dendrobates): some biological and chemical aspects. Science 156: 970–973.

Danielsson, Bengt
1949 Some attraction and repulsion patterns among Jibaro Indians. Sociometry XII(1–3):83–105.

Davis, Wade, and Andrew T. Weil
1992 Identity of a New World psychoactive toad. Ancient Mesoamerica 3(1):51–59.

Dean, Jeffrey S., A.J. Lindsay, Jr., and W.J. Robinson
1978 Prehistoric settlement in Long House Valley, Northeastern Arizona. In: Investigations of the Southwestern Anthropological Research Group: An Experiment in Archaeological Cooperation, edited by R.C. Euler and G.J. Gumerman, pp. 25–44. Museum of Northern Arizona, Flagstaff.

DeBoer, Warren R.
1981 Buffer zones in the cultural ecology of aboriginal Amazonia: an ethnohistorical approach. American Antiquity 46:364–377.

Descola, Philippe
1981 From scattered to nucleated settlement: a process of socioeconomic change among the Achuar. In: Cultural Transformations and Ethnicity in Modern Ecuador, edited by N.E. Whitten, Jr., pp. 614–646. Urbana: University of Illinois Press.

Descripción de Panamá y su Provincia sacada de la Relación que por
1908 Mandado del Consejo hizo y embió aquella audiencia (1607). Relaciones históricas y geográficas de América Central. In: Colección de Libros y Documentos Referentes a la Historia de América, Tomo VIII, pp. 137–218. Victoriano Suárez, Madrid.

Di Peso, Charles C.
1974 Casas Grandes: A Fallen Trading Center of the Gran Chichimeca, vol. 2. The Medio Period. The Amerind Foundation, Dragoon, Arizona.

Di Peso, Charles C., J.B. Rinaldo, and G.F. Fenner
1974 Casas Grandes: A Fallen Trading Center of the Gran Chichimeca, vol. 8. Bone, Perishables, Commerce, Subsistence, and Burials. The Amerind Foundation, Dragoon, Arizona.

Divale, William T.
1973 Warfare in Primitive Societies: A Bibliography. Santa Barbara, CA: ABC-Clio Press.

Dobkin de Rios, Marlene
1974 The influence of psychotropic flora and fauna on Maya religion. Current Anthropology 15(2):147–164.

Drennan, Robert D.
1991 Pre-Hispanic chiefdom trajectories in Mesoamerica, Central America, and northern South America. In: Chiefdoms: Power, Economy, and Ideology, edited by T. Earle, pp. 263–287. Cambridge: Cambridge University Press.

Drown, Frank, and Marie Drown
1961 Mission to the Head-Hunters. New York: Harper and Row.

Dussán de Reichel, Alicia
1979 Some observations on the prehistoric goldwork of Colombia. In: Pre-Columbian Metallurgy of South America, edited by E.P. Benson, pp. 41–52. Dumbarton Oaks, Washington, D.C.

Earle, Timothy
1978 Economic and Social Organization of a Complex Chiefdom: The Halelea District, Kaua'i, Hawaii. University of Michigan Museum of Anthropology, Anthropological Papers 63. Ann Arbor.
1987 Chiefdoms in archaeological and ethnohistorical perspective. Annual Review of Anthropology 16: 279–308.

Eddy, Frank W.
1966 Prehistory in the Navajo Reservoir District, Northwestern New Mexico. Museum of New Mexico Papers in Anthropology 15: pt. I and II. Museum of New Mexico Press, Santa Fe.
1974 Population dislocation in the Navaho Reservoir District, New Mexico and Colorado. American Antiquity 39(1):75–84.

Engel, Frédéric-André
1963 A Preceramic settlement on the central coast of Peru: Asia, Unit I. Transactions of the American Philosophical Society n.s. vol. 53, pt.3. The American Philosophical Society, Philadelphia.
1966 Paracas: Cien Años de la Cultura Peruana. Editorial Juan Mejía Baca, Lima.
1980 Prehistoric Andean Ecology: Man, Settlement, and Environment in the Andes, vol. 1. New York: Humanities Press.
1981 Prehistoric Andean Ecology: Man, Settlement, and Environment in the Andes: The Deep South. New York: Humanities Press.

Espinosa, Gaspar de
1864 Relación hecha por Gaspar de Espinosa, Alcalde Mayor de Castilla de Oro, dada a Pedrárias de Avila, Lugar Teniente General de aquellas provincias, de todo lo que le sucedió en la entrada que hizo en ellas de órden de Pedrárias (1516). In: Colección de Documentos Inéditos, Relativos al Descubrimiento, Conquista y Colonización de las Posesiones Españolas en América y Oceanía, Sacados, en su Mayor Parte, del Real Archivo de Indias, Vol. II, comp. D.J.F. Pacheco et al., pp. 467–522. Imprenta Española, Madrid.
1873 Relación e proceso quel Licenciado Gaspar Despinosa, Alcalde Mayor, hizo en el viaje que por mandado del muy magnífico Señor Pedrarias de Avila, Teniente General en estos reynos de Castilla del Oro por sus altezas, fue desde esta ciudad de Panamá a las provincias de Paris e Natá, e a las otras provincias comarcanas (1519). In: Colección de Documentos Inéditos Relativos al Descubrimiento, Conquista y Organi-

zación de las Antiguas Posesiones Españolas de América y Oceanía, Vol. XX, comp. D.J.F. Pacheco et al., pp. 5–119. Imprenta del Hospicio, Madrid.

Espinosa, Pedro de
1955 Carta de Pedro de Espinosa sobre la entrada a Buritica y otros asuntos del gobierno, y el borrador de la contestación, sin fecha (20 mayo de 1529). In: Documentos Inéditos para la Historia de Colombia, Vol. II, ed. Juan Friede, pp. 57–60. Academia Colombiana de Historia, Bogotá.

Evans, Clifford, and Betty J. Meggers
1960 Archaeological Investigations in British Guiana. Smithsonian Institution Bureau of American Ethnology, Bulletin 177. Smithsonian Institution, Washington, D.C.

Falchetti, Ana María
1987 Desarrollos de la orfebrería tairona en la provincia metalúrgica del norte colombiano. Museo del Oro 19:3–23.

Feinman, Gary, and Jill Neitzel
1984 Too many types: an overview of sedentary prestate societies in the Americas. Advances in Archaeological Method and Theory 7:39–102.

Ferguson, R. Brian
1990a Explaining war. In: The Anthropology of War, edited by J. Haas, pp. 26–55. Cambridge: Cambridge University Press.
1990b Blood of the Leviathan: Western contact and warfare in Amazonia. American Ethnologist 17(2): 237–257.
1992a Tribal warfare. Scientific American 266(1):108–113.
1992b A savage encounter: western contact and the Yanomamö war complex. In: War in the Tribal Zone, edited by R.B. Ferguson and N.L. Whitehead, pp. 199–227. Santa Fe, NM: School of American Research Press.

Fish, Paul R., and Suzanne K. Fish
1989 Hohokam warfare from a regional perspective. In: Cultures in Conflict: Current Archaeological Perspectives, edited by D.C. Tkaczuk and B.C. Vivian, pp. 112–129. Proceedings of the Twentieth Annual Chacmool Conference. The Archaeological Association of the University of Calgary, Calgary, Alberta, Canada.

Flannery, Kent V.
1968 The Olmec and the Valley of Oaxaca: a model for interregional interaction in Formative times. In: Dumbarton Oaks Conference on the Olmec, edited by E.P. Benson, pp. 79–110. Dumbarton Oaks, Washington, D.C.

Flannery, Kent V. (editor)
1976 The Early Mesoamerican village. New York: Academic Press.

Flannery, Kent V., and Joyce Marcus
1983 The earliest public buildings, tombs, and monuments at Monte Albán, with notes on the internal chronology of Period I. In: The Cloud People, edited by K.V. Flannery and J. Marcus, pp. 87–91. New York: Academic Press.

Flinn, Lynn, Christy G. Turner, II, and Alan Brew
1976 Additional evidence for cannibalism in the Southwest: the case of LA 4528. American Antiquity 41(3):308–318.

Fried, Morton
1967 The Evolution of Political Society. New York: Random House.

Friedman, Jonathan, and M. Rowlands
1978 Notes toward an epigenetic model of the evolution of "civilization." In: The Evolution of Social Systems, edited by J. Friedman and M. Rowlands, pp. 201–276. Pittsburgh: University of Pittsburgh Press.

Gähwiler-Walder, Theres
1988 Archaeological investigations in the Pavas-La Cumbre region. Pro Calima 5:50–60.

Gibson, Jon
1974 Aboriginal warfare in the southeast: an alternative perspective. American Antiquity 39:130–133.

Gregor, Thomas
1990 Uneasy peace: intertribal relations in Brazil's Upper Xingu. In: The Anthropology of War, edited by J. Haas, pp. 105–124. Cambridge: Cambridge University Press.

Gross, Daniel R.
1979 A new approach to central Brazilian social organization. In: Brazil: Anthropological perspectives: Essays in honor of Charles Wagley, edited by M. Margolis and W. Carter, pp. 321–342. New York: Columbia University Press.

Haas, Jonathan
1989 The evolution of the Kayenta regional system. In: The sociopolitical structure of prehistoric Southwestern societies, edited by S. Upham, K.G. Lightfoot, and R.A. Jewett, pp. 491–508. Boulder: Westview Press.
1990 Warfare and the evolution of tribal polities in the prehistoric Southwest. In: The Anthropology of War, edited by J. Haas, pp. 171–189. Cambridge: Cambridge University Press.

Haberland, Wolfgang
1984 The archaeology of greater Chiriquí. In: The Archaeology of Lower Central America, edited by F.W. Lange and D.Z. Stone, pp. 233–254. Albuquerque: University of New Mexico Press.

Hames, Raymond B.
1983 The settlement pattern of a Yanomamö population bloc: a behavioral ecological interpretation. In: Adaptive Responses of Native Amazonians, edited by R.B. Hames and W.T. Vickers, pp. 393–427. New York: Academic Press.

Hansell, Patricia
1987 The Formative in Central Pacific Panama: La Mula Sarigua. In: Chiefdoms in the Americas, edited by R.D. Drennan and C.A. Uribe, pp. 119–131. Lanham, Maryland: University Press of America.

Harner, Michael J.
1972 The Jívaro: People of the Sacred Waterfalls. Garden City, NY: Doubleday/Natural History Press.

Hearne, Pamela
1992 The story of the river of gold. In: River of Gold, edited by P. Hearne and R.J. Sharer, pp. 1–21. The University Museum, University of Pennsylvania, Philadelphia.

Helms, Mary W.
1979 Ancient Panama: Chiefs in Search of Power. Austin: University of Texas Press.

Hendricks, Janet W.
- 1988 Power and knowledge: discourse and ideological transformation among the Shuar. American Ethnologist 15:216–238.
- 1993 To Drink of Death: The Narrative of a Shuar Warrior. Tucson: University of Arizona Press.

Ichon, Alain
- 1980 Archaeologie du Sud de la peninsule d'Azuero, Panama. Etudes Mesoamericaines, Serie II, No.3. Mission Archaeologique et Ethnologique Française au Mexique.

Johnson, Allen W., and T. Earle
- 1987 The Evolution of Human Societies. Stanford: Stanford University Press.

Johnson, Frederick
- 1948 The Caribbean lowland tribes: the Talamanca division. In: Handbook of South American Indians, vol. 4: The Circum-Caribbean Tribes, edited by Julian H. Steward, pp. 231–251. Smithsonian Institution Bureau of American Ethnology, Bulletin 143. New York: Cooper Square Publishers, Inc.

Johnson, Gregory A.
- 1982 Organizational structure and scalar stress. In: Theory and Explanation in Archaeology, edited by C. Renfrew, M. Rowlands and B. Segraves, pp. 389–421. New York: Academic Press.

Karsten, Rafael
- 1923 Blood Revenge, War, and Victory Feasts among the Jibaro Indians of Eastern Ecuador. Smithsonian Institution Bureau of American Ethnology, Bulletin 79. Smithsonian Institution, Washington, D.C.
- 1935 The Head-Hunters of Western Amazonas. Societas Scientiarum Fennica. Commentationes Humanarum Litterarum. VII. 1. Centraltryckeriet, Helsingfors.

Kelekna, Pita
- 1981 Sex Asymmetry in Jivaroan Achuara Society: A Cultural Mechanism Promoting Belligerence. Ph.D. dissertation, University of New Mexico. University Microfilms, Ann Arbor.

Kimura, Hideo
- 1985 Andean exchange: a view from Amazonia. In: Andean Ecology and Civilization, edited by S. Masuda, I. Shimada, and C. Morris, pp. 491–504. Tokyo: University of Tokyo.

Kirchhoff, Paul
- 1948 Patangoro and Amani. In: Handbook of South American Indians, vol. 4: The Circum-Caribbean Tribes, edited by J.H. Steward, pp. 339–348. Smithsonian Institution, Bureau of American Ethnology, Bulletin 143. Washington, D.C.

Klepinger, Linda L.
- 1979 Paleodemography of the Valdivia III phase at Real Alto, Ecuador. American Antiquity 44(2):305–309.

Kolata, Gina
- 1986 Anthropologists suggest cannibalism is a myth. Science 232:1497–1500.

Las Casas, Fray Bartolomé de
- 1951 Historia de Las Indias, vol. III. Edición de Agustín Millares Carlo, Fondo de Cultura Económica, México.

Lathrap, Donald W.
- 1970 The Upper Amazon. London: Thames and Hudson.
- 1973 The antiquity and importance of long-distance trade relationships in the moist tropics of Pre-Columbian South America. World Archaeology 5:170–186.

Lehmann, Henri
- 1953 Archéologie du sud-ouest colombien. Journal de la Société des Américanistes n.s. XLII:199–270, Paris.

Lévi-Strauss, Claude
- 1969 The Elementary Structures of Kinship. London: Eyre and Spottiswoode.

Linares, Olga F.
- 1976 Animals that were bad to eat were good to compete with: an analysis of the Conte style from ancient Panama. In: Ritual and Symbol in Native Central America, edited by P. Young and J. Howe, pp. 1–19. University of Oregon Anthropological Papers 9. Eugene, Oregon.
- 1977 Ecology and the Arts in Ancient Panama: On the Development of Social Rank and Symbolism in the Central Provinces. Studies in Pre-Columbian Art and Archaeology 17. Dumbarton Oaks, Washington, D.C.
- 1980a Miscellaneous artifacts of special use. In: Adaptive Radiations in Prehistoric Panama, edited by O.F. Linares and A.J. Ranere, pp. 139–145. Peabody Museum Monograph 5, Harvard University, Cambridge.
- 1980b Ecology and prehistory of the Aguacate peninsula in Bocas del Toro. In: Adaptive Radiations in Prehistoric Panama, edited by O.F. Linares and A.J. Ranere, pp. 57–66. Peabody Museum Monograph 5, Harvard University, Cambridge.
- 1980c The Aguacate sites in Bocas del Toro: excavations and stratigraphy. In: Adaptive Radiations in Prehistoric Panama, edited by O.F. Linares and A.J. Ranere, pp. 292–306. Peabody Museum Monograph 5, Harvard University, Cambridge.
- 1980d La Pitahaya (IS-3) in the Gulf of Chiriquí: mapping and excavation. In: Adaptive Radiations in Prehistoric Panama, edited by O.F. Linares and A.J. Ranere, pp. 306–315. Peabody Museum Monograph 5, Harvard University, Cambridge.

Linares, Olga F., P.D. Sheets, and E.J. Rosenthal
- 1975 Prehistoric agriculture in tropical highlands. Science 187:137–145.

Linares, Olga F., and P.D. Sheets
- 1980 Highland agricultural villages in the Volcán Barú region. In: Adaptive Radiations in Prehistoric Panama, edited by O.F. Linares and A.J. Ranere, pp. 44–55. Peabody Museum Monographs 5, Harvard University, Cambridge.

Lizot, Jacques
- 1977 Population, resources and warfare among the Yanomamö. Man 12:496–517.
- 1985 Tales of the Yanomamö: Daily Life in the Venezuelan Forest. Cambridge: Cambridge University Press.
- 1989 Sobre la guerra. La Iglesia en Amazonas 44:23–34.

Lothrop, Samuel K.
- 1937 Coclé: An Archaeological Study of Central Panama, Part I. Memoirs of the Peabody Museum of Archaeology and Ethnology 7. Harvard University, Cambridge.
- 1942 Coclé: An Archaeological Study of Central Panama, Part II. Memoirs of the Peabody Museum of Archaeology and Ethnology 8. Harvard University, Cambridge.
- 1954 Suicide, sacrifice and mutilations in burials at Venado Beach, Panama. American Antiquity 19:226–234.

Lumbreras, Luis G.
- 1974 The Peoples and Cultures of Ancient Peru. Washington, D.C.: Smithsonian Institution Press.

Lyon, Patricia
1989 Archaeology and mythology II: a re-consideration of the animated objects theme in Moche art. In: Cultures in Conflict: Current Archaeological Perspectives, edited by D.C. Tkaczuk and B.C. Vivian, pp. 62–68. Proceedings of the Twentieth Annual Chacmool Conference, the Archaeological Association of the University of Calgary, Calgary, Alberta, Canada.

Mackey, James, and R.C. Green
1979 Largo-Gallina towers: an explanation. American Antiquity 44(1):144–154.

Marcos, Jorge G.
1978 The Ceremonial Precinct at Real Alto: Organization of Time and Space in Valdivia Society. Ph.D. dissertation, University of Illinois at Urbana-Champaign. University Microfilms, Ann Arbor.

Marcus, Joyce
1992 Mesoamerican Writing Systems: Propaganda, Myth, and History in Four Ancient Civilizations. Princeton: Princeton University Press.

Mason, J. Alden
1931– Archaeology of Santa Marta, Colombia: The Tairona Culture. Field
39 Museum of Natural History, Anthropological Series 20. Chicago.
1942 New excavations at the Sitio Conte, Coclé, Panama. Proceedings of the Eighth Pan-American Scientific Congress, vol. II:103–107. Department of State, Washington, D.C.

McManamon, Francis P.
1984 Discovering sites unseen. Advances in Archaeological Method and Theory 7:223–292.

Meggers, Betty
1971 Amazonia: Man and Culture in a Counterfeit Paradise. Chicago: Aldine-Atherton.

Meggers, Betty J., and Clifford Evans
1957 Archaeological investigations at the mouth of the Amazon. Smithsonian Institution Bureau of American Ethnology, Bulletin 167. Smithsonian Institution, Washington, D.C.

Métraux, Alfred
1949 Warfare, cannibalism, and human trophies. In: Handbook of South American Indians, vol. 5, Smithsonian Institution Bureau of American Ethnology, Bulletin 143, edited by J.H. Steward, pp. 383–409. Smithsonian Institution, Washington, D.C.

Milner, George R., E. Anderson, and V.G. Smith
1991 Warfare in late prehistoric west-central Illinois. American Antiquity 56(4):581–603.

Minnis, Paul E.
1989 The Casas Grandes polity in the International Four Corners. In: The Sociopolitical Structure of Prehistoric Southwestern Societies, edited by S. Upham, K.G. Lightfoot, and R.A. Jewett, pp. 269–305. Boulder: Westview Press.

Morey, Robert V., Jr., and John P. Marwitt
1975 Ecology, economy, and warfare in lowland South America. In: War, its Causes and Correlates, edited by M.A. Nettleship, R.D. Givens, and A. Nettleship, pp. 439–450. The Hague: Mouton Publishers.

Murphy, Robert F.
1960 Headhunter's Heritage: Social and Economic Change among the Mundurucú Indians. Berkeley: University of California Press.

Myers, Charles W., John W. Daly, and Borys Malkin
1978 A dangerously toxic new frog (Phyllobates) used by Emberá Indians of western Colombia, with discussion of blowgun fabrication and dart poisoning. American Museum of Natural History Bulletin 161:307–366.

Myers, Charles W., and John W. Daly
1983 Dart-poison frogs. Scientific American 248(2):120–133.

Nicholas, Francis G.
1901 The aborigines of the province of Santa Marta, Colombia. American Anthropologist 3:606–649.

Oberg, Kalervo
1955 Types of social structure among the lowland tribes of South and Central America. In: Peoples and Cultures of Native South America, edited by D. Gross, pp. 189–210. Garden City, NY: Doubleday/The Natural History Press.

Olson, Alan P.
1967 A mass secondary burial from northern Arizona. American Antiquity 31(6):822–826.

Otterbein, Keith F.
1970 The Evolution of War. New Haven: Human Relations Area Files Press.

Oviedo y Valdés, Gonzalo Fernández de
1851 Historia General y Natural de las Indias, Islas y Tierra-Firme del Mar Océano I. Imprenta de la Real Academia de la Historia, Madrid.
1852 Historia General y Natural de las Indias, Islas y Tierra-Firme del Mar Océano II. Imprenta de la Real Academia de la Historia, Madrid.
1853 Historia General y Natural de las Indias, Islas y Tierra-Firme del Mar Océano III. Imprenta de la Real Academia de la Historia, Madrid.
1855 Historia General y Natural de las Indias, Islas y Tierra-Firme del Mar Océano IV. Imprenta de la Real Academia de la Historia, Madrid.

Oyuela Caycedo, Augusto
1987 Implicaciones de las secuencias locales y regionales en los aspectos culturales de los Tairona. In: Chiefdoms in the Americas, edited by R.D. Drennan and C.A. Uribe, pp. 213–229. Lanham, Maryland: University Press of America.

Peebles, Christopher S., and Susan M. Kus
1977 Some archaeological correlates of ranked societies. American Antiquity 42:421–448.

Piedrahita, Lucas Fernández de
1942 Historia general de las conquistas del nuevo reino de Granada I. Biblioteca Popular de Cultura Colombiana, Bogotá.

Powell, Mary Lucas
1988 Status and Health in Prehistory: A Case Study of the Moundville Chiefdom. Washington, D.C.: Smithsonian Institution Press.

Proulx, Donald A.
1971 Headhunting in ancient Peru. Archaeology 24(1): 16–21.
1989 Nasca trophy heads: victims of warfare or ritual sacrifice? In: Cultures in Conflict: Current Archaeological Perspectives, edited by D.C. Tkaczuk and B.C. Vivian, pp. 73–85. Proceedings of the Twentieth Annual Conference of the Archaeological Association of the University of Calgary. Calgary, Alberta, Canada.

Quilter, Jeffrey
    1989    Life and Death at Paloma: Society and Mortuary Practices in a Preceramic Peruvian Village. Iowa City: University of Iowa Press.
    1991    Late Preceramic Peru. Journal of World Prehistory 5(4):387–438.

Ranere, Anthony J.
    1980    Preceramic shelters in the Talamancan range. In: Adaptive Radiations in Prehistoric Panama, edited by O.F. Linares and A.J. Ranere, pp. 16–43. Peabody Museum Monographs 5, Harvard University, Cambridge.

Rappaport, Roy A.
    1971    Ritual, sanctity, and cybernetics. American Anthropologist 73:59–76.

Ravesloot, John C.
    1988    Mortuary Practices and Social Differentiation at Casas Grandes, Chihuahua, Mexico. Anthropological Papers of the University of Arizona 49. Tucson: University of Arizona Press.

Ravesloot, John C., and Patricia M. Spoerl
    1989    The role of warfare in the development of status hierarchies at Casas Grandes, Chihuahua, Mexico. In: Cultures in Conflict: Current Archaeological Perspectives, edited by D.C. Tkaczuk and B.C. Vivian, pp. 130–137. Proceedings of the Twentieth Annual Chacmool Conference, the Archaeological Association of the University of Calgary, Calgary, Alberta, Canada.

Redmond, Elsa M.
    1983    A Fuego y Sangre: Early Zapotec Imperialism in the Cuicatlán Cañada, Oaxaca. University of Michigan Museum of Anthropology, Memoirs 16. Ann Arbor.

Reichel-Dolmatoff, Gerardo
    1951    Datos Histórico-Culturales sobre las Tribus de la Antigua Gobernación de Santa Marta. Instituto Etnológico del Magdalena, Santa Marta. Banco de la República, Bogotá.
    1953    Contactos y Cambios Culturales en la Sierra Nevada de Santa Marta. Antares Imprenta Editorial, Bogotá.
    1965    Colombia. New York: Frederick A. Praeger.
    1972    San Agustín: A culture of Colombia. New York: Praeger Publishers.
    1977    Estudios Antropológicos. Biblioteca Básica Colombiana. Colcultura, Bogotá.

Reichel-Dolmatoff, Gerardo, and Alicia Reichel-Dolmatoff
    1956    Momíl, excavaciones en el Sinú. Revista Colombiana de Antropología vol. V:109–333.

Renfrew, Colin
    1973    Monuments, mobilization and social organization in Neolithic Wessex. In: The Explanation of Culture Change: Models in Prehistory, edited by C. Renfrew, pp. 539–558. Pittsburgh: University of Pittsburgh Press.
    1982    Socio-economic change in ranked societies. In: Ranking, Resource and Exchange: Aspects of the Archaeology of Early European Society, edited by C. Renfrew and S. Shennan, pp. 1–8. Cambridge: Cambridge University Press.

Restrepo Tirado, Ernesto
    1929    Ensayo Etnográfico y arqueológico de la Provincia de los Quimbayas en el Nuevo Reino de Granada. Imprenta y Librería de Eulogio de las Heras, Sevilla.

Rodríguez, Carlos Armando
    1985    Archaeological excavations in a prehispanic cemetery in Guabas, Cauca Valley, Colombia. Pro Calima 4:49–52.

Roosevelt, Anna C.
    1987    Chiefdoms in the Amazon and Orinoco. In: Chiefdoms in the Americas, edited by R.D. Drennan and C.A. Uribe, pp. 153–185. Lanham, Maryland: University Press of America.
    1991    Moundbuilders of the Amazon: Geophysical Archaeology on Marajo Island, Brazil. San Diego: Academic Press.

Roper, Marilyn K.
    1975    Evidence of warfare in the Near East from 10,000–4,300 B.C. In: War, Its Causes and Correlates, edited by M.A. Nettleship, R.D. Givens, and A. Nettleship, pp. 299–343. The Hague: Mouton Publishers.

Ross, Jane B.
    1980    Ecology and the problem of the tribe: a critique of the Hobbesian model of preindustrial warfare. In: Beyond the Myths of Culture, edited by E. Ross, pp. 33–60. New York: Academic Press.
    1984    Effects of contact on revenge hostilities among the Achuara Jívaro. In: Warfare, Culture, and Environment, edited by R.B. Ferguson, pp. 83–109. New York: Academic Press.

Sahlins, Marshall D.
    1968    Tribesmen. Englewood Cliffs, NJ: Prentice-Hall, Inc.
    1972    Stone Age Economics. Chicago: Aldine Publishing Company.

Salazar, Ernesto
    1981    The Federación Shuar and the colonization frontier. In: Cultural Transformations and Ethnicity in Modern Ecuador, edited by N.E. Whitten, Jr., pp. 589–613. Urbana: University of Illinois Press.

Serje, Margarita
    1987    Arquitectura y urbanismo en la cultura tairona. Museo del Oro 19:87–96.

Service, Elman R.
    1962    Primitive Social Organization. New York: Random House.
    1968    War and our contemporary ancestors. In: War: The Anthropology of Armed Conflict and Aggression, edited by M. Fried, M. Harris, and R. Murphy, pp. 160–167. New York: The Natural History Press.

Shapiro, Judith
    1972    Sex Roles and Social Structure among the Yanomamö Indians of Northern Brazil. Ph.D. dissertation, Columbia University.

Sharer, Robert J.
    1978    The Prehistory of Chalchuapa, El Salvador, vol. 3, Pottery and Conclusions. The University Museum, University of Pennsylvania.

Sheets, Payson D.
    1980    The Volcán Barú region: a site survey. In: Adaptive Radiations in Prehistoric Panama, edited by O.F. Linares and A.J. Ranere, pp. 267–275. Peabody Museum Monographs 5, Harvard University, Cambridge.

Shennan, Stephen
    1982    Exchange and ranking: the role of amber in the earlier bronze age of Europe. In: Ranking, Resource and Exchange, edited by C. Renfrew and S. Shennan, pp. 33–45. Cambridge: Cambridge University Press.

Shook, Edwin M., and Alfred V. Kidder
1952 Mound E-III-3, Kaminaljuyú, Guatemala. Contributions to American Anthropology and History, vol. XI, no. 53. Carnegie Institution of Washington Publication 596. Washington, D.C.

Sillitoe, Paul
1978 Big men and war in New Guinea. Man (n.s.) 13: 252–271.

Simón, Fr. Pedro
1882 Noticias Historiales de las Conquistas de Tierra Firme en las Indias Occidentales. Primera Parte. Tomo I. Imprenta de Medardo Rivas, Bogotá.
1891 Noticias Historiales de las conquistas de Tierra Firme en las Indias Occidentales. Segunda Parte. Tomo II. Casa Editorial de Medardo Rivas, Bogotá.
1892a Noticias Historiales de las conquistas de Tierra Firme en las Indias Occidentales. Segunda y Tercera Parte. Tomo III. Casa Editorial de Medardo Rivas, Bogotá.
1892b Noticias Historiales de las Conquistas de Tierra Firme en las Indias Occidentales. Tercera Parte. Tomo IV. Casa Editorial de Medardo Rivas, Bogotá.
1892c Noticias Historiales de las Conquistas de Tierra Firme en las Indias Occidentales. Tercera Parte. Tomo V. Casa Editorial de Medardo Rivas, Bogotá.

Siskind, Jane
1973 To Hunt in the Morning. New York: Oxford Press.

Siverts, Henning
1972 Tribal Survival in the Alto Marañon: the Aguaruna Case. IWGIA Document 10, Copenhagen.
1975 Jívaro head hunters in a headless time. In: War, Its Causes and Correlates, edited by M.A. Nettleship, R.D. Givens, and A. Nettleship, pp. 663–674. The Hague: Mouton Publishers.

Smole, William J.
1976 The Yanoama Indians: A Cultural Geography. Austin: University of Texas Press.

Spencer, Charles S.
1982 The Cuicatlán Cañada and Monte Albán: A Study of Primary State Formation. New York: Academic Press.
1987 Rethinking the chiefdom. In: Chiefdoms in the Americas, edited by R.D. Drennan and C.A. Uribe, pp. 369–390. Lanham, Maryland: University Press of America.
1993 Human agency, biased transmission, and the cultural evolution of chiefly authority. Journal of Anthropological Archaeology 12:41–74.

Spencer, Charles S., and Elsa M. Redmond
1983 A Middle Formative elite residence and associated structures at La Coyotera, Oaxaca. In: The Cloud People: Divergent Evolution of the Zapotec and Mixtec Civilizations, edited by K.V. Flannery and J. Marcus, pp. 71–72. New York: Academic Press.
1992 Prehispanic chiefdoms of the western Venezuelan llanos. World Archaeology 24(1):134–157.

Staden, Juan
1944 Vera Historia y Descripción de un País de las Salvages Desnudas Feroces Gentes Devoradas de Hombres Situado en el Nuevo Mundo America (original German edition 1557). Translated and edited by Edmundo Wernicke. Museo Etnográfico, Universidad de Buenos Aires. Buenos Aires: Imprenta y Casa Editora "Coni."

Steward, Julian H.
1948 Preface. In: Handbook of South American Indians, vol. 4, Smithsonian Institution Bureau of American Ethnology, Bulletin 143, edited by J.H. Steward, pp. xv-xvii. New York: Cooper Square Publishers.

Steward, Julian H., and Louis C. Faron
1959 Native Peoples of South America. New York: McGraw-Hill Book Company.

Stirling, Matthew W.
1938 Historical and Ethnographical Material on the Jívaro Indians. Smithsonian Institution Bureau of American Ethnology, Bulletin 117. Smithsonian Institution, Washington, D.C.
1950 Exploring ancient Panama by helicopter. National Geographic 97 (2):227–246.

Stothert, Karen E.
1985 The preceramic Las Vegas culture of coastal Ecuador. American Antiquity 50(3):613–637.

Stout, David B.
1948 The Cuna. In: Handbook of South American Indians, vol. 4, Smithsonian Institution Bureau of American Ethnology, Bulletin 143, edited by J.H. Steward, pp. 257–268. New York: Cooper Square Publishers, Inc.

Taylor, Anne-Christine
1981 God-wealth: The Achuar and the missions. In: Cultural Transformations and Ethnicity in Modern Ecuador, edited by N.E. Whitten, Jr., pp. 647–676. Urbana: University of Illinois Press.

Taylor, Donna
1975 Some Locational Aspects of Middle-Range Hierarchical Societies. Ph.D. dissertation, City University of New York. University Microfilms, Ann Arbor.

Topic, John R.
1989 The Ostra site: the earliest fortified site in the New World? In: Cultures in Conflict: Archaeological Perspectives, edited by D.C. Tkaczuk and B.C. Vivian, pp. 215–228. Proceedings of the Twentieth Annual Chacmool Conference, the Archaeological Association of the University of Calgary, Calgary, Alberta, Canada.

Topic, John, and Theresa Topic
1987 The archaeological investigation of Andean militarism: some cautionary observations. In: The Origins and Development of the Andean State, edited by J. Haas, S. Pozorski and T. Pozorski, pp. 47–55. Cambridge: Cambridge University Press.

Trimborn, Hermann
1949 Señorío y Barbarie en el Valle del Cauca. Translated from the original German version by José María Gimeno Capella. Consejo Superior de Investigaciones Científicas, Instituto Gonzalo Fernández de Oviedo, Madrid.

Turner II, Christy G.
1983 Taphonomic reconstructions of human violence and cannibalism based on mass burials in the American Southwest. In: Carnivores, Human Scavengers and Predators: A Question of Bone Technology, edited by G.M. Le Moine and A.S. MacEachern, pp. 219–240. Proceedings of the Fifteenth Annual Chacmool Conference, the Archaeological Association of the University of Calgary. Calgary, Alberta, Canada.

Turner II, Christy G., and Nancy T. Morris
1970 A massacre at Hopi. American Antiquity 35(3):320–331.

Turner II, Christy G., and Jacqueline A. Turner
1992 The first claim for cannibalism in the Southwest: Walter Hough's 1901 discovery at Canyon Butte Ruin 3, Northeastern Arizona. American Antiquity 57(4):661–682.

Up de Graff, F.W.
1923 Head Hunters of the Amazon. New York: Duffield and Co.

Upham, Steadman, and Paul F. Reed
1989 Inferring the structure of Anasazi warfare. In: Cultures in Conflict: Current Archaeological Perspectives, edited by D.C. Tkaczuk and B.C. Vivian, pp. 153–162. Proceedings of the Twentieth Annual Chacmool Conference, the Archaeological Association of the University of Calgary, Calgary, Alberta, Canada.

Valero, Helena
1984 Yo Soy Napëyoma. Fundación La Salle de Ciencias Naturales Monografía No. 35, edited by E. Fuentes, Editorial Texto, Caracas.

Vencl, Sl.
1984 War and warfare in archaeology. Journal of Anthropological Archaeology 3:116–132.

Verrill, A. Hyatt
1927 Excavations in Coclé province, Panama. Indian Notes 4(1):47–61. Museum of the American Indian, Heye Foundation, New York.

Villa, Paola, Claude Bouville, Jean Courtin, Daniel Helmer, Eric Mahieu, Pat Shipman, Giorgio Belluomini, and Marilí Branca
1986 Cannibalism in the Neolithic. Science 233:431–437.

Vivante, Armando, and Nestor Homero Palma
1966 Venenos de anuros (sapos y ranas) empleados para emponzoñar dardos y flechas. Revista del Museo de La Plata (Nueva Serie), Sección Antropología, tomo VI:81–106.

Vogel, Joseph O., and Jean Allan
1985 Mississippian fortifications at Moundville. Archaeology 35(5):62–63.

von Schuler-Schömig, Immina
1981 A grave-lot of the Sonso period. Pro-Calima 2:25–28.

Wafer, Lionel
1903 A New Voyage and Description of the Isthmus of America. Edited by George Parker Winship. Cleveland: Burrows Brothers Co.

Wassén, S. Henry
1934a The frog-motive among the South American Indians. Anthropos XXIX:319–370.
1934b The frog in Indian mythology and imaginative world. Anthropos XXIX:613–658.
1957 On Dendrobates-frog-poison material among Emperá (Chocó)-speaking Indians in Western Caldas, Colombia. Etnografiska Museet Arstryck 1955–1956:73–94. Göteborg.

Webster, David
1975 Warfare and the evolution of the state: a reconsideration. American Antiquity 40:464–470.

Werner, Dennis W.
1980 The Making of a Mekranoti Chief: The Psychological and Social Determinants of Leadership in a Native South American Society. Ph.D. dissertation, City University of New York. University Microfilms, Ann Arbor.
1982 Leadership inheritance and acculturation among the Mekranoti of central Brazil. Human Organization 41:342–345.

White, Tim D.
1992 Prehistoric cannibalism at Mancos 5MTUMR-2346. Princeton, NJ: Princeton University Press.

Whitehead, Neil L.
1988 Lords of the tiger spirit: a history of the Caribs in Colonial Venezuela and Guyana 1498–1820. Koninklijk Institut Voor Taal-, Land- En Volkenkunde, Caribbean Series 10. Dordrecht, Netherlands: Foris Publications.
1990 The snake warriors-sons of the tiger's teeth: a descriptive analysis of Carib warfare ca. 1500–1820. In: The Anthropology of War, edited by J. Haas, pp. 146–170. Cambridge: Cambridge University Press.
1992 Tribes make states and states make tribes: warfare and the creation of colonial tribes and states in northeastern South America. In: War in the Tribal Zone, edited by R.B. Ferguson and N.L. Whitehead, pp. 127–150. Santa Fe, New Mexico: School of American Research Press.

Whitten, Norman E., Jr.
1976 Sacha Runa. Urbana: University of Illinois Press.
1978 Ecological imagery and cultural adaptability: the Canelos Quichua of Eastern Ecuador. American Anthropologist 80:836–859.

Whitten, Norman E., Jr. (editor)
1981 Cultural Transformations and Ethnicity in Modern Ecuador. Urbana: University of Illinois Press.

Wilcox, David R.
1989 Hohokam warfare. In: Cultures in Conflict: Current Archaeological Perspectives, edited by D.C. Tkaczuk and B.C. Vivian, pp. 163–172, Proceedings of the Twentieth Annual Chacmool Conference, the Archaeological Association of the University of Calgary, Calgary, Alberta, Canada.

Willey, Gordon R.
1971 An Introduction to American Archaeology, vol. 2. South America. Englewood Cliffs, NJ: Prentice-Hall.

Wilson, David J.
1987 Reconstructing patterns of early warfare in the lower Santa Valley: new data on the role of conflict in the origins of complex north-coast society. In: The Origins and Development of the Andean state, edited by J. Haas, S. Pozorski, and T. Pozorski, pp. 56–69. Cambridge: Cambridge University Press.
1988 Prehispanic Settlement Patterns in the Lower Santa Valley, Peru. Washington, DC: Smithsonian Institution Press.

Wing, Elizabeth S.
1980 Aquatic fauna and reptiles from the Atlantic and Pacific sites. In: Adaptive Radiations in Prehistoric Panama, edited by O.F. Linares and A.J. Ranere, pp. 194–215. Peabody Museum Monographs 5, Harvard University, Cambridge.

Wobst, H. Martin
   1977  Stylistic behavior and information exchange. In: For the Director: Essays in Honor of James B. Griffin. University of Michigan Museum of Anthropology, Anthropological Papers 61, edited by C.E. Cleland, pp. 317–342. Ann Arbor.

Wright, Henry T.
   1977  Recent research on the origin of the state. Annual Review of Anthropology 6:379–397.
   1986  The evolution of civilizations. In: American Archaeology Past and Future: A Celebration of the Society for American Archaeology 1935–1985, edited by D.J. Meltzer, D.D. Fowler, and J.A. Sabloff, pp. 323–365. Washington, D.C: Smithsonian Insitution Press.

Young, Philip D.
   1971  Ngawbe: Tradition and Change among the Western Guaymí of Panama. Illinois Studies in Anthropology No.7. Urbana: University of Illinois Press.
   1976  The expression of harmony and discord in a Guaymí ritual: the symbolic meaning of some aspects of the balsería. In: Frontier Adaptations in Lower Central America, edited by M.W. Helms and F.O. Loveland, pp. 37–53. Institute for the Study of Human Issues, Philadelphia.

Young, Philip D., and John R. Bort
   1976  Edabáli: the ritual sibling relationship among the western Guaymí. In: Ritual and Symbol in Native Central America, edited by P. Young and J. Howe, pp. 79–90. University of Oregon Anthropological Papers No. 9. Department of Anthropology, University of Oregon, Eugene, Oregon.

Zeidler, James A.
   1983  La etnoarqueología de una vivienda Achuar y sus implicaciones arqueológicas. Miscelánea Antropológica Ecuatoriana 3:155–193.
   1984  Social Space in Valdivia Society: Community Patterning and Domestic Structure at Real Alto, 3000–2000 B.C. Ph.D. dissertation, University of Illinois at Urbana-Champaign. University Microfilms, Ann Arbor.

Zier, Christian J.
   1976  Excavations near Zuni, New Mexico: 1973. Museum of Northern Arizona Research Paper 2. Flagstaff.

Zikmund, Miroslav, and Jirí Hanzelka
   1963  Amazon Headhunters. Prague: Artia.

Zucchi, Alberta
   1975  Caño Caroní: Un Grupo Prehispánico de la Selva de los Llanos de Barinas. Universidad Central de Venezuela, Caracas.

Zucchi, Alberta, and William M. Denevan
   1979  Campos Elevados e Historia Cultural Prehispánica en los Llanos Occidentales de Venezuela. Universidad Católica Andrés Bello/Instituto de Investigaciones Históricas, Caracas.

# Notes

In an attempt to render the descriptions of tribal and chiefly warfare in Chapters 2 and 3 more readable, with fewer page citations, I decided to try to reduce the number of page citations. Not wanting to lose what I consider to be additional data entries on subjects like raids, weapons, poisoned arrows, and defensive fortifications, I created these Notes, where supplementary (but usually redundant) references about the listed topics can be found, and the relevant page in Chapters 2 and 3 where these topics are discussed. I urge anyone interested in examining the ethnohistoric and ethnographic sources on tribal and chiefly warfare to consult these supplementary references as well.

## Tribal Warfare

*Jívaro*
    *Warfare strategies, weapons, tactics*
        retreat (Cotlow 1953:48, 147) p. 7
    *Post-war rituals and practices*
        abstinence (Cotlow 1953:149) p. 11
        trophy-head preparation (Up de Graff 1923:286-287) p. 11
        tsantsa feasts (Karsten 1935:89-93) (Cotlow 1953:229-230) p. 12
        tsantsas' uses (Cotlow 1953:112, 230) p. 12

*Yanomamö*
    *Nature and objectives of warfare* (Chagnon 1968a:129) (Valero 1984:52-53) p. 15
        club fights (Valero 1984:39-40, 219-221, 319-321, 328-329, 484) p. 15
        incentives (Valero 1984:50, 369, 382, 409, 506) p. 15
        female captives (Valero 1984:51) p. 15
    *Preparations for war*
        palisades (Valero 1984:338-339, 415) p. 16
    *Warfare strategies, weapons, and tactics*
        weapons (Valero 1984:37, 512-513) p. 17
        bewitching tactics (Valero 1984:135-135) p. 17
        raiding tactics (Valero 1984:341, 376, 380-382, 417, 475) p. 17
        treacherous feast (Valero 1984:432) p. 19
    *Defensive strategies*
        palisade (Valero 1984:241) p. 20
        other fortification measures (Valero 1984:352) p. 20
        guarding trails (Valero 1984:433) p. 21
    *Post-war rituals and practices*
        purification observances (Valero 1984:122-123, 237, 239, 241, 349-350, 376) p. 21
        waiteri, consequences of being (Valero 1984:329) p. 22
    *Mortuary treatment*
        distinguished warriors (Valero 1984:365-367, 437) p. 23
        mourning ceremonies before revenge raid (Valero 1984:100) p. 23

## Chiefly Warfare

*Cauca Valley*
    *Nature and objectives of warfare* (Trimborn 1949:201-203, 258) p. 25
    *Preparations for war*
        war councils, feasts (Trimborn 1949:150-151) p. 27
        fighting force size (Cieza de León 1947:370, 456) p. 27
    *Warfare strategies, weapons, and tactics* (Trimborn 1949:339) p. 27
        poison-tipped darts and arrows (Castellanos 1850:535-537, 541, 550) p. 29
        female participation (Trimborn 1949:323, 389) p. 29
    *Defensive strategies*
        taking flight, hiding valuables, burning settlement (Simón 1892b:121, 274, 337) p. 30
        defensive warfare tactics (Trimborn 1949:304-306) p. 30
    *Post-war rituals and practices*
        treatment of sacrificial victims (Cieza de León 1947:368-369) (Simón 1892c:66,69) p. 30
        public displays of trophies (Cieza de León 1947:365, 372) p. 31
        distinguished warriors (Trimborn 1949:404) p. 31
    *Mortuary treatment* (Cieza de León 1947:373, 378-380, 384) p. 31

*Tairona*
    *Preparations for war*
        spies (Simón 1892c:27, 30) p. 32
        war councils (Simón 1892c:27,186) (Castellanos 1850:336-337, 355) p. 32
    *Organization of war parties* (Castellanos 1850:335, 355) p. 34
        military paraphernalia (Castellanos 1850:297, 329, 355) p. 34
    *Warfare strategies, weapons, and tactics*
        strategies (Castellanos 1850:271, 298, 324, 326, 335, 347, 356) (Simón 1891:44) (Simón 1892b:283, 360) (Simón 1892c:47, 53, 181, 195, 207, 209, 210) (Aguado 1916:141) p. 34
        poison-tipped arrows (Aguado 1916:130, 142, 147, 151-152, 153-155) (Castellanos 1850:273, 293, 326, 329, 340) (Simón 1891:37, 46) p. 35
        Spanish armor (Castellanos 1850:324, 326) p. 35
        multiple attacking units, intimidation tactics (Castellanos 1850:268, 293-295, 322-323, 333-335, 353) p. 35
        fire-tipped arrows (Castellanos 1850:272-273, 281, 293) (Simón 1891:41) (Simón 1892c:31, 211) p. 35
    *Defensive strategies*
        inaccessible hilltop settlements (Castellanos 1850:293, 330, 339) p. 36
        obstacles (Simón 1892c:190, 210-211) p. 36
        taking flight, burning settlement (Castellanos 1850:298, 329) (Simón 1891:45) (Simón 1892b:357) (Simón 1892c:190) p. 36
        defensive warfare tactics (Castellanos 1850:324-325, 330-331, 340-342, 344-345, 356) p. 37
    *Post-war rituals and practices*
        treatment of sacrificial victims (Castellanos 1850:346) (Simón 1892c:27-28, 53, 187) pp. 37

*Panamanian Chiefdoms*
    *Defensive strategies* (Espinosa 1864:511, 518) p. 46

# Appendix
# Author's Translations of Spanish Text

## Chapter 2

*p. 16 Ustedes sabían...*
You knew that this is the best time for going to war.

*p. 19 No estoy contento...*
I am not happy... I can't understand why you killed all those people. What a lot of corpses in that village! You shot men, women, children with arrows... You should not have killed the way you killed.

*p. 19 Por estar matando...*
For the sake of killing people, look how we have had to come from Konata, from Wareta, from Namowei, from Hahoyaope, in order to live far from the other Yanomamö now, working so hard. Now that we are at peace, we should not look for more trouble. If we return to war, we will have to abandon these gardens, and go to other places and begin anew.

*p. 20 tan poquitos, era...*
being so few, it was dangerous to remain there

*p. 20 no sé por qué...*
I don't know why the Witokaya-theri abandoned this place later; perhaps for fear of the Hii-theri.

*p. 22 Soy hombre valiente...*
I am a brave man. The Peccary Spirit gives me strength. I don't take pity on anybody. I can kill even my son. Killing people is a pleasure for me.

*p. 22 Yo soy valiente...*
I am brave, the bravest of the Puunapiwei-theri. Wherever I go, I spill human blood. This is why the Mahekotho-theri always invite me to go to war with them.

*p. 22 la lógica implacable...*
the implacable logic of the system demands that the achieved status and fierceness be questioned constantly, in such a way that they can only maintain it by means of ever more daring exploits. The shadow of death looms on the horizon, a terribly efficient system since it prevents the establishment of any real power.

*p. 22 Yo no voy...*
I am not going to burn my father's body far from the the shapono. ...He is not just any dead man. However far we may be, we must carry him home to burn his body in the shapono.

*p. 22 No voy a pilar...*
I am not going to consume the ashes here in the wilds. I want to consume them in my shapono... He was a big man. His ashes cannot be consumed here.

## Chapter 3

*p. 28 con singular orden...*
with singular order, composed of squadrons, marching in time and nine to a row, with their outstanding ones, all very fierce, quivers full of poisoned arrows, lances with fire-hardened points, clubs of very hard palm-wood.

*p. 29 Unos palos de palma...*
sticks of black palm-wood, very hard, an arm and a half in length, that they call macanas, four fingers in width, with two cutting edges at either end.

*p. 29 palo blanco, recio*
white, hard wood

*p. 29 12,000 hombres con picas...*
12,000 men with lances of more than 40 spans in length above, and below the interlaced lances, between two [men armed with] lances, was one carrying a broadsword, which there is called a macana, who stepped forward from among the squadron of lances to fight, and then retreated beneath the lances, and those on horseback could neither never break through anywhere, nor thrust spears.

*p. 29 de veinte en veinte...*
of twenty by twenty by their order and measure, like streets

*p. 30 les cortaban las cabezas...*
they would cut off their heads and quarter their bodies, and even in smaller pieces, so that they might share more of the spoils of victory.

*p. 30 un dia le cortaban...*
one day they would hack off an arm and another they would remove an eye, and on another they would slash the lips, and in this way his male being was consumed, until his life came to an end and he was buried in the bellies of those who killed him.

*p. 31 A las puertas...*
At the entrances of the chiefs' houses there are small plazas, surrounded by thick canes, from the height of which they have the heads of enemies hanging, which is something frightening to see, as there are many, and fierce with their long hair, and their faces painted in such a way that they look like those of demons. At the bottom of the canes they make some holes through which the wind can pass when it blows; they produce a big sound, like the music of devils.

*p. 31 Halláronse en las casas...*
They found themselves in the principal houses of the lord of this province of Lile, as tall as three or four persons in height all around the main room, from 400 bodies or those that could fit in that room were heaped, flayed and filled with ash, not lacking any figure and some seated together in a chair and others with their weapons placed in their hands, as if they were alive.

*p. 31 en señalándose uno...*
having distinguished oneself with valor in warfare or on another occasion, they would kill him with the brave one's great pleasure and cut him to pieces and they would give one [piece] to each of the other Indians, by means of which they said they would become brave like that one had been.

*p. 32 sin que se hallase...*
with no nation within this area and the one that extends from the highest peaks to the seashore, that was not under the protection or the domain of these taironas, more or less subject to their hostilities.

*p. 32 por grado ó por fuerza*
by degree or by force

*p. 32 por ser el más abundante...*
for being the most bountiful and rich of all that land, of which it was the court and capital.

*p. 34 De largas plumas...*
With long feathers their heads full,/Diadems of gold on their foreheads,/On their chests rings or breastplates,/Which the sun's rays show clearly,/With other ornaments of golden sources/Hanging from their ears and nose,/Painted red, dressed up and sprightly/And with bows and arrows in their hands.

*p. 34 arma comun de todos es la flecha*
the common weapon belonging to all is the arrow

*p. 35 hierba ponzoñosa*
poisonous herb

*p. 35 Porque los moradores...*
Because the inhabitants of this heartland/Do not always have at hand/The herb nor the deadly poison/Used by the neighboring Indians:/They also say that it didn't grow/For already being in cold country.

*p. 35 Cuando vieron bajar...*
When they saw come down a slope/A handsome good-for-nothing wearing a headdress./In all his movements and appearance/He had exceptional agility:/He had the proportions of a giant,/And no less fierce in his attitude,/With a quiver full of arrows,/Covered only at the waist,/Bow that hangs from his shoulders,/And in his hands a mighty club./Each Spaniard is in disorder/Watching him descend with such eagerness,/With the weapons and equipment that they use,/Which are the bow, arrows, and club.

*p. 36 Porque viendo venir...*
Because seeing armed people coming,/Arobaro then sounded his horn,/At whose blare suddenly/His people appear,/With so many darts, arrows and stones thrown,/Like the thick drops that fall in winter,/In such a way, that whoever considers defeating/Achieves a great victory in its defense.

*p. 37 porque en algunas...*
because in some houses that day were found pieces of flesh and body parts of men or of women, as well as arms and legs and a hand prepared and salted and cut.

*p. 39 terná mas tierra é señorio*
will have more land and domain

*p. 41 Quando van á la guerra...*
When they go to war, they take their chiefs or captains: these are sacos or cabras, and they are already men of experience in matters relating to the weapons that they use.

*p. 41 porque es costumbre...*
because it is the custom in those parts that the chiefs and members of the ruling elite wear in battle some gold ornament on their chests or on their heads or on their arms, in order to be distinguished and recognized among their own and even among their enemies.

*p. 42 en las cosas...*
in matters of warfare I have noticed that these people pride themselves very much; ... and in no other way as much as in warfare do they pride themselves in looking like gentlemen and in going as dressed up as they can.

*p. 43 los cuales asaetaban...*
who would shoot and kill many of the fierce Indians, although the said Indians had such spirit that when they [crossbowmen] would kill one, they [Indians] would send ten forward.

*p. 43 en su ordenanza...*
in their orderliness in the manner of Germans

*p. 43 una bien rezia...*
a very tough guaçabara, or battle, the ones with the others, which was quite hard fought.

*p. 44 fechas á la manera...*
made in the manner of pikes, as long and as thick as those that the Germans use, studded, about a yardstick's length [or .836 m], towards the point, with shark teeth and the teeth of other fish.

*p. 44 con que se haçe...*
with which the poison of the Carib bowmen is made, in the Gulf of Urabá as well as on the coast of Darien and of Acla.

*p. 44 raizes de las de caña...*
shields of interwoven cane strips and round.

*p. 45 sáleles al encuentro...*
they confronted them [Espinosa's men] with so much effort and ferocity as if they were tigers or lions against cats that would scratch them.

*p. 45 á los que pueden...*
they kill as many as they can kill.

*p. 46 porque no teniendo...*
because not having enough to eat, we would all die of hunger.

*p. 47 y por ser tanta...*
because of the quantity of bones that were left there it retained the name as the province of bones.

*p. 47 tajada á tajada*
slice by slice [bit by bit].

*p. 48 por el camino...*
along the way they dug pits into which they would throw the dead

## Chapter 4
*p. 51 guerra de todos contra todos*
all-out warfare.

## Chapter 6
*p. 84 Y díjome que...*
He told me that along the sea coast, next to the trees that we call manchineels, they would dig below ground, and from the roots of that noxious tree they would remove those [roots]: which they cook over a fire in some ceramic jars and prepare a paste, and they search for some ants as large as a beetle of the kind that are found in Spain, very black and very nasty, ... They also search for some very big spiders to make this bad stuff, and likewise they add some furry caterpillars, thin and about half-a-finger long.... They also make it with bat wings and with the head and tail of a small fish of the sea, which has as its name the tamborino fish, very poisonous; and with toads and tails of snakes, and some small apples that in their color and smell are like those of Spain... They also add other herbs and roots to this poison; and when they want to make it they light a bonfire on a plain far from their houses or dwellings, and arrange some jars; they find some female slave or woman held in low regard, and that Indian cooks it.

*p. 85 mançanillos de aquellos...*
those small apples, with which the poison of the Carib bowmen is made, in the Gulf of Urabá as well as on the coast of Darien and of Acla, and in many islets thereabouts

*p. 85 Hay muchos y muy grandes...*
There are many large toads; they don't bite but when they are beaten they exude a white juice like milk, which if drunk or eaten is deadly.

*p. 85 En vn vaso o tinajuela...*
In a vessel or ceramic jar they put any poisonous snakes they can find and a large quantity of red ants that for their poisonous bite are called Caribs, and many scorpions and poisonous caterpillars of the kind mentioned above, and all the spiders they can find of a type that are as big as eggs and very fuzzy and very poisonous, and if they happen to have some human testicles they add them there along with menstrual blood, and they keep everything together in that vessel until anything alive dies and everything

*p. 85 [cont.]*
rots, and after this they take some toads and keep them confined for some days in a vessel without giving them anything to eat, after which they remove them, and one by one they place them on top of a ceramic jar or sherd, tied tightly by each leg with four strings to four stakes, in such a way that the toad is stretched over the middle of the jar without being able to move, and there an old woman beats it with some sticks until she makes it exude, in such a way that the exudate drips into the jar, and all the toads that have been collected for this purpose are processed in this order, and when enough of the toads' exudate has been collected, they add it to the vessel containing the now rotten snakes and other bugs, and to that they add the sap of certain ceibas or thorny trees that have a certain berry to purge, and they mix it and shake it all together, and they apply this blend to those arrows and lances that cause so much harm. And when over the course of time this poison becomes weak, they add a little of the sap of ceibas or of manchineels, and with this alone the poison regains its strength and vigor.

*p. 86 Los indios acostumbraban...*
The Indians used to skin some frogs alive, pulling the skin over the neck; after this barbarous operation they let the poor animal loose so that it would go away and grow a new skin so that they might skin it again or so that it might breed.... They would deposit the skin of the frog in a jar where the poison remained, and who knows what other poison they added; later they inserted the tips of the arrows and they became poisoned.

*p. 94 con los brazos en cruz...*
with their arms crossed, and calm demeanors, as if in the position of stoically awaiting the death they were going to confront.

*p. 103 Son estos indios caribes...*
These Carib Indians are bowmen and they eat human flesh; and this was learned because in some houses that day were found pieces of flesh and body parts of men or of women, as well as arms and legs and a hand prepared and salted and stored in a jar, and necklaces of human teeth, which the Indians wear in order to look well dressed, and the skulls of others mounted on stakes and driven into the ground in front of the doors of their houses as trophies and as a record of victory of the enemies that they have killed or that they have eaten.

*p. 104 yo les vi un dia...*
one day I saw them eat more than one hundred men and women whom they had killed or captured in warfare.

*p. 104 cuando quieren matar...*
when they want to kill some of those unfortunates in order to eat them, they make them kneel down on the ground, and lowering their head, they deliver a blow on the back of their neck, which leaves them stunned and they neither speak nor complain ... I have seen what I describe enough times.

*p. 104 luego se bebieron...*
then they drank her blood and ate her heart and entrails raw, carrying off the quarters and the head to eat the following night.

*p. 104 Dentro de las casas...*
Within the houses of the chiefs [the chiefly precinct] they have thick canes that I have mentioned above, which when dry are extremely strong, and they make an enclosure like a cage, wide and short and not very high, so tightly fastened, that there is no way for those who are put in to escape; they put the captives they seize when they go to war in there and they order them to be very well fed, and when they are fat, they are taken out to their plazas, which are next to their houses, and on holidays they kill them with great cruelty and eat them; I saw some of these cages or jails in the province of Arma.

*p. 104 en mitad desta...*
in the center of this fortress they have, or they used to have when I saw it, a tall platform and well built from the same canes, with its ladder, where they carried out their sacrifices.

*p. 104 y á algunos dellos...*
and in the case of some of them they removed their hearts and offered them to their gods, to the devil, in whose honor they made those sacrifices, and then, without much delay, they would eat the bodies of those whom they had thus killed.

*p. 104 hallaron una olla grande...*
they found a big jar full of cooked meat; and so hungry were they that they thought of nothing but eating, ... but when they were all very full, a Christian took out a hand with its fingers and nails from the jar; without which, they later saw pieces of the feet, and two or three quarters of men that were inside the jar.

*p. 105 Junto á las puertas...*
Next to the doors of their houses, because of their greatness, they have hanging from inside of the facade many feet of the Indians they have killed, and many hands; apart from which, so as not to waste anything, they preserve the intestines by stuffing them with meat or with ashes, some like blood sausages and others like long pork sausages, in great quantities; therefore, the heads are displayed as are many entire quarters.

*p. 105 Y si yo no hubiera...*
And if I had not seen myself what I am writing about, and if I did not know that there are so many people in Spain who know about it and who saw it many times, surely I would not tell how these men carried out such large-scale massacres of other men only to eat them; and thus, we know that these Gorrones are bloodthirsty for eating human flesh.

*p. 105 así como entraban dentro...*
as one entered inside, high up there was a long plank, which spanned the house from one end to another, on which many dead bodies of those men whom they had defeated and captured in warfare, all cut open; they cut them open with flint knives and they flayed them, and after having eaten the flesh they stuffed the skins with ash and fashioned wax faces on their heads, placing them on the shelf in such a way that they seemed alive.

*p. 105 Al punto arremetieron...*
At once four rushed forth, and stripping him, they cut off his head, and they drank his blood to see who could drink the most, like dogs in the slaughterhouse. In a moment they quartered his body and they ate the guts there later, without cooking them, dividing up the flesh among the most illustrious:

*p. 105 Aquí era la gran...*
Here was the big slaughterhouse of human flesh of these natives, who killed the slaves by stretching them over a stone for this purpose, where they cut their chests open while they were still alive, and removed their fat in order to make small oil lamps for the tunnels of the mines, and they traded and ate the meat.

*p. 105 fue sabroso almuerzo...*
his unfortunate body was a delicious meal.

*p. 105 los dichos caciques...*
the said chiefs and Indians performed their songs and dances, and slice by slice, and little by little their hands and arms were cut, until they killed them.

*p. 106 Mezclados con los restos...*
Mixed with the remains of food and the artifacts, a smashed mandible, as well as some skull fragments and long-bone fragments were found. It is probable that the people of the Copa de Oro complex practiced cannibalism, since these bones, like the animal bones, had had their marrow extracted.

*p. 106 A título explicativo...*
By way of explanation, if it is taken into account that the cannibalistic practices were usually associated with warfare activities, it follows that the individual buried in the urn could have died in one of these attacks; whereas the burned bones belonged to some prisoner taken in the same attack and sacrificed later, on the occasion of the ceremony marking the secondary burial of the deceased member of the group.

*p. 106 En los Niveles...*
In Levels 11, 9 and 8 some human bones were found scattered. It's a question of highly deteriorated long-bone fragments, mixed with the dirt and the cultural remains. These bone remains were found widely separated one from another and it doesn't appear to be a question of burials. It should be noted however that in Levels 9 and 8 the bones were associated with small flecks of ash and tiny particles of charcoal.

*p. 116 el del centro lo habían...*
the Indians had burned the one in the center right there, in this way: he was the first to be laid down, without bedclothes, with the body stiff; later they placed fuel on top of him and burned him; the survivors honored these ashes, for they were found in just the way they had been left by the fire. Later they buried his funerary retainers.

## Chapter 7

*p. 118 en realidad, los señores...*
in fact, the rulers of the Cauca Valley, like the Cueva chiefs, exercised a despotic rule, which especially in warfare, or rather, as a consequence of the continual state of war, grew to an unbounded power.

*p. 119 Sus guacábaras ó peleas...*
Their guacábaras or fights are often without purpose; but not without the devil giving them cause, because they are people that although they have differences and passions between one ruler and another, rarely are they provoked with good reason, and the most well-intentioned motives are induced by the tuyra and his tequina, giving them to understand that the war that he advises is divinely intended.

*p. 119 comenzaron luego a hacer...*
began then to perform displays of words and body movements in pursuit of what had been decided.

*p. 119 é lo ponen por obra...*
and they put it into effect, as if they were obliged by a firm and sufficient contract or an inviolable oath and tribute.

*p. 120 los señores más principales...*
the principal chiefs, who were the richest and bravest (because among them there is no other supreme authority, than that which is founded on these two things),

*p. 120 Sus guerras eran...*
Their wars were incessant, some provinces and towns against others, because the enemy of peace whom they served didn't let them rest one moment without going about spilling human blood, even though this made them braver.

*p. 120-21 eran un poco amigos, pues*
they were a little friendly, then.

*p. 121 quiero oír el canto...*
I want to hear the singing of Shama-thari women. I want my women to learn their songs.

*p. 121 Osheoshewë, porque...*
Osheoshewë, because he had seen the airplane closely, was now a white man.

*p. 123 Quando los indios...*
When the Indians are not at war, all their exertion is spent trading and bartering all they have with others; and in this way from some places to others those who inhabit the sea coasts or along rivers, travel in canoes to sell what they have in full and abundance, and to buy what they lack. In the same way they trade by land, and they transport their loads on the backs of their slaves: some take salt, others maize, others mantles, others hammocks, others spun cotton or cotton to be spun, others salted fish; others take gold... . In short, what the Indians lack is what they most value.

*p. 123 para que sea...*
so that warfare between them may be more sure and perpetual.

*p. 128 á donde entraron...*
to which the most illustrious entered into, two nephews of his named Yutengo and Arama, who although young men, had already given indications of their courage in heroic military deeds.

*p. 128 á fuego y sangre cruel guerra*
cruel warfare with fire and blood.

*p. 128 Qué es lo que...*
What were you doing amidst these people? You knew that this is the best time for going to war and that I was coming to kill my enemies.